D0891581

# JOHN CONSTABLE

## *A Kingdom of his Own*

# JOHN CONSTABLE
## A Kingdom of his Own

### ANTHONY BAILEY

Chatto & Windus

LONDON

Published by Chatto & Windus 2006

2 4 6 8 10 9 7 5 3

First published in Great Britain in 2006 by
Chatto & Windus
Random House, 20 Vauxhall Bridge Road,
London SW1V 2SA

Random House Australia (Pty) Limited
20 Alfred Street, Milsons Point, Sydney,
New South Wales 2061, Australia

Random House New Zealand Limited
18 Poland Road, Glenfield,
Auckland 10, New Zealand

Random House (Pty) Limited
Isle of Houghton, Corner of Boundary Road & Carse O'Gowrie,
Houghton 2198, South Africa

The Random House Group Limited Reg. No. 954009

www.randomhouse.co.uk

A CIP catalogue record for this book is available from the British Library

ISBN 0 7011 7884 1
EAN 9780701178841 (from Jan 07)

Papers used by Random House are natural, recyclable products made from wood
grown in sustainable forests; the manufacturing processes conform to the
environmental regulations of the country of origin.

Typeset by SX Composing DTP, Rayleigh, Essex
Printed and bound in Great Britain by
William Clowes Ltd, Beccles, Suffolk

*Maps by Reginald Piggott*

# *Contents*

# Illustrations

SCOTLAND

Constable's
England

Lake District

0        50        100 miles
0     50    100    150 km

North
Sea

The Peak
District

E N G L A N D

NORFOLK
Norwich

Birmingham  • Coleorton

SUFFOLK

W A L E S

Helmingham
Ipswich  • Woodbridge

Stoke by Nayland    • Harwich
Colchester  • Wivenhoe

MIDDLESEX

R. Thames

B E R K S H I R E

ESSEX

Hampstead  Hadleigh
Harrow
London    • Southend-on-Sea

WILTSHIRE
Stonehenge •   Old Sarum
Salisbury

Petworth
Arundel   SUSSEX
• Hove   Brighton

DORSET
Osmington
Weymouth
Portland Island

N

S U F F O L K

to Ipswich

Higham

Stratford
St Mary

East
Bergholt

Fen Bridge

Langham

Lock
Dedham
Mill

R. Stour

Lock

Flatford
Mill

Lock

Dedham

THE STOUR
VALLEY

E S S E X

1 mile

1 km

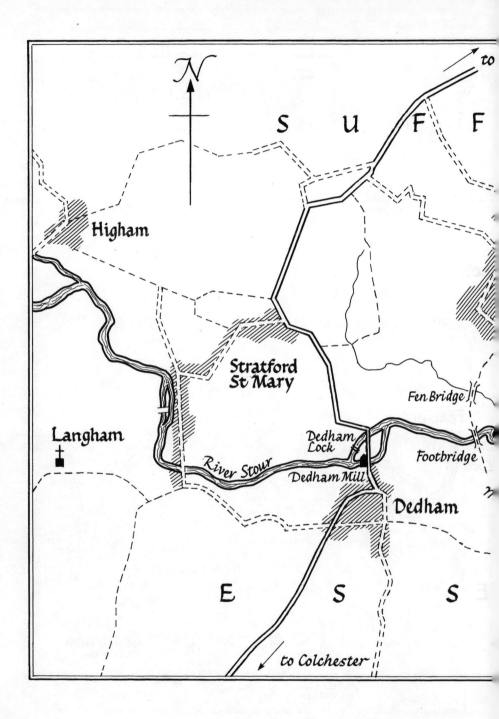

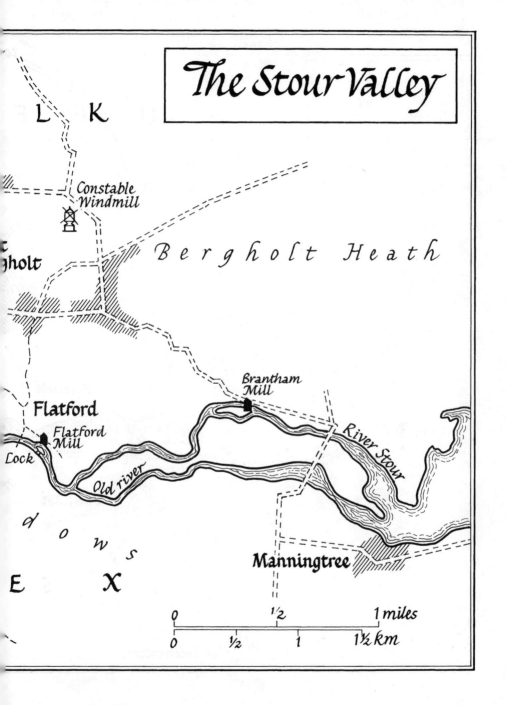

The Stour Valley

L K

Constable
Windmill

gholt

B e r g h o l t   H e a t h

Brantham
Mill

River Stour

Flatford

Flatford
Mill

Lock

Old river

d
o
w
s

E          X

Manningtree

0                    ½                    1 miles

0          ½          1          1½ km

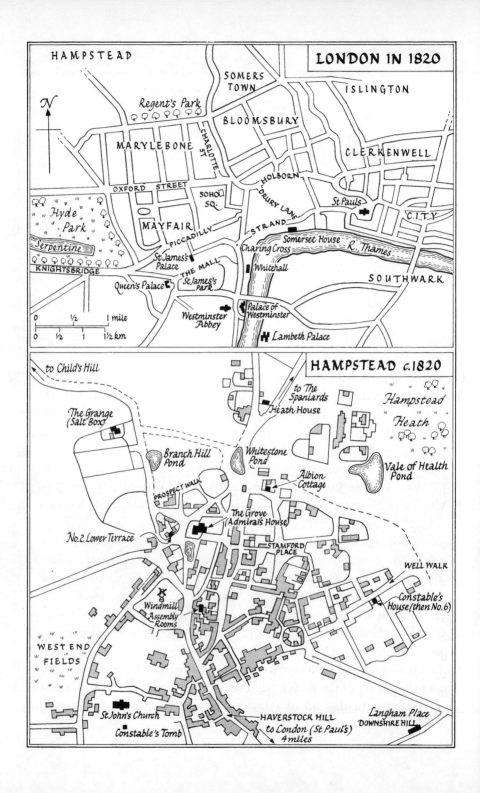

**LONDON IN 1820**

HAMPSTEAD

SOMERS TOWN

ISLINGTON

N

Regent's Park

BLOOMSBURY

CLERKENWELL

MARYLEBONE

CHARLOTTE ST

OXFORD STREET

SOHO SQ.

HOLBORN

DRURY LANE

St Pauls

C·I·T·Y

Hyde Park

MAYFAIR

PICCADILLY

STRAND

Charing Cross

Somerset House

R. Thames

Serpentine

KNIGHTSBRIDGE

St James's Palace

THE MALL

St James's Park

Whitehall

SOUTHWARK

Queen's Palace

Westminster Abbey

Palace of Westminster

Lambeth Palace

0   ½   1 mile
0   ½   1   1½ km

**HAMPSTEAD c.1820**

to Child's Hill

to The Spaniards

Heath House

Hampstead Heath

The Grange (Salt Box)

Branch Hill Pond

Whitestone Pond

Albion Cottage

Vale of Health Pond

PROSPECT WALK

The Grove (Admiral's House)

No.2 Lower Terrace

STAMFORD PLACE

WELL WALK

Windmill Assembly Rooms

Constable's House (then No.6)

WEST END FIELDS

St John's Church

Constable's Tomb

HAVERSTOCK HILL
to London (St Paul's)
4 miles

Langham Place
DOWNSHIRE HILL

# *Acknowledgements*

I am indebted to many people. Most especially, to Anne Lyles at Tate Britain, whose great knowledge of Constable matters has been generously shared, and to the late Leslie Parris, who encouraged me to embark on this book. I gratefully acknowledge the help of Brian Allen, Sarah Barnes, Hugh Belsey, Marcus Bicknell, Heather Birchall, David Blaney Brown, the late John Constable and Freda Constable, Richard and Val Constable, Sarah Cove, Natalie Finch, Angela Green, Anne Helmreich, Tom Hodgson, Judy Ivy, Celia Jennings, the late Evelyn Joll, Susan Morris, Annabel Obholzer, Pippa Parris, Charles Rhyne, Ian St John, Frank Salmon, Norman Scarfe, Sarah Speight, Allen and Olive Synge, David Thomson, Pieter and Elizabeth van der Merwe, Barry Venning, Ian Warrell, Andrew Wilton, Joan Winterkorn, and Patricia Wright. My thanks to the Yale Center for British Art in New Haven for a visiting fellowship and the Mellon Centre for British Art in London for a grant for research expenses. At Yale, I was much assisted by Constance Clement, Jules Prown, Elisabeth Fairman, Scott Wilcox, Gillian Forrester, Susan Brady, Mary Beth Graham, Lori Misura and Denise McColgan. The Suffolk Records Society kindly gave permission for me to quote from its published volumes of Constable correspondence. The Suffolk Records Office in Ipswich gave me access to many books and documents. The staff of the London Library provided their habitual skills and patience. My thanks also to the Wellcome Library and the library of the Royal Academy. This book has come into being with the particular aid of Penelope Hoare, Katherine Fry, Poppy

Hampson, Mary Gibson, Diana Phillips, Reginald Piggott and Neil Olson. Margot Bailey has once again been a presiding angel.

Constable's spelling was idiosyncratic, his punctuation erratic; and I have not aimed at complete consistency in rendering his words. For example, phrases he emphasised in handwritten correspondence and journals were often underlined by him, while in published form emphasis was italicised.

# *Preface*

Constable laboured for many years with little popular success. The Royal Academy treated him haughtily as just a landscape painter, barely deserving recognition. But then the French took him up – gold medals were bestowed – and the London art world slowly opened its eyes to what he was up to. He had a select following at the time of his death and then the world came to his works and adopted them as images of an England that suddenly fitted its picture of itself (or aspiration for itself) as green and pleasant. Constable became quintessential. During the First World War, Maurice Baring wrote to Ettie Desborough about her journal, in which she had discussed the deaths of two of her sons in Flanders. 'It sums up all that is best in England, and English things, like a Constable landscape or a speech in Shakespeare.'[1] Later, there seems to have been a reaction against this at once aesthetic and patriotic admiration of Constable, as if it were all too overwhelming, swamped by nostalgia, even a bit old hat. But now one senses the tide turning again. Perhaps rightly it was in Paris in 2002 that a selection of Constable works – *Le Choix de Lucian Freud* – was displayed at the Grand Palais and forcefully reminded us of the revolutionary in Constable as well as what now seems traditional – indeed, reminded us of his single-minded passion for landscape at a time when painting water meadows and river banks was regarded as not quite the thing. Without him we wouldn't have as essential parts of our beings the out-of-doors elements of an England that he saw, felt and painted.

It isn't much of an exaggeration to say that the last biography of

John Constable was published 163 years ago. In the years since, a great amount has of course been written about Constable, including several brief lives and much art history in the shape of critical studies, scholarly monographs, and exhibition catalogues. But Charles Leslie's *Memoirs of the Life of John Constable* of 1843, an astute selection of letters to and from Constable linked by a friendly commentary, has remained the text to conjure with, both charming and persuasive. However, the lacks in Leslie's *Life* have also become increasingly evident: his tendency to see the best or least-troubled side of Constable; and his habit of excising anything that might strike an early-Victorian reader as coarse or indiscreet, such as getting rid of the words 'cow-dung' in a letter Constable wrote to the engraver David Lucas or leaving out the names of artists Leslie felt would be embarrassed by being featured in an anecdote.[2] And though Leslie chose cleverly from the letters available to him, he didn't have to hand the massive amount of correspondence which Ronald Beckett edited into half a dozen volumes in the 1960s and to which two supplementary volumes were soon added. Unfortunately also missing in Beckett's haul are many letters to the Dunthornes, father and son, that were apparently destroyed in the 1920s.[3] Nevertheless, the Constable correspondence assembled by Beckett is probably the biggest trove of documentation concerning any English artist and it has remained a vital resource and rather intractable tool for getting at John Constable.

Beckett's work was comprehensive yet forbidding. It arranged the hundreds of letters not in one chronological sequence but in a series of volumes divided by theme: family, friends, fellow artists, letters to Leslie and so on. To find out what was happening to Constable in, say, 1827, the reader has to consult eight books and collate the findings, together with details from other sources that Beckett chose to interpolate between the letters. So Beckett's masterwork was both boon and bother. It gave some Constable scholars, sitting with the pale green volumes (splendidly published by the Suffolk Records Society) on a shelf near their desks, the right to say no other biographical text was needed: Leslie was charming and, as for the rest, it was all in Beckett . . . Yes. But. In the numerous volumes of the *Correspondence* there are so many trees that the wood which is John Constable is hard to discern.

I have enjoyed Leslie's *Memoirs* and have adopted a year-by-year framework much like his for this book. Yet, although some of the same material has gone into this account, I have all in all selected differently from the correspondence. I have – to make use of an artistic term, *chiaroscuro*, that Constable bandied about – given equal stress to the *chiaro* and the *scuro*, feeling that Leslie downplayed the darkness visible in Constable's life and works, particularly in the latter part of his career. And while naturally concerned with the work which brought him, in England, a largely posthumous renown, I have devoted substantial attention to his protracted love affair with Maria Bicknell, from their first meeting when she was about twelve (and he was a grown man) to their eventual marriage and tragically abbreviated married life. I have dealt at greater length with the ups and downs of their many children and Constable's concerns for them. He was torn between his two ambitions, between trying to perfect his life and perfect his work, though he hoped that his realm encompassed and was enriched by both his art and his family.

*Spring*: East Bergholt Common. Mezzotint engraving by David Lucas, after John Constable, 1830.

# 1. *Day-Spring (1776-99)*

The lane slopes gently from the village to the river, grassed ridge in the middle and wheel-ruts to either side with muddy spots and slithery patches. Gravity makes the feet go faster. On the right the trees in the lane-side hedge are thinning out. Dark furrows in the ploughed field beyond create long converging lines before vanishing together in the early morning sun. A pheasant whirrs off over a fence to a pasture where cattle are grazing. A bird's nest can be seen; the hedge needs re-laying. The leaves have begun to turn and the last blackberries look dry and dusty. For a moment a prospect opens along the broad valley westward and the grey tower of Stratford church comes into view, marking what is still the highway – Colchester south, Ipswich north, outposts of the metropolitan world. Then Fen Lane closes in again; the shadows thicken and one feels suddenly colder.

John Constable as a boy hurrying to school would have been tempted to pause for a few seconds on the bridge, Fen Bridge, which crosses a stream coming from Stratford to join the Stour. From the bridge one can look down on dark green water, with patches of scum and out-of-focus shapes of fish below the surface, flickering from refuge to refuge. With the trees left behind he could walk fast along the raised bank to the next bridge over the Stour, the span just high enough for one of his father's barges to get under. This is the Staunch, Bridge Meadow to its left, the Fen to the right, and ducks and a few swans browsing as usual, with several willows growing out of the bank and old stumps, the remains of the willows' predecessors, sticking up like blackened teeth. Across this bridge he was in the open and on the flat, skirting a water meadow. The raised edges of the valley rise on three sides, south, west, and north. A slight soft wall of clouds is forming to the south-west, and there's the hint of a breeze which two centuries ago would have had the men at the family windmill on East Bergholt Common hauling on ropes and tackle, setting the mill in the right direction and opening up the sails. Hastening along the path, young Constable could get a bearing he didn't need from Dedham church tower before passing a farmyard on his right, farmhouse and barn on his left, and then come between the outlying houses of Dedham village. Soon there was the inn sign of the Duke of Marlborough swinging gently on the right and Dedham church looming to the left. From the big brick building this side of the church the bell would be ringing. He would clatter up the steps, jostling with a few equally out-of-breath pupils as he dashed into the schoolroom. With luck, he would be standing at his desk as Dr Grimwood came through the door in his black scholar's gown, as prayers were said and announcements made. Then John Constable let himself be wrapped into the school-day as into a dream, allowing the pictures in his mind of lane and fields and river to fill his head until it was time to be outside again for the walk home.

John Constable came into the world on 11 June 1776 in East Bergholt, Suffolk. The parish record of his christening on that date includes the additional, exceptional word '*Born*' – that is, he was baptised on the actual day of his birth. The story he later heard was that he wasn't expected to live, and the Reverend Walter Driffield had to turn out at eleven o'clock at night for a swift walk 'over the heath' to the Constables to make a Christian of the weakly infant.

His parents were Golding Constable, grain merchant, mill owner and farmer of ninety-three acres, and Ann Watts Constable, daughter of a London barrel-making manufacturer. Golding Constable's childless Uncle Abram, who had interests in Suffolk and London, had named him as the heir to much of his estate. As for Ann, provided with a good dowry, she married Golding in 1767, when she was eighteen. In 1776 the Constables already had two daughters and a son, all born in the mill house by the river at Flatford. John was the first to be born in their grand new village residence, East Bergholt House, which had four large rooms and some smaller on each of the three floors, as well as stables and a coach house. Despite his uncertain first hours, Constable was soon a healthy, thriving child. Golding Constable could begin to hope that he had a capable heir as miller and merchant. His daughters Ann and Martha were eight and seven years older than John, and their brother Golding, born in 1774, was disappointingly slow – epilepsy was mentioned.

East Bergholt lay in the extremely fertile countryside of southern Suffolk, on sandy soil rather than the more irksome clay, and perched on the northern rim of the shallow Stour valley. This was just upstream from where the placid river broadened out into a tidal estuary – a few miles east were the seaport of Harwich and the North Sea. The Stour, as the Reverend Grimwood would have told his pupils, had been the ancient boundary between the Angles and the Saxons. East Bergholt was a diffuse village, with a skein of houses threaded along a curving main street. Constables had been living in the Stour valley for generations and Golding Constable didn't mind calling it home; he claimed he found it hard to breathe when close to the city, in fact as soon as he reached Ilford in Essex. Moreover, East Bergholt, like most Suffolk villages, had its own energies and preoccupations in farming and trades linked to it. In the past cloth-making had made for local prosperity. One effect of that could be seen in the fine early-Tudor church, squatting where the street took a right-angle bend; while the rapid winding-down of cloth fortunes was evident in the fact that the church had never been given an upper tower or spire.

Dedham Grammar School was John Constable's third school and his favourite so far. In 1783, aged seven, he had been plucked from the family bosom and sent as a weekly boarder fifteen miles away, to Aldham, just west of Colchester. There, at Pound House, in Ford Street, which ran down to the River Colne, he had gone to Mr

Stilleman King's establishment; this taught the three Rs to children aged eight or nine.[1] From there, his father having ambitions to make him a clergyman or his successor in the Constable business, he was removed to Lavenham, about twelve miles from East Bergholt. Lavenham School was meant to be run by Mr Blower, a man unfortunately headlong in love, and there young Constable came up against the brutal cane of an usher who was the stand-in pedagogue for the distracted headmaster. Ever after Constable thought of Lavenham School as a prison. (The experience was to make him reluctant to impose a formal education on his own children.) But an appeal to his father and mother was successful – the Constables were by and large doting parents – and Constable was transported to close-at-hand Dedham as a day boy. Here, for the next five years, his failure to shine academically was tolerated. Dr Thomas Grimwood, forty-six in 1786, managed to instil in him some knowledge of the Bible and the classics, and some Latin, Greek and French. Indeed, Constable's Latin later sufficed for keeping up with his friend John Fisher, a bishop's nephew, when they read Horace together.[2]

Dr Grimwood possibly remained indulgent because Constable showed a talent for penmanship and calligraphy, skills most teachers favour.* Constable seemed to think in pictures, before he ever drew or painted, and Dr Grimwood, good at his job, recognised that his dreamy pupil might have other than conventional talents. 'Honest John,' as he called the boy, might indeed be too much of a 'genious' to become a merchant. When Constable, abstracted in the classroom, didn't realise he had just been asked a question, Dr Grimwood exclaimed with a forgiving smile, 'Oh, I see you are in your painting room.'[3]

What he remembered of his childhood came occasionally into view, when afterwards he recalled what he had seen, almost as if framed, from windows of the family house. The prospect, for example, across

*Later readers trying to decipher Constable's adult correspondence may have wished he had kept up those skills.

the kitchen garden or flower garden to outbuildings and then fields. The porch and the sundial over the entrance to the church, the building that was their immediate neighbour to the south-east, or the grassy strip of common land across the way, on which fairs were held in summer. The windmill belonging to his father that stood on the near horizon, at the edge of East Bergholt Common, a white-painted wooden postmill with dark sails, a village landmark that he looked at every morning to see what it told him about the weather, where it was coming from and how hard it was blowing. Landmarks and benchmarks. Various lanes radiated from the village centre out to the hamlets of Gaston End, Burnt Oak, Baker's End, Pittis End and Flatford. About a thousand people lived in this community, with a dense stratum of farm workers and their families at the base and a few notables at the top, including the squire Peter Godfrey, who lived across the street at Old Hall, and the rector whose fine house and long driveway was visible through the trees beyond the church, the rectory grounds forming the territory along the eastern border of the Constable estate. Here was a known order of things. Here was a security that for a long time didn't manifest its claustrophobic aspects. Everyone knew young John Constable, and he knew everyone: the family servants, his father's workers, village people, local gentry. The tilling of land and the harvesting of crops, the shipping of grain out and coal in, created a structure to life: what happened when. You knew what seasons betokened particular events and how you'd be expected to handle them, what clothes to wear, what food to eat.

The house seemed to him a mansion. It had not only Georgian symmetry but size enough to give a boy lots of scope. As other siblings came on the scene – another sister, Mary, in 1781, and a younger brother, Abram, two years later – and as his two older sisters either cosseted him or kept telling him what to do, he found its space useful; there were rooms to hide in, to read or draw in; there were the gardens and nearby fields for further refuges. John grew up with an unquestioning sense of where he stood in the local order of things: near the top. This confidence was no doubt aided by the fact that he was the heir apparent: Golding, though older, had his handicaps; Ann

East Bergholt House, *c.*1810

and Martha were girls. (Ann remained boyish-looking; she never married but was devoted to her horses and dogs. Mary, also a spinster, seemed to get increasingly scatterbrained with the years.) However, their father's fortunes fluctuated with trade, with the price of grain and coal, with peace or war, and Golding Constable let his children know it, even though the family was cushioned against the worst slumps and downturns. It wouldn't do them any harm to prepare for occasional frugality.

As well as the windmill across the common, his father owned two watermills, one at Dedham and the other at Flatford, inherited from Uncle Abram, the corn-factor in London. 'Corn' was not American maize but any sort of grain, particularly wheat used for flour. There were also two yards and a wharf at Mistley, on the Stour estuary, where the Constable coastal vessels *Telegraph* and *Balloon* – modern names for traditional sailing craft – loaded grain for London and

brought back bricks and manure. Several canal barges carried these goods further inland, to and from Dedham and Sudbury. Although 'trade' underpinned his family's existence, and the Constables wouldn't have considered themselves gentry, they were well connected. Mrs Constable knew the widowed Lady Beaumont, now remarried to Mr John Gates and living in an elegant house in Dedham High Street.[4] The Cobbold brewing family in Ipswich were friends. Mrs Constable's brother David Pike Watts, a wine merchant and brewery owner in London, eventually had a fortune of £300,000. Several military and naval men were relations. John's sister Martha, nicknamed Patty, his only sibling ever to marry, became Mrs Nathaniel Whalley and provided another substantial family foothold in the City of London – the Whalleys were cheesemongers in Aldgate. The Constables had an eminent neighbour in Dr Durand Rhudde, who became rector of East Bergholt in 1782, when John was six. Dr Rhudde (pronounced Rudd) was a chaplain to George III. His daughter Maria Elizabeth married Charles Bicknell, lawyer to the Admiralty, and his sister had married a wealthy Suffolk landowner, William Bogdani. This relationship would eventually enhance Dr Rhudde's fortunes.[5]

For the time being, young John Constable was at the centre of his own world. Dr Grimwood, despite his concerns with parsing and declensions, was no fierce taskmaster; the boy, he thought, would get on quietly one way or another. John's mother hoped he would grow up pious and well mannered, but she herself was not just pious but practical and shrewd. John's father continued to assume that, with John's brother Golding being what he was, John would come into the business. No one objected if John's training for doing the accounts, for the intricacies of buying grain or selling coal, appeared to include helping out with barges at Flatford lock, sitting with a fishing pole beside the Stour backwater below Fen Bridge, and walking to the windmill on a day of scudding clouds to watch the sails swish by, while the grinding stones within sounded a rough susurrus. The Stour countryside was in good heart. Something to be proud of even if the world beyond, from what the Ipswich papers said about it, was in a parlous state, with the French murdering their monarch and the English fleet the only bulwark to prevent Jacobin hordes from swarming on to our shores. Even so, it would be good if the mate of the *Telegraph* could escape his impressment and go back to serving the Constables rather than the Crown.

What John Constable took in from his father, and didn't at first react against with any passionate contrariness, was a sense of the necessities in their lives: people needed food and fuel, and the family themselves got their livelihoods from supplying this need. The land, one way or another, had seasonal rhythms that had to be honoured, and the river its varying levels and tides that must be served. Much of this was unspoken. And equally, when he was sixteen, there was scarcely a decision made: he started work alongside the clerks in his father's office and the workmen at the mills. Like most youths he wanted to leave his mark and used his penknife to carve the outline of a windmill on a beam of their postmill; nearby with the same implement he added an inscription, '*John Constable, 1792*'. He knew about mills inside and out, and brother Abram later boasted, 'When I look at a windmill painted by John, I see that it will go round' – for Abram, this wasn't apparently the case with windmills drawn by other artists. John's early reading interests and rudimentary drawing skills were evident in a book, *A Juvenile Introduction to History*, in whose margins he made clumsy illustrations: two windmills behind the brow of a hill, on one page, and on another, a sketch for a bloody tale called 'Fraternal Affection'. In this a ship had been wrecked and lots were drawn for places in the ship's small boat. One boy gave up his place to his older brother, but then, in the icy water, he changed his mind and tried to clamber on board. His crewmates chopped off his hands to prevent him swamping the boat, but the lad continued to tread water so bravely that his mates relented and saved him – they made land next day. The drawing shows the desperate boy's handless stumps. It provides no evidence of artistic talent but possibly suggests fraternal feeling for brother Golding.[6]

Constable, though hardly demonstrating it, was all the while storing up data. What the sky looked like on a spring day; the look of East Bergholt fields being lashed by rain and hail; high skies with masses of cloud above and bits of cloud below that were moving faster – these, he later noted, were called 'messengers' by millers and sailors, and foretold bad weather. A millworker kept his eyes on the shapes of clouds – thunderheads, cauliflower clouds, anvil shapes – so that he was ready to get the sails right for what was coming, and if necessary put the brakes on. Saw-blades needed to be kept sharp; gears and blocks had to be greased; blocks and tackle were on hand to be hooked into the right eye-bolt for hauling the mill round into the prevailing wind. Working at the Pitt's Farm windmill, named after a nearby homestead, and at the two watermills could have given the tall good-looking boy the opportunity to live up to the fertility lore attached to his occupation, or at least appreciate the humour of it. In several European languages to 'mill' was also to copulate. In ancient Greek *myllein* meant to grind, to press the lips together, or, figuratively, to have sex. 'Even today in vernacular German,' writes Anita Albus, 'to "mill" is equivalent to "engaging in sexual intercourse".' Constable undoubtedly made an impression on the local girls, but the story handed on by an old-timer from Dedham that, claiming a God-given droit de seigneur, Constable got one impressionable though pro-testing lass into trouble and sired a reminder of his insistence, is unsupported by anything other than gossip and our knowledge of what lads normally get up to, if they can.[7]

In late adolesence Constable had a frequent companion: John Dunthorne. Constable was eighteen in 1794 and Dunthorne twenty-four, the six years' seniority making him a useful adviser on several counts. Dunthorne lived in a cottage close by in The Street, facing the junction with Cemetery Lane, across from the Red Lion Inn, and just north of the Constables' entrance gate. Dunthorne had married Hannah Bird the year before. Ann Constable later claimed that Hannah took in Dunthorne 'from an advertizement, without a change of raiment, or a shilling in his pocket', and although the marriage had its ups and downs the couple had four children (Ann, James, John and Hannah). Dunthorne worked as a jack of all trades, as plumber, house painter, signboard artist, glazier, handyman and, at one period, village constable. For Constable, Dunthorne's chief fascination was his desire to be a painter, not just as a maker of signs but pictures: no one else in the Constable family had such an interest. Moreover, Dunthorne struck his East Bergholt fellow residents as a maverick. The rector regarded him as a dangerous atheist. For Constable, this may have added to Dunthorne's appeal.[8]

They were soon companions on the road to art, going off on local painting expeditions together. Golding Constable was at first amused by his son's harmless hobby and said, when he saw the pair arrive back in the village carrying their sketching gear, 'Here comes Don Quixote with his Man Friday!' (He may just as easily have said, 'Here comes Robinson Crusoe with his friend Sancho Panza.') With Dunthorne, Constable learned diligence, observation and technique. The engraver David Lucas later wrote (in a note made in his copy of Leslie's *Life*), 'Both were methodical in their practice, taking with them into the fields their easels and painted only for a certain time each day. When the shadows from objects had changed their position the sketching was postponed untill the same hour, the following day.' Constable afterwards recalled the importance of East Bergholt and its scenery in what he became: 'I associate my "careless boyhood" to all that lies on the banks of the Stour. They made me a painter.' In this John Dunthorne was a vital prop, providing the physical help and cheerful encouragement an adolescent boy might need. Dunthorne, although untrained himself, was also a practical instructor, demonstrating what to do with pigments and linseed oil, brushes and canvas. Together they solved problems of focus and composition, colour and contrast.[9]

Nothing of Constable's work from those apprentice days shows any great talent. He must have been in at least two minds about what he was going to do, but he didn't seem completely repelled by the destiny of grain merchant that hung over him. His father worked hard, put his shrewd mind to problems of shipping and milling, and was a thoughtful parent. His son was impressed by Golding Constable's consideration for his workers. On one occasion a bargee had refused a move from one Constable-owned cottage to another, telling his employer, 'If I remove from this place I shall never be able to shave again.' How so? asked Mr Constable. The bargee replied that he sharpened his razor every Sunday on the top step of the stairs and couldn't do without it. Well, said Mr C, in that case 'my carpenter will take up the step for you to carry with you, and the stairs too if you want them.' John's mother managed the large household, organised the domestic brewing and dairy work, was well informed about village affairs and kept in touch with her London relatives. She remembered birthdays and sent useful gifts. But she regarded John Dunthorne as by no means a suitable companion for her son. Moreover, she wished young John could be more sociable and spend time at home with his family rather than stay out sketching in the fields till nightfall.[10]

Even so, Ann Constable's contacts in Dedham and the next village, Langham, helped set her son on a path that bypassed the grain and coal business. Perhaps there was an element of maternal cleverness here, if not a little social climbing. She may have thought that if John were going to be mixed up with painting and painters, why not ensure that he got to know a grandee or two, not just an artisan? In 1795 Mrs Constable arranged for John to call on the twice-widowed dowager Lady Beaumont in Dedham High Street when Lady Beaumont's son Sir George, whom Mrs Constable had known as a boy, was staying there. The baronet was now a very wealthy man, his riches founded on coal mines, with a house in Grosvenor Square, London, and a country estate first in Dunmow, Essex, and then Coleorton, Leicestershire. More crucially, Sir George was a distinguished collector of paintings, a dedicated amateur artist and a connoisseur of high taste; he had done the Grand Tour and had *objets* and stories to show for it; he had known such artistic luminaries as Reynolds, Gainsborough and Wilson; and Alexander Cozens himself had taught him art at Eton.[11]

In Dedham, Sir George agreed to let Constable, nineteen that summer, show him some pen-and-ink copies the young man had made of engravings (by Dorigny) of some Raphael cartoons. In turn, Sir George showed Constable watercolours he owned by Thomas Girtin, a rising star in London – 'examples of great breadth and truth', that Beaumont advised Constable to study. He also displayed a small painting which he carried everywhere in a travelling case. It was an Annunciation scene painted in 1646 by Claude Lorrain. In an Italianate landscape – bright water, bright sky – a young woman sat beneath some overarching trees with an angel beside her making meaningful gestures. This was Hagar, whose story is recounted in Genesis: after Abraham got her pregnant, she quarrelled with Abraham's wife Sarah and then ran off into the wilderness. There she met the angel by a spring. The angel told Hagar her child would be a boy named Ishmael, who would lead a great tribe. Meanwhile, the angel said, Hagar should return home to live with Sarah. The angel pointed the way to a small town on a hilltop.

Sir George may have asked Constable if he noticed how Italian the scene was – not exactly biblical! But Sir George's enthusiasm for his little picture must have been the primary thing demonstrated. Constable should note how Claude – the son of a pastry cook from a place near Nancy, in France – had split up the painting, with the foreground a dark green-brown, the middle distance a lighter green and the background a hazy blue. The sun blazed at the viewer; the trees made a feathery frame. The two small figures were posed stagily, with Hagar in her bright blue dress leaning back in alarm, startled by the angel whose wings looked as if they were stage props. The hilltop town, the lake, the river, the bridge and a man rowing a small boat – not at all like the Stour, though some similar elements may have sparked recognition with Constable. What atmosphere!

The little painting had a lifelong effect on Constable. He later copied *Hagar and the Angel* several times. One example of the master's influence was visible in a weak sepia sketch Constable made soon after seeing the work, but it was not for some seven years that Claude's impact truly made itself felt with the *Dedham Vale* of 1802 – an enchanted landscape. The introduction to Claude would have been reason enough for Constable to be for ever grateful to Beaumont, but the baronet continued to play a part in Constable's life, not least by the love of paintings he plainly radiated. Yet the celebrated art lover had his blind side: he never appreciated Turner's genius and he didn't seem to understand what he was dealing with in Constable. No real patronage was offered apart from one small commission in 1823, which a then overworked Constable declined. The young man from East Anglia was always a potential protegé, but Beaumont's commitment remained a social one, with an element of condescension to his mother's friend's son – a country relationship, of the sort a superior being might enjoy with an inferior.[12]

Right then it would have taken a leap of vision to detect a future master in the student artist. He copied in an exercise book a number of grotesque heads from Lavater's *Physiognomy*. An early attempt at landscape, *A Country Road*, was perhaps sketched during a 1794 tour to Norfolk he made with one of his father's clerks. He went on working for his father while in his spare time painting alongside Dunthorne and studying what he hoped were the right books. In October 1796, as the evenings once again grew longer, he was deep in Count Algarotti's *Essay on Painting* and Leonardo's *Treatise*. These texts had been suggested to him while staying with an aunt and uncle in Edmonton, on the northern outskirts of London. Thomas Allen, a brewer married to Ann Constable's sister Jane, was like many of John Constable's relations in what might be called well-to-do trade. The Constables' idea seems to have been to expose John to useful contacts in the grain business but the immediate effect at the Allens was to introduce him to their friend John Thomas Smith. Smith was a portrait painter, engraver, author, teacher, and collector of antiquities, who became Keeper of Prints at the British Museum.

When Constable later pledged that all that lay on the banks of the Stour made him a painter he told only a partial and somewhat identity-enhancing truth. What also made him a painter was stimulation received from suburban London – from Thomas Allen, a scholar as well as a brewer, and from friends of the Allens interested in the arts and antiquities. Among these were J.T. Smith and the painter John Cranch. For a while Smith (1766–1833) played Polonius to Constable's Hamlet. He was ten years older, a native of the city born in a London hackney carriage, who claimed to have been patted on the head as a child by Dr Johnson. He loved talking about art. He took Constable around in London and suggested Algarotti and Leonardo to him for reading. He also got Constable to do artistic chores for him, seeking out picturesque rural scenes and copying prints. Smith was particularly interested in decayed cottages covered with mossy thatch. Where Sir George Beaumont had held out glimpses of the Golden Age in the form of enchanted palaces, Smith offered raggle-taggle rustic dwellings in which even Marie-Antoinette's ladies would have struggled to keep their shepherdess clothes clean. John Cranch was likewise into the picturesque, picturing interiors of cottages showing homespun activities. (He achieved a fleeting celebrity for his painting of the death of the tragic young poet Chatterton.) Cranch also gave Constable a list of books he should read – not just Leonardo and Algarotti, but de Piles, the Richardsons, Hogarth and Reynolds, whose *Discourses* were essential reading. Cranch told Constable: 'The "Discourses" are a work of unquestionable genius . . . They go . . . to establish an aristocracy in painting.' However, Cranch thought quite smartly that Reynolds had led many students 'into a contempt of everything but <u>grandeur and Michael Angelo</u>: the force . . . with which the precepts are inculcated, makes us forget that the truth of Teniers and the wit and moral purposes of Hogarth have been, and will for ever be, at least as useful'. Cranch's painting skills were also made to serve as a learning tool. Constable wrote to Smith in November 1796 to say that he had just painted 'a small moonlight' in Cranch's manner; this showed gypsies camped at night round a fire near Hadleigh church.[13]

If not a gypsy's, an artist's life beckoned the twenty-year-old Constable while in London. His father – perhaps beginning to suspect his son's commitment to the family business – reproved him for a hastily scribbled letter. John replied affecting to set Golding Constable right on what he saw as an error. He didn't want a job in town other than for the purpose of learning a business like his father's and this might be of service to both of them. In fact, this reply was disingenuous; although part of John Constable felt Suffolk – his Suffolk – was the necessary framework of existence, part sought a new world. He loved his family and the security it provided. He was also repelled by the loving confinement created by parents and siblings, by knowing how his mother and father would react to any question. Like many a young man before him, he wanted to stay and he wanted to escape.

Although Constable went back from Edmonton to East Bergholt, and set to work in his father's office, his mind was only half on the job. Constable tried to get J.T. Smith to lobby on his behalf. He wrote to Smith in March 1797: 'My dear Friend, I must now take your advise and attend to my Father's business, as we are likely soon to lose an old servant (our Clark) . . . And now I certainly see it will be my lot to walk through life in a path contrary to that which my inclination would lead me.' He clearly hoped that Smith would support his artistic leanings. But Smith – also got at by Constable's mother – seems to have hedged his bets, promoting loyalty to the family while conducting a correspondence art course with Constable. Smith sent books and prints which Constable should copy and encouraged the young man in his first clumsy attempts at etching. Another educational venture proposed by Smith was for Constable to find out for him details of Gainsborough's life; Constable said he would ride over to Sudbury, Gainsborough's birthplace, for that purpose. He was also put to work collecting suitable subject matter – ramshackle cottages preferred – for a book Smith was putting together, *Remarks on Rural Scenery*. Constable seemed to enjoy the growing sense of an art world to be explored, to be touched, with luck to be immersed in. He wrote to Smith to say he believed the present Royal Academy exhibition was very good, and, proud to mention an artist he knew personally, 'I understand Sir G. Beaumont excels.'

As the publication date of Smith's book got closer, Constable acted out of gratitude to find subscribers for it at half a guinea a copy. Friends were pestered, among them the amateur artist and banker's wife Mrs Elizabeth Cobbold in Ipswich and the attractive Miss Lucy Hurlock in Dedham; local acquaintances were signed up, including the poet Robert Bradstreet in Higham and Ben Strutt, a collector in Colchester; relatives were waylaid for their ten shillings and sixpence – Constable's sister Martha Whalley subscribed as did his cousin James Gubbins and his uncle David Pike Watts. Constable himself put his name down for two copies. *Remarks on Rural Scenery* appeared on 13 July 1797 – Bonaparte's armies had just outmanoeuvred the Italian and Austrian Armies while the British Navy, the nation's great deterrence against the French, had been paralysed by mutinies at Spithead and the Nore. Smith's work now seems a dusty enough little volume plugging the picturesque, but it serves as a footnote to what interested Constable at the time and as a memento of his pupillage with Smith. (Constable had apparently already been reading William Gilpin's influential essay *On Picturesque Beauty*.) Smith offered some practical advice: a painter had no need to invent figures for a landscape when real people would make better models; and he should try to imitate the colours of nature as realistically as possible, studying closely the innumerable degrees of green and noting how natural objects partook of the colours around them, a doctrine Constable heeded. Fondness for a particular locality he took for granted. He was now putting Smith's advice into practice with John Dunthorne and also with an amateur drawing master from Ipswich, George Frost, whose day job for fifty years was clerking for the Blue Coach firm, which ran services to and from London.[14]

Smith pleased Mrs Constable by praising her son, but she deftly deflected his compliments, saying that if Smith knew her husband he wouldn't wonder that they had such a son. Indeed, she counted on seeing John back in Bergholt soon and hoped he would then 'attend to business – by which means he will please his Father, and ensure his own respectability, comfort & accommodation'. But it was Smith, who visited East Bergholt in the autumn of 1798, whose influence and leverage seemed to count. Constable drove him over to see Mrs Cobbold, subscriber to Smith's *Remarks* and another, if unpaid, believer in Constable's artistic promise. All things seemed to be suddenly conspiring in favour of the path he was really inclined to take. Abram had just turned sixteen and was willing to work in the family business. At Mrs Cobbold's on 29 January 1799 Constable met a well-connected Quaker lady from Tottenham, Priscilla Wakefield. In her diary she described him as 'a pleasing modest young man – who had a natural genius for painting'. And she furnished him with a letter of introduction to Joseph Farington, the secretary of the Royal Academy of Arts – a man with power to open the magic doors. Mrs Constable allowed her hopes for John's respectability to be temporarily put aside. Mr Constable agreed that John could go to London with a small allowance, to study art. The young man might have put it more definitely: he was going to town 'to become a painter'.[15]

## 2. A Hero in Distress (1799–1802)

John Constable signalled his success in a joyful letter to John Dunthorne in early March 1799. He wrote from 23 Cecil Street, off the Strand: 'I am this morning admitted a student at the Royal Academy; the figure which I drew for admittance was the Torso . . . I shall begin painting as soon as I have the loan of a sweet little picture by Jacob Ruysdael to copy.'

Saying this, he was getting ahead of himself. Farington, regarded by some as Dictator of the Royal Academy, had looked at Constable's rural sketches and introduced him to Joseph Wilton, the elderly Keeper. Classical art still set the fashion, and drawing the Belvedere Torso was the standard challenge set for would-be students. Constable, coming up to twenty-three years old, had been admitted as a Probationer, not yet a full-fledged student; but he was allowed to use the Antique Academy, full of plaster casts of ancient statuary, and did so until the end of the Academy year. He went to anatomy lessons, drew from the casts and – continuing to teach himself the techniques of painting – made copies not only of Ruysdael but of Poussin and Claude. He shared rooms with another young hopeful, Richard Ramsay Reinagle. Reinagle was not an RA student but a pupil of his father, who was an associate of the Academy and a skilful copyist of old masters. Constable went looking for art he could find publicly on view – sparser in those days, before great museums. Loyalty, if not simple curiosity, took him to Old Bond Street to see an object John Cranch was exhibiting, admittance half a crown. This was not a painting but 'an old, rusty, fusty head, with a spike in it', that Cranch, one of three partners who owned it, declared to be 'the real embalmed head of Oliver Cromwell'. A change from the Belvedere Torso.[1]

Constable returned to East Bergholt for the summer holiday and in mid-August was sketching in the countryside near Ipswich. He wrote from there to J.T. Smith, the mentor with whom he was still in touch, 'It is a most delightful country for a painter. I fancy I see Gainsborough in every hedge and hollow tree.' Constable made no secret of his heroes and their pull on him. When Richard Ramsay Reinagle came up to Suffolk to visit him, the weather was wet and they walked to Dedham to sketch the flooded fields. (Reinagle's painting, *Dedham in Flood*, was shown at the Academy in 1801.) Reinagle, a year older than his fellow lodger, was also taken to meet some young ladies of the neighbourhood who admired the handsome young miller who wanted to be an artist. Among these was Miss Lucy Hurlock, daughter of the Reverend Brooke Hurlock, rector of Lamarsh, who also stood in as curate for the absentee rector of Langham, close to Dedham, Dr John Fisher. We don't know whether it was again Constable's mother's skill at drawing useful people into her son's ken that functioned here, or whether it was simply a warm glance from Miss Hurlock. But in a fateful, knock-on way, through the Hurlocks young Constable met Dr Fisher, whose primary post at this point was as a canon at Windsor. Dr Fisher was also an amateur artist and art devotee; he was acquainted with the King; he had a London townhouse, in Seymour Street, and pretty soon he too was taking an active interest in Constable's career.

The daughters of a dissenting minister and engraver named Taylor who had recently moved from Colchester joined the number of Constable's feminine fans. The Taylors were renting a small house in Dedham from Golding Constable. Ann Taylor – later known as a writer of verse for children and in particular of 'Twinkle, Twinkle, Little Star' – went over to East Bergholt in December 1799 hoping to see the paintings of the young man she'd heard so much about and with luck the young man in person. Rumours which had reached her 'conferred upon him something of the character of a hero in distress'. Constable's father, she understood, wanted 'to confine him to the drudgery of his own business – that of a miller. To us this seemed unspeakably barbarous, though in Essex and Suffolk a miller was commonly a man of considerable property, and lived as Mr Constable did, in genteel style.'

Mr Constable in fact was continuing to give his second son every chance to prove his mettle. He had allowed John to use a spare bedroom in East Bergholt House as a studio and soon let him have the small but more self-contained Moss Cottage, with a twenty-five-foot by twelve-foot upstairs room to paint in, just up the street. Mrs Constable seemed equally inclined to be unbarbarous and when the Taylor girls called one December morning they found her at home, 'a shrewd-looking, sensible woman'. Ann Taylor later recalled the meeting: 'There we were, five girls, all "Come to see Mr John Constable's paintings", and as we were about to be shown up into his studio, she turned and said dryly, "Well, young ladies, would you like to go up all together to my son, or one at a time?" I was simpleton enough to pause for a moment, in doubt, but we happily decided upon going en masse.'

Ann Taylor said nothing about the young hero's paintings, but she noted that in one respect Constable lived up to romantic expectation: 'So finished a model of what is reckoned manly beauty I never met with.'[2]

Mrs Constable used to go up to London to visit her many relatives at least once a year; the relatives came down to Suffolk in return. As noted, the extended family in London included Constable's sister Martha, her husband Nathaniel, and their children, at 15 America Square in the Minories, and they frequently invited him for a meal and cheerful company. Ann Constable generally brought to town East Bergholt gossip and hampers of Suffolk food (such as turkeys), took her son's shirts home for mending, and left him plenty of good advice. She trusted he would avoid debt, 'that earthly Tartarus' – she probably had in mind Golding Constable's brother-in-law, the MP Christopher Atkinson, who had swindled the army while a victualling contractor and been expelled from the House of Commons for perjury. If John had to become a painter, she hoped he would create masterpieces that would 'be nothing short of perfection'.

Johnny, as his younger sister Mary continued to call him, had moved soon from Cecil Street to 52 Upper Norton Street, off the Portland Road. His rooms-sharing arrangement with Reinagle hadn't lasted long. In later years Reinagle claimed to have been instrumental in getting Constable started as a painter. Reinagle was evidently eloquent and personable, had studied abroad, and with his family background in the art business and metropolitan sophistication won the young Suffolk man's confidence. Moreover, the portrait of Constable (now in the National Portrait Gallery) that he painted around this time does a skilful job of conveying Constable's moodiness. Constable repaid the compliment with a portrait of Reinagle, though soon after he let the portrait painter John Hoppner paint over it in return for help Hoppner had given him with a picture. Obviously it wasn't a treasure Constable wanted to keep. As in many such acquaintanceships formed when two young hopefuls meet, cracks had quickly appeared. Constable's growing sense of vocation came up against the wheeler-dealing attitude of his friend. Instructed by Reinagle *père*, whose 'restoration' of old paintings raised troublesome questions, Reinagle's eight sisters apparently copied sections of old masters without the permission of the owners and touched up the oil paint they used with watercolours. Thus they worked very quickly. Farington recorded their comment: 'Picture painted one day – sold the next – money spent the third.'[3]

Constable appears in the register of students admitted to the Royal Academy on 21 June 1800; he was twenty-four. He had passed the tests of drawing in chalk an antique figure, an anatomical figure and a skeleton, and was given a circular ivory badge, or 'ticket', with his name and date of admission on it. The Academy was housed in part of Somerset House, the great pile designed by William Chambers that in 1780 mostly replaced the old mansion that had stood at the eastern end of the Strand. There the Academicians fulfilled the Academy's self-imposed obligation to train young artists without charge. Among the dozen or so who were Constable's fellow pupils were many who never found fame, though one who remained in close touch with him to the end was Samuel Lane, a would-be portrait painter who was profoundly deaf and needed to be communicated with in sign language. (Reinagle, though not a RA student, had been exhibiting at the Academy since 1788.) Thomas Uwins, William Mulready and George Jones appear in the lists of this and adjacent years, though they were all younger than Constable. Andrew Robertson, B.R. Haydon and David Wilkie were also students during Constable's time. The rising star at the Academy was J.M.W. Turner, only a year older than Constable but already a ten-year veteran there and, as of 1799, an Associate Academician. Constable's apprenticeship, begun in the Antique or Plaister Academy (named after the battered plaster casts of classical pieces from which the students drew) was continued in the School of Living Models or Life Academy; in this twenty-five of the students attended in the evenings to draw a pair of models. The Keeper, Joseph Wilton, nicknamed 'Squire', was a nattily dressed but decrepit elderly man, no use at discipline. The RA Council had had to rule in 1792 that students were no longer to be provided with free bread for rubbing out sketching mistakes because they threw lumps of it at each other when fights broke out. Henry Fuseli, who became Keeper in 1804, on one occasion cried out during a student disturbance, 'You are a pack of wild beasts!' To which a student replied, 'Yes sir, and you are our keeper.'[4] In one respect Fuseli set the prevailing tone when, in a lecture, he referred disdainfully to 'the last branch of uninteresting subjects, that kind of landscape which is entirely occupied with the tame delineation of a given spot.'[5]

The Visitors, who set poses for the models and supervised Life instruction, included such notable Academicians as Stothard, Northcote and Flaxman. Under them, Constable worked hard at his drawing – one later friend, C.R. Leslie, admired his Life School nudes for having 'breadth of light and shade', though Leslie also thought they were sometimes 'defective in outline'. At this stage Constable was picking up hints from wherever, whomever, he could. In early 1800 he was making copies of paintings by A. Carracci and Richard Wilson; he wrote to John Dunthorne, 'I find it necessary to fag at copying, some time yet, to acquire execution.' Joseph Farington had lent him Wilson's *Hadrian's Villa* to copy.[6] He worked again in front of Sir George's little Claude and copied a Ruysdael which he and Reinagle had bought as a business venture for £70. But around the beginning of 1801 he was expressing to Dunthorne his disenchantment with the work of his old acquaintances (Reinagle not mentioned but undoubtedly in the frame); indeed, he was 'disgusted . . . with their cold trumpery stuff. The more canvas they cover, the more they discover their ignorance and total want of feeling.' Reinagle's landscape of Dedham, painted in East Bergholt, was one such; Constable, who never in his life lacked feeling, described it as 'very well pencilled' and with 'plenty of light without *any light at all*'.

Although from time to time he felt like someone from a different world, a well-to-do young man whose need to be a professional painter wasn't clear to his contemporaries, he couldn't complain about the access and advice he was being given. Beaumont admonished him to read Sir Joshua's *Discourses*, as if offering him a route to the heart of things.[7] The then President of the Academy, Benjamin West, took a painting of Flatford Mill by Constable that had been turned down for an exhibition and drew on it in chalk to demonstrate the necessity of chiaroscuro. West – himself the painter of stagy, somewhat static pictures – told him, 'Always remember, sir, that light and shadow *never stand still*.'[8] West realised that Constable might be disheartened by the rejection of his picture and urged him not to be. 'Young man,' he said, 'we shall hear of you again. You must have loved nature very much before you could have painted this.'[9] And practical support came from below as well as from on high. Another Suffolk person in town was Sam Strowger, a former ploughman. Strowger had recently served as a soldier in the Life Guards, and while doing so had like other guardsmen occasionally modelled at the Academy; he was regarded as 'the most symmetrical' of models and featured in many paintings including David Wilkie's *Rent Day*, in which he is shown as a seated farmer with one finger raised. For Strowger, who came from a farm near East Bergholt and in 1802 became a full-time porter at the Academy with a salary of £25 a year, Constable was not an outsider. Strowger was charmed by Constable's Suffolk views and vouched for the accuracy with which they represented all the operations of farming.[10]

Besides Sir George's collection, Constable had free admission to Michael Bryan's commercial art gallery. He told Dunthorne that he went there once a week, to look at the Orléans collection and particularly 'some landscapes by Gaspar' (this was Gaspar Dughet, 1615–1675, brother-in-law of Nicolas Poussin). He also went to auction rooms to look at old masters and he naturally attended the annual Academy exhibition; this afforded instruction, amusement, abhorrence and – now and then – admiration. In 1801 he told Farington that he thought highly of Turner's *Dutch Boats in a Gale* and sounded proud of knowing the van de Velde it resembled.[11] Nevertheless, despite this gadding about, he complained to Dunthorne that he didn't know much about what was going on in the art world. He had moved early in 1801 to rooms of his own at 50 Rathbone Place, off Oxford Street, with one room specifically reserved as his 'shop' for painting, and now, contrary as ever, claimed to be a stay-at-home. He told Dunthorne that he seldom went out: 'I paint by all the daylight we have, and that is little enough . . . I sometimes however see the sky, but imagine to yourself how a purl must look through a burnt glass. All the evening I employ in making drawings, and reading, & I hope to clear my rent by the former. If I can I shall be very happy.'

Once in a while his longing for home welled up. He told Farington of this and Dunthorne heard a similar *cri de coeur* in the winter of 1800. 'I hope to see you in the spring, when the cuckoos have picked up all the dirt. Every fine day makes me long for a walk on the commons . . . This fine weather almost makes me melancholy; it recalls so forcibly every scene we have visited and drawn together. I even love every stile and stump, and every lane in the village, so deep rooted are early impressions.' Clearly he visualised his experiences as 'scenes', and many of his later pictures were of scenes he must have first encountered with Dunthorne. Dunthorne, although still in place, shared Constable's sense of loss. In March 1802 the village handyman had just finished making a cello but wasn't feeling well, and complained to Constable that he missed him: 'I have no comfortable companion for any serious or instructive conversation.' Constable had just seen his mother who was visiting London; he wrote to Dunthorne, 'I never hear of an arrival from E. Bergholt but I forthwith take my hat & stick and trudge off for the news.' Mrs Constable had given him 'a good account of most of my neighbours', but Constable was told that Dunthorne didn't look well. He put this down to the 'unwholesomeness' of Dunthorne's business – presumably working with lead pipes and lead-based paint – but he hoped spring would bring his old friend a new lease of life.

The Academy year already imposed its constraints. 'As the season advances it becomes more difficult to leave London,' Constable reported. There were numerous picture sales and 'much is to be seen in the Art'. However, summer arrived with the end of the Academy exhibition, Suffolk awaited, and he went to Helmingham Park beyond Ipswich to draw the old oaks. Helmingham Hall belonged to the Earl of Dysart, a member of the Tollemache family which had originally lived at Bentley near East Bergholt. The connection with the Tollemaches was a lasting and fruitful one for Constable; looking ahead a little, work copying family portraits was to come his way, as were commissions for house portraits from Tollemache relatives; moreover, the Earl of Dysart bought a landscape from Constable in 1810 – his first exhibition sale. After the Earl's death in 1821 his sister Lady Louisa Manners became Countess of Dysart and inherited Ham House, another family property near Richmond, Surrey. She eventually took on Constable's hard-to-employ brother Golding as warden of her ill-managed Bentley woods; gifts of venison from a thankful Lady Dysart were a by-product.

In Helmingham Park Constable was on his own, sleeping at the parsonage, eating at the farmhouse and 'left at liberty to wander where I please during the day'. The solitude was inspiring. The drawings he made he thought 'may be usefull'. He used black chalk as for Life class nudes though his models here were trees and his influence was Gainsborough. Art out of doors wasn't too far removed from farming,

A girl in a bonnet,
believed to be the
young Maria
Bicknell, *c*.1800

using your hands, breathing open air, and while you did so dreaming
in an attached, concentrated way. Some of the drawings of trees he did
at Helmingham began to show talent, an ability to see the skeletons
within the forms, visualising the negatives that could be used to create
positive images. Then it was back to East Bergholt. Back to the family
and his ally John Dunthorne. And this year there was a new face
nearby – that of a twelve-year-old girl, Maria Bicknell, the rector's
granddaughter. We don't know where Constable first saw her,
perhaps in the village street, running through the fields between the

gardens of East Bergholt House and the rectory, or maybe in church, with Maria fidgeting up front and Constable in the family pew perusing a newly acquired Book of Common Prayer. During the 1800 Christmas holidays Maria may have been among the assembled Rhudde relatives. Constable was twenty-four and Maria half his age, a lot younger than Lucy Hurlock or any of the other girls who had taken his fancy. He may not have recognised the spark that flashed – he might even have been horrified by any flicker of erotic impulse – but something happened; it is visible in the painting he made of young Maria apparently about this time. The daughter of Charles Bicknell, an important London lawyer (he was solicitor to the Admiralty) who had married Dr Rhudde's daughter Maria Elizabeth as his second wife, Maria at that age could also have had no conscious sense of what was to come. And yet between painter and sitter a current passed. He saw that small pale face with big dark eyes framed by a bonnet, a single tight curl of hair on one side of her forehead, her left hand on her hip. She looked at him so thoughtfully but impatiently – perhaps wishing he'd hurry up and finish painting her so that she could run outside and play.

When he was back in London in Rathbone Place Constable seemed to have a stronger sense of his own direction. Reinagle had exchanged the Ruysdael they had bought together for some other pictures and promised to pay Constable his share when they'd been sold; but Constable refused an invitation to dine with his former business partner whose work he thought mechanical.[12] He told Dunthorne that it 'would be reviving an intimacy which I am determined never shall exist again, if I have any self command. I know the man and I know him to be no inward man.' Even so, predicting Constable's future from the work he was involved in at this time would have been difficult. At the end of 1800 he had finished four watercolours of Dedham Vale, a sort of small-scale local panorama for Lucy Hurlock on her marriage. He was doing a lot of drawing, and was pleased when J.T. Smith offered to take some of his work and try and sell it in his shop. Yet March found him melancholy, according to Farington, and he seems to have needed as much family support as he could get: he spent a lot of time with the Whalleys in the spring and summer of 1801. Golding Constable still wasn't convinced of John's vocation; he thought his son was 'pursuing a shadow', Farington reported, and wished to see him 'employed'. Constable might have countered that he had been employed, for instance in painting Old Hall, the manor house just across from East Bergholt church. Farington, although seeing a lot of Sir George Beaumont's influence in the somewhat ghostly picture of the mansion and surrounding parkland, had pleased him by saying he should ask not five but ten guineas for it.[13] During the summer and autumn he spent what for him was an exceptional amount of time away from both Bergholt and London. It was almost as if he were trying to test to the limit his own commitment to his roots.

Daniel Whalley, his sister Martha's father-in-law, had a house in Derbyshire. From there, accompanied by Martha's brother-in-law, also named Daniel, Constable went on a three-week sketching tour of the Peak District, averaging a couple of pencil and sepia drawings a day. In Dovedale, which Constable sketched as a narrow cleft running into a steep hillside, they bumped into Farington, a veteran in the picturesque, on a very hot day. Constable's drawings were improving, though still a bit wispy, and he found his morale improved too. Possibly he felt more in touch with nature than he might have expected this far from the Stour valley; the local Derbyshire quarries provided millstone grit, the material which provided the stones that turned in the watermills and windmills of England and ground the Constables' flour.[14] He wrote to Dunthorne after this trip: 'My visit to the Whalleys has done me a world of good – the regularity and good example in all things which I had the opportunity of seeing *practiced* (not talked of only) during my stay with that dear family, will I trust be of service to me as long as I live. I find my mind much more decided and firm . . .'

Back in London he attended a series of lectures given by the anatomist Joshua Brookes (RA students were admitted free) and he let the lectures prompt him to thoughts of 'the Divine Architect'. He told Dunthorne – adopting a somewhat superior tone – 'a knowledge of the things created does not always lead to a veneration of the Creator. Many of the young men in this theatre are reprobates.' Constable gave no hint of any such thinking or any untoward behaviour. On the contrary, he was buckling down to all sorts of work. He got paid for painting the background of a picture of an ox that Mary Linwood, a celebrated embroiderer, was copying in needlework. Dunthorne was pleased to hear that he was also 'doing something in the Portrait way' and passed on the cheering news that Constable's father was speaking of his son's recent efforts in 'quite a different way'. And then a painting called *The Edge of a Wood* was accepted for the 1802 Academy exhibition: it showed a thick stand of trees in which one could just make out a man sketching and a donkey and its foal peeking out from the gloomy underbrush; above, only a tiny patch of sky. Nice, but Gainsborough had been here before. And it was a pity that landscape was still on a low level in the hierarchy of art, inferior to history painting and even portraiture; landscape – so such pundits as Jonathan Richardson believed – didn't greatly improve the mind or excite noble sentiments. At this time Dr Fisher proferred a professional post: a new drawing master was needed for the Royal Military College at Marlow. Tempted, Constable went for an interview and stayed with the Fishers at Windsor. Several fine drawings of Windsor Castle showed what he could now do. But though he was offered the job, he took soundings and several influential people advised against acceptance. Farington was one such, and Benjamin West said that if Constable accepted the post he would have to give up all hope of future distinction.[15]

Into May 1802 Constable spent several weeks thinking about what was the surest way to excellence as an artist. Sir George Beaumont's collection once again proved a vital resource in decision-making. After a visit to *Hagar and the Angel*, Constable wrote to Dunthorne, the one person he could really unburden himself to:

I am returned with a deep conviction of the truth of Sir Joshua Reynolds's observation that 'there is no *easy* way of becoming a good painter'. It can only be obtained by long contemplation and incessant labour in the executive part.

And however one's mind may be elevated, and kept up to what is
excellent, by the works of the Great Masters – still Nature is the
fountain's head, the source from whence all originally must spring – and
should an artist continue his practice without refering [*sic*] to nature he
must soon form a *manner*, & be reduced to the same deplorable situation
as the French painter mentioned by Sir J. Reynolds, who told him that
he had long ceased to look at nature for she only put him out.

For these two years past I have been running after pictures and
seeking the truth at second hand . . .

He was determined instead to concentrate on first-hand truth. He
was going to make no more 'idle visits' this summer or give up time to
'common place people'. Farington backed him up in one aspect of
this: he told Constable he should study nature and pay less attention
to particular works of art.[16] Constable wrote to Dunthorne that he was
soon coming back to Bergholt to make 'laborious studies from nature'.
Although he was conscious of the benefits he had got from exhibiting
at it, the Academy exhibition had showed him little or nothing worth
looking up to. 'There is room enough for a natural painture. The great
vice of the day is *bravura*, an attempt at something beyond the truth
. . . *Fashion* always had, & will have its day – but *Truth* (in all things)
only will last and can have just claims on posterity.'

Constable wrote to his most appreciative listener with a young
man's dogmatic idealism, and he may not have suspected how uncomfortable things might get for him, with these colours nailed to the
mast. He also wrote with difficulty, having pains in his teeth and lower
jaw that caused one cheek to swell. Among his laborious studies from
nature made that summer was a painting, *Dedham Vale*, a prospect of
the Stour valley apparently from Gun Hill, near Langham. We look
past a clump of trees beneath which a countryman sits with legs
outstretched. Farington, when he saw the picture, thought it 'rather
too cold'.[17] Turner used the term 'elevated pastoral' for many prints
in his *Liber Studiorum* but this pastoral scene is of a rural landscape not
so much elevated as cultivated – a glimpse of an English Arcadia.

# 3. *Nature's Proper Interest (1802–10)*

Many war-weary people in England felt more cheerful in March 1802. The Treaty of Amiens was ratified and nine years of conflict with France were interrupted by a period of peace. The Channel could once again be crossed without fear of battle or captivity. Those who had been hungry for the Continent and its culture now took their chance to journey there: to board a packet boat from Dover to Calais, to take a diligence to Paris, to wander around the Louvre and admire the paintings which had been liberated from Italy by the armies of the Corsican monster, and then, pushing on across this country which seemed to promote both mob-terrorism and the sweetest charms of civilisation, to traverse the sublime, beautiful, fearsome Alps and visit the land which harboured so many vestiges of the classical world. Many artists in London jumped at this chance: the RA President Benjamin West, Henry Fuseli, Joseph Farington, and J.M.W. Turner, already a full Academician at twenty-seven, were among the cross-Channel voyagers. John Constable was not. Despite his admiration for Claude and Rubens, he had resolved to avoid imitation of and even exposure to other artists, and he stayed put in England. He seems to have had none of the restlessness that causes many to pack their bags and seek other lands; he never crossed the Straits of Dover. He had got as far as Derbyshire, and a few years on would actually reach the Lake District in the north-west of England; but, impelled to quit London, his main ambition was to catch the Ipswich stage and eight hours later find himself at home in Suffolk, there to walk with Dunthorne and sketch the woods, fields and streams around East Bergholt.

He was a stay-at-home artist, but he wasn't entirely stuck in the mud. Captain Torin, a friend of his father, was to make his last voyage to the Orient for the East India Company in the spring of 1803 and invited Constable to join his ship *Coutts* for the first part of the passage. Turner was to say later, with his usual competitiveness, that Constable knew nothing about ships, but that wasn't true. He may not have been a small-boat sailor like Turner but he had seafaring kinfolk. His mother's brother John Watts had sailed with Captain James Cook. His cousin Sidey Constable captained the family's coasting barge *Telegraph* on its voyages delivering grain and coal between London and East Anglia. He had watched river barges being built in the dry dock at Flatford and he knew how boats sat and moved in the water. Constable's voyage with Captain Torin didn't take him out of sight of England – it was largely in the Thames estuary and the inshore approaches to it, behind the Goodwin sands – but it lasted nearly a month. Constable told Dunthorne, 'I saw all sorts of weather. Some the most delightfull, and some as melancholy . . . When the ship was at Gravesend, I took a walk on shore to Rochester and Chatham. Their situation is beautifull and romantic, being at the bottom of finely formed and high hills, with the river continually showing its turnings to great advantage. Rochester Castle is one of the most romantic I ever saw.'

At Chatham the viewer of romantic medieval ruins became a student of modern warships. He hired a boat and went down the River Medway to look at the men-of-war moored in it. He sketched three views of the *Victory* (this was two years before Trafalgar). 'She was the flower of the flock,' he continued enthusiastically in his 23 May 1803 letter to Dunthorne, 'a three-decker of (some say) 112 guns. She looked very beautifull, fresh out of Dock and newly painted. When I saw her they were bending the sails – which circumstance, added to a very fine evening, made a charming effect.' His nautical language was roughly correct – such as bending on the sails – and the drawings he made showed personality and skill of observation. For a better view he seems to have climbed to the top of a mast on one ship, maybe the *Coutts* herself. Unfortunately when the *Coutts* got around the North

Foreland she ran into a south-westerly gale and had to shelter in the lee of the Kent coast for three days. 'Here,' wrote the artist (obviously not an aspiring sailor), 'I saw some very grand effects of stormy clouds.' As the *Coutts* got under way again for her voyage to China, Constable was landed by boat on the shingle beach at Deal and in the confusion of disembarkation left all his four weeks' sketching on board – about 130 drawings, mostly small. From Deal he walked the ten miles to Dover and took a coach to London next day. His drawings were happily shipped on to him before the *Coutts* left the Channel and he later used some of the Medway sketches for a watercolour of the *Victory* at Trafalgar engaged with two French ships of the line.

The war with France was soon being waged again; the Peace of Amiens had ended in May 1803, and the people of Britain once again slept uneasily. Militias drilled and beacons were prepared. On 17 July Farington recorded: 'I had the last night the most distinct dream of Invasion . . . Of seeing the French boats approach in the utmost order, and myself surrounded by them after their landing. I thought they preserved great forbearance not offering to plunder, & that I was in the midst of them some conversing in broken English. It seemed to me that they came upon the Country quite unprepared, and met with no resistance . . . There was during my dream a sense of great negligence in not being better prepared to receive such an enemy.'[1] Constable was more concerned about the state of the Art and his own place in it. The Academy exhibition that year struck him as 'very indifferent' and 'in the landscape way most miserable'. And yet this state of things intensified a feeling of his own possibilities. He wrote to Dunthorne, 'I feel now, more than ever, a decided conviction that I shall some time or other make some good pictures. Pictures that shall be valuable to posterity, if I reap not the benefit of them.' He had enough money to splash out and buy a dozen prints and four drawings by Waterloo and two small landscapes by Gaspar Dughet. (Leslie later noted Constable's zeal as a collector: 'If a book or print he wanted came in his way, the chances were he would buy it, though with the money that should pay for his next day's dinner.') He noted that R.R. Reinagle was following the latest fad – panorama painting – and would be exhibiting, in the Strand, a view of Rome. The panorama was, Constable observed a shade maliciously, a type of painting that suited Reinagle and kept his defects somewhat hidden. But Constable wasn't in the main current of things. Talking to some younger artists, he was startled to hear of their admiration for Turner's work and surprised they thought it by no means extreme.

The Royal Academy meanwhile was gripped by civil war. Some members, including Farington, thought the King had too much influence through patronage. The monarch's supporters wanted to get rid of Benjamin West, who was not only American by birth but allegedly pro-Napoleon. Rows broke out between members on any pretext – for example on Christmas Eve, during an argument about the giving of gold medals for architecture and sculpture, Sir Francis Bourgeois and Turner furiously slanged each other, Bourgeois calling Turner 'a little reptile' and Turner telling Bourgeois he was 'a great reptile with ill manners'. Constable was out of the way in Suffolk well into the following year, sketching with George Frost ships and warehouses on the Orwell River at Ipswich, the East Anglian corn shipping centre, and making what seems to have been his first drawing of a rainbow. He didn't exhibit at the Academy in 1804. He told Farington it was futile to compete with mediocrity; he had nothing to gain 'by putting pictures in competition with works which are extravagant in colour and bad taste, wanting truth.'[2]

Banking down his own fires but impressing his father with his diligence, he found plenty of local people ready to engage his talents. The small cottage near the Red Lion was his village studio. Portraits painted in the mornings left time for landscapes in the afternoons. The portraits were often life size, head to waist three guineas, head and shoulders two guineas. He told Farington that these low prices allowed the farmers in the vicinity to indulge their ambitions to have their children and other relatives painted.[3] Among the families who sat for Constable at this time were the Cobbolds and the Bridges: he sketched Harriet and Sophia Cobbold in Ipswich in 1804 and 1806, and in 1804 he portrayed Mr and Mrs George Bridges and their eight children, arranged around a harpsichord; they lived near Manning-

Constable's mother, Ann

tree. He managed to find time now or a little later to paint a portrait of his mother, sitting in an upright armchair with a spaniel on her lap. And he tackled a self-portrait for which he donned a high-collared coat and a cravat. There is just a touch of belligerence in his expression, as if he isn't sure of the patience of the person he is staring at in the mirror – how long does he want to hold this pose? The self-portrait makes one question Lady Beaumont's opinion, expressed to Farington this spring of 1804, that Constable 'seemed to be a weak man'.[4] (Constable, one recalls, didn't always agree with everything Sir George Beaumont said.) Difficult, possibly; weak, no.

If there was weakness in any aspect of Constable's art at this moment, it was manifest in several altarpieces he was talked into by influential local people. Dr Rhudde was rector not only of East Bergholt but of nearby Brantham church and for Brantham Constable painted a tall canvas of Christ blessing the children – a rather sickly picture much indebted to the style of Benjamin West. This, and a painting of Christ blessing the bread and wine, made for Nayland church a few years later at the behest of his well-meaning aunt Mrs Martha Smith, were to be taken as proof by Charles Leslie that Constable – after the Nayland attempt – was wise to stop making 'incursions into this walk of the art'.[5] Constable's uncle, David Pike Watts, thought the artist had used his own brother Golding as a model for the Nayland Christ, and Golding may also have served for the Brantham altarpiece – eyes rolled heavenwards, cheeks almost cosmetically pink.[6] Otherwise, the fact that Golding's epilepsy didn't disqualify him for this role is one element of Constable's religious 'incursion' that we can be less critical about.

The support Constable got from his relatives was lifelong. 'Doing something for John' seems to have been a commitment on which the whole family agreed. His mother's sister Mary Watts married James Gubbins, a surveyor, and Constable was frequently invited to their house at Epsom; there he sketched the Common in early August 1806, and there, several years later, he painted out of doors in oils a landscape of a shallow valley, a long meadow bordered by low escarpments and clumps of trees in thick summer leaf. A happy picture, it marked a moment in which Constable found his own way as a landscape painter. Claude, Rubens, Cozens, Gainsborough – they had served their turn. But around 1806 he may still have received some useful tips from Dr William Crotch, Professor of Music at Oxford and a professional drawing master, who was only a year older than Constable and seems to have given him hints on drawing trees of full bulk. David Pike Watts, a wealthy wine merchant, was a collector of art, Gainsborough included, and in his avuncular way attempted to push forward his nephew's career. Watts threw Constable and Crotch together at several dinner parties at his house in Portland Place. In return, Constable occasionally passed on to Uncle David news of the art world (and talked to Farington about Watts's activities). In April 1806 Farington learned from Constable about some trouble Watts was having with Benjamin West.[7] Watts was interested in a painting West had exhibited in his own gallery but they couldn't agree a price. Eventually West said he would accept a lower price if Watts kept the sum secret; Watts, offended, declined to buy it under such a constraint. The waves rippling out from this grumpiness apparently reached out to nephew John as a journeyman in what Watts seemed to think was the important but murky world of paintings and painters.

Constable's reputation as a portraitist had by now reached London. Through Mrs Priscilla Wakefield, the lady who had opened his way to the RA, he spent several weeks in the summer of 1806 with the Hobson family in Tottenham. Markfield House was new, the mansion of William Hobson, a Quaker contractor, who built London docks and coastal defences and fathered sixteen children. In two small calf-bound sketchbooks and on detached sheets Constable sketched the house itself, the Hobson sons and daughters, and various domestic scenes. He also made a coloured pastel sketch of clouds above a barely suggested horizon – a precursor of many sky studies a decade and a half later. Whether a family portrait of the Bridges sort was intended we don't know – apparently it didn't come about – but Constable built up a large inventory of Hobson material: a young man lounging; the girls sewing and reading, sitting together and apart, playing a spinet and having tea. One brilliant oil sketch painted by an apparently entranced artist shows a young woman from the rear, a black stole dipping across a red dress that reveals her shoulders, bare back and neck – the vertical furrow in her neck leading the eye up to dark brown hair piled high in a bun.

In the autumn of 1806 David Pike Watts suggested that his nephew might try some pastures new: instead of the Stour valley, the fellsides

of the Lake District.[8] Uncle David would pay his way. Constable
stayed with friends of friends and with Watts's agent, Mr Worgan,
who looked after a property Watts owned, Storrs Hall, near Bowness.
He toured the rugged countryside with George Gardner, son of David
Gardner, the friendly and fashionable portraitist who had painted
Constable ten years before and who came from this area. However,
George Gardner had less tolerance for the picturesque than his
companion and soon went back to Borrowdale, leaving Constable
sketching. In seven weeks, not all of fine weather but of dedicated
labour, Constable finished nearly ninety drawings and watercolours.
At Brathay Hall, at the north end of Lake Windermere, he also made
portraits in oils of his hosts Mr and Mrs Harden. John Harden did
several drawings of Constable in their music room, attentive to Mr
Worgan playing the harpischord and at work on a rainy-day portrait
of Jessy Harden, who found Constable 'a genteel, handsome youth'.
(The 'youth' was now thirty.)

Did this tour do Constable much good? Certainly the scenery –
novel to him – was as close to the thrilling tremors of the sublime as
you could find in England. He went to such remote places as Taylor
Gill Force, a waterfall in Borrowdale. Many of his sketches were large,
on tinted paper, and on many he recorded the date, the weather and
particular aspects of the occasion. For example, on one pencil and
watercolour view he made the inscription, '*Borrowdale 2 Sept 1806
morning previous to a fine day.*' Again in Borrowdale on 25 September
he wrote: 'Fine cloudy day, to me very mellow, like the mildest of
Gaspar Poussin and Sir G.B . . . from the eastern slope near
Rosthwaite, looking south to Glaramara and the other hills which
block the end of the valley.' On 4 October he noted: 'Dark Autumnal
day at noon . . . the effect exceeding terrific – and much like the
beautiful Gaspar I saw in Margaret Street.' Later, Charles Leslie
recalled hearing Constable say that the solitude of mountains
oppressed his spirits. Leslie thought Constable's 'nature was
peculiarly social . . . He required villages, churches, farmhouses, and
cottages.'[9] But though Constable never went back to the Cumbrian
fells, visiting them was certainly beneficial for him. He might not

quite have emulated Thomas Girtin – whom Sir George Beaumont had proclaimed the exemplar of great breadth and truth – yet the Watts-sponsored tour seemed to free him up. A number of the Borrowdale drawings and watercolours have a power until now unseen in his work and an ability to show the bones of the worn mountains poking through their rough skins. On his drawing *Esk House* of 12 October the son of the Stour valley wrote unloyally, 'The finest scenery that ever was.'[10] Everything he did here was superior to what his mentor Sir George would have been capable of.

This was country that the Romantic writers claimed for their own. John Keats, staying in the Lake District in 1818, thought the mountains around Borrowdale as fine as anything he had seen. He wrote, 'I have been very romantic indeed, among these mountains and lakes.'[11] Coleridge wrote to a friend in September 1802, soon after climbing Scafell, 'Nature has her proper interest; & he will know what it is, who believes and feels, that everything has a life of its own, & that we are all <u>one life</u>.' Constable would have understood Coleridge's belief that 'a Poet's <u>Heart & Intellect</u> should be <u>combined, intimately combined & unified</u>, with the great appearances in Nature – & not merely held in solution & loose mixture with them, in the shape of formal Similes'.[12]

At Old Brathay a neighbour of the Hardens, Charles Lloyd – a minor poet and son of a Birmingham banker – got Constable to paint several members of his family, including his pretty wife Sophia and their child. Lloyd's sister Priscilla was married to Christopher Wordsworth, a Lambeth vicar and brother of William, and it was through the Lloyds that Constable met the Lake poets, Coleridge and Wordsworth. The latter brought out the sardonic rather than romantic in Constable. Farington wrote in his diary the following year: 'Constable remarked upon the high opinion Wordsworth entertains of himself. He told Constable that while he was going to Hawkshead school, his mind was often so possessed with images, so lost in extra-ordinary conceptions, that he was held by a wall not knowing but he was a part of it.' As Constable stood nearby, Wordsworth asked Mrs Lloyd to note the singular formation of his skull, a shape which Coleridge remarked was 'the effect of intense thinking'. If that was the case, Farington observed, Wordsworth must have started thinking in his mother's womb.[13] Keats arrived at a similar verdict, writing in a letter, 'Wordsworth has left a bad impression where ever he visited in town by his egotism, vanity, and bigotry. Yet he is a great poet if not a philosopher.'[14]

This northern excursion of Constable's was exceptional for the region it took him to but in another respect it came to fit a pattern: if he found it hard to leave home, once away he found it hard to return. Going south in November he called on other members of the Lloyd family to paint portraits and stayed long enough to outwear his welcome. Charles Lloyd wrote from Brathay to his brother Robert in Birmingham, 'Is Mr Constable gone yet? I do hope he will not become troublesome.'[15] When in the midst of a painting job, Constable had a way of forgetting other engagements; an obsessional concentration seized him, which could be disconcerting for his hosts or his family.

A drawing Constable did of himself in this busy year shows his assurance – a confident profile, aquiline nose, firm chin, long sideburns.[16] He had sent to the RA exhibition a fine watercolour of the *Victory* sandwiched between two French ships at Trafalgar, the only error being in his subtitle which made E. Harvey (of the *Temeraire*) rather than T. Hardy the captain of Nelson's flagship. Back in London from Birmingham he saw a lot of David Wilkie and Benjamin Haydon; they regularly had dinner together at Slaughter's in St Martin's Lane. 'This period of our lives was one of great happiness,' recorded Haydon, thereafter not often happy. 'Painting all day, then dining at Old Slaughter's Chop House.' Constable's three entries for the 1807 Academy exhibition sprang from his tour of the Lakes; he told Farington that in one 'he thought he had got something original'. The paintings attracted his first press notice. The *St James's Chronicle* was struck by his *View in Westmoreland* and wrote that Constable 'seems to pay great attention to Nature and in this picture has produced a bold effect.'[17] Encouraged by this, Constable asked Farington whether he should put his name in for the Academy

Self-portrait of 1806

elections as a candidate for Associate membership. Thomas Stothard, Academician and brilliant draftsman, had apparently raised the subject with him. Farington told Constable that he wasn't likely to be elected, 'but he might put down his name to make [it] familiar to the members'. Farington added rather earnestly that the best impression was made by meritorious works. Constable said that for the present he would decline to put down his name.[18]

The summer of 1807 saw Constable so busy in London he was unable to get to East Bergholt. An invitation had come from the Earl of Dysart – whose domains included Helmingham Park, a London house in Piccadilly and Ham House in Richmond – to copy family portraits.[19] This was hack work, but reasonably paid, and since some of the paintings being copied were by Reynolds and Hoppner, Constable willy-nilly learned a good deal more about portrait painting. Charles Leslie afterwards said he thought it a pity that these chores kept Constable from painting landscapes, but he certainly got to appreciate Reynolds's sense of colour and the contrast between light and dark, or chiaroscuro. Moreover, Constable continued to be a keen RA student. Farington on 16 November 1807 heard from the horse's mouth that Constable was spending every evening at the Life Academy in Somerset House, that he was 'settled' as a painter, and that his father was now reconciled to his artistic career. David Pike Watts, whose portrait he had recently painted, also uttered sententious words of approval, declaring that 'J.C. is Industrious in his profession, Temperate in his diet, plain in Dress, frugal in Expenses . . . and in his professional character has great Merit'.[20] The paragon was among a number of eminent artists Uncle David invited to a dinner party in December 1807. Farington was there, and so were Northcote, West, Stothard, Anthony Carlisle (the RA Professor of Anatomy) and Dr Crotch, the composer and drawing master, in some senses a professional guest since at these Watts dinners he played for a fee. Farington in his diary bit the hand that had fed him by noting that Watts had 'an habitual reverence for rank & title'. But Watts did his best to grease the ways for his nephew's advancement in the Art. And Constable showed diplomacy he didn't always display with his contemporaries by turning the other cheek to Watts's critical comments on his work – although he had the temerity to say he couldn't understand why Watts had chosen to live in Portland Place, which hurt his uncle's feelings. Watts was also unhappy at changes Constable made to the Brantham *Christ Blessing the Children*; a more finished picture may have resulted but it didn't interest Watts any more. He said, 'The *mind* of the Picture has fled.' Later, in 1810, Uncle David sent Constable a long letter packed with details of how he might improve his Nayland altarpiece – this had begun as an *Agony in the Garden* but on Watts's advice became *Christ Blessing the Bread and Wine*. The general tone of the letter was as always outspoken but friendly and Constable didn't let it upset him.[21] In any event, Mrs Constable congratulated her son on a picture which she hoped would make certain his fame.

Despite his uncle's help, 1808 didn't bring Constable any notable accession to fame and fortune. In fact, even with his frugality, he was having trouble making ends meet on what his father gave him. Mrs Constable was apparently asked to use her influence to have the parental allowance boosted without giving Golding Constable reason to demand John abandon his artistic career. Abram, his younger brother, was also an intermediary. He sent on 'the *needful*' cash which Mr Constable now provided and wrote in a letter, 'You know money comes loath from our Father, & that he thinks any sum a great one.' Well into 1810 Golding Constable continued to believe that his son was pursuing a shadow in wanting to be a painter, and he wasn't wrong in thinking that most of the work his son managed to get came from the kindness of friends. John sent – as requested by Abram – a grateful acknowledgement for the money to his father. This got him a pleased thanks from his mother, who also sent some shirts she had made for him; she was concerned about the depth of the cambric frills which fashion seemed to demand and which were deeper than any she had ever made. She had more serious anxieties about Mr Constable's health: he had a bad cold, shortness of breath, and a troublesome cough, all of which she blamed on his work on the new floodgates at Flatford Mill. Other health news in the village included the prevalence of measles. It had 'proved fatal only to Mrs Barnard's little boy, which caused her great vexation', wrote Ann Constable, 'but the loss *appears* as if it would ere long be supply'd'.

Constable was now living in Percy Street off Tottenham Court Road and seems to have been summoned for possible military duty to protect his native soil. But actual service was avoided; a clerk in the Middlesex Militia provided a certificate that he had found a substitute to act for him, one James West.[22] It makes one wonder just how accurate was the judgement of Bishop Fisher's wife at this time in commenting that Constable looked guileless, 'like one of the figures in the works of Raphael'.[23] Our hero reappeared in East Bergholt in the late summer of 1808 and walked to his favourite sites to once again paint and draw. An oil-on-paper painting of Dedham Vale from Gun Hill with simplified trees and broadly observed meadows seems to date from this time. *Plein-air* painting was becoming fashionable and even paintings of agricultual scenery were beginning to be seen with less objection. Albeit primarily still 'only' a landscape painter, Constable for a change was for once not entirely fighting the tide when he returned to open-air oil sketching.[24]

Farington continued to encourage him, though sometimes the help took a negative form. On 3 April 1809 the Dictator of the Academy advised Constable not to send in a large painting he had done of Borrowdale, because it looked unfinished. On 28 March 1810 Farington called on Constable '& saw 3 Landscapes painted for the Exhibition (rural subjects) & recommended to him to imitate nature & not to be affected by loose remarks of critics'.[25] Constable would probably have been glad of any critical notice, but so far the press hadn't bothered with him much: as noted, only the *St James's Chronicle* in 1807 had given him more than a passing mention. But his 1810 submisssions were pruned from three to two. One was a painting of the porch and graveyard of East Bergholt church, showing a group of figures in conversation by a tomb and the porch sundial in bright sunlight – the motto on the dial, *Ut umbra sic vita* (Life is like a shadow) – Constable reserved for a later mezzotint. It was a lovely painting of strong contrasts, and didn't make a meal of the symbolism of time passing and life's inevitable end. The other painting he sent in was a landscape which *The Examiner* described as 'a chaste, silver toned picture . . . a singular but pleasing view of water flowing between two trees'. Constable was probably more thrilled by the fact that he sold this picture for thirty guineas to the Earl of Dysart, admittedly his patron as a portrait copyist but also the collector of Reynolds and Gainsborough, and someone recognised by the *Ipswich Journal* as 'an advocate for native genius'.[26] Constable's cup no doubt ran over when Farington and Stothard both advised him to put his name in for the next elections of Associates of the Academy. Progress! – or so it seemed until November, when he failed to be elected.

In March 1810 he moved to new accommodation at 49 Frith Street. Among his acquaintances was Henry Monro, a nineteen-year-old RA student and son of Dr Thomas Monro whose patronage and hospitality had assisted many young artists, including Tom Girtin and William Turner.[27] Constable was occasionally invited to dinner at Dr Monro's quarters in the Adelphi, and this gave him a sense of having his foot on an important ladder. He had also been seeing a lot of Wilkie, Haydon and Jackson. Wilkie in particular became a good friend, strolling with Constable to Somerset House, going to the theatre with him, getting Constable to model for him (as the doctor in his painting *The Sick Lady*), and taking an admiring interest in some of Constable's sketches.[28] Haydon presented a more difficult challenge. Constable felt that Haydon, the self-proclaimed practitioner of High Art, had too much influence over Wilkie. But any long-term friendship between Constable and Haydon had two further obstacles: Constable, despite little initial success, remained devoted to the Royal Academy, while Haydon's animosity against that institution was growing self-destructive. Friendly relations were further undermined by Haydon's immense vanity. He once asked Constable why he was so anxious about what he was achieving as an artist. 'Think,' said Haydon, his megalomania admitting of only one possible subject of interest, 'of what *I* am doing!'[29] In April 1809 Haydon – coming up against Constable's own fierce sense of self-worth – renounced Constable's acquaintance; he had learned that Constable had been telling people (specifically Northcote) that he had warned Haydon not to belittle John Jackson – another fellow RA student and a portrait-painting protegé of Sir George Beaumont's. Constable thought Jackson had generously helped Haydon get ahead. Haydon said that he was furious he had allowed Constable to wind himself into his acquaintance. Jackson like Wilkie was a fine talent but – unlike Haydon – modest with it; he wrote to Constable in 1810 hoping that Constable could join him in the New Forest for a couple of weeks of sketching and exploring, and though this invitation went begging, Jackson put Constable up in his Newman Street rooms in 1811 while Constable was looking for new lodgings.[30]

Constable travelled to various connections and relations in the summer of 1809. He went to Malvern Hall, near Solihull, to stay with Henry Greswolde Lewis, its owner and brother of the dowager Countess of Dysart. There he painted a portrait of Lewis in a cravat and turned-up fur collar and several pictures of the Hall, with rooks flying overhead. (Constable noticed rooks: he later told Bishop Fisher's nephew John that the cawing of a rook was a 'voice which instantaneously placed my youth before me'.) His main job at Malvern Hall was to paint a portrait of Lewis's thirteen-year-old ward, Mary Freer. Apart from the hands and arms, which seem unfinished or have been badly cleaned, this stunning picture makes one feel that Constable could have been one of the best portrait painters of the age, up with Reynolds, Romney and Lawrence. Sitting brush in hand a few feet in front of the vibrant Mary Freer did he feel an echo of another young woman, Maria Bicknell, who had been about the same age as Mary when he first met her? Constable also spent time during the summer with the Gubbinses in Epsom – two of his Gubbins cousins were in the army, as were two of his Watts cousins – and the picture he painted there now showed his growing originality as a landscape artist as well.

The Gubbinses were planning an East Bergholt trip, as were the Whalleys, and Mrs Constable encouraged John to turn up as well, bringing home with him anything that needed mending; new collars and wristbands could be stitched on. She kept him abreast of family news, telling him of the repairs Golding was planning at Dedham Mill 'for the benefit of *succeeders*', i.e. his children. She let John know that the Constable vessel *Telegraph* was loading at Mistley and that his old headmaster, Dr Grimwood, had died 'after a fortnight's severe indisposition'. East Bergholt was much the same as ever, 'oft times a christening, seldom a burying', and she hoped a catalogue of the RA exhibition would make its way there by 'some friendly means!!' Dunthorne was as impecunious as ever but he and his family were well; his new inn sign for the Duke of Marlborough in Dedham was capital. She made a point of enclosing some cash 'for travelling extras from an affectionate mother'.

Constable got to East Bergholt that autumn. In early October the weather was fine, good for sketching out of doors. He stayed in Suffolk into December, and his reluctance to leave the village for London was not just because of outdoor sketching or getting together with his old friend Dunthorne. Staying again at the rectory was Dr Rhudde's granddaughter, Maria Bicknell. The sometimes intimidating rector had been 'unusually kind & courteous', according to Constable's mother in mid-June, even taking a letter from Mrs Constable to her son in London; but Dr Rhudde may not have realised that the reason for Constable's continued presence in East Bergholt lay in the rector's household. Nine years had passed since Constable had first met Maria Bicknell, a mere girl, who was now twenty-one. That Constable, thirty-three, took a new and perhaps suddenly amorous interest in her may simply have been because she had become a pretty young woman. Or it may have had to do with the fact that she had rematerialised as such on his own doorstep, just over the hedge that divided the Constable gardens from the rectory land; she was, evidently, an indispensable part of his world. In the next few weeks they met often and strolled together in the wooded gardens of the rectory and the more open gardens of East Bergholt House. They walked through the surrounding fields and along the small stream called the Rhyber. And at some point he told her he loved her.[31]

Was it mere chance that two high points in Constable's life coincided? Finding out that he loved Maria Bicknell seems to have come together with the end of his long journeyman stage as a landscape painter. Of course, we can't say which was cause and which effect – it may be that being in love liberated his abilities as an artist; or, perhaps, finally 'finding himself' as a painter gave him the confidence to approach Maria as a suitor.

# 4. *A Cure for Love (1810–13)*

At the start the relationship met with approval all round. Mrs Constable thought Maria very much the right thing and invited her and one of her sisters to tea at East Bergholt House. However, like most mothers she also felt the need to urge caution on her son who was, apart from a small commission or sale now and then, entirely dependent for his livelihood on the allowance from his father. On 15 March 1810, while applauding what seemed to her the expression of more energy than usual in John's last letter, she warned him against being – as Dr Grimwood would have had it – dreamy: 'You must exert yourself if you feel a desire to be independent – and you must also be wary how you engage in uniting yourself with a house mate, as well as in more serious & irrevocable yokes.' Back in London, Constable called at the Bicknells' house in Spring Gardens Terrace, a fashionable address near St James's Park. His mother twice reminded him to pay his respects to Maria's grandfather at his town house in Stratton Street when he was in residence there as a chaplain-in-ordinary to George III. (East Bergholt church was often left in the care of one of several curates Dr Rhudde retained.) With one such nudge, Mrs Constable added, 'How soon and how easily is friendship shipwreck[ed].' Mr Constable had recently had a neighbourly difference with Dr Rhudde, which Mrs Constable presumably recalled when she wryly referred to the rector as 'the Great Pacificator', and she didn't want these difficulties affecting John and Maria. Meanwhile, John Constable went walking in the park with Maria. Her father was an important man, a solicitor to the Prince

Regent and a lawyer for the Admiralty. Maria's mother was his second wife; there were three children from his first marriage and five from this, with Maria – born in January 1788 – the eldest. For a while the Bicknells seemed pleased with Maria's admirer. Constable called at Mr Bicknell's office – in Norfolk Street, off the Strand – as well as in Spring Gardens, and Mr Bicknell – checking up? – dropped by at Constable's lodgings in Frith Street. (Mrs Constable now worried about the suitability of these rooms. They were, she thought, 'not respectable enough for the money you pay'.)

The crucial figure in what might happen, as Mrs Constable had recognised, was Maria's grandfather. Durand Rhudde, from a clerical family, had been a poor scholar at Cambridge and had had to work part-time in order to graduate. He had served in several ecclesiastical posts before being made incumbent of East Bergholt and Brantham in 1782. These livings had brought him a free house and a considerable income, but his present wealth and consequent power had largely come about through the marriage of his sister to an extremely wealthy man, William Bogdani. Mr and Mrs Bogdani had both died in 1790 without children, leaving their Suffolk farms to the Reverend Rhudde and his daughter, Charles Bicknell's wife.[1] So the Rector had the wherewithal to keep good horses and buy fancy carriages in which he drove around the countryside, travelled back and forth to London, and went for holidays in up-and-coming seaside resorts such as Cromer. In the village, where the fact that he had *two* curates made an impression and the sermons he gave when in residence were admired by large congregations, he was regarded with humour, awe and even a touch of terror. John Lott, brother of the Flatford farmer Willy Lott, called Dr Rhudde 'the Grand Caesar'.[2]

Such an imperial power had to be kept sweet and Mrs Constable made an effort. She welcomed the rector's invitations to ride in his carriage with him on her way home from London after visiting the Whalleys, and she accepted his offers to carry letters and parcels to town for John to collect. She kept an eye on doings at the rectory and let John know about them. In early January 1811 she wrote, 'The Revd Doctor complains very much of rheumatism & old age – but I scarcely ever saw him looking better, or preach with more delightful energy than on Xmas Day and that after assisting Mr Kebbell [one of the curates] in the Sacrament to 150 communicants.' But the rector's wife was 'very sadly', suffering it seems from senile dementia. Word reached Mrs Constable via William Travis, the village physician, who had heard it from Thomas, one of the Rhuddes' servants, that Mrs Rhudde thought some of the Bicknells were poisoning her food. Her place as hostess at the rectory began to be taken by a local widow, Mrs Everard, whose attentions to the curates had been noted by Mrs Constable – was Mrs Everard aspiring to higher things?

Mrs Constable received from her son a watercolour he had recently done of East Bergholt church and she immediately recognised this drawing as a useful weapon. She had Abram take it back to London so that John could make a copy of it. The copy came to East Bergholt a month later, and John Dunthorne was asked to inscribe a small plaque for the frame: '*A South East view of East Bergholt Church, a drawing by John Constable & presented in testimony of respect to Durand Rhudde D.D. the Rector. February 26, 1811.*' Mrs Constable herself took the watercolour round to the rectory, where Dr Rhudde declared it was 'most beautiful' and expressed his pride in possessing it. However, when it dawned on him that he was especially obliged to Constable, its begetter, for the gift, he felt things were getting out of balance; he wrote, sending Constable a banknote, and attempted to smooth over any awkwardness by suggesting that the artist might use the money to purchase 'some little article by which you may be reminded of me, when I am no more'.

Mortality was indeed making itself felt all round. Dr Rhudde's wife died on 19 March 1811. Their daughter, Maria's mother, wasn't well, and Maria's twenty-year-old brother, also named Durand, succumbed to tuberculosis and died in April this same year. Maria, distressed, went to Worcestershire to stay with her half-sister, Mrs Sarah Skey. The Bicknells may have begun to feel the John–Maria attachment could do with cooling off. Meanwhile, the winter was long and icy, with deep drifts of snow and the *Telegraph* frozen in at Mistley. Mrs Constable sent her son money for coal and worried about him on many counts, some real, some imaginary; she was anxious both about his being smitten by Maria and by dangers to his health. Was he keeping his feet dry in the dreadful London streets? Sitting in damp shoes and stockings brought on sore throats, lung inflammation and toothache, she said. But Mr Constable, suffering from a nasty cough and neuralgia, had other concerns: in late April the mate of the *Telegraph*, Zacariah Savell, had been taken by a Navy press gang and despite being a 'protected person' because of his duties in the coastal trade, was being held on shipboard at the Nore anchorage. Golding Constable asked his son to call on Mr Bicknell at the Admiralty and find out if strings could be pulled to save Savell. What resulted from this intervention is unknown, but in 1818, after the war was over, Savell was in command of a Constable vessel.

The 1811 Academy exhibition made Constable uneasy. He had entered the largest painting he had so far submitted, *Dedham Vale: Morning*, a wide-angle view of the Stour valley, a view out of shadow into early-morning light, showing cattle browsing as they are led by a herdsman along the lane from Flatford to Bergholt, with a milestone (which he had used in this way before) showing the name of the place, Dedham Vale, inscribed as on a classical monument. A Claudean tree frames the scene on the left. If this was the morning of his life, he should have been happier, but he gave the impression of being love-sick and badly pining with it. The painting wasn't placed to his satisfaction at the Academy – he complained to Farington that it was hung too low in the ante-room. He thought this showed his stock was low with Academicians. Farington tried to encourage him, telling him that Lawrence, the celebrated portrait painter and later the RA President, had twice mentioned the picture approvingly.[3] However, as Leslie was to note, the painting didn't clamour for attention. Constable was up against the fact that people found his works unobtrusive; they didn't at once spot the originality and quality that coexisted with being low-key.

Maria was not at Spring Gardens, London, but at Spring Grove, near Bewdley, Worcestershire, with Mrs Skey, so Constable had nothing to keep him in Frith Street. He went to Bergholt for three weeks in May and painted 'from nature'. When he returned to town in early June he obviously felt unsettled. He told Farington that on coming back to London he had gone at once to the exhibition again to see what effect art had upon him after a period of studying nature. At Somerset House he had seen 'many pictures which were altogether works of art, such as might be painted by studying pictures only'.[4] And yet he wasn't immune from the vice, if such it was, of thinking in terms of pictures. In Suffolk, he said, 'a most delightful landscape for a painter . . . I fancy I see Gainsborough in every hedge and hollow tree'.[5] In fact, despite his proclaimed attachment to Nature, his view of the country became increasingly sophisticated; and his eye was far from innocent. The engraver John Burnet later wrote of Constable that 'No one, perhaps, has given a greater look of studying Nature alone . . . but he told me he seldom painted a picture without considering how Rembrandt or Claude would have treated it'.[6]

On 6 June he again talked to Farington, telling him of 'the particular circumstances of his situation in life'. They also discussed Constable's uncle David Pike Watts, who wanted him to pass on to the architect (and Academician) Robert Smirke information about a new church in Marylebone. Watts had recently lost his second son Michael, an ensign in the Coldstream Guards, at Barrosa, south of Cadiz; his oldest son David, also an army officer, had died on shipboard going to Jamaica in 1808.[7] Watts bore the new loss firmly, thought Constable, and his uncle went on concerning himself with the fortunes of his artistic nephew. For Constable's thirty-fifth birthday Watts sent him a printed leaflet, 'A Cure for Love', and a lengthy homily he had written on his nephew's health and happiness, salted with biblical and of-the-moment political references:

> It is signified by the inspired writer of the Psalms, that in times of public calamity, when War distresses a Kingdom from without, and Dissipation corrupts it within, when the Necessities of Life become expensive, and Rents & Taxes consume a great share of Income; that the natural Affection of Love and the endearments of conjugal union, suffer disappointment and are often cross'd by Circumstances . . .[8]

A second letter lectured Constable on his art:

> That dread of being a mannerist, and that desire of being an original,
> has not, in my imperfect judgment, produced to you the full advantage
> you promised yourself from it . . . My opinion is, that cheerfulness is
> wanted in your landscapes; they are tinctured with a sombre darkness.
> If I may say so, the trees are not green, but black; the water is not lucid,
> but overshadowed; an air of melancholy is cast over the scene, instead
> of hilarity.[9]

One might resist the suggestion that Constable make his works
hilarious, but the thrust of Uncle David's remarks – 'Lighten up,
John!' – can be admitted. And perhaps could have been admitted by
the artist himself if Constable hadn't been the person he was, touched
with darkness.

Watts continued to take Constable's part in his feeling for Miss
Bicknell and tried to bolster his confidence. He wrote, 'Though you
are miserable yet you are a *man*. If you weakly sink that heroic
character, you would have been a feeble Prop to a Woman who puts
herself in your Protection. Arise! revive! . . .'[10]

Constable went down to Bergholt again in time to catch the village
fair at the end of July. While there he painted several vivid, atmospheric oil sketches that would perhaps have struck Uncle David as
cheerful. He then spent three weeks in September with Bishop Fisher
and his family at the Bishop's Palace, Salisbury, where he was commissioned to paint the Bishop's portrait and got to know the Bishop's
nephew, also John, and also a churchman. He made sketches of
Salisbury and its cathedral from Harnham Hill, a view that provided
one of his RA exhibits in 1812 – *Salisbury, Morning*. Maria was still
with the Skeys and no one answered when he called for news at Spring
Gardens; Constable was desperate at not hearing from her or even
hearing about her. So he took a giant step – Maria's father hadn't
given his formal permission for Constable to write – and sent Maria a
letter. Some of the strict rules then governing a relationship between
a young man and woman were laid out in a novel published that year,

Jane Austen's *Sense and Sensibility*: 'A correspondence between them by letter could subsist only under a positive engagement.' Maria was not officially engaged and she replied to Constable with off-putting caution: 'Let me beg and entreat you to think of me no more but as one who will ever esteem you as a friend.' She didn't want to make her parents unhappy. What she called 'the delusion' to which she had long given way must have an end. Constable at this stage buckled; he was sick, and felt he hadn't been properly well since the last time he saw her. However, when she had returned to London and Constable called on the Bicknells, her father gave permission for John to write to her.

This looked like a great advance, and Mrs Constable took it as such. But Maria was less optimistic. Her father was going to give her his thoughts and she warned Constable she would be guided by her father in every respect. And Mr Bicknell's thoughts, when they came, were kind and reasonable and put forward but 'one objection'. Maria wrote about this from the Skeys' on 4 November 1811. Beginning the letter 'My dear Sir', she wrote that the problem was 'that necessary article Cash . . . To live without it is impossible, it would be involving ourselves in misery instead of felicity.' The problem was insuperable, she believed, and they had therefore better not write one another. The painful trials of life would have to be borne with resignation. 'You will still be my friend, and I will be yours . . . We should both of us be bad subjects for poverty, should we not? Even Painting would go on badly, it could not survive in domestic worry.' (She was a well-read young woman, and might have known the lines in *The Winter's Tale* where Camillo says, 'Besides, you know / Prosperity's the very bond of love.')

Far from being thrown off his stride by this common sense, Constable was galvanised by it. His health improved. He went to Epsom to stay for a few days with the Gubbinses and breathe country air. He continued to attend life classes at the Royal Academy.[11] He moved to 63 Charlotte Street, to rooms above the premises of an upholsterer, Richard Weight, and nearly opposite the house of his counsellor Joseph Farington. He seemed undaunted by the fact that in this year's poll for Associate Members, he got no votes.[12] He wrote to Maria from Charlotte Street – 'Dear Miss Bicknell' – confident he

Life drawing, female nude

still had her unalterable affections: 'Be assured we have only to consider our union as a circumstance that must happen and we shall yet be happy.' How he wished he could see her! Then he went to East Bergholt to see his father, who had had a bad cold, and give his anxious mother an account of things. On his return to Charlotte Street in mid-December he wrote to Maria that he was still painting: 'Nothing so much as employment will keep the mind from preying on itself.' And he had hopes that good would result from all this, including 'advancement in the art I love, and more deserving of you'. For him there was, evidently, no necessity to choose between Art and Love, one or the other.

For the moment, however, Maria wasn't to be budged. She was grieved and surprised that he persevered with 'an idea that must terminate in disappointment'. Her father thought they should put an end to their correspondence and that this would make them happier! Maria begged Constable to stop thinking of her; he should forget that he had ever known her; and she concluded her letter with the forlorn words, 'Fare well, dear Sir, and ever believe me, Your sincere and constant well-wisher, M.E. Bicknell.'

Quite what this rejection was meant to bring about, perhaps Maria alone knew. Unless that is she had been discussing the situation with her half-sister Sarah Skey and had some tactics in mind, particularly on how to circumvent the lack of Cash. But surely she didn't expect Constable to knuckle under meekly. As it was, Uncle David would have approved the manly character he now showed. Five days before Christmas 1811 Constable took a coach to Worcester and went on to Bewdley and Spring Grove. Despite bad weather, he had a happy weekend with Maria, although sadness from knowing that she was worried about her parents' attitude intruded from time to time. But Sarah Skey, five years a widow and the mother of two small boys, was all kindness. Constable was cheered by seeing Maria in her calming and supportive company. On getting back to Charlotte Street, he wrote to Maria (addressing her once again as 'My dear Miss Bicknell') on Christmas Eve, 'I too well know the effect that hours of desponding have upon the health not to see the necessity of making every exertion for the present – 'till it shall please providence to bring us together.'

Thomas Stothard called on Constable on the same day and thought the younger artist was depressed from being too much on his own. Constable agreed and invited his sister Mary to come and stay with him. She arrived on 2 January. He also had a loving end-of-year letter from his father. Golding Constable asked his son if he could really afford a wife and children. Mr Constable suggested that John not give up his 'female acquaintance in toto' but defer a permanent connection 'until some removals had taken place'. He didn't specify which removals, but the deaths of some older people would undoubtedly help Constable's circumstances. Moreover, he wished John would think of what parts of his profession paid best. He believed his son's anxiety to excel made him raise his aspirations too high. 'Think less and finish as you go,' was his pragmatic advice. Three weeks later this 'parent and sincere friend', as he called himself, sent his son practical help in the form of a twenty-pound cheque, which John for some reason failed to cash. Meanwhile, his mother continued to do her own worrying. She wrote on 16 February to say that she hoped Maria would become 'another amiable and good daughter' for her in her lifetime, and she urged Constable to use the now lengthening days of the six-week period before the next Academy exhibition to work hard and 'secure his fame'.

Maria returned to London in early January and Constable took every opportunity to see her, often hanging around in St James's Park in hope of meeting her. She wrote on one occasion to say she was happy enough knowing she was in the same town as he; she preferred accidental meetings to painful premeditated appointments (which her parents didn't know about and which couldn't always be kept). But eventually the strain told, and she felt it was better for her health and peace of mind to be in Spring Grove rather than Spring Gardens. In Worcestershire she could look at a portrait he had given her of himself and think of him 'steadfastly pursuing painting'. In town she would be distressed and he would be tormented. 'Think my dear Sir of the number of wasted hours spent in the Park, think what an unsettled being I am rendered.'

It is unclear whether Maria's health entered the reckoning at this stage or whether her family's desire to keep her at a safe remove was the main factor. In any event, it was off to Worcestershire for her again; on 20 February she wrote from Spring Gardens to say adieu. Constable seems to have waited a whole month before replying to her, no longer 'Dear Miss Bicknell' but 'My dearest Maria'. He had an astonishing ability to put his painting before everything, and now he was absorbed with a view of Salisbury and three other landscapes for the Academy exhibition as well as some portrait commissions. His letter of 21 March said he was trying to follow her advice and this commitment, together with hard work, had to support him 'in this gloom of solitude'. But in April, May and June the letters flashed back and forth between Charlotte Street and Spring Grove. In one, he said that though he was denied the pleasure of talking to her as they walked, with her arm locked in his, 'yet we have had that pleasure and may yet again for many years'.

Mrs Constable through all this tried to ensure that the rector was kept on side. She worried that although Dr Rhudde was all politeness, smiling and bowing when he encountered her and her husband, 'yet something still <u>rankles</u> at his heart', and she feared that whatever it was might burst out. She may also have been concerned about how Dr Rhudde's rheumatism might effect his equilibrium. Yet when she wrote to her son on 12 April 1812, she was pleased that John had called at the rector's London residence in Stratton Street and left his card; it was the sort of courtesy that might help avoid any impending rupture. She also passed on a bit of news that might amuse Constable: the rector's gardener, Peck, had the previous week rearranged the raised flower beds outside Dr Rhudde's study windows so that they took the form of two large hearts. This had provoked the rector's new self-appointed helpmeet Mrs Everard to exclaim, 'Truly ridiculous!' But Mrs Constable had no objection to the doctor being touched by Cupid: 'It may cause him to have a fellow feeling for <u>others</u> in the same situation.'

Mrs Constable made sure that the rector heard of the portrait her son was painting of Dr Fisher, the Bishop of Salisbury. At the same time, Mr Constable was worried by a newspaper article critical of John's work – it complained of lack of finish – but he put this down to his son's unhappy love life. Constable's paintings were in fact garnering approval. West, the Academy President, praised the four he exhibited at the Academy; Constable thought they were decently hung, and he turned the other cheek to Callcott's comment that they looked 'rather dark and heavy'. *The Examiner* particularly liked his *Flatford Mill from the Lock*, though 'it wants a little more carefulness of execution'.[13] Writing to Maria at the end of May, John said he hoped to get to Suffolk soon and paint there for most of the summer: 'You know I have succeeded most with my native scenes. They have always charmed me & I hope they always will – I wish not to forget early impressions.'

Nevertheless his burgeoning popularity as a portrait painter made for chores. The Godfreys in East Bergholt liked Constable's portrait of their son and recommended the artist to General Rebow, in Wivenhoe, and he asked Constable to paint his seven-year-old daughter Mary. The Dysart portrait-copying duties also paid a dividend: the Countess wanted him to paint her, and so did her daughter Lady Heathcote. Captain Thomas Western of the Royal Navy, who lived not far away in Suffolk, was soon on the list, and there was a copy to make of the portrait of Bishop Fisher. One portrait seemed to prompt another; word of mouth reported that Constable was talented, and no doubt it was added quietly that his charges were reasonable. For him the portraits brought in 'cash' and therefore were rewarded with Golding Constable's approval. But he felt John should stop concentrating on unpropitious landscapes and feared the connection with Maria would be his son's ruin. He now made an effort to tempt him to leave London – if Constable did so, he could have the mill house at Dedham to live in. However, Constable wrote to Maria that he wouldn't leave the field while he had a leg to stand on. As for his father's suggestions, 'His ideas are most rational, but you know Landscape is my mistress – 'tis to her that I look for fame.'

In Bergholt in mid-June Constable looked from his window and wrote to Maria in Worcestershire, telling her of the prospect before him. 'I see all those sweet feilds where we have passed so many happy hours together.' (Constable was always an 'e before i' person, whatever the preceding letter.) He was especially pleased that 'the scenes of my boyish days should have witnessed by far the most affecting event of my life', i.e. falling in love with her. He detailed his doings, such as his walks with his 'three little mates', the Constable dogs; one was a pug named Yorick who took an almost ridiculous pleasure in such walks. He told Maria about his neighbour John Dunthorne, who was thriving, his family growing up delightfully: 'One of his little boys (my namesake) has been grinding colours for me all day – he is a clever little fellow and draws nicely all "of his own head".' Fourteen-year-old Johnny, so introduced, would become possibly John Dunthorne Senior's greatest gift to the artist for whom he had already provided companionship, support and practical experience in painting. And Constable reverted to what for him and Maria had to be the main subject: he had paid several visits to the curates and to 'the Doctor' at the rectory. On one such call 'the Doctor was unusually courteous, and shook hands with me on taking leave – am I to argue from this that I am not entirely out of the pale of salvation?'

He had meant to go up to London in July, hearing that Maria would be there. But she changed her plans. Sarah Skey's ten-year-old son Samuel had died. Then for a whole month Maria failed to write and Constable reflected on the two hundred miles separating them. On 22 July he wrote to her to say that he had been living like a hermit, 'though always with my pencil in my hand' ('pencil' in this case meaning brush). He thought he had either got better in 'the art of seeing Nature' – a phrase of Sir Joshua's – or Nature had become more generous to him in unveiling her beauties. However, any delight he got from this was affected by sadness because she wasn't nearby.

> In your society I am freed from the natural reserve of my mind – 'tis to you alone that I can impart every sensation of my heart – but I am now too apt to dwell on this melancholy side. Should I not rather think on the thousand blessings which I possess? I am hourly receiving every kindness from the best of parents – have I not health and time to pursue my darling study? – and above all I have your great love and esteem.

He went on sketching and painting in and around East Bergholt until mid-August. He now found the village dull. But his melancholy was suddenly alleviated: Maria was in town. They met several times and Constable seems to have imparted every sensation he felt for her. When they said an ardent goodbye on 25 August, she for the seaside at Bognor, he for East Bergholt, he went off with her gloves in his pocket.

This London visit left him in the dumps. On getting back to Bergholt, he was grieved to hear from Maria that she was also in low spirits. He wrote that she had so far borne with fortitude the greatest share of their sorrows; he hoped their present sufferings arose simply from the strains of again being parted. His heart was entirely and for ever hers. His love for her increased every day. He hadn't attempted a landscape since returning to Bergholt; he wasn't equal to it. 'My pursuits in landscape have been disturbed, this summer, and I find myself driven into the autumn without much to show for it.' He was going to Wivenhoe, near Colchester, for a few days to paint Mary Rebow, a portrait which gave him trouble though the Rebows liked it and he managed to get 'a good deal of Landscape' into the picture. Then it was on to Captain Western at Tattistone Place. All this of course pleased his parents. His mother wrote to him in late November, when he was back in London, 'You can now so greatly excell in Portraits, that I hope it will urge you on to pursue a path, so struck out to bring you Fame and Gain.'

Landscape might be his Mistress, but Maria must have wondered occasionally if for Constable this wasn't a good deal more than a figure of speech. Who really figured first in his affections? (Nine months later, she put it to him directly: Who had he thought most of that summer, 'landscape or me?') On his return to London in early November 1812 Constable, as usual, reported to Farington on what he had been up to, 'studying Landscape and painting some portraits'.[14] He and Maria were still apart, with him in Charlotte Street and her in Bognor. But she didn't advise him to visit her in Sussex: 'Prudence whispers you had better not come.' The Bicknell family was again upset about the attachment. Writing to Maria on 25 October Constable had referred to a call his mother had made at Spring Gardens a month earlier when she learned that the Bicknells were expected at the rectory at Christmas, and Mr Bicknell had promised he would call on the Constables then. Constable continued, 'But let us not flatter ourselves (even if he should call) on that account. You know perfectly well that the impression your family has towards me is not to be affected by a few outward civilities.' We are reminded of the age difference between them – he was thirty-six, she was twenty-four – when he wrote ten days later to say to her, 'Time however . . . must help us . . . Remember, my dear child, that our business is with ourselves, and that while you love me I shall consider every circumstance attending this unpropitious scene but as the dust on my shoes.'

Yet the circumstances piled up; the dust thickened. When she came back to town in early December Constable went round to Spring Gardens but wasn't allowed in. Maria wrote to explain: 'I have a cold that slightly attacks my chest.' Her mother – who was also ill –

wouldn't let her go out. But Maria said she would try to meet him; she would be walking in St James's Square on Friday at two o'clock. In fact, they managed to meet twice before he went to Bergholt for a family Christmas, village 'balls and routs', and finishing work on Captain Western, full-length in naval uniform.

When Constable returned to Charlotte Street in mid-January guilt at being out of touch with Maria drove him to frequent queries to Spring Gardens about her health. It may have dawned on him that not only her mother but several of her siblings were seriously unwell and when she talked of a cold attacking her chest, she sent ominous signals. But Mr Bicknell got to read Constable's letters first, and he seemed more and more fed up with his daughter's suitor. Maria wrote again to suggest that Constable attend more to his painting and less to her. She was afraid that other artists of less ability would outstrip him in the race for fame; he would then regret the neglected time, the opportunities lost, and blame her. Guilt consumed her too. 'Believe me,' she wrote, 'I shall feel a more lasting pleasure in knowing that you are improving your time and exerting your talents for the <u>ensuing Exhibition</u>, than I should do while you were on a <u>stolen march</u> with me round the Park.' (Her sister Louisa was generally brought along as a chaperone on these occasions.) Maria thought they should resolve to not see each other for a period, and she closed with an emphatic, '<u>Please do not answer this</u>'.

She had apparently got the word from her father, usually the mildest of men, that Constable wasn't welcome. Constable was sent word of this and Maria, ever dutiful, told him they should wait – wait with quiet resignation. A merciful Providence would dispose of them. She bade him 'farewell'.

Mrs Constable had already picked up the signs. Maria's brother Sam had been at the rectory but hadn't called at East Bergholt House. Constable's mother was offended that despite the 'virtuous & honourable love' her son and Maria had for one another, John had been refused 'the admittance of a gentleman to her father's house'. Nevertheless she told him to hang on: 'Patience is the only advice I should give & you I hope pursue.' The two women in his life were at least agreed on what he should do.

# 5. *Avoiding Notice (1812–15)*

The relationship between Maria and Constable was at the centre of both their lives, but other factors impinged. Maria's health, for one thing: there were frequent signs it was shaky, though her bouts of frailness never caused Constable to slacken his wooing. Moreover, he had domestic problems of his own. In the small hours of 10 November 1812 a fire broke out at 63 Charlotte Street, where he lived above the apartment and upholstery workshop of Richard Weight and his family; the artist and his belongings had to be evacuated. One of the first things he did next day was write to Maria in Bognor in case she had somehow heard of the fire and was worried about him. He had lost nothing; he was troubled only by the alarm, bustle and inconvenience. His Uncle David offered him a bed in Portland Place, and the dentist across the street, John Henderson, lent him a room to paint in while the Weights' premises were repaired. A week later Constable had leisure to write again to Maria giving her more details of the minor calamity. The fire had spread fast through Weight's workshop and the back of the house, and he had made a point of first rescuing his writing desk, 'containing my most <u>valuable letters</u>' (we can guess from whom). Half dressed, without shoes or waistcoat, he managed to calm the distraught Weights and then help neighbours move bits and pieces into the street. The fire engine took an hour to arrive and stop the flames from spreading further. While Constable was carrying a large picture belonging to Lady Heathcote down the stairs, a window blew in and showered him with glass. He took the picture over to Joseph Farington's. On getting back, he found the Weights' servant woman in great distress: her savings were in the garret, under her pillow. Constable ran upstairs through the smoke and rescued what she called her 'pockets', the purses which contained 'all her fortune'.

Constable never had a wide circle of acquaintance but he always had several good friends. At this time he was getting to know better one who would be among the very best – John Fisher, nephew of the Bishop of Salisbury, who had been ordained as a priest in June 1812. He had written to Constable in May, unsuccessfully trying to tempt him to Salisbury again: 'We will rise with the sun, breakfast, & then out for the rest of the day – if we tire of drawing we can read or bathe and then home at nightfall to a short dinner.' Young Reverend Fisher wasn't afraid to give Constable the benefit of his judgement on the artist's paintings. Shortly after the Charlotte Street fire he thanked Constable for a painting which, gift or not, had struck one observer as gloomy. Furthermore, wrote Fisher, 'It does not *sollicit attention.* And this I think is true of all your pictures & the real cause of your want of popularity.' Fisher suggested Rubens as a painter whose works illuminated a room and hence gave a sense of cheerfulness. He thought Constable had the same fault as his pictures, being too unassertive, 'too honest and high-minded to push himself'. However, he enjoyed the three landscapes Constable sent to Somerset House in 1813. One of them, *Boys Fishing*, was one of the largest works he had yet painted, and according to Robert Hunt in *The Examiner* (30 May 1813) was 'silvery, sparkling, and true to the greyish-green colouring of our English summer landscapes.' (To modern eyes it looks rather ye olde quaint, though that may be partly because it has been much overpainted and retouched.)[1] Fisher, after seeing the exhibition, wrote to say that of all the exhibits, 'I only like one better & that is a picture of pictures, the Frost of Turner. [This was Turner's *Frosty Morning.*] But then you need not repine at this decision of mine; you are a great man like Buonoparte and are only beat by a frost.' At the Academy dinner, Constable sat opposite Benjamin West and Thomas Lawrence, and next to Turner, his celebrated contemporary, whom he saw as a fellow painter seemingly for the first time. He reported to Maria, 'I was a good deal entertained with Turner. I always expected to find him what I did – he is uncouth but has a wonderfull range of mind.'

At close quarters with celebrity and genius, Constable must have felt he was at last on the verge of real acceptance, if not popularity. His failure – despite Stothard's backing – to get elected as an Associate in 1812 was put behind him. West said that the Council thought he had made a very great advance this year. The Stour, painted large, seemed to offer a way ahead. David Pike Watts, a governor of the British Institution and relentless booster of his nephew, gave him a ticket to the banquet opening a big BI exhibition of Reynolds's works. At this Constable talked to Bishop Fisher and Sir George Beaumont, and he saw Mrs Siddons and Lord Byron. *Childe Harold's Pilgrimage* had come out the year before to immense applause, and Constable was not immune to the almost tangible aura of fame. He wrote a few days later to Maria, as if with fellow feeling for Byron, 'His poetry is of the most melancholy kind, but there is great ability.'

Constable had complained in late 1811 about the loneliness of his vocation and how his mind preyed on itself. Both the sunny moments and the dark periods got into his painting. Stothard, whose deafness also isolated him, was twenty-one years older but liked Constable and had a remedy for his depressions: long walks. One day in early June 1812, he set off with Stothard at 6 a.m. from central London. He wrote to Maria, 'We breakfasted at Putney – went over Wimbledon Common – & passed three hours at least in Coomb Wood (Stothard is a butterfly catcher), where we dined by a spring – then back to Richmond by the park, and enjoyed the view – and home by the river.' Their friendship didn't preclude arguments about Art. Farington recorded in his diary Constable's expression of surprise that 'so ingenious an Artist [as Stothard] should be solely engrossed in imitating Rubens. Stothard, on the contrary, equally disapproved Constable's choice of landscape in painting simple scenes, Mills, &c.'[2]

Some Academicians were beginning to see the merit of Constable's so-called simple scenes. Farington himself approved of *Boys Fishing* and Henry Thomson told Constable he would get his vote for Associate membership, though Constable had little expectation of being elected. Perhaps the most pleasing thing of all, when *Boys Fishing* was shown at the British Institution six months after its RA appearance, a purchaser appeared who was neither a relative nor close friend: James Carpenter, bookseller in Old Bond Street, wanted the picture, though he couldn't pay entirely in money. He offered twenty guineas and 'Books to a certain amount beyond that Sum'. Constable accepted, and often bought books from Carpenter thereafter.[3] His portrait efforts (at £15 a head) for Lady Louisa Manners, Lady Heathcote, H.G. Lewis and the Reverend George Bridgeman, among others, were bringing in cash. When Constable left London for what he called his beloved Bergholt at the end of June 1813, he was able to write proudly to Maria that for the first time in his life he did so with 'pockets full of money. I am entirely free of debt . . . and I have required no assistance from my father for some time.'

Constable had addressed Maria as 'Miss Bicknell' in May as he tried to obey her strictures on their corresponding by at least curtailing the fondness he expressed, but she cracked first: in early June she began a letter to him, 'My dear John'. In late August she wrote from Richmond, 'I wish I could divest myself of feeling so like a culprit when I write to you.' (She knew she was breaking the rules.) 'I think of you equally if I write, or do not write . . .' She read, probably to please him, James Northcote's *Memoirs of Sir Joshua Reynolds, Bart.*, which had just been published.[4] When he got back to Charlotte Street in November, with many drawings and a tiny sketchbook crammed with 'hasty memorandums' of places and prospects and items he had picked up in the Stour valley – 'plants – ferns – distances' – he appears to have accepted that they should meet at most once a month; he was consoled, he said, by the thought that 'our hearts are one.' But consolation didn't come easy. On 22 December 1813 prowling around St James's he saw Maria and her mother in the street; Maria wasn't looking well. The next day he wrote to her to say he had been out searching for her again all morning. Finally he was lurking by the railings across from their house when he had the mortification of seeing her and her sister Catherine go into the Bicknell residence and failed to get them to notice him. 'You may judge how I feel when I return to my room,' he complained. He had been half frozen, since he had been out for hours without his greatcoat. 'I detest the sight of my wretched pictures.'

Some of his old certainties were collapsing. He had been brought up as a communicant in the Church of England: 'Ever since I have been of age to receive the Sacrament I have never failed of receiving it on X'mas day . . . I really fear that my mind is not in a fit state for so solemn an occasion.' He had told the Gubbinses that he would spend Christmas with them in Epsom, but he seems to have stayed in London because he was worried about Maria's health. Fortunately John Fisher came to see him just before Christmas and talked comfortingly. And Fisher's uncle, the Bishop, continued to give support – Constable spent a pleasant day with the Bishop and his wife in early February 1814. But he declined to go to a party at his uncle David's: since, he said, parties only increased his melancholy, 'I am turned hermit.'

It was a winter of bitter cold. The Thames iced over, the streets were full of dirty, frozen slush, and the contents of chamberpots were frozen under beds. The snow prevented the lovers from seeing each other and the Bicknell fireside provided Maria with no cheer; both her mother and sister Louisa were ill. In mid-February, after a short thaw, Maria wrote to Constable to say she couldn't write to him weekly (as he wanted) but would write as often as possible; she hadn't been well. 'This sudden change again to extreme cold has affected my chest.' She hoped he would see 'the impropriety of our walking together circumstanced as I am'. Constable seems to have felt suddenly that time was passing, the fates unrelenting. Was there ever going to be a way out of this? He wrote to John Dunthorne asking him to send young Johnny to Charlotte Street. 'I think he may be usefull to stimulate me to work, by setting my palate [sic] &c. &c. – which you know is a great help and keeps one cheerfull.' Constable's mother didn't think this a good idea: Johnny, now sixteen, might be 'company, but he cannot be a companion, & that is what you want to ascend, my dear John – not descend.' Maria the solicitor's daughter was the way ahead, the artisan Dunthornes were not. Constable disagreed with his mother's judgement: he wrote to Maria that Johnny 'is not at all vulgar and [is] naturally very clever – but had he not these good qualities I should love him for his father's sake'. Johnny came but didn't stay long; he left with tears in his eyes, promised another visit by Constable.

In mid-February Maria told Constable that she wouldn't see him again until May. He prayed she would at any rate write to him: 'No lover will ever think no news good news.' She replied it was improper for them to walk out together. But a young woman's right to change her mind was soon manifest. In March she reserved some seats at Covent Garden Theatre and wrote to Constable, 'Can you my dear John brave these cold nights without any danger of getting cold?' She had 'secured places in box 36 up one pair of stairs. March 17th.' The play the lovers saw was 'not calculated to cheer one', John wrote, hoping 'the next will be a comedy'. Meanwhile, he was fence-mending with the rector. Constable called on Dr Rhudde in Stratton Street and found him coolly polite as always and not exactly encouraging.

Towards the end of April Constable handed in two landscapes as his entries for the Academy exhibition. The first, *Ploughing Scene in Suffolk*, shows a field on the Bergholt slopes of Dedham Vale, with a team of horses pulling a plough. After summer ploughing the field remained fallow until it was manured in the autumn and sown for the winter. The picture was given a quotation in the exhibition catalogue – the first time Constable had done this, perhaps taking note of how successful Academicians such as Turner promoted their pictures that way. Constable used two lines from *The Farmer's Boy* by the best-selling Suffolk poet Robert Bloomfield: 'But unassisted through each toilsome day, / With smiling brow the ploughman cleaves his way.' Just how smiling the ploughman might be after a day's toil is a moot point – his brow is invisible – but the painting itself is a wonderful example of how Constable could mimic the conditions of one season in the country while working in the city in another. A small low copse makes a not-quite-horizontal slash of darkness across the picture's middle ground. Large loose clouds allow pools of sunlight to illuminate distant meadows and part of the 'summerland' field in which the ploughman stoops over his plough. England was probably never better and more beautifully cultivated than now, and Constable caught the moment.

After handing in this, and a slightly darker and moodier scene showing Willy Lott's cottage and a ferryman poling his boat across the Stour at Flatford, Constable went up to Suffolk for a week. He told Maria that Bergholt looked 'uncommonly beautifull'; he took 'several beautifull walks' and rode with his sister Mary to visit the Earl and Countess of Dysart at Helmingham Hall. When he returned to London he called at Somerset House to check on his creations. Sam Strowger, one of his best friends there, had been pleased to tell him that some paintings had been moved since their proximity injured the effect of Constable's.[5] Constable himself was happy with 'the look and situation' of *Ploughing Scene*. Although Turner's *Dido and Aeneas* was getting a lot of attention, he said that he would rather be the author of his own landscape with the ploughman. Many Academicians thought his *Ploughing Scene* 'as genuine a peice of study as there is to be found in the room'. John Allnutt, wine merchant and stockbreeder of Clapham Common, a perceptive art patron, liked it too and bought it at the following winter's BI exhibition. Allnutt, even more than James Carpenter, was a complete stranger to the artist, and this lack of prior connections particularly delighted Constable. Was a public coming to him at last?

The 1814 Academy exhibition involved Constable in one disagreeable incident. Maria visited it with her father, and when Constable encountered them, he failed to greet Mr Bicknell with a bow. His omission was taken for disrespect. Constable thought that, as the younger man (albeit almost thirty-eight), he was merely refraining from pushing himself forward in an impertinent manner. Maria was cross, but Constable explained and apologised; he hadn't intended any slight. Then she relented – the way Constable now mentioned her father made her happy, and it was a pity that 'existing circumstances should preclude your being better acquainted'. The circumstances, a note from her on 18 May made clear, included their continued lack of 'that most necessary evil, money'. (A lack spelled out a month later when she added that 'people cannot live now upon four hundred a year'.) And the circumstances made both parties ultra-sensitive. When Constable suggested he might visit Maria when she and Louisa were staying at Richmond, she said no; he complained she wasn't the Maria he once knew, and this made her miserable. But a few weeks later, when he was again in Suffolk, she wrote him a 'truly affectionate' letter that made him happy.

East Bergholt in June: although cut off from her, he knew that he was 'among every blessing and endearment that can be found in this world'. Not only was he with his family but he had 'health and leisure to pursue my "longings after fame", in these dear scenes which I must always prefer and love to any other . . . The village is now in great beauty. I think I never saw the foliage so promising.' Constable spent most of the summer there. He made one trip in June to visit the Reverend W.W. Driffield at Feering. Reverend Driffield, who had christened Constable as an endangered infant, took him south to Maldon and Southend. Constable walked along the banks of the Thames estuary and delighted in 'the melancholy grandeur of a seashore'. He wrote to Maria, 'At Hadleigh there is a ruin of a castle which from its situation is a really fine place – it commands a view of the Kent hills, the Nore and North Foreland & looking many miles to sea.' He spent the second half of July in London, where he lobbied Farington about becoming an Associate and Farington told him a common objection to his pictures was that they were unfinished – Constable should study Claude's manner of completing. This was advice Constable could go along with – and it was no hardship to look at the two Claudes of J.J. Angerstein in Pall Mall.[6]

Maria had been invited to Wales in the autumn and Constable entreated her – 'my beloved Child' – to go. But instead she went with Louisa first to a house her father had rented in Wimbledon and then to Brighton, for sea air. She and Constable managed to meet once in London. He was very low in spirits, particularly as she told him she wouldn't see him again for a time: 'It would not you know have <u>been right</u>, for <u>Louisa and I</u> only to have admitted so formidable a personage under our roof, the village would have rose in arms to our relief.' So he spent the following few months mostly in East Bergholt, avoiding people other than such visiting relatives as the Whalleys and the Gubbinses. James Gubbins, now an army captain, was his favourite cousin and had stories to tell of his brother Richard, who had been at the capture of Washington. His family was anxious 'lest he should be knocked on the head by those wretched Americans.' Constable knew he was being unsociable, for example when he begged to be let off a dinner with the curate Mr Robertson, and he was happy to be – as he told Maria – 'almost entirely in the fields'. He had an object to pursue that filled his mind and precluded melancholy. The landscapes he was at work on were better than usual – his work was consolation for not being with her – and though he had seen her only once since spring, he hoped winter would bring more cheering prospects. 'And when this unnatural and useless persecution which now embitters both our lives, shall have [ceased] we shall yet be happy . . . I can hardly tell you what I feel at the sight from the window where I am now writing of the feilds in which we have so often walked. A beautifull calm autumnal setting sun is glowing upon the gardens of the Rectory and on adjacent feilds where some of the happiest hours of my life were passed.' He didn't need to add 'with you'.

Among the paintings he did that wonderfully fine summer and autumn were several that had old subject matter but seemingly new inspiration. Farington might have claimed his admonition to study Claude was paying off. Constable, impelled by love, was perhaps simply digging deeper in his own ground. A manure pile, symbol of good husbandry, figured in the foreground of a picture of the Stour valley that he painted for Philadelphia Godfrey, daughter of Peter Godfrey of Old Hall; it was a gift from her husband-to-be, a landowner named Thomas Fitzhugh, so that she would have at her new home in London a view from her old home in Suffolk. Constable usually wrote to Maria on Sundays but occasionally gave in to the temptations of fine weather, as on 25 October when he walked through the woods to Nayland to visit his invalid aunt. He knew Maria's curiosity was piqued by Miss Godfrey's marriage and several times he wrote to pass on titbits. He let her know, for example, that Mr Fitzhugh was 'extremely rich . . . and a college friend of Mr Godfrey's. I beleive he is near thirty years older than Miss G [he was in fact forty-four years old] but in the plenitude of his wealth that was not <u>thought</u> of . . . I am told there is a very great attachment between them.'

The chief product of his Bergholt painting season was *Boat-Building*. A pencil sketch for this was made in early September beside the excavated dry dock, near Flatford Mill, where barges were constructed for Constable's father's grain and coal business. The actual painting was done entirely in the open air; as he later told the engraver David Lucas, he worked all afternoon until smoke from a nearby chimney announced fire being lit for the preparation of supper.[7] As with the painting for Miss Godfrey, Constable dealt in the detail of work, though here it was not moving manure but making a barge in its pit – a massive wooden-shoe of a craft, almost an ark, being born. Timbers were being hewn with saw and adze, and pitch was being heated in an iron pot for caulking the planking. The fabric of the huge boat is precisely rendered. The green shadows suggest it is afternoon. The fertile ground here was not Squire Godfrey's but Golding Constable's, whose artist son may have been honouring some of the tools of the trades that were used in Constable businesses and helped pay his own allowance.

When he left the village in early November, Constable told Maria that his mother thought regretfully that her son's propensity to avoid notice seemed to have increased. He acknowledged that although five or six years before he had been 'a little on tiptoe for fame and emolument', he wasn't any longer seeking honours. This attitude made Maria cross. She didn't see how he could congratulate himself on it. She believed it strange that a professional man should shun society the way he did; it wouldn't help him get ahead. If he wanted to remain single, fair enough. But *she* wanted him noticed, and, arranging to meet the recluse in mid-November in St James's Square, she added: 'I must have you known, and then to be admired will be the

natural consequence.' Possibly Constable was preparing himself for
what by now seemed natural disappointment, which quickly came. In
the elections for Associate members of the Royal Academy, he once
again failed. Worse, one of the two successful candidates was Richard
Ramsay Reinagle, who had an easy victory; this was anguish indeed.[8]

While Constable readjusted to London's 'brick walls and dirty
streets', Mrs Constable wrote to tell him of the 5 November
celebrations in the village: 'plenty of squibs and crackers . . . but no
bonfires.' She was worried about Maria returning from her stay in
Brighton and the effect on her son: 'I dread your waiting jobs under
the Lady's window for fear of colds & pains in the face & teeth.' A
month later she let him know that his father had again been thinking
about the uncertainties of John's profession and – to 'make *his death
bed easy*' – was planning to put one or two thousand pounds into an
annuity for his son. Mr Constable wasn't well during the early winter;
in the new year he was bothered by poor circulation resulting in
chilblains, though he retained a 'composed state of mind – no per-
plexities within, & every comfort without'. Constable was warned his
father showed 'symptoms of dissolution' – even Dr Rhudde sent to
ask how he was – and he made a quick visit to Bergholt to see the
seventy-seven-year-old merchant. However, by mid-February Mr
Travis, the local doctor, decided that Mr Constable was out of the
woods; the poultice on his foot was removed; his toes were healed.
Soon he was having 'tollerable good nights' and was behaving 'very
mild and kind'.

The fact that Constable and Maria Bicknell exchanged few letters
in the first months of 1815 suggests that they were managing to meet
quite frequently. In any event, Mr Bicknell now decided to stop
fighting fate. Maria wrote on 23 February to give Constable the glad
news that her father had given permission for her to receive him in
their Spring Gardens house as 'an occasional visitor'. This was
insufficient for Constable, who held out for a personal invitation from
Mr Bicknell. He had been formally dismissed, 'with expressions the
most mortifying to a man of honor', and he wanted to be formally
assured he would be welcome. (He could be just as unbending as

Maria's father and grandfather.) Constable's mother didn't make too much of this semi-acceptance of her son as a satisfactory suitor. She reminded Constable to remember Dr Rhudde's birthday in early March with all due respects. She also took the side of Hannah Dunthorne in a contretemps she had had with John Dunthorne, her husband, telling Constable that she didn't agree with him when he said, 'Dunthorne's *old woman's* conduct has always been of the worst kind towards him.' Mrs Constable protested that Hannah had taken in Dunthorne without a shilling and married him, putting him 'in possession of her house, furniture, trade, and what very property she had'. He ought to be grateful. 'I assure myself Miss B. would not countenance *for a moment* such a character.'

This was the last bit of maternal diplomacy Constable was subject to. On the cold morning of 9 March, Dr Rhudde's 81st birthday, Ann Constable went outside after breakfast to do some gardening and felt giddy. She collapsed. It seems to have been a stroke for her voice was affected and her left side partly paralysed. Mr Travis attended to Mrs Constable on her sofa; he bled her, which proved a temporary relief, but she continued to weaken. Prayers were said for her at the Sunday evening service conducted by Reverend Robertson. Abram sent word to London to his brother John, who apparently followed their sister Martha to Bergholt. But Ann Constable lingered on, and they had both returned to London – Martha to look after her young family, John to work on his paintings for the upcoming RA exhibition – when they heard of their mother's death at the end of March. She was not quite sixty-seven. She was buried on 4 April in the churchyard next door to her house.

Constable was not at the graveside. Possibly he felt it enough that he had been home just before when she was still alive and he was needed most. Possibly he was up to his neck in his painting and simply unable to do as Abram suggested, throw himself into the mail coach on Monday night to be with his family for the funeral on Tuesday. And possibly the sudden loss of his mother had shattered him, rendered him immobile; it was a Constable trait to turn inwards, in private grief, at such moments, as later events would show. Abram

understood – John shouldn't be uneasy about it – and sent news that
Dunthorne went on as usual and their father was all the better for a
letter John had written to him; he had got Abram to read it twice to
him and 'quite lighted up with pleasure'.

Soon Mr Constable had recovered enough from the loss of his wife
to call in William Mason, the Colchester solicitor and husband of their
relative Anne Parmenter. Mr Mason came several times to redraw
Golding Constable's will and lessen any difficulties that might arise on
*his* death. Mr Constable wanted to leave Abram in charge of the
business but give all his children equal shares in it. And on 6 May he
wrote his son John a heartfelt letter. Addressing him as 'Honest John',
he said his wife's death had brought him also nearly to the grave but
he was now stronger and had been out several times in his gig. 'My
breath at times is very short, but not more so than usual.' He sounded
particularly pleased with news of John's paintings at the Academy.
'Mrs Coyle of Dedham lent us a Catalogue of the Exhibition. She saw
your pictures & spoke highly of them.'

That year Constable showed eight pictures, the maximum per-
mitted. *Boat-Building* was one and the view of the Stour valley for
Philadelphia Godfrey another. There were good notices with
'reservations' – 'coarsely sketchy' was *The Examiner*'s qualified
admiration of Constable's 'sparkling sunlight' and 'general character
of truth', while *The New Monthly Magazine* liked his freshness and
colouring but regretted that his performances, 'from want of finish,
are sketches rather than pictures'.[9]

Dr Rhudde was remarkably attentive to the Constables through
this period. He enquired several times from Abram about Golding
Constable during his illness, and when Constable went up to East
Bergholt in mid-May to visit his father and paint his portrait, the
rector spoke to him at the door of his pew in church and asked for
news of Mr Constable. Was the rector's bark worse than his bite? Or
was the Great Caesar influenced by his own immediate grief. He had
just preached 'a most consolatory sermon'; his own daughter, Maria's
mother, had died nine days before in London. She had been an invalid
for the past ten years but it was still a shock for many, including

Constable. He wrote to Maria on 21 May, 'That we should both of us have lost our nearest friends (the nearest we can ever have upon earth) within so short a time of each other is truly melancholy.' It made him miss Maria all the more.

In the unsettled world beyond, where 'that scoundrel Bonaparte' as Abram called him was once again at large, other losses now affected the Constables. On 18 June the Battle of Waterloo took place. Constable spent the day at the Whalleys in East Ham, taken there by David Pike Watts. Two of Constable's cousins, sons of his mother's sisters, Lieutenant Thomas Allen and Captain James Gubbins, were on the bloody field. After a long and anxious wait, their families learned that Thomas had survived but James had not. James Gubbins, Constable said a few months after this, was one of the most interesting men he had known. Gubbins had run up great debts as a cavalry officer, but Constable's mother had nevertheless been impressed by her nephew's sense of style and had the previous Christmas sent John some home-made shirts, with collars cut in the up-to-date fashion approved by James Gubbins. It was first reported, in the *Gentleman's Magazine*, that the captain had died after being hit by a cannonball, while leading his troop in a charge. Later, it was announced that his frightened horse had carried him into enemy lines where, although he surrendered, a French officer killed him. Constable's pleasure that the day was saved for Britain (and for the forces of legitimate monarchy), preventing the overthrow of much he held dear, was thus balanced by his distress at the death of his cousin and so many of James's comrades.

For the second year running it was a lovely summer. But Constable spent the first part of it indoors, in London, working twelve, sometimes fourteen hours a day on the background for a portrait by another artist: George Dawe's portrait of the actress Eliza O'Neill, a current Juliet, propped up winsomely against a massive balustrade. At least being in London gave him the opportunity to see Maria, now staying in a cottage her father had rented in Putney; he met her on Putney Bridge on 3 July, a few days before leaving for Suffolk. From

Constable's father, Golding

there he reported, 'I never saw dear old Bergholt half so beautifull before as now.' His father had felt buoyant enough on his son's birthday to raise a glass, drinking the health of 'the painter and his pictures', but Travis the surgeon warned the family to beware of sudden change. As it was, Mr Constable was going on his usual rides and going to church, taking the sacrament. The village rumour mill was also working hard: word had it that Dr Rhudde had made a new will, leaving what had been intended for his daughter, Maria's mother, to his son-in-law, Mr Bicknell, and granddaughters. The rector gave the impression of having a new broom to sweep with. On the Sunday after Mrs Bicknell's death he told the congregation in his sermon that it was wrong at such points to have long lamentations.[10]

After being stuck in the studio at Dawe's, painting in the open air was wonderful for him – as Maria noted almost jealously in a letter of 20 July. Constable did an oil sketch at the annual village fair, when the locals celebrated the great victory over Napoleon with beef, beer, a band and fireworks, and by hanging the Corsican upstart in effigy.[11] Among several out-of-doors scenes he painted slightly further afield were a sketch of Stoke-by-Nayland and a view of the hamlet of Brightwell, near Woodbridge. The latter was the result of a request from a clergyman and antiquary, the Reverend F.H. Barnwell, and Constable went there on an excursion that took in Framlingham Castle and Ipswich. The Brightwell picture shows 'the church as it appears above a wood' (as he wrote to Maria). It is a little gem, six and a half by nine inches, oil on panel. A lane winds into a dip between fields and scattered trees, with farm buildings on the right and the red-tiled roof and greystone tower of the church on the ridge-line horizon. It is a bright though slightly overcast day, the scene rendered boldly and simply, almost as if enamelled, with sharply contrasted areas of green vegetation and grey cloud. Happiness seemed to have improved Constable's powers of concentration and focus. In late August, he wrote to Maria, 'I live almost wholly in the feilds and see nobody but the harvest men.' By mid-September, he was 'perfectly bronzed'.

Two domestic views were apparently painted just before and after Brightwell: outdoors painted from indoors. They show the Constable family's kitchen garden and flower garden, seen from an upstairs window in East Bergholt House, respectively in the morning and evening. They have the same intensity and brilliance as the Brightwell picture, cut into by deep areas of darkness. In the kitchen-garden painting, the rectory – Dr Rhudde's house – can be seen in the central

distance, with the Constable windmill on the horizon to the left.[12]
Although the fields where he and Maria had met in the first years of
their getting to know one another may have been in his mind, it seems
likely that his parents were in the forefront of his thoughts. Mrs
Constable had been working in the gardens when she was struck with
her fatal giddiness. Constable never exhibited or tried to sell these
paintings. They give an almost elegiac sense of things he wanted to
register as permanently as he could. It was as though he was looking
at them for the last time, before they disappeared or he went away.

# 6. *Ready to Marry – Perhaps (1815–17)*

The Bicknell summer household at Putney Heath had an addition. Maria, who was fond of dogs, reported happily, 'We have got a little terrier, Frisk is his name, a *great torment*, and a *great pet*, he bites & destroys every thing he can lay hold of, we flatter ourselves that as he grows older, he will leave off all these tricks, even in trifles hope befriends us, it is the rainbow of the shower.' But the sunny period of the dog's life was short. He wasn't well, and this made Constable worry in East Bergholt. (Frisk died in December.) Moreover, when Constable got back to town for a few days in early November and saw Maria at Spring Gardens, he wasn't happy with the cold manner with which her father greeted him. He also had no encouragement in the Academy elections for Associates: he got no votes at all; Mulready and Jackson were elected.[1] So it was back to Bergholt, to work on pictures for the next exhibition, and to be with his father, who was seriously ailing again. For once there is a hint that, despite saying he was anxious to hear from Maria, he got a strange reassurance from *not* being near her. Having her at a distance took away 'the anxious desire . . . to meet, perhaps too often at least for each other's comfort 'till we can meet for once, and I trust for good'. It was now he, not she, who advised patience. 'We have certainly got the worst over – and as we have borne so much and so long, would it not be wiser yet to listen to the voice of prudence?'

He was worried about money, about being able to support her and a family. Her expectations from the rector might help in future, as might his from his father, but he wasn't 'quite at liberty on that subject'. And she – while knowing he was right in staying with his father – found at the cold turn of the year that exasperation broke in. Painting seemed to take all his time and attention. 'How I do dislike pictures,' she exclaimed three days after Christmas. 'I cannot bear the sight of them.' John, on the contrary, loved making pictures but found himself on the last day of the year distressed because he wasn't able to paint. His father was once again in a 'very dangerous state', with all his children within a minute's call of his bedside. Constable was beginning to wonder whether he would ever have children of his own. William Hurlock, fourth son of the former curate of Langham and ten years younger than Constable, was visiting Dedham with his family and called on the painter, who walked him back to Dedham and met Hurlock's two lovely boys. Constable wrote enviously and gloomily to Maria about this, and it made her gloomy too. Meanwhile, Mr Travis continued to ease Golding Constable 'down the hill of life', bringing two bottles of medicine on each visit. On one such call Mr Constable was alert enough to ask, 'Why two bottles?' Travis replied, 'One is to do you good, one to do me good.'

Bergholt was 'quite in a bustle', with the Common being enclosed and the resulting fields being reapportioned. Constable wrote to Maria, 'Some amongst us have shown such extreme greediness and rapacity to "lay feild to feild" as to make themselves obnoxious.' Some did well out of the enclosure, others did poorly; any immediate cash gain may have seemed acceptable but long-held grazing and growing rights were lost. During the long war with France arable land had greatly increased in value. The price of wheat had soared in a generation, from 45 shillings a quarter in 1789 to 102 shillings in 1814.[2] Landowners were correspondingly wealthier. Drawings and oil sketches which Constable had done of the Common were eventually put to use in one of a series of landscape engravings of his work; now he gave his tiny bit of allotted land near the Constable windmill to his brother Golding. He managed to get away for a weekend in London at the end of January when he saw Maria. On his return to Suffolk he had some books sent to her, one being a 'beautifully written' life of Claude Lorrain. He was also on the lookout for a spaniel for her to take the place of Frisk.

On the occasion of this London visit, Maria had apparently discussed the vexed question of her dearest's friendship with John Dunthorne. She regarded the plumber/ glazier/artist as an unfitting companion for John Constable. He was 'destitute of religious principle' – a verdict that may have reflected what her grandfather said about Dunthorne – and was in every way his inferior. This put Constable on the spot. He struggled with what to do. Old friend on one side, dearly beloved young woman on the other. At last he decided that as Dunthorne was 'determined to continue in his perverse and evil ways', he would get Mr Travis to tell him not to come to the Constable house again, except on business (possibly, as a close-at-hand plumber, Dunthorne could not be spared); their neighbourly and artistic relations were at an end. According to Constable, Dunthorne at this point was as upset with him as he with Dunthorne. 'The sight of me became a monster to him, and he wished to be rid of me.'

One wonders how much this imbroglio was kindled by Constable's desire to appease the rector. The episode leaves a sour taste, and didn't in any event affect the state of things for the lovers. Dr Rhudde was again 'entirely inveterate' against Constable as a potential husband for Maria, and equally against was his daughter (and Maria's aunt) Mrs Harriet Farnham. Banishing Dunthorne into outer darkness didn't help. The rector's attitude was further reinforced by a completely tactless act by Constable. He had learned from Maria that the Bicknells were looking for a new school for her fourteen-year-old sister Catherine. Miss Taylor's school in East Bergholt was suggested as a possibility. Constable heard Miss Taylor saying she hadn't got enough pupils and thereupon mentioned Catherine to her. He obviously thought Miss Taylor wouldn't use his name; any sensible person should have known that the recommendation of John Constable would not be the way to Dr Rhudde's heart. But Miss Taylor wasn't sensible. The chance of a new pupil was all that mattered. She went at once to the rectory and canvassed the subject of Catherine joining her school. Dr Rhudde erupted. What had John Constable got to do with his family's private affairs? With his granddaughter's schooling? Surely Constable was still banned from visiting Spring Gardens? Dr Rhudde wrote a fierce letter to his son-in-law Charles Bicknell, and Maria had to tell Constable not to come to town just yet. His recent visits to the Bicknell house had been kept a secret from the rector, who was now fully apprised and furious about it. 'How it will end,' sighed Maria, 'God only knows.'

Resolution was approaching faster than she knew. When Constable heard from Maria that 'the kind Doctor says he "considers me no longer as his grand daughter"', it was all he needed; his nerve stiffened. He and Maria had done nothing blameable. 'Our business is now more than ever (if possible) with ourselves.' Moreover, he had been talking with his brothers and sisters about William Mason's proposals for their father's estate and doing his arithmetic, all the while Mr Constable inexorably declined. 'I shall inherit a sixth part of my father's property, which we expect may be at least four thousand pounds apiece, and Mrs Smith [his aunt in Nayland] will leave about two thousand pounds more amongst us – and I am entirely free of debt. I trust [–] could I be made happy [–] to make a good deal more than I do now of my profession.' After this, 'my dearest Maria', he had nothing more to say, other than 'The sooner we are married the better'. No more arguments! 'We have been great fools not to have married long ago[,] by which we might perhaps have stopped the mouths of all our enemies.' He didn't mind who read this, including her father.

Constable had now stayed in East Bergholt longer than for many years and he remained another month, despite the need to get his pictures to the Academy and despite hearing from Maria that she had been ill. She had visited Greenwich, 'a damp, unhealthy place', and caught a cold. On 9 March she excused herself to him for not writing a long letter, 'for *thinking* hurts my chest', and then added lightly, 'I really think it does me good to be ill for a day or two, one enjoys so much the more returning to one's usual occupations, and the charm of breathing the fresh air.' Chest – breath – air. Intimations. She in fact seemed a trifle rattled in late March, complaining when he wrote to her too often and when he wrote too little (a contrariness Constable pointed out to her).

The pictures he took to town at the end of March for the Academy exhibition were *A Wheat Field* and *A Wood, Autumn*. The wheatfield was part of his customary territory, land on the slopes below Bergholt with the Stour valley leading up to Stratford St Mary, with what looks like the remains of the 'runover dungle' in a far corner of the field and a closer than usual view of people harvesting: five men working around the walled edges of the wheat; a boy carrying an armful of wheat up the slope; a woman and two girls gleaning; and a boy with a dog sitting beside a pile of clothes and baskets, no doubt containing food and drink; above, a serene summer sky. Despite the human interest, it is a less focused picture than the *Stour Valley and Dedham Village* painting of a year before. As for *A Wood*, it is now lost to sight but was bought immediately by Constable's uncle, David Pike Watts, for forty guineas; it may have illustrated Constable's former haunts in Helmingham Park.[3] Although he exhibited only two paintings at Somerset House, this year was to be his most productive ever. Among other pictures he had worked on were a long-promised copy of a Reynolds portrait for Lady Louisa Manners – a good patron who, however, kept interrupting his landscape work when he was in London and gave him added reason for staying in Bergholt as long as possible. Press reaction to his Academy exhibits was not wholehearted. *Ackermann's Repository of Art* said, 'From extreme carelessness this artist has gone to the other extreme, and now displays the most laboured finish.' *The Examiner*'s critic thought differently, approving Constable's eye for nature but believing 'his execution is still crude'.[4]

Golding Constable was given a private view of the *Wheat Field* before his son took the paintings to town. The older man was failing: his dropsy had increased and Mr Travis was powerless to help. For several months Constable was a shuttlecock. At the end of February he made a trip to London on art business and to see his 'beloved and ever dearest' Maria, then returned to Suffolk to be with his father and was joined by his sister Martha Whalley who came to Bergholt to cheer up the family. At the end of March he returned to town, where, according to Maria, there was much sickness and 'horrid black, cold, raw, easterly winds'. But in early May he was called again to Suffolk by Abram, to the bedside of their father who said he was ready 'to be released'. The brief visit of his artist son pleased the old man. Constable was back in Charlotte Street when on 14 May his father died. He wrote to Maria when he got to East Bergholt on 19 May, the day before the funeral, to say:

> My dear Father's end was so happy – he died whilst sitting in his chair as usual, without a sigh or a pang, and without the smallest alteration of his position or features, except a gentle inclination of his head forwards – and my sister Ann who was near had to put her face close to his to assure herself that he breathed no more. Thus it has pleased God to take . . . this good man to Himself – the rectitude of his conduct through life had disarmed the grave of its terrors, and it pleased God to spare him the pang of death.

Constable now had few doubts as to what his course of action must be. His father's death left him an equal share with his brothers and sisters in the Constable estate. Abram would continue to run the family business and would hand out to his siblings equal parts of the annual profits; John Constable reckoned he would be getting roughly two hundred a year from this, twice the allowance he had been receiving from his father. Moreover, he could expect a share in what East Bergholt House fetched when sold, there were other well-to-do relatives who might leave him something, and his paintings were starting to bring in regular money. He and Maria might count on at least four hundred a year and that, with careful housekeeping, should be enough. His expectations from David Pike Watts were greater in the eyes of some beholders than in Constable's, which was as well, for when Uncle David died at the end of July, aged sixty-two, the bulk of his fortune of nearly £300,000 went to his daughter.[5] Dr Rhudde was said to be 'full of indignity' about this, partly because he had decided that Mr Watts had been a greater monetary benefactor to Constable over the years than was in fact the case. In mid-August, reporting from East Bergholt this sub-plot to Maria in Putney, Constable added wryly that, still, 'the Doctor is quite well & may live to see things in their right light yet'.

It appeared that Dr Rhudde's reactions had ceased to matter as much as before. Another factor that had impelled Constable was the wedding of his friend John Fisher, a ceremony conducted on 2 July by Fisher's uncle the Bishop of Salisbury. Constable saw Farington that day, told him of Fisher's marriage, and said that 'under all the circumstances He had made up his mind to marry Miss Bicknell without further delay & to take the chance of what might arise'.[6] With his heels dug in, Constable was not about to put up with any further harasssment from Maria's father. He had been visiting Spring Gardens fairly frequently and on one such occasion was seen by Mr Bicknell holding hands with Maria. Mr Bicknell said, 'Sir, if you were the most approved of lovers, you could not take a greater liberty with my daughter.' Constable replied, 'And don't you know, Sir, that I *am* the most approved of lovers?'[7]

Though unapproved by Mr Bicknell, Constable with his mind made up was 'happy in love'. Close at hand in East Bergholt he kept a portrait he had done of Maria, which was the first thing he saw in the morning and the last at night; he said it calmed his spirits. He sent Maria a book of the letters of Saloman Gessner, the Swiss poet and painter, whose essay on landscape had been given him by J.T. Smith nineteen years before and provided early encouragement. And he gave her a new dog, Dash, from his sister Ann's kennels in East Bergholt. His instructions to Maria were that Dash should be fed 'bread or a little barley meal well scalded with extream boiling water, and a bit of fat mixed with it', and he should have very little meat. This made for a healthy dog. (Dash turned out to be not fond of barley meal, though he choked it down.) Constable's bad news from Bergholt in mid-August was the weather, with the hay and corn a month late. Mount Tambora, a volcano in Indonesia, had erupted the previous year and its spreading ash clouds made 1816 in Europe 'the year without a summer'.

On 30 August Constable wrote to Maria in Putney Heath from Wivenhoe Park, near Colchester, where he was making a painting for General Rebow, to tell her 'I live in the park and Mrs Rebow says I am very unsociable'. On 6 September he wrote to her again from the

Rebows', enclosing a letter from his friend Fisher. Fisher told Constable he would be in London on 24 September happy to marry them – so stop shilly-shallying. 'Follow my example, & get you to your lady, & instead of blundering out long sentences about the "hymeneal altar" &c., say that on Wednesday September 25 you are ready to marry her. If she replies, like a sensible woman as I suspect she is, well, John, here is my hand I am ready, all well & good . . . I am at her service.' Fisher wanted them to spend their honeymoon at Osmington, near Weymouth, where he was vicar. The supporters of the couple included Mr Driffield, who had christened Constable and now said he would marry them if Fisher couldn't. Mr Driffield picked up Constable from the Rebows and drove him to East Bergholt.

Maria was indeed as sensible as Fisher suspected, and although she thought a wedding date a few days later than that proposed by Fisher suited her better, *she* wasn't thinking in terms of postponements. She wanted Constable to put himself on the line and undertake the unpleasant task of letting the Doctor know their plans. She had shown Fisher's letter to her father, 'in hope they would make some impression upon him, [but] he merely says that without the Doctor's consent, he shall neither retard, or facilitate it, complains of poverty & so on'. Constable wrote to Dr Rhudde in 'the most respectful manner'. The Doctor had recently been sending mixed messages, one moment calling Constable an 'infidel,' the next – according to Abram – suggesting via Mr Travis that Constable should go into the Church. It was easy to get into, the Doctor said, and being a clergyman was less objectionable than being an artist. When Dr Rhudde returned from his annual trip to Cromer, he actually bowed graciously to Constable from his coach, while his coachman Thomas, holding the reins, gave Constable a knowing grin from the seat above.

Through this closing period of his bachelorhood, Constable seems to have been a good deal distracted. Was he in fact ready to marry Maria? Should the wedding be postponed? He now gave the impression of putting his professional obligations before her. Excusing himself, he told her he had been busy on pictures which he hoped would provide funds for their future together. A few portraits might assist with living expenses through the winter. The Rebows obviously intended their commission – they hoped for several paintings – to help the couple on their way. Constable had been working on a large picture of Flatford Mill for the next Academy exhibition, and his mind was much on the problems of painting *Wivenhoe Park*. As if hoping she would understand, he wrote to Maria that he was getting on well with it, albeit with a struggle: 'The great difficulty has been to get so much in as they wanted . . . On my left is a grotto with some elms, at the head of a peice of water – in the centre is the house over a beautiful wood and very far to the right is a deer house, which it was necessary to add, so that my view comprehended too many [distances]. But to day I have got over the difficulty, and begin to like it *myself*.' Possibly the Rebows wanted some of these 'necessities', perhaps he wanted them himself. The painting needed to be wider to accommodate things and so he added strips of canvas at each side. He seemed to have been taking note of how grassy the grass looked, and how bright green and how almost edible it could be. He was painting a natural scene, painting 'from nature', but also transfusing the scene with light. Wrestling with the real, he heightened the actual into the ideal.[8]

Far from wanting the marriage put off, Maria asked for Constable's opinion of what she should wear on the day. She wasn't pleased when he replied that he always wore black and thought she looked well in that colour. This apparent lack of nuptial enthusiasm made her remind him that, even now, if he wanted to, it wasn't too late to follow her father's advice and wait. But as she probably guessed it would, resolution once again seized Constable. Fisher wrote to suggest the first of October. In East Bergholt the village was abuzz with the impending union and Constable was congratulated as though he were already a married man. Then, of course, came a late difficulty: a portrait to be done of an elderly clergyman in Brightwell who was expected to die at any minute and a sitting requested; Constable couldn't say no. However, on Saturday 28 September, only a day later than promised, he went up to London on the 'Times' coach, and on the following Monday Maria and her aunt Mrs Charles Arnold – a stalwart supporter of Maria in her proposed union – called in

Maria Bicknell, 1816

Charlotte Street to discuss final arrangements. Maria had told him to
make his own invitations to family and friends, and although he now
wrote to his sister Martha Whalley to ask her to attend the ceremony,
he had left it too late; she couldn't come. Constable sent his kindest
love to Maria's sister Louisa, who he hoped forgave him for taking
Maria from her family. After this Maria had a last talk on the subject

with her father, and 'warm words' were exchanged. Did she make a final, fruitless attempt to get Papa's blessing? For whatever reason, the wedding was put off one more day.

But at last, on Wednesday 2 October, according to the parish register of St Martin-in-the-Fields, 'John Constable of the Parish of Saint Pancras a Bachelor and Maria Elizabeth Bicknell of this Parish a Spinster were married in this Church by Licence . . .' It was the first wedding solemnised that day in St Martin's; the others all conducted by the church's curate John Tillotson, this by 'John Fisher, Prebendary of Sarum'. The long-term bachelor groom was forty, the bride twenty-eight. If Maria had hoped to the last minute the church doors would swing open and a procession of Bicknells would come in, she was disappointed; her immediate family, who lived a few hundred yards away, were noticeably absent, and apparently none of his family showed up either. The witnesses in the great near-empty church were his close neighbours from Charlotte Street the apothecary William Manning and his wife Sarah. In the absence of other well-wishers, the Mannings were left to bid the happy couple long life and good fortune.[9]

At the end of May 1816 Constable had put his name forward once again for election that autumn as an Associate of the Academy; thirty-six other artists did so too. Farington told him that he intended to suggest to several influential members that the Academy 'fill at least 4 of the 5 vacancies by electing such Artists as had been sometime on the list and were of considerable standing *in years*'.[10] Constable certainly qualified on both counts. Moreover, now that Constable's marriage was an accomplished fact, his father-in-law felt he had a stake in his success. Mr Bicknell met the Academician William Owen at Putney and, knowing how some naval officers were advanced by the Admiralty, asked him if any outside influence would be useful in getting Constable elected. Owen, so Farington reported, said 'nothing of the kind would have any effect, but that the general feeling was so much in favor of Constable that whenever it could be done with propriety He would have friends ready to support him'.[11] But despite Farington and Owen, once again at the November elections Constable got no votes.[12]

For the moment Constable had other things on his mind. He was on an extended honeymoon and happily drawing, painting and making up for lost time with Maria. They went first to stay with Bishop Fisher and his wife in Salisbury, then to his aunt Mary Gubbins and her family in Southampton. From there they made an excursion to the picturesque ruins of Netley Abbey.[13] After that they joined Prebendary Fisher and his wife in Osmington, a small Dorset village tucked into a cleft of the land half a mile from the sea. They stayed for seven weeks. In his invitation Fisher had commended the place: 'The country here is wonderfully wild & sublime & well worth a painters visit. My house commands a singularly beautiful view & you may study from my very windows. You shall [have] a plate of meat set by the side of your easel without your sitting down to dinner: we never see company: & I have brushes paints & canvas in abundance.' He knew Constable's obsessiveness and apparent unsociability. But in the small vicarage there wasn't room for much except the contentment of the two newly-married couples.

From the wooded valley of Sutton and Preston, a small amphitheatre formed by hills, you could see (so Fisher said) 'a peep of the blue sky in the distance with Portland: and two old forlorn ash trees in the foreground. The place is very sequestered & is frequented by kingfishers & woodcocks.' From Osmington Mills, where fishing boats were hauled up, they walked along the shore westward to Redcliff Point and round the end of it into Weymouth Bay and Bowleaze Cove. There, Constable painted an oil showing a stream called the Jordan snaking across the beach to the sea. The Constables and Fishers also took higher walks on the downs above, where old drystone walls enclosed the grassy fields and there were far views along Chesil Beach to Portland Island. Monarchical enthusiasts among the locals had carved in the chalk hillside overlooking Weymouth an image of George III on horseback – but that wasn't conspicuous from Osmington and Constable's royalist sympathies weren't put into conflict with his tangible sense of the Dorset landscape. Indeed, any assumption that he could only paint Suffolk or Stour valley scenes would now have been quickly overturned. Channel clouds, Channel skies. Wide views with

Weymouth Bay

lonely figures and small flocks of sheep. Fisher – as he had said he would – provided canvases and paints. Constable carried a sketchbook everywhere and painted daily, mostly in fair weather but sometimes in foul. When conditions were really bad he moved indoors and kept on painting: a portrait of a buxom, ringletted Mary Fisher, wearing a low-cut dress and a pearl necklace with a pendant crucifix, was one from this time. Fisher had promised in his letter of invitation, 'My wife is quiet & silent & sits & reads without disturbing a soul & Mrs Constable may follow her example. Of an evening we will sit over an autumnal fireside[,] read a sensible book perhaps a Sermon, & after prayers get us to bed at peace with ourselves & all the world.' One suspects that Fisher spoke with his ecclesiastical tongue slightly in cheek, and the two newly-wed pairs had other things to occupy and amuse them. Certainly Fisher and Constable discussed each other's drawings. Any pensiveness on Mary Fisher's part may have been prompted by occasional thoughts of her cousin John Wordsworth, brother of the poet, whose ship the East Indiaman *Abergavenny* had been wrecked off this shore in February 1805. Seeking shelter after a partial dismasting, the vessel had run aground and several hundred men had been lost, including John Wordsworth. Toll for the brave.

John and Maria Constable stayed longer than they had intended. The couples got on well and the two men shared confidences about the Established Church and the art establishment whose heart was the Royal Academy. Fisher, even more than his helpful uncle, the Bishop, perceived qualities of genius in the often self-doubting Constable. He overrode the artist's moments of low esteem with intelligent praise and criticism. He helped Constable set a higher value on his own worth and eventually – by buying paintings at good prices – became Constable's first major patron. On the last Sunday of his extended honeymoon Constable sat in a choir stall of Preston church, near Osmington, where Fisher also performed parish duties, and sketched his friend in the pulpit as he delivered a sermon.[14]

Married life began properly back in Charlotte Street in mid-December. Maria was married to a painter, and these were his working quarters. Constable had got his landlord Richard Weight to repaint the staircase and front rooms; a new wallpaper was still to be selected for the back drawing room, for which Lady Heathcote had earlier approved a salmon colour – a good choice as a background for pictures. Constable's sister Ann invited them to spend Christmas in Bergholt, sister Mary wrote sending her affection and congratulations on their marriage, and Abram turned up in town in person to do the same. But Bergholt itself raised the question: how did the great Caesar, Dr Rhudde, feel about them now?

He was still blowing hot then cold. Mr Travis 'sounded' the rector when he encountered him and mentioned that 'Mr and Mrs Constable would much like to visit Bergholt'. The rector, seemingly relishing his power, replied, 'If they do, and call upon me, I will not see them.' The couple postponed their trip. Nevertheless, other signs suggested hope. Dr Rhudde's servant Thomas brought Abram a fine turkey for Christmas, with the Doctor's compliments, and this was seen as a peace offering. Mary sent news on 12 January 1817 that Mr Travis understood that the rector simply wanted Constable 'to make a proper apology' to Mr Bicknell and himself, presumably for Constable's conduct in general and in particular for stealing away Maria; then 'all would be well'. So Constable wrote a letter to Mr Bicknell, which did the trick, and another to the rector, which did not. Abram reported that Dr Rhudde told Mr Travis, 'If you can see a simple apology in that letter it is more than I can.' The Doctor further accused Constable of laughing at him in church and drawing caricatures of him. It was obviously time to bow and scrape, never easy for Constable, but Abram and Mr Travis advised it, and for Maria no concession was too great. Constable did his humble duty and wrote again to the rector, sending a copy of his submission to Abram. On 19 January Abram met Dr Rhudde who said he had had a letter from John. Would Abram tell his brother the Doctor would be coming to town in February and would have come to a decision by then? He wasn't displeased by Constable's second letter; in fact, 'I wish them both happy and shall try to make them so.' Abram thought the rector was softening: 'He must have his way, it is no use to oppose him, & by giving way & humoring him, any thing may be got over.'

Dr Rhudde was eighty-four and cranky; he was seen to have trouble getting up to and down from the pulpit. The Constables' suspense continued. The Doctor's February trip to town didn't help and he returned home, so Constable told Farington, 'in as ill a humour as ever'. But, Constable added, the rector had had a new will drawn up in which he had made provision for any children Constable might have. In that respect Constable and Maria had apparently been doing their natural best since John Fisher joined their hands at St Martin-in-the-Fields. Although Maria unfortunately had a miscarriage in mid-February, she was soon pregnant again. In April, sister Ann sent Maria her good wishes and love, and recommended for her condition the remedy of Bergholt air. First, however, Maria tried East Ham air at the Whalleys', and Constable made a quick and almost undercover trip to Bergholt on his own. While there he wrote Dr Rhudde a 'most respectful' letter which was counter-productive: in fact, the Doctor was made really miserable by it. Ann, Mary and Abram all made a point of calling at the rectory but no progress was achieved.

# 7. *Housekeeping (1817–19)*

Before a summer holiday in Suffolk, decisions had to be taken about a new place to live in town. Constable's lodgings with the Weights, despite repainting, would no longer do. Farington's advice was sought, and a house further up Charlotte Street considered, but Farington thought the price being asked for goodwill, lease and annual rent too dear.[1] Maria's father was giving her an allowance of £50 a year, and this with Constable's private income of £200 meant he needed to bring in about £100 from painting to meet their expected expenses. For the time being Maria took shelter with Mr Bicknell and her sister in Putney Heath, at what Constable called 'Louisa Cottage'. Meanwhile, spurred by the absence of his wife, Constable hunted for a new home.

He soon found one. Number 1 Keppel Street, north of the British Museum and between Gower Street and Russell Square, had a view of fields, ponds and a pig farm; it was almost country.[2] It was only seven or eight years old and Constable told Maria it was a 'charming, snugg place & a great bargain'. John Fisher soon dubbed it Ruysdael House, in honour of one of his friend's favourite Dutch painters.[3] In late June Constable told Maria, still in Putney, 'The more I see of the house the better I like it – I know it will suit us exactly'. But he cautiously sent a surveyor – who found nothing amiss – and a painter to give him an estimate for rooms that he wanted to be redecorated. He signed a seven-year lease at £100 a year, 'including taxes', a copy of which was approved by Mr Bicknell's legal partner Anthony Spedding. Constable said later that the five years they spent there were the happiest of his life.

\*

His Academy entries that year were almost all from his native scenery. It was as though he knew an epoch – his own time in his own place – was about to end, and he was putting together the evidence of it. Flatford Mill was again a subject, though the title was less specific, *Scene on a Navigable River*; it was the largest painting he had so far exhibited. Among the others was the small, startling and rather surreal *Cottage in a Cornfield*, a close-up picture with some of the simplified qualities of his view of Brightwell. On view but not for sale was *Wivenhoe Park*, his panoramic prospect of General Rebow's house and grounds, the commissioned result of his 'living in the park' the previous summer. His portrait of John Fisher was an entry from beyond East Anglia. Together with the portrait of Mary it hung in the Fishers' house in a room where the clergyman kept up with his correspondence – in one such letter he told Constable the portraits were much admired. During this summer Constable also painted a through-the-trees view of East Bergholt church and a moody Dedham lock-and-mill scene, with a stormy sky making dark reflections on the surface of the Stour. Charles Leslie, his future biographer, met

John Fisher, 1817

Constable about this time and thought Constable's art was 'never so perfect as at this period of his life'. Leslie took particular notice of the cottage in the cornfield (corn being a term for all sorts of grain; in this case it was wheat). The cottage, he wrote, was 'closely surrounded by corn which, on the side most shaded from the sun, remains green, while over the rest of the field it has ripened'.[4] It was the sort of close observation in a painting that most of Constable's viewers weren't aware of. The newspaper critics that year thought he was improving but buyers weren't particularly evident.[5]

Another picture was formed in embryo at this time. In late June Constable walked over the new Waterloo Bridge shortly after it had been opened and named by the Prince Regent. He had been going daily to Somerset House for the exhibition and apparently saw the opening ceremony from its terrace. Taken by the radiance of the sun on the water and the red and gold standards of the royal barges, he seems to have decided then and there that this was the subject for a painting. He made sketches and then continued to work away at the subject on and off: in July 1819 he wrote to Fisher, 'I have made a sketch of my scene on the Thames – which is very promising.' Various paintings featuring the bridge followed in the next thirteen years, some bowing to Canaletto, others to Turner, who – as will be seen – became extremely competitive about the high-key of Constable's eventual painting, which threatened Turner's status as the reputed doyen of 'white painters'.

In early August Constable and Maria – more than four months pregnant – forsook London for the country. They stayed for nearly three months, for the most part in East Bergholt, presumably with Abram, Ann and Mary in the old family house (which there was now talk of selling), and Maria blossomed. Dr Rhudde was quiet, though there were fears he might be biding his time before exploding. Out of doors and in, Constable worked hard, building up a stock of useful drawings and oil sketches, using both a four-and-a-half-inch by seven-and-a-quarter-inch sketchbook and larger loose sheets. His territory extended to Dedham, Ipswich and Mistley; they visited the

Elms in Old Hall Park, East Bergholt

Rebows in Wivenhoe and in Feering called on the Reverend Driffield, who was keen to know how things stood with the Doctor. Constable walked, as always, down Fen Lane, and on 25 July he sketched the entrance to the lane. This seems to have been the occasion of the unfinished picture (now in Tate Britain); he perhaps meant to finish it in town. The viewer is attracted down the lane along the shadowed side of a hedge, the rutted lane itself in sun as it curves downhill through trees. Beyond are the valley and Dedham church tower. In the sunlit field on the left, over the hedge, are seen the heads and white shirts of a gang of mowers and reapers at work in the wheat. Sam Strowger had applauded the correctness of Constable's vision in such a picture, pointing out to the agriculturally ignorant members of the arranging committee how the appointed leader or 'lord' of the gang moved ahead of the rest – as he was doing here. This practice prevailed in many parts of the English countryside. In north Oxfordshire, the 'lord' was called 'king of the mowers' and was generally the tallest and most experienced man, according to Flora Thompson. 'With a wreath of poppies and green bindweed trails around his wide, rush-plaited hat, he led the band down the swathes as they mowed and decreed when and for how long they should halt for "a breather".' A stone jar to drink from was kept under a hedge in the shade.[6] On the back of another open-air oil sketch Constable painted at East Bergholt this year, the artist wrote, 'Made this sketch, Oct.1817. Old Joseph King, my father's huntsman, came to me at this time – there was a barn on the right in which he had thrashed that time 70 years.'[7]

When Constable and Maria returned to town in late October, he showed his Suffolk studies to Farington and others; W.R. Bigg liked them, and Constable was judged to have had a successful campaign. His star was at last rising. Rumours were heard that he would become an Associate at the next RA elections. Sir William Beechey, the portrait painter, told David Pike Watts's daughter Mary Watts-Russell that her cousin was 'a general favourite' and would have 'plenty of votes'. Constable made light of this, explaining to Maria that 'poor, good-natured Beechey' must have said the same of twenty candidates. When the elections took place, on the evening of 3 November, five out of the twenty-four members voted for Constable in the first poll, which was won by the sculptor E.H. Baily, and in the second he got eight votes in the contest won by the animal and battle-scene painter Abraham Cooper. But Constable was cheered; this was better than he had ever done before. And Farington, although no longer an across-the-street neighbour, went on being a confidant: he and Constable talked in December about Haydon and 'his continued abuse of the Academy'.[8] Constable, albeit married, was still invited to dinner at Farington's, as on the occasion in March 1818 when other guests were Henry Thomson RA, Samuel Lane and the American Gilbert Stuart Newton.

The big event of the winter, three weeks before Christmas, was the safe arrival in Keppel Street of John Charles Constable – 'a fine boy', according to Farington. The infant was delivered on 4 December 1817 at 9 a.m., so Constable later recorded in the family Bible. East Bergholt was quickly informed and from there the news went out to the aunt at Nayland. Ann Constable also wrote to pass on the important fact that the intelligence had reached the rectory. Mr Travis had called there and Dr Rhudde had asked him, 'What news?' Travis replied, 'You are a great grandfather, Doctor,' at which Dr Rhudde didn't seem at all displeased. He said, 'You must now approach me with additional respect, as I am a Patriarch.' The Doctor then told Mr Travis that he intended to leave *it* something in his will.

Ann Constable immediately began to look among the local girls for a nursemaid. But Constable himself, according to Charles Leslie, proved to be an exceptionally attentive father. John Charles 'might be seen almost as often in his arms as in those of his nurse, or even his mother. His fondness for children exceeded . . . that of any man I ever knew.' The baby was christened on 19 March, the godparents being Maria's father, the Bicknells' friend Charles Phillips of Pall Mall, and Mary Watts-Russell of Portland Place.

Whether being a father had anything to do with it is uncertain, but in 1818 Constable began to think of pictures on a bigger scale – a scale which might finally get him the recognition he felt he deserved. Family letters are sparse for this period. He was absorbed with Maria, the baby and painting. However, the pictures he showed at Somerset House that year were still mostly small-scale: two drawings and four landscapes in oil, one of which may have been a view of Dedham Lock and Mill he painted several times; a wonderfully fresh version of this shows a cloudy sky beginning to clear after a shower and the red-brick

Dedham mill and lock

mill reflected in the water below lock gates. Several reviewers talked
of his extraordinary pencilling and peculiar felicity. The critic of the
*Morning Herald* thought *Landscape – breaking up of a shower* displayed
'much genius'. The *Literary Gazette* called it 'a remarkably sweet
production' which had 'something . . . of the glittering freshness . . .
of summer rain'.[9] Constable was preoccupied to the point where he
forgot to put his name down as a candidate for the November
elections, but an official of the Academy assumed he had meant to and
did so for him. He shared the good news with Farington that he had
sold two landscapes, one for forty-five, another for twenty guineas; it
was better, he agreed, for them to be seen and sold at moderate prices
than held on to unsold.[10] It was also a busy year for portraits. He
finished one of Mrs Pulham, the Woodbridge solicitor's wife, and
others of Dr John Wingfield (headmaster of Westminster School), Dr
William Walker (rector of Layham, a few miles from East Bergholt),

the Reverend Dr James Andrew (a governor of Addiscombe College, in Kent) and his wife; and he started a new portrait of Dr Fisher, the Bishop of Salisbury, to whose daughter Dorothea he also gave painting lessons. Portraits brought in ready money in small but useful amounts, and because Constable's fees were modest, he was in demand. Portraits kept him so busy during the summer that there was only time for short trips to Suffolk between his imperative visits to see Maria and John Charles in Putney. East Bergholt House was being put on the market and family discussions involved him in prices, disposal of furniture, and new places to live for his brothers and sisters. He was in the village briefly in late October when he managed to spend some time in the churchyard sketching his parents' tomb and to make his last drawing of the house from the fields at the back.

The year's Academy elections for Associates went normally. Despite the hopes raised earlier, and despite some canvassing he did in June, Constable – still regarded as *only* a landscape painter – performed poorly. His friend Samuel Lane, a portrait painter of middling talent, was regarded as having stronger chances in the run-up to the contest in November. In the end Constable got one vote – less than he had done the year before – and the single vacancy went to the American Washington Allston, who was at sea, en route to Boston. One election Constable won was for a directorship of the Artists' General Benevolent Institution; Turner was in the chair at the May meeting where this occurred.[11] Clearly this was a body that didn't hold Constable's supposed cushion of income against him, and rightly so. He was always a giver: alike to poor musicians, impoverished painters, in-need farm workers, elderly hard-up East Bergholt folk, and young women selling flowers in London streets.

The family house was sold in early November. The buyers were a neighbouring couple, Mr and Mrs Walter Clerk, and forty-five years' worth of possessions had to be cleared out. Constable wasn't able to make a visit and Abram bore the brunt of the work. Their sister Ann set about getting an old cottage on the heath repaired for herself, with Golding as a rather uncomfortable companion for a time. He was away

Constable's
brother, Abram,
c.1806

during the house transaction, unwell, probably with epilepsy – Abram
a few years later noted that Golding sometimes had fits which made
him momentarily senseless and left his mind 'very weak'. But Golding
returned to East Bergholt in August 1819 and was able to resume his
favourite sport, shooting game; he stayed until he went to a house on
the Dysarts' estate at Helmingham as live-in land warden. Mary joined
Abram at the old house attached to Flatford Mill, once again within
earshot and touching distance of the river. William Mason, the family
solicitor in Colchester, did the conveyancing. The furniture, books,
tools and agricultural implements were auctioned over three days in
mid-March 1819 in two hundred lots, for good prices. The livestock,
wagons and farm carriage were sold on the first day. Abram bought two
of the horses for seventy-five guineas and Mary bought her three
favourite cows, Cherry, Tibby, and Feresty. Ann reported that the
toys were in particular demand: 'the doll's bed with tatter'd garniture
sold for a guinea, the child's wagon and sundry other toys 17s. – the
windmill &c., 15s.6d.' John Constable didn't attend the auction.[12]

Dr Rhudde's disposition was still a constant concern. Sometimes

Constable's
sisters, Ann and
Mary

he seemed affable until the dreaded words 'John Constable' were mentioned. Yet in December, around the time of the birth of John Charles, Dr Rhudde drew up a new will in which he left his granddaughter Maria the same share in his estate as her siblings. It was perhaps just in time. The Doctor was seen several times searching the rectory for his late wife, and on one occasion in early March 1819 was discovered by his coachman Thomas at 6.30 a.m. sitting by the kitchen fire before any of the other servants were downstairs. Abram thought he often seemed very lost.

Constable was particularly busy in the first few months of 1819. He was at work on a single large picture for the Academy exhibition, the first of what became a sequence of six-footers: a 'Scene on the River Stour', soon known as *The White Horse*. He painted the picture entirely in his Keppel Street studio, not in the open air, but used some earlier sketches from Willy Lott's house and the river below Flatford Lock, and beforehand made a full-size oil sketch, as became his practice with his biggest paintings. The sketch is a darker picture, with rain threatening; the finished, exhibited work has some clouds but a largely sunny sky, bringing out the whiteness of the horse being ferried by barge around the end of the Spong, an island at this point in the Stour. Farington was asked to look at it and he offered several suggestions that Constable said 'he would attend to'. Whatever alterations Constable made were, for other viewers of the moment, all to the good; he saw Farington a few days after his visit and was 'in high spirits from the approbation of his picture'.[13]

His offering to the British Institution at the start of the year hadn't been acclaimed. *Osmington Shore* was described by one critic as 'a sketch of barren sand without interest'. But now his reversion to his native scenery took the reviewers' fancy. As well as the horse, the painting shows one of the bargees leaning against a quant pole, the surface of the river barely ruffled, a few cattle standing at the water's edge. Despite having only one focus of 'action', on the barge, the painting was awash with bucolic detail: houses amid the trees; a skiff moored at the river bank in front of a thatched boat shed; posts and reeds; white clouds tethered overhead; on one side the river surface reflective, on the other shadowed.

At the time the full-size oil sketch received attention only from the painter and any callers who saw him at work on it, as he tried to resolve various problems the picture presented. Later it was to become the first example in the series of preliminary paintings, the six-foot oil sketches that many were to think Constable's 'supreme achievement'.[14] In 1819 the finished picture on show at Somerset House attracted more attention than any he had exhibited hitherto. It wasn't hung in the best room, some of his supporters complained, but it was – as Leslie observed – 'too large to remain unnoticed'. There were signs that Constable was coming at last into his kingdom. Robert Hunt, critic of *The Examiner*, wrote on 27 June 1819 that the artist 'has none of the poetry of Nature like Mr Turner, but he has more of her portraiture'. The art reviewer of the *Literary Chronicle* exclaimed, 'What a grasp of everything beautiful in rural scenery!' and declared that 'this young artist' – now forty-two – was 'rising very fast in reputation'. Martin Archer Shee, who was to become President of the Royal Academy, later said he thought it the finest of Constable's works. The painter himself was in high spirits at this upbeat reception; the painting, 'a placid representation of a serene grey morning' in summer, was (he thereafter said), 'one of my happiest efforts on a large scale'.[15]

Even so, there was no rush of buyers. It took the indispensable John Fisher to set the seal on Constable's success. He had been made an Archdeacon of Berkshire at the end of 1817 and Prebendary of Salisbury Cathedral in the same period. His obligations included giving sumptuous dinners to the Bishop and resident canons, but he also had numerous perquisites, including lifetime use of Leydenhall, a fine house in the cathedral close, with a garden running down to the River Avon. Fisher wrote in July, enquiring as if for an interested friend about the asking price of Constable's 'great picture'. He said, 'We will call it if you please "*Life* and the pale Horse", in contra-distinction to Mr West['s] painting [which was called *Death on the Pale Horse*].' Constable replied that the price was a hundred guineas, not including the frame. Fisher wrote back saying he wanted to purchase it. The opposite of a hard bargainer, Constable – now that he knew who the potential buyer was – wanted to charge less for *The White Horse*, but Fisher wouldn't agree. 'Why am I to give you less for your picture than its price? It must not be.' It was Constable's first big sale and gave a great boost to his confidence.[16]

Maria was well gone in pregnancy again. Suffolk plans had therefore been put aside. But in early May Abram told Constable he was really needed in East Bergholt to settle the house business with the Clerks in William Mason's presence. Moreover, the rector could not 'continue long, not many day's [*sic*], in all human probability'. Constable took the Ipswich coach but got to the village a few hours too late on 6 May; it would have been his mother's birthday and the church bell was tolling. He wrote at once to Maria: 'The poor Doctor breathed his last about 5 o'clock this morning . . . Mr Travis did not think he suffered much pain though he was so long in dying.'

Two days later the *Ipswich Journal* printed an obituary of the Doctor:

Thursday last died, in his 86th year, the Rev. Durand Rhudde, D.D.,
Rector of Brantham with Bergholt, and of Great Wenham, in this
county, and Chaplain in Ordinary to His Majesty. He was formerly of
King's College, Cambridge . . .

In East Bergholt all seemed much quieter without the Doctor and
the gossip and comings and goings that had attended him. Constable
took the chance of being there to go for a contemplative walk up to
Langham through the fields and along the river. He wrote to Maria:
'I never saw Nature more lovely . . . Every tree seems full of blossom
of some kind & the surface of the ground seems quite lovely – every
step I take & on whatever object I turn my eye[,] that sublime
expression in the Scripture "I am the resurrection & the life" &c.,
seems verified about me.' Although the Doctor may have lost some of
his wits towards the end, his last will treated Maria fairly. Like the
Bicknells' other three children (Samuel, Catherine and Louisa), she
was left £4,000 of government 3 per cent stock. Her father
discontinued her allowance of £50 a year, but with the Rhudde
legacy giving her £120 a year the Constables were ahead by £70.
Constable specified strictly how the executors should make over the
money and the government stocks. He said, 'The hand of Providence
has been with us.'

If they had more income, they also soon had a new expense. Maria
gave birth to a girl on 19 July. She was christened Maria Louisa on
20 August with her aunts Ann and Louisa as godmothers and John
Fisher as godfather, a role he was to take seriously; her given names
were replaced by a variety of pet names through childhood – Minna,
Minny, Nummenum and Ladybird, among others. And they also
had new worries: the first-born John Charles was weak, and Maria
wasn't springing back after the confinement. A 'change of air' was
called for; Hampstead was proposed, a large village still in
countryside, just outside the great wen. There was a good ten-a-day
coach service into town. Anthony Spedding, Charles Bicknell's legal
partner, had a house in Hampstead[17] and Constable had walked that
way on several excursions with Thomas Stothard. For the next few

months he rented Albion Cottage, on a road called Upper Heath, at the north end of the village. Hampstead had a reputation as a spa, with a 'Vale of Health' and springs, wells, and a pump room that Dr Johnson, Fanny Burney, and David Garrick had patronised. Many of the ponds on the Heath had been dug in Henry VIII's time and since enlarged. The artists William Blake and John Linnell for a while lived close by – Blake contrarily used to complain about the fresh Hampstead air, so unlike the London smoke. And John Keats, the tubercular poet, had recently been lodging in Well Walk and Wentworth Place. Other writers followed, including Charles Dickens: members of the Pickwick Club were shortly to be treated to a lecture from their chairman entitled 'Speculation on the Source of the Hampstead Ponds, with some Observations on the Theory of Tittlebats'.

The new scene gave Constable new subject matter. From Hampstead southwards you could see London with the dome of St Paul's on the horizon. From London – for example from his old lodgings in Charlotte Street – the hills of Hampstead were visible. He was soon out on the high ridge of the Heath, painting the ponds, the sheep and their shepherds, the treelined paths and the houses such as Mr Spedding's to be glimpsed through the trees – and on those relative heights, taking new notice of the sky.

Leaving Maria behind, he got to East Bergholt again in the autumn. Abram met him at Colchester and drove him home to Flatford in the gig. Never again East Bergholt House. Next morning he looked out on a world covered deeply in snow. After walking around the village he wrote immediately to Maria about the ravages done to the trees by the wind and weight of snow: 'One would think there had been a battle of Waterloo in Mr Godfrey's park, and the roads are impassable for the broken boughs & fallen trees.' Abram and Mr Revans, his father's elderly steward, brought him up to date on money matters, and Constable felt thankful: 'How many comforts are within our reach – & should any thing happen to me, I should leave the world with the consolation that you & our darling angels would be above want . . .'

Following his old route to school, he walked down to Dedham to post the letter. A few days later he wrote to Maria again to describe how they had divided the family silver: 'I have got the beautifull coffy pot and washer on which it stands – a pair of very noble candlesticks – a handsome soup ladle – & two gravy spoons – all of which were my Grandmother's present to my Mother on her marriage.' There was a good deal of linen if Maria felt they wanted it. Discussing 'family matters' had quite worn them all out, but the brothers and sisters (including Martha Whalley who had come up for the occasion) had got on very amicably.

He returned to London and Hampstead on the eve of the election of Associates, in time to call on Farington. How stood his chances? On 23 August Thomas Phillips had told Farington that although Constable 'had produced his best picture at the last Exhibition . . . he is still an artist unsettled in his practice'. To Constable, Phillips recommended the study of Turner's *Liber Studiorum* in order 'to learn how to make a whole'. Samuel Lane, the deaf portrait painter for whom Constable had been learning sign language, had called on Farington earlier in the day and agreed not to push his own claim – thus helping Constable's chances. Farington declared that he had been telling Academicians they'd do best to consider the merits of 'those who were of long standing in the Art' – a plug for Constable. There were thirty-eight candidates, with only one place available for a painter and one for an engraver. In the preliminary balloting at a meeting thinly attended by full members of the Academy, Constable had a tight tussle with his new friend Charles Leslie, the good-natured American narrative painter. But in the final ballot he pulled ahead: the result was Constable eight, Leslie five. Perhaps 'long standing' finally paid off. Perhaps, as Farington told Constable's father-in-law, it was also 'a due acknowledgement of his professional ability'.[18] *The White Horse* and becoming a director of the AGBI undoubtedly helped. Whatever – he had at last broken through the portcullis. He wrote to Abram the following day to let the family know of his success. From Salisbury the Fishers sent their congratulations, John Fisher writing on behalf of the Bishop as well to tell Constable he owed his place in the Academy 'to no favour but solely to your own unsupported unpatronised merits. – I reckon it no small feather in my cap that I have had the sagacity to find them out.' On 8 December Constable and Maria called in person on the RA secretary to acknowledge Farington's assistance.

Why had it taken so long? Richard Redgrave later recalled that although Constable could be 'soft and amiable in speech, he yet uttered sarcasms which cut you to the bone'.[19] Was it a defensive tactic he had learned at school, and never stopped deploying? Was he, like many inherently shy people, prone to fits of fierce outspokenness? He was fully aware of his sarcastic side and sullen moments, noting to Fisher on one occasion (8 May 1824), 'a good deal of the devil is in me'. His friendship with Fisher (not a painter) lasted, but the friendships with the artists Reinagle, Haydon and William Collins did not. Collins in 1814 had been impressed enough by Constable to note in his journal: 'Two days since Constable compared a picture to a *sum*, for it is wrong if you can take away or add any figure to it.'[20] But quarrels and coolness followed, owing in part to Constable's inability to curb that devil in him. In a letter to Fisher Constable mentioned Collins as 'an unpleasant person' he was minded to rid himself of. When Collins became a full Academician in 1820, well before Constable, he became – said Constable – 'too great a man'. Constable was also outspoken in his belief that Collins painted works that were 'too pretty to be natural'. Leslie thought Constable was unable to 'conceal his opinions of himself and others; and what he said had too much point not to be repeated, and too much truth not to give offence'. Therefore 'some of his competitors [NB competitors, not colleagues] hated him, and most were afraid of him. There was also that about him which led all who had not known him well and long to consider him an odd fellow, and a great egotist . . . But . . . he was not a *selfish* egotist.'[21]

Constable rarely stopped to reflect before making a sharp rejoinder, particularly about his fellow artists. He thought Bonington's 'dash' and 'compleation' were assumed without the

necessary painful study.[22] (Anyone might be jealous of Bonington's
dash.) Eastlake's works, done in Italy and Greece, had 'wonderful
merit and so has watch-making'. When he was eventually an RA and
a member of the Arrangement Committee, he upset a fellow
Academician by telling him the frames of his pictures bulked too
large. The painter, H.W. Pickersgill, defended himself by saying his
frames were just like those the brilliant portraitist Sir Thomas
Lawrence had used. Constable replied, 'It is very easy to imitate
Lawrence in his *frames*.' He often failed to react with simple pleasure
to a compliment. When William Blake looked at some Constable
sketches and praised one of an avenue of trees in Hampstead, saying,
truthfully, 'This is not drawing but inspiration,' Constable snapped,
'I never knew it before. I took it for drawing.'[23] When a pension for
senior Academicians was being discussed, Constable said it would be
no bad thing on condition they relinquished their easels. The critic
Edward Dubois was often unfair and malicious in his reviews of
Constable's works but one can see the justice of his description of
Constable as 'a crab stick'.[24]

   Money, as suggested earlier, may have been a factor in the long
delay in his recognition by the Academy. He seemed to many
members too comfortably off, with no need to struggle – not that he
saw himself that way. Moreover, he wasn't a historical or literary
artist like Wilkie, or even primarily a portrait painter; he was a
landscape painter, and although educated taste was cottoning on to
landscape,[25] most RAs still saw it as 'low art'. (Constable's view of the
Academicians was that they knew 'as much about landscape as they
do about the kingdom of heaven'.)[26] And his landscapes weren't
exactly Claudes or Poussins: to many they seemed rough and ready,
the handling too free, the finish unfinished.

   Finally, there was his prickly personality. He knew his approach
was right. And possibly as a talented child he had got used to
approbation, and thought he deserved nothing less. Perhaps too, after
quitting Suffolk for London, he felt that he had known Eden, and was
thereafter sulky at having lost it. Melancholy became a habit – the
grumpy melancholy of one uprooted from a perfect place. That, at any

rate, was his condition as an artist. As for the husband and father, he could for the moment bury himself in domestic activity and happiness in Keppel Street. Might it last for ever!

# 8. *All but the Clouds (1820–21)*

Early in the new year the old King died. The staff of the Royal Academy donned mourning clothes in honour of George III, the deceased founder and patron of their institution. Bishop Fisher in Salisbury was among many who felt someone close to them had departed. Benjamin West, the King's exact contemporary, said he had lost his best friend – and died too, six weeks later. A cast of West's painting hand, taken as if holding a brush, was made within an hour of his death, to mark his passing. Whatever his limitations as a painter, West – a celebrity – always encouraged younger artists, including Constable. Encountering him in the street one day in 1812, Constable asked whether West thought he was pursuing his studies so as to lay 'the foundation of real excellence'. The RA President replied, 'Sir, I consider you have achieved it.'[1] Sir Thomas Lawrence, the fashionable portrait painter, succeeded West as President. George IV, nicknamed Prinny, even more of an art lover than Farmer George, was the new King.

Constable seems to have been a straightforward monarchist and pro-Hanoverian. He took the fourth George's part against his consort, Caroline, who had left the country as an outraged princess in 1813 and now returned to England to claim her rights as Queen. In July Parliament enacted a bill to deprive her of her title and dissolve the marriage. In London mobs roamed the streets in support of the Queen, demanding illuminations and breaking windows; soldiers had to keep the peace. On 1 September Constable wrote to Fisher from Keppel Street that he was glad he had got his wife and children out to Hampstead: 'Things do not look well though I fear nothing – but the Royal Strumpet has a large party – in short she is the rallying point (and a very fit one) for all evil minded persons.' She was also a rallying point for such important opposition figures as William Cobbett – a dangerous radical as far as Constable was concerned. Constable continued, 'I hear the Duke of Wellington was yesterday in the most imminent danger – & had nearly lost his life by the hands of an <u>Old Woman</u>.' For Constable, Wellington – barring the bad luck of assassination – was a trustworthy hero.

An 'old woman' closer to the artist was one of his father's sisters, Aunt Martha Smith, aged eighty and slowly declining in Nayland. Constable had been to see her a few months earlier and her eyes had filled with joyful tears when he told her of Minna's birth and his happiness with Maria. In 1810 she had commissioned Constable to paint the altarpiece for Nayland church and now on her death in January 1820 she left him £400 as the promised payment for this.

Stour scenes figured again in Constable's Academy campaign of 1820. His two paintings showed the Stour, one upriver at Stratford St Mary, the other at its North Sea mouth. He had sketched children fishing by the Stratford watermill in 1811 and his painting now extended the view to more of the river, a barge and the meadow across the way. The water surface alternates between pools of shadow and reflection; the trees along the left-hand bank are similarly broken up, here sunlit, there in deep shade; the sky's blue partly covered by stacks of white cloud. As with *The White Horse*, Constable made a full-size sketch as well as painting his six-footer for Somerset House, and to present taste the sketch is (as with most of his six-footers) livelier than the finished product; in the latter the pains taken seem to reduce the spontaneity and energy. Energy, of course, is part of the subject. A watermill with its side-mounted wheel may now appear merely a picturesque element in a sylvan landscape. But in that time mills – water or wind-powered – worked machinery for grinding, sawing, pumping and pressing. Stratford Mill then made oil (Constable tells us so on the back of a little oil sketch he painted in 1811). Thereafter it was used for the production of paper and macaroni. It would not have seemed as 'picturesque' to Constable as to us.

Before sending it in, Constable told Farington he didn't mean to 'consult opinions' about the painting.[2] Was he fearful that Farington might talk him into changes he'd regret? Later that year Farington succeeded in convincing Constable to put aside his newly begun painting of the opening of Waterloo Bridge for another big Stour picture. In any event, *Stratford Mill* was a success at the RA exhibition. It was noticed flatteringly by *The Examiner*, which dared to brave 'the jealousy of some professors and of some exclusive devotees of the Old Masters' by saying that Constable's picture 'has a more exact look of nature than any picture we have ever seen by an Englishman'.[3] Constable was pleased: viewers were responding to the way he saw landscape. His second, smaller picture (based on a drawing of 1815) showed the lighthouse at Harwich, a sparer, less cluttered and possibly to modern eyes lovelier scene.

*Stratford Mill* also succeeded in acquiring a buyer, the faithful John Fisher. Early in 1821 he won a court case and bought the picture for one hundred guineas to give to his Salisbury lawyer, John Tinney. Tinney became an ardent fan: he tried to buy at least one further large Constable and several smaller ones, and he put up with frequent requests from the artist to send back *Stratford Mill* to be exhibited or improved or simply to rest in Constable's studio once more. Constable, despite having been paid for it, seemed to think it still rightly belonged there, sitting on an easel and impressing visitors. Poor Tinney had to keep asking for the return of his picture. He was taken advantage of until his patience snapped. He had wanted another work from Constable, but Constable masochistically refused to paint one. Tinney's wants were a burden to him. Constable wrote to Fisher (17 November 1824), 'I am now free & independent of Tinney's kind & friendly commissions – these things only harrass me. You know my disposition is this – in my seeming meekness, if I was bound with chains I would break them – and – if I felt a single hair round me I should feel uncomfortable.' A lot of Constable's self-acknowledged obduracy is evident here.

At the new King's birthday dinner in Somerset House on 3 July Sir Thomas Lawrence, the new President, was in the chair at the centre of the long table. Collins was at one end and Turner at the other, with Constable and Samuel Lane to his right. (Farington did a diagram in his diary of the seating arrangements.)[4] Constable conversed as well as he could with Lane, using sign language; with Turner he had to cope with the great man's grunts, sybillic utterances and occasional bursts of brilliance – it helped to be able to hook into Turner's streams of associated thoughts. Constable and Turner – linked by posterity as the twin masters of nineteenth-century British art – were never friends. Constable said of Turner's *Hannibal* in 1812 that he found it 'scarcely intelligible in many parts' and yet as a whole 'novel and affecting'. A year later, in 1813, he dined beside Turner in the RA Council Room with various other exhibitors and, as already noted, wrote to Maria that 'I always expected to find him what I did – he is uncouth but has a wonderfull range of mind.' Given that both men were at the forefront of the movement to paint landscape out of doors, both believed poetry and painting were closely connected, both had friends in common like Leslie and heroes in common like Claude – and both were commonly attacked by such critics as John Eagles and were in the end applauded together by Delacroix – it is strange how problematic their acquaintanceship was.[5] Constable put on record more compliments about Turner's work than Turner did of his, Constable referring for example to Turner's 'golden visions' in a letter to Fisher in 1828. But he undoubtedly suffered from working so long in Turner's shadow. His envy of Turner's success sometimes showed, as when he called Turner's book of mezzotint engravings the 'Liber Stupidorum'. Possibly there were temperamental and even political differences between the more ruthless unmarried London-born artist whose father had been a barber and the Suffolk grain-merchant's son who had married the daughter of an Admiralty lawyer.

In July 1820 Constable took Maria, John Charles, and Minna to Salisbury to stay with John and Mary Fisher for six weeks. The archdeacon now had one vicarage in Osmington and another at Gillingham, west of Salisbury, as well as Leydenhall his large house in the cathedral close. The cathedral with its great spire, the highest in

England according to Defoe, overlooked the well-endowed community of ecclesiastics; and the Constables didn't complain at being guests there. *The White Horse* was in the Fishers' drawing room, hung – Fisher had told the artist in late April – 'on a level with the eye, the lower frame resting on the ogee: in a western side light, right for the light of the picture, opposite the fireplace. It looks magnificently. My wife says that she carries her eye from the picture to the garden & back again & observes the same sort of look in both.' Fisher and Constable made sketching trips near and far: down the garden to the River Avon; across the water meadows to West Harnham and the low downs of Harnham Ridge beyond, with its prospect of Salisbury and the cathedral; to Gillingham with its quaint bridge and mill; to the megaliths of Stonehenge; and to Old Sarum, the loaf-shaped hill which had been the site of a fortified camp in earlier times and was still a prime rotten example of parliamentary corruption, being a barely populated 'borough' with the right to send two MPs to the House of Commons (Cobbett called it 'the Accursed Hill').[6] Constable drew and painted both close-at-hand and panoramic views, some with rich detail, others done with quick touches. In one of the sketchbooks the archdeacon wrote down a translation of some Latin lines which Constable later used in the text for a mezzotint of East Bergholt House:

> This spot saw the day spring of my life,
>     Years of happiness and days of Joy.
> This place first tinged my boyish fancy
>     With a love of the art.
> This place was the origin of my fame.

But the countryside had more distant views than Suffolk's, and the skies got his attention differently. He stood just outside the gateway to Fisher's house and looked across the lush green meadow to the grey-white cathedral spire rising some four hundred feet out of the old trees to brush the clouds: Heaven-aspiring – on a far grander scale than Dedham. When the Constables returned to London in late August, Fisher reminded his friend to paint the eclipse forecast for 7

September. He seemed to know that skies were going to be an increasing part of Constable's agenda.

Constable sent Maria and the two children up to Hampstead while he attended the life classes at the RA and got on with several paintings. He worked again on his 'Waterloo Bridge', which Fisher was encouraging. He made a copy of a Claude for Fisher and painted a sketch of Leydenhall's garden and the cathedral as the basis for a picture Bishop Fisher wanted. Wonderful patrons, the Fishers, though the relationship involved having to give 'the good Bishop's' daughter Dorothea copying tips and tolerating the senior Fisher's quirks. On 3 January 1821 the archdeacon wrote to Constable about the commissioned work: 'The Bishop likes your picture – "all but the clouds" he says. He likes "a clear blue sky".' Constable also had orders for portraits and house-portraits piling up (they included Lady Dysart, the Reverend Thomas Walker – the chaplain of Lincoln's Inn – and Henry Greswolde of Malvern Hall.)[7] Meanwhile, Farington argued that Constable should work on another full-size Stour painting rather than the Waterloo Bridge.[8] Part of him was already there on the Essex–Suffolk border: in what was already a very productive year he found time to complete another version of one of his favourite Stour valley subjects, *Dedham Mill and Church*.

Archdeacon Fisher had several shocks in February 1821. His mother-in-law died suddenly. Then, while in the graveyard discussing with the elderly clerk of Osmington church where she should be buried, the old man exclaimed, 'I cannot stand, sir!' and fell dead into Fisher's arms. When Constable heard of this he wrote to his friend, 'The poor clerk's sudden death . . . must have called for a great exertion of your fortitude and piety.' He went on to tell Fisher about what obviously meant more to him: the friendship and approbation that kept him going when standing – as he was these days – before a large canvas. 'I shall never be a popular artist – a Gentlemen and Ladies painter but . . . your hand stretched forth teaches me to value my own natural dignity of mind above all things.' Fisher had cheered up three weeks later when he wrote to Constable from Salisbury about Gilbert

White's *Natural History of Selborne*. 'It is a book that should delight you & be highly instructive to you in your art if you are not already acquainted with it. White was the clergyman of the Place & occupied himself with narrowly observing & noting down all the natural occurrences that came within his view: and this for a number of years . . . It is in your own way of close natural observation: & has in it that quality that to me constitutes the great pleasure of your society.' Fisher recognised that, like White, Constable had his own specific locale; he painted his own places best.

Constable went at once to Bond Street, to his friend the bookseller James Carpenter, and bought *Selborne*, first published in 1789. He wrote to Fisher, 'The single page alone of the Life of Mr White leaves a more lasting impression on my mind than that of Charles the fifth or any other renowned hero – it shows what a real love for nature will do – surely the serene & blameless life of Mr White, so different from the folly & quackery of the world, must have fitted him for such a clear & intimate view of nature . . . This book is an addition to my estate.' Twelve years later *Selborne* was also put into the hands of his son John Charles, who was given his own copy.[9]

In Hampstead another addition to the Constable estate had just arrived – 'a beautiful boy', born on 29 March and christened Charles Golding Constable, after both his grandfathers. According to Constable, Maria had grown 'unusually large' this time, but the delivery went well, with Dr Robert Gooch in attendance. Maria was averaging nearly one child a year.

Constable had been working on four entries for the RA annual exhibition: *Hampstead Heath*, *A Shower*, *Harrow* and *Landscape: Noon*, which was to become known after the most prominent object in it as *The Hay Wain*. This was his big offering for the exhibition and he had been keeping the archdeacon (and Farington) informed about it. But earlier in the year he had realised that he needed some details about its central feature: the four-wheeled farm wagon, or 'wain', which at a late stage he had decided to introduce. The empty wagon was on its way through the shallow millstream to the ford by which it would cross the main river channel, heading for the meadows where haymakers were at work. A fisherman (or boy fishing under a man's hat) was on the far bank among the grass and reeds, where the bows of a boat could be seen. Perhaps because of the constraints Maria had put on his friendship with John Dunthorne, Constable asked Abram to get Dunthorne's son Johnny to draw him the 'outlines of a scrave or harvest wagon'. Johnny, now twenty-three, had a cold job doing this out of doors in February, but according to Abram, Dunthorne Senior – now fifty-one, and with a hernia problem – 'urged him forward saying he was sure you must want it as the time drew near fast'. Johnny was apparently doing this 'free from sordid motives', i.e. without pay, but Abram said he would hand on any recompense Constable cared to give him. At the time in February Abram was 'extremely apprehensive' about the state of the painting and thought his brother still had 'everything to do' to get it ready by 10 April, when it was to go to Somerset House. And when William Collins saw *Landscape: Noon* on 9 April, he said he liked it but regretted that Constable had lacked 'time to enable him to finish the picture more accurately'.[10] The sashes of a window on the stairs at Keppel Street had to be removed to get the painting out. When Farington went to the Academy on 1 May, one of the varnishing days, he saw Constable at work putting in final touches. He signed the painting '*John Constable pinxt London 1821*'.

Constable went up to Bergholt in mid-April, leaving Maria, the two older children and the newborn. He took a parcel of hot-cross buns as an Easter gift and told Maria his old haunts were 'sweet and beautiful'. The trees and blossom were coming out, and swallows were appearing. At the Whalleys', he felt the urge to live in Dedham too. 'Here is so much entertainment to be found for the children, & if I was absent you would be near Martha.' But he encountered his sister Ann in Bergholt in a prickly mood and thought her companion unpleasant. Maria had her own family problems. Her brother Sam died from consumption on 22 May and her sister Catherine had 'many bad symptoms', and looked likely to follow him (she died about four years later).

Then it was into the fray at Somerset House, into what Fisher called 'the crowded copal atmosphere of the Exhibition: which is always to me like a great pot of boiling varnish'. Constable was pleased with his big landscape, though unusually for him with a new painting he didn't claim it as his best to date. He told Fisher it wasn't 'so grand' as *Stratford Mill*, 'the masses not being so impressive – the power of the Chiaro Oscuro is lessened – but it has rather a more novel look than I expected'. And several critics were enthusiastic. Robert Hunt in *The Examiner* said that *Landscape: Noon* approached 'nearer to the actual look of rural nature than any modern landscape whatever'. The *Observer* thought it deserved a high place and admired the 'fine freshness' of its colouring, and *Bell's Weekly Messenger* approved but added, 'Why all that excess of piebald scambling [*sic*] in the finishing, as if a plasterer had been at work . . .? The Artist may say, "I intend what I paint always to be viewed at a certain distance, you will then get rid of my white spots." This is certainly an affectation and trickery of art unknown to our best painters.'[11] What one saw as Constable's 'sparkle' was to another Constable's 'spottiness' – and in time more would be heard on that score.

Among the visitors to the Academy exhibition were two from France: Théodore Géricault, one of the leaders of the French avant-garde, and the writer-critic Charles Nodier. Géricault, who had brought *The Raft of the Medusa* to exhibit privately in London, was overwhelmed by *The Hay Wain*. And Nodier mentioned only one painting in an essay he wrote on his trip to Britain:

The palm of the exhibition belongs to a large landscape by Constable, with which the ancient or modern masters have very few masterpieces that could be put in opposition. Near, it is only broad daubings of ill-laid colours, which offend the touch as well as the sight, they are so coarse and uneven. At the distance of a few steps it is a picturesque country, a rustic dwelling, a low river whose little waves foam over the pebbles, a cart crossing a ford: It is water, air, and sky; it is Ruysdael, Wouvermans or Constable.[12]

No one bought the painting at Somerset House. Constable

exhibited it again at the British Institution in January 1822 with a price of 150 guineas; it was seen by a French art dealer with a British name, John Arrowsmith, who went to Keppel Street to call on Constable and offer him £70 for the painting, 'without the frame'. The artist said no to this, though he claimed he needed the money 'dreadfully'. Whether Abram was having difficulties paying sums due to family members because of the prevailing agricultural depression, we don't know, but Constable's friend and major patron John Fisher was also strapped. Constable said the painting of *The Hay Wain* had impoverished him and asked his friend to lend him twenty or thirty pounds – Fisher sent five pounds, all he could afford. The archdeacon also took Constable along in early June to sketch while he visited rural deaneries. What Maria thought about being left with the new baby and two small children, while Constable took this fortnight-long working holiday, we have to assume; judging from later, similar occasions, her patience wasn't infinite; on the other hand, perhaps she was now grateful not to be bothered in bed by her loving husband. Fortunately she had to assist her a 'treasure', a nurse/governess/ family-help named Elizabeth Roberts – nicknamed 'Bobs' or 'Old Lady Ribbons' – whose devotion to the Constables was demonstrated over many years.[13]

Yet Constable always missed home terribly and came back repenting his absence. He quickly decided Maria needed country air again – having been stuck in Keppel Street – and it was briefly back to Hampstead, to a house in Lower Terrace rented for four guineas a week, furnished. He wrote to Fisher on 3 November: 'The last day of Octr was indeed lovely so much so that I could not paint for looking – my wife was walking with me all the middle of the day on the beautifull heath.' Out on the Heath he found a new subject for painting, but he also now had to address a number of traditional chores. He was commissioned to paint an altarpiece for the church in Manningtree, a few miles east of Bergholt, where the Stour opens out into an estuary; it was 'a job' that would help meet the expenses of his expanding family and two homes. Salisbury continued to vie with the Stour, however, and in early November when his family was moving down to Keppel Street he joined Fisher again for a week or so, drawing the cathedral and the close, and visiting Winchester with its cathedral. Compared to Salisbury, he found it 'more impressive but not so beautifull'. And he wrote to Maria with his passionate regrets: 'Kiss my darlings . . . I am quite home sick (perhaps love sick) . . . I am uncomfortable away so long.'

Back in Keppel Street he worked on his next painting for Somerset House, a six-footer; it was a view on the Stour centred on some barges being moved just below the footbridge at Flatford. Farington was one of his chief supporters in this field – he felt big Stour pictures should be Constable's way ahead – but on the penultimate day of 1821 the 'Dictator' of the Academy ceased to matter. Descending from the gallery of a church near Manchester he fell and died. Farington was therefore not available to support Constable's candidacy for full RA membership in February 1822, when one place went to Richard Cook (who had given up exhibiting three years before but married well) and another to William Daniell whose uncle was the Academician Thomas Daniell. Literally nepotism.

# 9. *Skying (1821–22)*

Despite his concern for his friend's artistic success, John Fisher could be as self-absorbed and demanding as Constable. In August 1821 Fisher had decided that he needed a boat, to use on the Avon at the foot of Leydenhall garden. The obvious thing was to find one locally, new or second-hand, but Fisher reckoned it wouldn't be too much of a chore for Constable to arrange the purchase. After all, he was a river man by birth and could find the right boat for him on the Thames. So Constable obligingly sent Fisher sketches of various types of small craft. He also went to some boatbuilders near Westminster Bridge and fixed on a sixteen-foot rowing skiff, price twenty-five guineas, including oars. At which point Fisher decided he didn't have the money. Constable, in any event, had enough to do in Hampstead. He had rented a room from a glazier to use as a studio, where he was working on a large picture, presumably a preliminary study for *A View on the Stour*. He had also cleaned out the coal, mops and brooms from a shed at Lower Terrace for use as 'a place of refuge'. Although Maria was 'placid and contented', and Mrs Roberts was now nurse and governess, two small children and a baby in the house created a zone of turmoil that could envelop the artist. The best refuge of all – the best place to get some sketching done – was out of doors, on the Heath.

At the end of summer and in the early autumn he frequently walked on to the Heath and looked upwards, then to his sketching paper pinned to the lid of his paintbox, again and again, drawing and painting. He wrote to Fisher on 20 September to say that he had 'made many <u>skies</u> and effects . . . We have had noble clouds & effects of light & dark & color.' He would have liked it said of himself, 'as Fuseli says of Rembrandt, "he followed nature in her calmest abodes and could pluck a flower on every hedge – yet he was born to cast a stedfast eye on the bolder phenomena of nature."' And again, on 23 October: 'I have done a good deal of skying . . . That Landscape painter who does not make his skies a very material part of his composition . . . neglects to avail himself of one of his greatest aids.' Constable wasn't the first artist to note this. Willem van de Velde the Younger, of the father-and-son team of marine painters who moved from Holland to England, used to have an old Thames waterman take him out on the Thames in all weathers, to study the sky. William Gilpin wrote: 'These expeditions Vanderveldt called, in his Dutch manner of speaking, going a-skoying.'[1] Charles Leslie said Van de Velde also used to go up to Hampstead Heath to observe the weather.[2] Turner often walked out into the open and lay on the ground, looking up at the sky. Constable was therefore part of a tradition of painters taking supposedly picturesque elements and looking at them in naturalistic detail, defining their changes and differences. He looked harder and more precisely than most. And he noted that this know-ledge would affect the complete painting. Constable continued his 23 October letter to Fisher by quoting Sir Joshua Reynolds on land-scapes by Titian, Salvator Rosa, and Claude: '"Even their skies seem to sympathise with the Subject."' Constable went on, 'Certainly if the Sky is *obtrusive* – (as mine are) it is bad, but if they are *evaded* (as mine are not) it is worse, they must and always shall with me make an effectual part of the composition . . . The sky is the "*source of light*" in nature – and governs every thing.'

Perhaps he felt a bit guilty about this new obsession. Did Hampstead skies challenge his old watery loyalties? He told Fisher (in the same letter) that he had imagined himself with his friend on a recent trip which Fisher had made to fish in the New Forest. 'But the sound of water escaping from Mill dams [moves me]' – he omitted some words in his enthusiasm – 'so do Willows, Old rotten Banks, slimy posts, & brickwork. I love such things . . . As long as I do paint I shall never cease to paint such Places.' He would have been delighted to be with Fisher on his Hampshire river: 'But I should paint my own places best – Painting is but another word for feeling. I associate my "careless boyhood" to all that lies on the banks of the *Stour*. They made me a painter (& I am gratefull) – that is I had often thought of pictures of them before I had ever touched a pencil . . .'

But skies were also an old interest. The apprentice at his father's windmill on Bergholt Heath had learned to study the sky for portents of the changeable East Anglian weather – for calm, for gales, for reliable grain-grinding breezes. Years before he had read Leonardo's *Trattura*, in which painters are advised to get inspiration from shapes seen on damp walls, in the embers of fires and in cloud patterns.[3] Like many, he felt simple gratitude for sky, for clouds, for sunlight shining on and through them. Now on the relative heights of Hampstead he had open air and became a regular sky-watcher again: in 1821 and 1822 he painted nearly one hundred sky studies. He often took note of the exact time he made such sketches, involving an hour or so each, though the skies could change rapidly while he worked. The wind was 'very brisk' and the clouds 'running very fast', he recorded on one study, 'very appropriate for the Coast at Osmington'. This was one of twenty Constable sky studies in oil that eventually came into Charles Leslie's hands and which Leslie said were painted 'on large sheets of thick paper, and all dated, with the time of day, the direction of the wind, and other memoranda on their backs'.[4] Occasionally a thin strip showing land or tops of trees at the bottom of the sketch anchored the clouds and sky. Rarely a few birds wheeled. Most often the scudding, drifting or towering clouds and gaps of sky were the sole subject – and one could read (between the lines as it were) the weather of the moment – rain showers, impending thunder, clearing skies, the sun coming out. It was a completely different routine from that involved in assembling the parts of an exhibition six-footer – parts which were static, formed already in his memory or imagination. Here he was dealing with impressions – moving elements, parts of the air – while the wind stirred the grass around him and smoothed or dishevelled the sky above.

Hampstead was the perfect place for this activity. It was at a height, slight but meaningful, over London. It provided expansive prospects from a continuous elevation and little interference from dramatic scenery nearby. Here he could keep what was almost a visual journal, in Fisher's words like Gilbert White 'narrowly observing and noting down all the natural occurrences that came within his view'. Exactly what other meteorological scholarship of the time became part of his thinking is uncertain, but Luke Howard's early essays and his *Climate of London* (1818–20), classifying different types of cloud, are in evidence. Howard named the clouds in a way which stuck; his Latinate term 'cirrus' has been made out by some experts on the back of one of Constable's 1822 studies. Moreover, Constable wrote Howard's name in notes he made while reading Thomas Forster's *Researches about Atmospheric Phaenomena*, first published in 1813. Constable's second-edition copy cost him six shillings. Its first chapter concerned the theories Howard expressed in his essays, and Constable's annotations to it suggested his disagreement with many of Forster's conclusions; one such note also uses Howard's term 'cumulostrati'. Later Constable wrote to a friend: 'Forster's is the best book – he is far from right, still he has the merit of breaking much ground.' One quotation from Howard in Forster's book drew attention to Robert Bloomfield's poem of 1800, *The Farmer's Boy*, a poem Constable later copied a long section from.[5]

Constable obviously didn't intend to exhibit his cloud studies. They seem to be closely observed expressions of wonder at the beauty and variety of creation. He may also have thought they would be items in his armoury – material that he could employ when he needed 'a sky' for an exhibition painting. Yet he wasn't totally successful in carrying over his spontaneous observations of skies into his finished pictures. Although in *The Lock* viewers can almost hear the air moving and the trees shaking, and in some paintings of Salisbury cathedral the tip of the spire – slicing the dark clouds that offended Bishop Fisher – seems to vibrate as the wind whistles around it, this wasn't always the case. In *The Hay Wain*, the sky isn't particularly inspired. We may of course think this because we have seen the picture too often, but Constable seems to have shared these doubts; he continued to work on the painting's sky, after he got it back from the Academy, and, as if

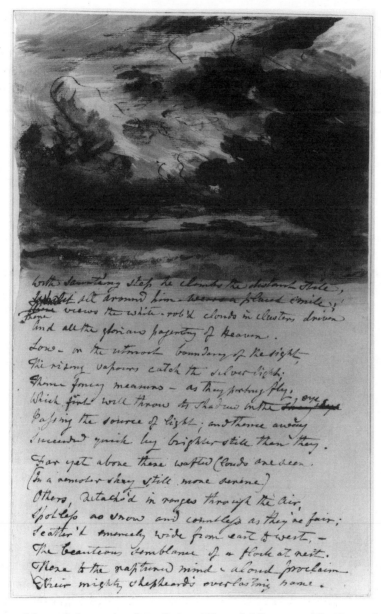

Constable copied a section from Robert Bloomfield's poem, *The Farmer's Boy*, to accompany his cloud study

aware that he needed to do more aloft, embarked on his skying season in Hampstead at the same time.[6]

In most of Constable's pictures of this period the dynamic conditions are brilliantly suggested. In 1821 he made several pencil sketches of East Bergholt heath that provided material for an oil sketch on a wooden panel: windmill facing into the wind; racing low clouds; rooks wheeling; a ploughman firmly steering the plough pulled by a pair of heavy horses, locked to the spinning earth by gravity. And this eventually formed the basis for one of a series of mezzotint engravings of Constable's works that he entitled 'English Landscape'. For the plate called 'Spring' Constable wrote that it:

> may perhaps give some idea of those bright and animated days of the early year . . . when at noon large garish clouds, surcharged with hail or sleet, sweep with their broad cool shadows the fields, woods, and hills; and by the contrast of their depths and bloom enhance the value of the vivid greens and yellows, so peculiar to this season . . . The natural history . . . of the skies . . . is this: the clouds accumulate in very large and dense masses, and from their loftiness seem to move but slowly; immediately upon these large clouds appear numerous opaque patches, which, however, are only small clouds passing rapidly before them . . . These floating much nearer the earth, may perhaps fall in with a stronger current of wind, which as well as their comparative lightness, causes them to move with greater rapidity; hence they are called by wind-millers and sailors 'messengers,' and always portend bad weather . . .

These clouds, wrote Constable, float midway in 'the lanes of the clouds' and are almost uniformly in shadow, receiving reflected light only from the clear blue sky above.

In several Hampstead pictures figures are to be seen walking along the ridge lines and near horizons, silhouetted against (and emphasising) the skies. Constable named some of the panoramic views from the Hampstead heights in a letter to Fisher of 3 November 1821, helping him with a circular diagram that showed the compass points. Hampstead was in the centre, St Alban's to the north, Gravesend to the east, Dorking to the south, and Windsor to the west. He also drew Fisher's attention to the presence of 'the finest foregrounds – in roads, heath, trees, ponds &c'. The altitude had got to him. He told Fisher that he had been reading a life of Nicolas Poussin (by Maria Graham). Poussin, obviously an artist after his own heart, proved 'how much dignity & elevation of character was the result of such patient, per-severing and rational study – no circumstances however impropitious could turn him to the right or left – because he knew what he was about – & he felt himself above every scene in which he was placed'. One of the most striking Hampstead paintings was an oil sketch on paper (at some point affixed to canvas) called *The Road to the Spaniards*, taken from a dip in the road across the Heath leading to the Spaniards Inn, with some trees on the left amid which stood the house of the lawyer Anthony Spedding. It is a view seemingly from below ground level looking up to the top of the sandy track, with agitated thundery clouds tumbling above a few isolated people and animals. The horizon curves – there is a sense of the earth being round indeed. On the back a note records the atmospheric conditions of the day: 'Monday 29 July 1822, looking NE, three hours after noon . . . a stormy squall coming from the north-west.'

A resident in Hampstead a few years before had been John Keats. Keats and Constable just missed each other, but they had much in common. Keats wrote to his brothers George and Thomas from Hampstead at the end of 1817, 'The excellence of every Art is its intensity.' And in a letter to Benjamin Haydon in April 1818, telling of his plans for a 'pedestrian tour' of the north of Britain, Keats exclaimed, 'I will clamber through the Clouds and exist.' Constable, clambering also above every scene in the locality, found a new province of his own kingdom on the Heath as he looked up at the clouds soaring past, dawdling, or stuck almost still. He strolled every day to Prospect Walk – now called Judges Walk – to try to capture the atmosphere re-making itself. On 3 September 1821 he painted 'with large drops of rain falling on my palette'. On 10 September there was thunder and a heavy downpour. On the 11th, a brighter day, the small cumulus clouds were touched with sunlight. He painted the clouds at all sorts of angles, sometimes climbing, sometimes right overhead, sometimes parading directly at him in line ahead. Most of these sketches were oil on paper, and he sometimes made two a day.[7] He wrote to Fisher a year or so after, taking his own obsession lightly, discussing having children, and punning on the similarity between nubile (meaning marriageable) and nubilous (by which he seems to have meant shady or cloudy, from Latin *nubes*, a cloud), he told the archdeacon: 'You can never be nubilous – I am the man of clouds.'

# 10. *At the Summit of Earthly Ambitions (1822–23)*

'I am about Farrington's [*sic*] house,' Constable wrote to Fisher in April 1822. 'Ruysdael House' in Keppel Street had been wonderful – 'the 5 happiest & most interesting years of my life were passed in Keppel Street', he said later. 'I got my children and my fame in that house, neither of which would I exchange with any other man.' But the house was now too small for his family. They were, he said, 'like bottled wasps upon a southern wall'. Farington's – 35 Charlotte Street – was both well known to him and more spacious. It had been empty since Farington's death at the end of the previous year, and after going with Maria to look over it, Constable wrote to Samuel Lane that the house 'left a deep impression on us both. I can scarcely believe that I was not to meet the elegant and dignified figure of our departed friend . . . or hear again the wisdom that always attended his advice, which I do indeed miss greatly.'[1] After some hard bargaining with Mr Prior, who held the head lease, he took the house and some of the fixtures, fittings and furniture, including two small Richard Wilson paintings which he had copied at Farington's behest on his first arrival in London twenty-three years before.

Charlotte Street, named after George III's wife, had a church, Sass's School of Art, John Henderson the dentist, William Manning the apothecary, and various architects and artists (including R.R. Reinagle). Number 35 was a typical Fitzrovia terraced house, about thirty years old, standing on the east side of the street, three windows wide and four storeys high above a basement. It also had a one-storey studio at the back, joined to the main house by a small gallery with a barrel-vaulted skylight. Constable had moved in by mid-June, having

got an again heavily pregnant Maria and the three children and Mrs
Roberts into summer quarters at Hampstead – once more at 2 Lower
Terrace. The move was expensive, and Constable scurried for cash,
politely dunning Mary Watts-Russell for money she owed him and
taking on several commissions. The Manningtree altarpiece of Christ
rising from the grave was one; others were a large picture for the son
of his late uncle by marriage, Christopher Savile, and a *Salisbury
Cathedral* for Bishop Fisher.[2]

Moreover, the house involved unexpected outlays. Although the
painting room itself seemed 'light, airy, *sweet* & warm', bricklayers,
carpenters and plumbers had to sort out serious sanitation problems;
a hollow wall that connected with the studio floor turned out to be –
Constable told Fisher – 'immediately over the *well* of the *privy*. This
would have played the devil with the oxygen of my colours'. And
detracted from the supposed sweetness. There were also unsuspected
neighbour problems. The Priors and the Blatches, on each side of 35,
were friendly and soon got used to incursions by the Constable cats,
but two women across the street were running a brothel. In early
September Lucy Dale and Elizabeth Williams were charged at
Clerkenwell Sessions with keeping a common bawdy house, and
Constable was the principal witness against them. The case dragged
on for several months. Then Lucy Dale confessed her guilt and was
bound over to keep the peace for two years; Elizabeth Williams was
discharged. Constable had to appear in court on several days and
didn't get off unscathed since he agreed to pay all the costs, about
thirty pounds. On 6 December he told Fisher that 'the inmates have
long since fled, some of whom were the old womans *daughters* – & we
hope the business is well done'. Anything for a quiet life.

Fisher wrote to console Constable in February 1822 when, bested
by Cook and Daniell, he failed again to be elected a full member of the
Academy. 'The title of RA will never weigh a straw in that balance in
which you are ambitious to be found heavy, namely the judgement of
posterity. You are painting for a name to be remembered hereafter: for
the time when men shall talk of Wilson & Vanderneer & Ruisdale &
Constable in the same breath.' Constable thought 'the disgrace was

not mine', and was so busy he soon forgot his failure; he sent five paintings to the annual exhibition, among them *Malvern Hall* and *The Bridge*, his large picture of the year – his fourth six-footer; on no painting, he said, had he ever worked so hard. He had trouble composing the picture, telling Fisher that since the archdeacon had seen the painting 'I have taken away the sail, and added another barge in the middle of the picture, with a principal figure, altered the group of trees, and made the bridge entire. The picture now has a rich centre . . .' In the event, the scene now seems a touch too picturesque, and the activity about the barges melodramatic, though his sometimes hard-to-please sister Ann thought the painting 'beautiful'. It was renamed for the exhibition *View on the Stour, near Dedham*, and pleased many of the critics. Robert Hunt of *The Examiner* found in it, 'among the glare of gold frames, . . . the consoling recollection of the charms of nature'.[3] Constable thought his reputation was rising as a landscape painter. He wrote to Fisher, 'I am (as Farrington always said I should be) fast becoming a distinct feature in that way.' But Constable's naturalism wasn't always popular with his gold-framed colleagues.

In April he had made a brief visit to Suffolk and saw for himself the countrywide agricultural distress that prevented John Fisher buying *The Hay Wain*. Abram was uncomfortable about the state of things. Constable reported to Fisher that his brother thought the situation as bad as in Ireland – ' "never a night without seeing fires near or at a distance", The *Rector* & his brother the *Squire* (Rowley & Godfrey) have forsaken the village – no abatement of tithes or rents – four of Sir Wm. Rush's tenants distrained next parish – these things are ill-timed'. Constable's sympathy for the working peasantry seems to have been exceeded by his disdain for the local gentry. However, he was upset on his sister Ann's behalf that her house had been broken into while she was at church; she lost some spoons, a box Dr Rhudde had given her, and a watch which had been their father's.

Money was tight all round that summer and Constable might have been expected to welcome several generous gestures from clients. Fisher's friend Tinney, the lawyer, offered one hundred guineas for a

companion picture to *Stratford Mill*, the Constable Fisher had given
him. Constable didn't take this up. But he couldn't say no to the
Bishop of Salisbury, who sent a banker's draft to alleviate Constable's
financial troubles, adding 'Lawyers frequently receive retaining fees,
why should not painters do the same?' This advance payment may
have been a way of making up for Constable's kind tutoring of his
daughter Dorothea and a means of nudging along his new painting
*Salisbury Cathedral from the Bishop's Grounds*, which the Bishop hoped
would soon 'be ready to grace my Drawing Room in London'.
Constable's other big job of the moment was the altarpiece for
Manningtree. This had come about, he first believed, as 'a gift of
compunction . . . from a gentleman who is supposed to have defrauded
his family'. Then Constable learned that his patron, Edward Alston, a
brewer and distant relative of his, had in fact commissioned the picture
in order to placate the Archdeacon of Colchester, who was in charge of
licensing public houses in Manningtree. When the archdeacon died,
Alston considered abandoning the project. But in the end Alston's
offer of £200 to the parish of Manningtree was made good, and
Constable – who had already invested £5 in a large mahogany frame for
the piece – got on with the painting. *The Risen Christ* offers no rebuttal
to the view that Constable should have stayed away from religious
subjects: his red-bearded, bare-chested Christ rises with outstretched
arms from the dark earth into a golden swirl of clouds, grave-clothes
tied around his waist like a sarong, his expression suggestive of anxiety
to know how he had got here. His hands show the wounds from being
nailed to the cross and a disciple cowers at his feet. Benjamin West
seems again to have provided some religiose precedents.*[4]

Another summer, another child: Isabel, John and Maria Constable's
fourth child and second daughter, was born on 23 August 1822 at 2
Lower Terrace. Mary Constable sent to Hampstead from Flatford
Mill a chicken and a cake. Constable had meant to visit Fisher in

*The altarpiece was in St Michael's, Manningtree, until it closed in 1965; then it went to
All Saints, Feering, where Reverend Driffield had been resident curate; it is now in St-
Mary-the-Virgin, Dedham.

Salisbury soon afterwards – new babies needed Maria, not him – but he was still in Hampstead in early October and Fisher was moving back to Osmington. Constable wrote to his friend that he now had to shift his own family to Charlotte Street. 'I have got an excellent subject for a six foot canvas . . . but I have neither time nor money to speculate with, & my children begin to swarm.' What seemed to be a case of male post-partum depression left him gloomy about the new RA Associates – 'not an artist among them' – and the state of English painting – 'The art will go out – there will be no genuine painting in England in 30 years.' He thought the work of younger artists was influenced for the worse by the British Institution, whose directors favoured imitation old masters. And he wasn't happy about the proposed new National Gallery – more old masters. On 6 December he wrote to Fisher, with his usual mixture of shyness and bravado, that his chance of being elected a full member of the Academy was less than it had been a year before. 'I have nothing to help me but my stark naked merit, and although that (as I am told) exceeds all the other candidates – it is not heavy enough. I have no patron but yourself – and you are not the Duke of Devonshire – or any other great ass. You are only a gentleman & a scholar and a real lover of the art . . .' In his black mood he forgot about the Dysart family, Bishop Fisher, Tinney, General Rebow and other supporters.

Constable's worries may have sprung partly from having *The Hay Wain* and *The Bridge* still on his hands, partly from ill health, and partly from fears (a trifle exaggerated) of financial ruin: 'I shall want at least 400£ at Xmas.' Running two houses and supporting his wife and four children (with nurses, cook and housekeeper) made him on edge, or deeply despondent. He told Fisher that 'anxiety – watching – & nursing – & my own present indisposition' kept him from his easel through January 1823. Dr Matthew Baillie of Cavendish Square, one of George III's physicians, had joined Dr Gooch in looking after the Constables, though both doctors generally refused payment. (Gooch was given a painting, Baillie a print, for their services.) A particular concern was John Charles, now five years old and 'in a bad state'. Constable himself was emaciated and weak from bloodletting, while Maria ended the winter 'extremely delicate' and needing much care. Two of the servants were laid up. And Constable was dismally right about his Academy chances: despite the vacancy being for Joseph Farington's seat, his old mentor's influence was sorely lacking; he did less well than before and his former friend Richard Ramsay Reinagle was elected – 'the most weak and undesirable artist on the list', Constable thought. Reinagle later claimed (in a letter of 1850 to the *Literary Gazette*) to have helped Constable, whom he called 'a pupil of mine', by painting some cattle in a Constable landscape. When Reinagle made this assertion, it was after being forced to resign his Academy membership for exhibiting as his own somebody else's picture.[5]

Perhaps being run-down was a factor in an episode in March, when Constable's propensity to repeat gossip got him into trouble with William Collins and John Linnell. A complicated story, it involved a long-haired drawing master from Southampton called Read, an acquaintance of Linnell's, whom Constable had met at John Fisher's. Read, with painting ambitions, brought some studies to Hampstead to show Constable and apparently claimed to have been badly treated by Linnell, who was like Read a Baptist. Constable – no admirer of Dissenters – retailed this to colleagues at Somerset House and Linnell, who was standing for Associate membership, attributed to Constable his failure to be elected (an overestimate of Constable's influence). With Collins on Linnell's side, it was like a duel, though Constable seemed to realise he was in the wrong. He backed down, agreeing to put in writing his belief that Read's assertions were false. A comic moment in the drama occurred when Read had a large number of his paintings delivered to Charlotte Street, hoping for Constable's help in getting them exhibited. They were stacked up outside the door of number 35 and a crowd gathered to look at them, saying – Constable claimed – they made quite a show and were better than Constable's.[6]

Despite these distractions, Constable buckled down to work on a big canvas, this time upright and slightly less than five feet tall, showing a barge in Flatford Lock with the lock-keeper opening the shutter of the gates to release water and lower the craft. He worked as well on Dr Fisher's *Salisbury Cathedral from the Bishop's Grounds*. This, together with *A Study of Trees* and *A Cottage,* were his entries for the Academy exhibition; *A Barge passing a Lock* wasn't ready, and he thought he suffered from it. But the *Cathedral,* though smaller, made its effect. The cathedral looked like scrimshaw, carved from whalebone or ivory, framed by trees and with two figures on the path in the left foreground – the Bishop pointing out the spire to his wife, somewhat like donors in a medieval religious picture. 'I have not flinched at the work, of the windows, buttresses, &c.,' Constable wrote to John Fisher on 9 May. A number of white cumulus clouds were intruded on by one dark cloud, which bothered the Bishop; another version of the picture was made for the Bishop's daughter Elizabeth on her marriage later that year, with the clouds more diffused and with more of what Archdeacon Fisher spelled out as necessary sunshine. (Someone of the Bishop's persuasion was Henry Fuseli, the RA Professor of Painting, who liked Constable's landscapes but said that the painter made him call for his greatcoat and umbrella.) Another sunny-but-serene, white-clouds-only version of the cathedral was done by 1826 to replace the one the Bishop had commissioned but didn't like. Constable preferred to make a new one rather than alter the first. In any event the critics generally admired the exhibited Cathedral and its one dark cloud. The *Literary Gazette*'s writer thought it 'striking' though he also found it 'mannered' – this was a word which would dog Constable from now on. The *Morning Chronicle* would have liked less attention to detail in the architecture; apparently a little flinching might have been in order. Callcott told Constable he thought his fellow artist had managed the painting well, but Constable returned this compliment with his verdict to Fisher that the picture Callcott had on show was poor. However, Constable said that Turner's picture, *The Bay of Baiae,* seemed 'painted with saffron and indigo'. Turner, he thought, was 'stark mad – with ability'.[7]

Constable's health seems to have improved by this time; his pictures for the annual show were off his back and in late April he had managed a quick trip to Bergholt. Spring feelings warmed his 9 May letter to Fisher. He had much work to do, and finances to repair. 'However though I am here in the midst of the world I am out of it –

and am happy – and endeavour to keep myself unspoiled. I have a
kingdom of my own both fertile & populous – my landscape and my
children . . . Let me hear from you – soon.'[8]

That summer the Constables' out-of-town house in Hampstead was
Stamford Lodge in Stamford Place. There and in Charlotte Street
Constable got a great deal of work done, including two portraits for
the Countess of Dysart. In July he spent several days with an amateur
painter who was a great fan both of his and of Turner's. The Reverend
Thomas Judkin was pastor of the Somers Town Episcopal chapel and
exhibited from time to time at the Royal Academy. Constable told
Fisher in July 1823 after his stay in Southgate with Judkin: 'He is a
sensible man . . . but he will paint.' And was he sensible? Maria early
on had Judkin sized up as a time-waster, who kept dropping by
Charlotte Street to chat about Art; he and the occasional poet Peter
Coxe were numbered by her among Constable's 'loungers'.

Constable also had a 'great row' about this time with Turner and
Collins, apparently about Academy matters; something of a civil war
was going on at Somerset House, with Turner 'watchful and savage'.
Turner had helped put landscape painting in the front rank of art, and
Constable should have been grateful to him; but he lacked Turner's
bumptious self-confidence and his pride made him prickly and
resentful. Collins, whose works often featured 'happy urchins and
pious labourers', showed him a recent painting which Constable
disliked; it was 'insipid . . . and far too pretty to be natural'.

Fisher still wanted to buy *The Hay Wain* but still couldn't afford it.
He hoped to get Constable to Salisbury but thought his friend was
probably too tied 'to your family, your portraits, and the necessity of
carrying your dish between <u>fame and famine</u>'. But Constable found
time to buy for eight guineas a painting of fruit Fisher had wanted –
and was rewarded with instant repayment and a perceptive compliment: 'Where *real* business is to be done you are the most energetic
and punctual of men: in smaller matters, such as putting on your
breeches, you are apt to lose time in deciding which leg shall go in
first.' And Constable then got organised to visit Fisher. He left his

family well and arrived in Salisbury at 6 p.m. on 19 August, in time for dinner with his 'best friend in the world'. There was immediately pressure for him to stay on in Salisbury. Fisher's uncle, the Bishop, wanted to discuss the wedding-picture copy of the *Cathedral*, and the 'kind & friendly' Tinney wanted two upright landscapes at fifty guineas each. After making another quick sketch of the cathedral, however, Constable went on with Fisher to Gillingham where the archdeacon's family were in residence and where the company of Constable offered social support. Constable found Gillingham 'a melancholy place', its people poor and dirty. Fisher felt on his own there, seen by the locals as one of the tithe collectors who made life onerous, ordained to steal milk and butter from their mouths – although they welcomed Fisher's medical expertise for their wounds and illnesses. The fact that he was a part-time incumbent probably didn't help. Constable liked riding around with Fisher and listening to him talk about a special sermon he was working on, apparently for the cathedral, and he liked being at home with Mary Fisher and the Fisher children. He described them all in a letter to Maria, knowing she would be interested in comparing them with their own: Osmond stammered, Emma was bashful, William known as Belim was Constable's favourite, and Frank with delicate silk-like hair reminded him of Charley.

One jaunt Constable took with Fisher was to Fonthill, the folly-mansion the eccentric writer and traveller William Beckford had built, and which had recently been sold to a gunpowder manufacturer. From the top of Fonthill tower Constable saw the spire of Salisbury Cathedral fifteen miles away; it 'darted up into the sky like a needle'. The house was amazing, Constable told Maria. 'Imagine . . . any beautifull Gothick building magnificently fitted up with crimson & gold, antient pictures, in almost every nitch statues, large massive gold boxes for relicks . . . beautiful & rich carpets, curtains & glasses – some of which spoiled the effect – but . . . on the whole, a strange, ideal, romantic place – quite fairy land.' An immense sale of objects and paintings was going on that Constable called something of an 'auctioneer's job'. Harry Phillips, the auctioneer, had apparently added many items to Beckford's collection, knowing the Beckford name would help shift them. The sale went on for thirty-nine days. The Fishers turned up on one occasion to buy three lots of old china. Fisher teased Constable: 'One of them I bought on the speculation of swapping it with you for one of your little sea peices.'

At first the weather while Constable was in Gillingham made painting difficult. He wrote to Maria every four or five days, asking what was happening at home and telling her that from the Fishers' garden he could hear the Gillingham watermill, which rattled away as its machinery turned out cotton, the sounds making him think of Flatford. He had been too long away from her: 'I miss you at night and once I thought I had you in my arms, how provoking.' But despite several pledges to return, Constable as always found it hard to shake himself loose. Fisher's friendship was 'at once the pride – the honour – and grand stimulus of my life'. Perhaps thinking a news-filled letter would compensate for his absence, he told Maria about the perquisites the Fishers gave their servants: 'Mrs F. says 2 guineas is the usual allowance for [tea] & sugar.' He was at least two weeks overdue when he got back to Hampstead in mid-September and found his family 'better than I have ever had them'.

Back in Hampstead and Charlotte Street, he spent a bit more than a month working on Tinney's pictures and hanging his 'bridal picture' of Salisbury Cathedral in Seymour Street ready for the arrival of Elizabeth Fisher and her husband. He also did another favour for John Fisher, for a few days looking after a poodle the archdeacon had bought in town. But what are best friends for? Constable said his cook and the two cats would be able to amuse Fisher's dog. And then he once again left London. Maria had Mrs Roberts and other servants at Stamford Lodge to help with the children, so maybe she didn't mind too much, at first, when Constable went to stay with Sir George and Lady Beaumont in Leicestershire. He suggested he was going to Coleorton Hall for roughly a week. He wrote to Maria on getting there, excited by the loveliness of the place: 'Such grounds – such trees – such distances . . .'

On the way he had stopped in Leicester to call on his niece Alicia,

Martha Whalley's daughter, who was at school there. Family connections mattered to him. He reported to Maria that Alicia looked 'delightfully', her cheeks rosy from being surprised and kissed by a gentleman – her uncle John. But what he found at Coleorton was what really mattered: 'Only think that I am now writing in a room full of Claudes (not Glovers) [the RA painter of decorative landscapes] – real Claudes, and Wilsons & Poussins &c. – almost at the summit of my earthly ambitions. I cannot help asking myself how I came here.' On the one hand, he felt sad, thinking with tears in his eyes of his 'ducks' and her, 'my poor Fish'. On the other hand, the Beaumonts were so kind he gradually felt quite at home.

Or so he said. The relationship between Sir George and Constable was never simple. Beaumont was a great 'patron' even if he never bought anything from Constable; he was influential in the London art world and a collector of genius (his pictures were to help found the new National Gallery). He wanted to improve Constable's taste, and may always have felt slightly miffed that Constable wasn't open to that sort of improvement. The Beaumonts were among the grandest people Constable had close contact with, and he arrived in their house shouldering his background as the art-loving Suffolk boy whose family was in trade and whose mother had been acquainted with Sir George's mother in Dedham. Sir George's fortune was underpinned by Leicestershire coal mines.[9] However, as a 'leader of Taste', which Charles Leslie called him, he had weaknesses, the first being that the taste he preferred was gone by, and he bought neither of the most talented artists of his time. Beaumont actively disliked Turner's paintings and Constable was perhaps too close to him to be seen for the original he was. Turner looked on Sir George with an equally cold eye; his pictures were 'made-up', he thought. Constable didn't detect any threat to himself in Beaumont's derivative art and remained generous. 'I feel that I am indebted to him for what I am as an artist,' he wrote later to William Wordsworth – who also had cause to be thankful for Sir George's patronage.[10]

At Coleorton Constable looked at some sky studies by Alexander Cozens. He copied a small Claude, probably *Landscape with Goatherd and Goats*, 'a grove scene of great beauty . . . It contains almost all that I wish to do in landscape.' At night, after hearing Sir George reading Shakespeare aloud, say Jaques's speech from *As You Like It* about the seven ages of man, he slept with another Claude in his bedroom. He expected Maria to be jealous – she had counted on him being home by now. That she was fed up shone through a letter in which she wrote, seemingly compliant, 'As it is for your advantage I must put myself out of the question and submit without murmuring to my fate.' Her fate was unwittingly touched on a few lines later, when she said she had successfully cured Charley of an illness 'without Mr Drew', the apothecary, and added, 'I wish I could cure myself but everyone says how thin I am grown.' A week later, in mid-November, she wrote that his friends were beginning to wonder what had become of him. Constable, thick-skinned in these matters, replied next day mentioning other little jobs Sir George had for him, and adding that the Beaumonts wanted him to spend Christmas with them. This provoked Maria to write on 21 November that she would expect him 'the *end of next week* certainly, it was complimentary in Sir George to ask you to remain the Xmas, but he forgot at the time that you had a wife'.

A polite if obsessional host, indeed; but the question recurs: Why did Sir George never buy a Constable painting? Although they generally seemed to agree about the old masters, their tastes actually differed, so Leslie thought.[11] Sir George constantly communed with pictures whose tints were 'subdued by time', such as those by Gaspar Poussin, and this unsuited his eye 'for the enjoyment of freshness'. And Constable was 'too daring in the modes he adopted to obtain this quality'. When Sir George 'recommended the colour of an old Cremona fiddle for the prevailing tone of everything . . . Constable answered by laying an old fiddle on the green lawn before the house', to show Sir George that brown didn't work for trees and grass. Constable admired Beaumont's hard-working attitude in painting, even as an amateur. He wrote a touch optimistically to Fisher, 'Painting like religion knows no difference of rank.' He and Sir George became sincere friends but the social differences were buried rather than removed. It took him more than a week in the Beaumonts' company to lose 'all uncomfortable reserve and restraint', and he ended his six-week stay at Coleorton feeling greater self-esteem – but suffering nervous exhaustion.[12]

When Constable finally got back to town, to Maria and his 'ducks', all his pent-up anxiety exploded. His happiness at being with his family went up, as in a chimney fire. It was his old complaint, neuralgia, with severe pains in the teeth, face and head. His teeth and jaw problems apparently started in 1798 at the time of Mr Travis's dental operation, and often seemed to strike him just when he was getting down to work on his pictures for Somerset House. In later years he sympathised with Leslie about toothache because he knew what it was like: 'it is an entire illness with me at all times when I am so visited'. Beaumont wrote early in 1824, hearing the artist had been unwell, admonishing him to get 'air and exercise', otherwise he would never reach Sir George's age. For one who had been a very active child and youth, and despite his skying excursions on the Heath, Constable wasn't a great one for regular exercise. Leslie said, 'He loitered rather than walked, and his pace could scarcely be quickened into exercise, unless he was late for some appointment.'[13]

He must also have been very worried about Maria. When Fisher came to town in February he found her poorly. Perhaps she was suffering from let-down at the reunion with her fatigued husband after his absence at the Beaumonts. But there was more to Maria's illness than that. It is unclear whether Constable had a full idea what was wrong; if so he probably didn't want to believe it. He never used in his letters the word 'consumption' (or 'phthisis' as it was then generally called). However, Charles Leslie and Henry Syer Trimmer later did,[14] and Constable knew that there had to be something wrong with the Bicknells: her brother Durand, dead in 1811 aged nineteen; her mother, long an invalid, dead in 1815; and her brother Sam, who he had told Farington was suffering from consumption, dead in 1821, aged twenty-four. There were worries on the same score about her sister Catherine now. Consumption was known to run in families (as with the Brontës), though no one recognised until 1882 that it was an infectious disease caused by the tubercle bacillus, a microbe or bacterium. Cow's milk could carry and spread the bacterium and so could coughing, sneezing and spitting. Night-sweats, weight loss, tiredness and coughing up blood were all symptoms. It came on gradually, solemnly, and seemed, as Dickens noted, to prepare its victims for death 'grain by grain'. It was a disease, he thought, that 'medicine never cured, wealth never warded off'. Anaemia was an invariable feature of it. 'Youth grows pale, and spectre thin, and dies,' wrote Keats in 1819. Despite this the doctors of the age recommended bleeding and near-starvation as treatment. Arsenic, quinine, ergot and coal gas were among the remedies in vogue, while digitalis, tartar-emetic and laudanum were much prescribed.[15]

Bleeding in fact gave brief respite from the breathlessness that affected victims as their lungs were destroyed, but that was all. Many purported remedies were toxic. Patients were often kept in hermetically sealed rooms. Some 'cures' such as horse-riding were now and then in vogue, while Lady Denham in Jane Austen's *Sanditon* was sensibly prepared to supply asses' milk to consumptives sojourning at that embryonic coastal resort. Fresh air and sea air were sometimes proposed for sufferers, as were balloon-ascents. Constable's interest in clouds and the skies may have been increased by Maria's need for breathable air. One impressive aspect of the disease was that it seemed to affect more young women than men. There were consequently many nineteenth-century stage heroines speaking or singing their last as art copied life. One popular early photographic print was Henry Peach Robinson's *Fading Away* of 1858, which showed a young woman dying of consumption. Another feature of the disease was that it seemed to produce a surfeit of sexual energy; it was, according to one authority, 'the most lecherous of all illnesses'. Many of the female victims became pregnant; this seemed to bring in its train sudden remissions or more drastic, rapid deterioration. One other constant factor was the irrational optimism that seized consumptives. 'The hope of the tuberculous' was well known, part of their heightened awareness, and part of their tragedy. 'My poor Fish,' Constable had written to Maria from Coleorton, happy with the Claudes and Poussins, missing her with tears in his eyes. More than he yet knew, she was Poor Fish.[16]

# 11. *Trying the Sea (1824)*

The problem child, Constable's older brother Golding, wasn't so mentally or physically handicapped as some thought. In early February 1824 he wrote Constable a literate thank-you letter for putting in a good word for him with Lady Louisa Manners, now nearly eighty and Countess of Dysart since the death of her brother; the Earl had been a good patron to Constable as the painter of family portraits. The Dysart woods at Helmingham and Bentley, close by in Suffolk, were meant to be looked after by a steward named Wenn, who was looking after his own interests and overcharging Lady Dysart for fencing. Constable recommended Golding to Lady Dysart to replace Wenn as warden of her woods. Golding enjoyed hunting and shooting, and might prevent the misuse of her land. Wenn – 'a lying low fellow', according to Constable – complained to the Countess about this interference, but Constable went in April to take a personal look at the woods and back up Golding with his own report on matters (and also to take to the Whalleys and his brothers and sisters his Easter-time gift of hot-cross buns). Abram meanwhile urged Golding to place a notice in the Ipswich paper, before the shooting season started, warning people not to trespass or shoot game in the Dysart woods. Lady Dysart occasionally invited Constable to her houses in Pall Mall and Richmond; gifts of venison from her frequently arrived for the Constables; and Constable sent on to her Golding's letters.

Although John Fisher continued to advise Constable it was a bad time for his health to be in London, painting. Constable spent his usual winter-into-spring session of hard work in front of his easel in

Somerset House terrace and St Paul's, from the north end of Waterloo
Bridge

Charlotte Street. The Academy exhibition waited for no artist. For a
while his subject was Waterloo Bridge. He had been making sketches
for it since 1817, when the Prince Regent opened the bridge, and had
done several oil studies. However, he had had trouble fixing on the
point of view, particularly in determining how high the horizon
should be. Two of the oil sketches were impressionistic; two of the
paintings (one now in the RA, one in Cincinatti) were more finished,
the larger being – as Bishop Fisher noted – Canaletto-like in its
polished detail. One Waterloo Bridge picture took John Fisher's
fancy; in April 1820 he asked Constable not to let it go without
informing him – if he was 'strong enough in purse', he might buy it.
Constable completed this or another of the same subject on 17 January
1824, a painting he called 'a small balloon to let off as a forerunner of

the large one'. He took up the subject again several times in the following years, in November 1825 telling Fisher that he was 'hard and fast on my Waterloo which <u>shall be done</u> for the next exhibition'. And a week later: 'My Waterloo like a blister begins to stick closer and closer – & to disturb my nights . . .' Yet some things with him had to mature like old compost; it was not until 1832 that the 'great Bridge', now called *Whitehall Stairs*, reached the Royal Academy.[1]

In 1824 what surfaced instead – as though from a beyond-the-grave prompting by Joseph Farington – was a Stour subject that seems to have been roughed out a year earlier: *The Lock*. It was a 'large upright', about fifty-six inches by forty-eight. It showed the down-stream end of Flatford Lock with Dedham church in the distance – the tiny tower framed by the lock gate, a leafy tree branch and the brawny arms of a bargee working with a crowbar on the winch. (An Academy Life-class study of a muscle-straining nude man he had made sixteen years or so before apparently furnished material for the bargee's action, as did his own Stour-side memories of inland navigation.) To modern taste, the full-sized sketch – fleshed out in oils roughly brushed and palette-knifed – is happily less finished than the upright canvas which went to Somerset House by mid-April. *The Lock* was his sole entry that year. He had thrown himself fully into it; he wrote to John Fisher, 'It is going to its audit with all its deficiencies in hand . . . I have done my best.'[2]

For a change his best struck gold. Constable's colleagues liked it even though some were annoyed by his execution. He wrote to Fisher, 'Perhaps the sacrifices I make for *lightness* and *brightness* is too much, but these things are the essence of landscape . . . I do hope that my exertions may at last turn towards popularity; 'tis you that have too long held my head above water. Although I have a good deal of the devil in me, I think I should have been broken hearted before this time but for you.' *The Lock* was sold on the first day, the private view of the RA show. It was bought for 150 guineas, frame included, by James Morrison, a well-to-do businessman. John Jackson, the portrait painter, told Constable that Lord Fitzwilliam would have bought it if Morrison hadn't got to it first. The press generally approved, the

*Literary Gazette* declaring, 'The character of his details, like those of Wilson, appear as if struck out with a single touch,' and noting that this was something which 'comes only by great practice and much previous thought and calculation'. To top this, Constable reached agreement with John Arrowsmith, the Frenchman who had been after his *Hay Wain* for two years. The dealer now wanted that picture as part of a package of several paintings for which he offered more money and the promise of immense enhancement of Constable's reputation. Fisher, who had also wanted *The Hay Wain* but couldn't manage it because of the prevailing agricultural depression, liked the idea of it being sold to France: 'The stupid English public, which has no judgement of its own, will begin to think that there is something in you if the French make your works national property. You have long laid under a mistake. Men do not purchase pictures because they admire them, but because others covet them.' Constable agreed to let Arrowsmith have *The Bridge* and a smaller painting, *Yarmouth Jetty*, along with *The Hay Wain* for £250.[3]

'The Frenchman', as Constable referred to the Parisian dealer, was approved by Paul Colnaghi, the printseller, but Constable told Fisher he wasn't going to let the paintings out of his hands till paid. However, Arrowsmith sent the money promptly and Constable, with Morrison's payment, suddenly found himself more than £400 to the good. Arrowsmith – despite his English-sounding name – was only just conversant in that tongue but had good connections; his brother-in-law, the photographer Louis Daguerre, had exhibited a diorama in Regent's Park in 1823.[4] As well as dealing in paintings, Arrowsmith had a restaurant in Paris (one room was later called the Salon Constable). This may have helped him gauge the mood of the day, hearing over the table d'hôte what Delacroix, Géricault and Nodier had to say about Constable. Arrowsmith was soon back in London and brought a colleague, Charles Schroth. In late May seven more small pictures were commissioned from 35 Charlotte Street, three for Schroth, four for Arrowsmith. To crown the artist's feeling that not just France lay open for him, the director of the Antwerp academy called on Constable after seeing *The Lock* at the Royal Academy and assured him his pictures would 'make an impression on the continent'.

Although Constable at that moment showed no signs of going much further than Hampstead, the Continent was getting closer, and he was aware of it. He mentioned to Fisher in a round-up of London news at the end of May, 'The other day (what is it that this great town does not afford) two people flew over our heads in a balloon – and were knocked on their heads in a park near Croydon.' In fact, the balloonist Thomas Harris was killed but his aerial companion Miss Stocks survived. Another recent death had been that of Byron, 'martyr' to Hellenic freedom, on 10 April. Constable, in the unforgiving mood of a frequent reader of *John Bull*, the right-wing weekly, thought the world well rid of the poet and adventurer, 'but the deadly slime of his touch still remains'.

Someone who managed to cope well with Constable's ups and downs was Johnny Dunthorne. In May, now aged twenty-six, he came to work as Constable's assistant in Charlotte Street. He brought with him a breath of Suffolk air and the latest East Bergholt news. Constable's sister Mary was looking for a new lightweight carriage, perhaps a landaulet, and Johnny was roped in to the search Constable was asked to make in London. The Constable brothers all agreed Johnny was the right person for Charlotte Street. Abram wrote, 'He is certainly the most extraordinary young man within my knowledge, so clever, so active, & so innocent, 'tis marvellous.' In a letter to Golding of 3 December 1824, Constable said Johnny 'is very useful to me and is getting me forward in my things [–] he is handy and obliging – that he will do any thing [–] he will copy any of my pictures beautifully or go [on] the most trifling errand'.[5] Constable took him to see the 1824 Academy exhibition. Johnny had helped with *The Hay Wain* by providing sketches of a farm wagon and now he served as apprentice, preparing Constable's paints and palette, 'squaring up', tracing, putting in outlines, underpainting and copying. He helped lay in some of the versions of *Salisbury Cathedral* and eventually assisted Constable by working on some of his 'dead horses', thereby diminishing the number of forlorn canvases stacked up in his studio.

He sometimes took Constable's place at his easel, working on paintings of either the Stour or the Thames.[6] While there, he befriended the pigeons of a Charlotte Street neighbour that perched on the easel.[7]

Johnny was working too at becoming an artist. For Mary he painted a picture of the Constables' former home, East Bergholt House; he was painting landscapes of East Bergholt scenery, for instance *A Country Lane*, which looks very much like the lane to Flatford, with the view across Dedham Vale. In the ensuing few years, encouraged by Constable, he sent some of his paintings to the Academy and the British Institution – pleasant enough pictures judging by two in Colchester Museum's collection, though his skies are unexceptional and the light in them seems artificial. Mary and Abram went on worrying about him, anxious about his regular attendance at church but pleased that his painting was 'wonderfully improved'. With the passing of Dr Rhudde and Maria's absence from East Bergholt we hear no more of Dunthorne Senior's 'perverse and evil ways'. (In the village, the handyman-artist was as he grew older in fact respected for his integrity.) After the breakdown of the friendship between the older Dunthorne and young Constable, it was fortunate that the artist – now approaching forty-eight – was able to befriend young Dunthorne. Having 'my friend' Johnny around cheered up Constable as Maria's illness left him feeling stranded by fate. Maria wrote to him from Brighton in mid-June 1824, 'How lucky you have Mr Dunthorne.' Johnny was good at keeping at bay such unwanted visitors as Peter Coxe and the Reverend Judkin. Constable took him along to church services at Fitzroy Chapel and passed on to Johnny some of the chores Sir George Beaumont asked him to perform, cleaning and repairing pictures. Other distinguished clients followed, including Lord Westmorland, Lord Cadogan and the Marquess of Aylesbury. Constable might have taken credit as the begetter of Johnny Dunthorne's restorer's workshop in Grafton Street, off Fitzroy Square.

In Paris, in his absence, Constable had a splendid reception by way of the paintings Arrowsmith had brought there.[8] In the *Journal de*

*Paris* Stendhal welcomed these '*paysages magnifiques*'. Fisher sent him a paragraph from a Salisbury journal mentioning the success of two pictures exhibited in the Louvre by 'Mr Constable the eminent artist'. Arrowsmith reported directly that Constable's pictures were causing a sensation among French artists; the Paris correspondent of *The Times* had even mentioned their arrival.[9] One French critic, calling the paintings 'a miracle', was worried that they might seduce his compatriots from their proper allegiance. 'What is to become of the great Poussin?' was Constable's paraphrase of this warning. But he was obviously pleased by 'the great sensation they seem to have made'. He was also flattered by a letter from France addressed to him: '*Monsieur* John Constable, Peintre paysagiste, 35 Charlotte St, Fitzroy Square, à Londres.' He said nevertheless that he had 'not the least thought of going among them'.

He had enough to do where he was. He had written to John Fisher in early May about Maria's health: 'We are told we must try the sea.' He sent his ailing wife and his children to Brighton at once, accompanied by Mrs Roberts and Ellen, their chief maid. Sea-bathing had become fashionable, here and in other new resorts such as Sidmouth and Margate. The Prince Regent had frequented Brighton and as King had commissioned John Nash to remodel the Royal Pavilion. A good coach service got Londoners seeking salubrious air down in a morning or Brighton-based stockbrokers up to town, and this meant Constable could easily go back and forth to his studio. The family went to the west end of the expanding town, to a rented house in a relatively new enclave called Mrs Sobers' Gardens, in Western Place. Mrs Sobers lived next door, the beach was a short way to the south with the rote of the sea on the shingle easily heard and seagulls crying overhead, and open fields lay immediately to the west in the direction of Shoreham and Worthing.[10]

Because of Brighton, Constable was leading a split existence, down there for weekends and holidays, and up in Charlotte Street the rest of the time. Johnny helped pack Arrowsmith's pictures for shipment to Paris but was less successful – for once – in fending off the Reverend Judkin. Judkin called on 27 May bringing some of his pictures which Constable found 'very bad & cold. I should be glad that he never came again.' A few weeks later Constable encountered Judkin's painting *Stolen Moments* in a gallery; it was 'too bad & vulgar to look at'. Judkin then made the mistake of calling in Charlotte Street and asking Constable how he liked *Stolen Moments*. Constable couldn't help saying it wasn't a subject a clergyman should paint and, as a picture, was 'very far indeed from what it ought to be'. In 1825 Judkin aroused Constable again to say, 'I am sick of "Amateurs" – they are the greatest enemies the living art has.' Judkin was oblivious or turned the other cheek, and the following year penned a 'Miltonic sonnet' which set Constable on a pedestal alongside Wordsworth. Another hopeful in Charlotte Street was Mr Appleton, a tub-maker, who came to ask Constable to sell him 'a damaged picture . . . cheap' to hang in a room he was renting out.[11]

The double life left both husband and wife in need of news from one another. At Maria's urging, Constable kept a journal.[12] He started it on 19 May and sent it down about once a week, often courtesy of someone he knew who was heading for the seaside. He seems to have written up his diary on the night of the day concerned or the morning after, mentioning the sending-off of Arrowsmith's paintings, the cleaning and oiling of Tinney's picture, the arrival of mail from East Bergholt, and visits from Henry Sass, Thomas Stothard and W.R. Bigg as well as the usual loungers. He told Maria about his health – he had taken some doses of calomel in warm water for a bout of illness until Manning, the apothecary, advised against it – and told her what he had to eat. The undermaid Sarah had been left in London to look after 35 Charlotte Street and its busy occupants, Constable and Johnny Dunthorne. When Sarah was ill, on 2 June, Constable recorded: 'Mutton broth for dinner.' But she had clearly recovered the next day when he enjoyed a 'very nice' beefsteak pudding. Tinney had generously if reluctantly given up *Stratford Mill* again, and it was on display in the Charlotte Street studio where Constable tinkered with it despite Tinney's request that he leave well alone. After reading the journal Maria wrote back, telling 'My dear John' not to send any more butter; it wouldn't keep and in any case the Brighton butter was beautiful. A bit later she wished he hadn't wasted carriage charges on a box of things he sent down – not only some medical powders from Mr Drew but nine pounds of loaf sugar. She had taken several rides, had walked to the chalybeate wells, both those in Shoreham and that uphill nearby, and, what would surely please him, was studying skies all day. The noise the children were making made her forget what she meant to say next. She tried to keep the family accounts in order and was upset when she was two sovereigns out. She was reading a book on education so as to improve the children and added, 'I am perfectly satisfied with my four without wishing for any more.' Was this a hint to John?

He missed Maria. On 25 May he wrote, 'As good a night as could be expected without my Fish.' He ended another entry as if she were there: 'Goodnight my darling Fish.' He thought he needed sea air as much as she, complaining on 28 May, 'My cheeks are always disagreeable hot, and pains in my stomach and shoulders & eyes & throat.' And, two days later, 'a sort of heartburn after breakfast'. Indigestion or

Mouse

hypochondria; angina and/or high blood pressure? On the night of 6–7 June he dreamed of his dear Fish: 'I was in a bad way.' 35 Charlotte Street might have interested Gilbert White: a goldfinch had flown in and seemed to want to stay with the pet goldfinch of Sarah, the maid. Constable borrowed a cage for it. Then Sarah's 'new favourite cat' nearly got Sarah's pet bird. There were always several cats in the house that managed to coexist with a mouse, also an habitué; it was getting very fat, Johnny Dunthorne said, but then Constable would put rinds of cheese out for it. Generally at least one pair of pigeons was on hand and quarrelling over eggs. Two sparrows came into the house and let themselves be caught, then released by Constable. Birds liked him. A robin got washed in a dish of water set out for the pigeons to drink from in the back drawing room. Unfortunately Sarah was proving a problem, claiming to have pains in her head – was she drinking? – she was nearing forty. Ellen was sent to take her place and was kept busy catching up with the ironing.

Brighton: a rainstorm over the sea

It was a relief to take Johnny Dunthorne down to Brighton for a week in early June, and Johnny made himself useful there by preparing Constable's painting box for him. Constable took it to the beach where he rested it on his knees, the inside of the lid forming a working surface for his oil sketches. He generally used a coarse-wove paper, primed with two or three coats of oil paint – pink, brown or grey. Often his sketch was still wet when he unpinned it and put it away, and traces of paint stuck to the sheet above. A longer Brighton sojourn occurred in the second half of July. Minna's birthday was on the 19th and he got there two days before. He came meaning to have a month's working holiday and stayed for nearly three months. Constable found a great deal there for the painter: the beach, the sea, the breakers, the fishing boats and coal brigs, the chain pier, the sky. On Minna's birthday he went down to the beach, pinned his paper to his box lid, and in oils painted several of the coal-black colliers at the water's edge, unloading coal. He wrote on the back for John Fisher's benefit, '3d tide receding left the beach wet – Head of the Chain Pier Beach Brighton July 19 Evg., 1824 My dear Maria's Birthday Your Goddaughter – Very lovely Evening – looking Eastward – cliffs & light off a dark [?] effect – background – very white and golden light.' The chain pier (builder Captain Brown, Royal Navy) had opened the year before and Constable's drawings of it provided material for an oil shown at the RA in 1827. (Turner painted the pier a year later.) Later, one of Constable's beach sketches was engraved and he wrote that it was meant to convey 'one of those animated days when the masses of cloud, agitated and torn, are passing rapidly', while the wind 'meeting with a certain set of tide, causes the sea to rise and swell'.[13] He painted a picture of Mrs Sobers' Western Lodge, with its 'Gothic' features. He walked to Worthing and also up on to the Downs on a fine day to see the Dyke, the old Roman embankment, 'perhaps the most grand & affecting natural landscape in the world – and consequently a scene the most unfit for a picture. It is the business of a painter not to contend with nature & put this scene (a valley filled with imagery 50 miles long) on a canvas of a few inches, but to make something out of nothing . . .' One sketch catches superbly this natural – i.e. in Constable's eyes insufficiently cultivated – landscape, with the roll of the sparsely grassed Downs under low clouds, cattle grazing loosely, and a windmill off to the right in the shadowed foreground. It was curious how Constable could combine the creation of such a moving sketch (made on 3 August 1824) with the spleen he expressed on the back of it: 'Smock or Tower Mill west end of Brighton – the neighbourhood of Brighton – consists of London cow fields – and Hideous masses of unfledged earth called the country.'[14]

In late August he was still in two minds about even being in Brighton. He appreciated what seemed an improvement in Maria's health beside the sea but clearly wasn't attuned to all the pleasures of a seaside resort. Fisher received a surly blast at the end of the month:

> I am living here but I dislike the place . . . Brighton is the receptacle of the fashion and off-scouring of London. The magnificence of the sea, and its (to use your own beautifull expression) everlasting voice, is drowned in the din & lost in the tumult of stage coaches – gigs – 'flys' &c. – and the beach is only Piccadilly . . . by the seaside. Ladies dressed & <u>undressed</u> – gentlemen in morning gowns & slippers on, or without them altogether about <u>knee deep</u> in the breakers – footmen – children – nursery maids, dogs, boys, fishermen – <u>preventive service men</u> (with hangers & pistols), rotten fish & those hideous amphibious animals the old bathing women, whose language both in oaths & voice resembles men – all are mixed together in endless & indecent confusion.

It was high summer and perhaps the heat, the celebrated 'dippers' Martha Gunn and Old Smoaker, and the Piccadilly-like crowds didn't help his temper. Constable waxed on:

> The genteeler part, the marine parade, is still more unnatural – with its trimmed and neat appearance & the dandy jetty or chain pier, with its long & elegant strides into the sea a full ¼ of a mile. In short there is nothing here for a painter but the breakers – & sky – which have been lovely indeed and always varying.

While getting that off his chest, Constable shared some of his better news. His wife and children were delightfully well. He had made friends with Henry Phillips, a botanist, who was intelligent. He was also getting on with some of his 'French jobs', one of which was apparently a Hampstead view for Charles Schroth.

Back in London at the beginning of November, soon joined by Maria and the children, he had to deal with another bout of illness and depression. He told Fisher, 'All my indispositions have their source in my mind – it [is] when I am restless and unhappy that I become susceptible of cold – damp – heats – and such nonsense. I have not been well for many weeks – but I hope soon to rid myself of these things and get to work again.' *Restless and unhappy*. Yet the need to work. It was the artist's life. He was also again having trouble talking Tinney into lending *Stratford Mill* for the British Institution exhibition in January 1825 or getting Tinney to let him postpone fulfilment of a generous commission of two 'uprights'. Fortunately there was good news a few weeks later. He reported to Fisher that Johnny Dunthorne was helping him and cheering him up. Moreover, 'my wife is quite well – never saw her better and more active & cheerfull – but she is rather stouter than I could have wished. My children are lovely – and much grown. John I am sorry to say is a genius . . . droll & acute . . . Your goddaughter is so much the little lady that she delights every body.'

From Paris came further news that he was – in Fisher's words – 'the talk and admiration of the French'. W.H. Pyne had written colourfully in the *Somerset House Gazette* in July that Constable's three paintings – one being *The Hay Wain* – might have remained in Charlotte Street 'till *Doomsday*, had not a collector from Paris called upon their ingenious author, Mr Constable, and purchased them, in their accumulated dust, as they hung almost obsolete on his walls'. His pictures were first displayed at Arrowsmith's gallery, where Delacroix came twice to see them and repainted his *Massacre at Scio* as a result. At the Louvre, on 25 August, they joined an exhibition of works by living French artists. The director-general of royal museums, Comte Auguste de Forbin, was dissatisfied with where the Constables were first hung and moved them to 'a post of honor . . . in

the principal room'.[15] Reporting to Fisher, Constable expressed his
pleasure at this and at a comment he was told was overheard in the
Louvre: 'Look at these English pictures – the very dew is upon the
ground.' James Pulham, his old friend and patron in Woodbridge,
wrote to say that Constable's presence in the Louvre 'must invoke the
English Primacy to make you . . . a Royal Academician'. Mr Pulham
thought the purchase of works from such a famous artist must now be
beyond him. Constable was moved to give Pulham one of his pictures
of Harwich Lighthouse, which he finished on 15 July and Johnny
packed up and sent off the next day. The seal was set on Constable's
French success when the King, Charles X, visited the Louvre in
January 1825; he made Sir Thomas Lawrence a knight of the Legion
of Honour for his portraits, and awarded Constable a gold medal for
his landscapes.[16]

# 12. *The Leaping Horse (1825–26)*

On 5 January, in bleak midwinter, Constable told Fisher that he was 'writing this hasty scrawl [in the] dark before a six foot canvas – which I have just launched with all my usual anxieties'. This was his sixth six-footer, and he had been planning it for nearly two months. Fisher thought a bit more diversity in Constable's subject matter and mood would help, but the artist said he wasn't about to vary his plans 'to keep the Publick in good humour'. There were to be two pen-and-wash studies and a full-size oil sketch, and despite his confessed anxieties, in his next letter to his friend he said the subject was 'most promising . . . It is [a] canal, and full of the bustle incident to such a scene where four or five boats are passing with dogs, horses, boys, & men & women & children, and best of all old timber-props, water plants, willow stumps, sedges, old nets, &c&c&c.' But it didn't come easy. He was distracted by some portrait work: a group picture of the Lambert family of Woodmansterne, near Croydon, friends of the Bicknells. Then he didn't have a great deal of stuff in his store for this particular spot on the Stour, the so-called canal, and depended much on memories of the towpath along which he had walked to school in Dedham.[1]

The scene was at the Float Jump, where a low wooden barrier across the towpath kept cattle from getting by and the horses, which towed the barges, could be jumped over it. The artist looked from the south, on the land side of the river bank and a sluice which connected a field to the river; Flatford was well downstream to the right. A barge was being poled across the river to collect its horse. The first study shows a horse standing at the barrier. The second shows a riderless horse vaulting the Jump. The large oil sketch shows a youthful rider hanging on tight as the horse leaps over the Jump like a hunter or cavalry charger. Between the oil sketch and the exhibited painting there were further changes: a barge whose prow had just entered the picture in the sketch has passed by downstream; the first barge has sprouted a mast, with a sail ready for hoisting. The lad riding the horse is dressed distinctly in waistcoat and hat. A bent and pollarded willow on the near bank has been slightly straightened and moved from in front of the horse to behind it, removing the sense that it is getting in the way of the leap. Dedham church is at the right-hand edge of the painting, though it wouldn't have been visible from this angle. In all the pictures – studies, full-size sketch and finished piece – there is an excitement that mounts. In the first study it is evident in the vigorous pen work. In the second it is made clear in the turmoil of clouds and the upward thrust of the horse. Most suggestive of movement is the big oil sketch, with its cloud-dark, windy sky. But on this occasion one can approve the finished painting most (it isn't too finished). The jumble of matter on the river bank in the foreground – old timbers, the little bridge carrying the towpath over the sluice-gate, an eel trap, a net, a moorhen flapping frightened from its nest, various plants and weeds – were all detailed in a letter he wrote to a possible buyer later in the year. The moorhen, based on a Johnny Dunthorne sketch, was a late addition. As he drove the paint on to the canvas, he gave the impression that more senses were involved than just his sight: he could hear the Stour water splashing through the sluice and the wind stirring the willows; he could smell the mud and slime on the banks.[2] Nevertheless, he wasn't satisfied with it. It was a rush to get it to Somerset House; the painting should have stayed in his painting room several weeks longer; and after it had been sent in he wrote to Fisher, 'No one picture ever departed from my easil with more anxiety . . . ' Possibly its incompletion was part of its success.

Fisher was told Constable's news: 'My wife and I are going to *exhibit* at the same time.' But Maria beat him to it; her creation was indeed premature. Emily Constable was born at 10 p.m. on 29 March, the same date on which Charles Golding, her second brother, had been born four years before.³ It indicated a regularity in their marital getting-togethers in early summers, despite her frailty. Maria wasn't at all well during the later stages of the pregnancy, and she seemed knocked about by the birth of her fifth child. Afterwards she managed to breastfeed the baby but, Constable reported to Fisher, 'is in a sad weak condition – and we are obliged to watch her carefully'. Emily was to be also known as Emma, sometimes spelled Ema, and she figured in a sweet undated drawing Constable later did of her leaning over the arm of an elegant chair, looking up at the artist, her father, with large sad eyes.

Despite Mr Pulham's prognosis, there was no test of his reputation in the Academy elections that year: no member had vacated his seat, so there was no vote. There was also no sign of Fisher's hope being fulfilled that Constable's gold medal from France would cause 'the stupid English public' to think there was something in him. But Constable remained grateful for Fisher's 'early notice' and 'friendship in my obscurity'. He was sure 'My reputation at home among my brother artists [is] dayly gaining ground, & I deeply feel the honour of having found an original style & independent of him who would be Lord over all – I mean Turner . . .' (How Turner felt about Constable was kept, as was his way, well hidden.) Constable showed three paintings (including *The Leaping Horse*) at the Academy exhibition, which were generally admired; the *Morning Chronicle* mentioned 'the pleasing peculiarities of this artist's style'. The diarist Henry Crabb Robinson thought Turner's *Dieppe* magnificent but could 'understand why such artists as Constable and Collins are preferred' – even in a compliment, being linked with Collins would not have pleased Constable.⁴ The other two RA paintings were of Hampstead – views of Branch Hill Pond and Child's Hill – and were bought by the iron manufacturer Francis Darby after another purchaser backed out following 'serious losses in India'. Darby's father had built the celebrated Iron Bridge over the Severn at Coalbrookdale. Darby paid Constable 130 guineas for the Hampstead pair, getting a twenty-guinea discount on the asking price because Constable 'felt flattered that an application should be made to me from an entire stranger . . . for the pictures' sake alone'.⁵ With Johnny Dunthorne at hand to help,

Constable then set about making two sets of copies of the Hampstead paintings – one set for Charles Schroth in Paris, one for Darby.

Although *The Leaping Horse* found no purchaser in Constable's lifetime, the year became a good one for Constable. The French Embassy had handed him his gold medal in early April. Schroth had ordered three more paintings for his gallery and the reception they received was – Schroth thought – even warmer than that given Constable's pictures in the Louvre. A letter telling Constable about this arrived courtesy of Delacroix. Firmin Didot, a Parisian printer from the rue Jacob who was introduced by Arrowsmith, also ordered three, and Arrowsmith two more. 'These all make income,' Constable told Fisher, happily. In August he sent *The White Horse* and another painting to the Musée Royale in Lille; dear obliging Fisher had lent his prized picture for a show that year at the British Institution and perhaps expected its immediate return, but Constable sent it off to Flanders without asking. On 10 September he craved Fisher's forgiveness for this but assumed he would be glad *The White Horse* was to be seen by the art lovers of Lille in company with portraits by Sir Thomas Lawrence. One of Constable's worries hadn't been about himself or his family but the health of his old patron Bishop Fisher. The Bishop got 'cold in his loins' out riding in the sharp easterly winds of early April and died a month later. His cheerful demands for brighter skies over his cathedral were gone for ever.

Maria and the children were once again sent off to Hampstead for the summer, but it doesn't seem to have helped either Maria or Constable. He drew her around this time, her face looking rather unhealthily swollen. He complained to Fisher at the end of their stay, 'Hampstead is a wretched place – so expensive – and as it was so near I made my home at neither place – I was between two chairs – & could do nothing.' He wrote to Francis Darby, 'Could I divest myself of anxiety of mind I should never ail anything. My life is a struggle between my "social affections" and my "love of art"'. He recalled Lord Bacon's remark that 'single men are the best servants of the publick'. He – Constable – had a wife in delicate health and five small children. 'I am not happy apart from them even for a few days, or hours, and the summer months separate us too much, and disturb my quiet habits at my easil.' Fisher had come to a similar diagnosis and wrote, 'Whatever you do, Constable, get thee rid of anxiety. It hurts the stomach more than arsenic. It generates only fresh cause for anxiety, by producing inaction and loss of time.' Constable acted. On 31 August he moved his family down to Brighton. They stayed first in Russell Square, an enclave of two-storey terraced houses with a central garden, a short block from the seafront, and then moved to Canne Street in December.[6]

In Charlotte Street Constable resumed his journal for Maria. What he had had for dinner, visitors from Flatford, painting matters, their wedding anniversary, the cats and the hens. Master Billy had been pestering the goldfish, putting his paw in their bowl and frightening them, but next day was himself severely alarmed by the crowing of the cock. Friday 16 September was headlined by the journal writer '*A Grand Epoch*':

> This morning was ushered by a prodigious battle with the fowls in the garden – the black hen making a great to-do & cackling – the cock strutting about and crowing – and Billy looking at them in great astonishment from the back kitchen window. When all was quiet I looked into the brew house & saw her on the nest which I had made, and at breakfast – Elizabeth [Sarah's replacement as maid] brought me in a beautifull egg – probably the first hen's egg ever laid on the premises.
>
> How much we have changed the circumstances of this house from what it was in Mr Farrington's time – his attics turned into nurseries – a beautifull baby born in his bedroom – his washhouse, turned into a brew house – his back parlor, which contained all his prints, turned into a bed room – his painting room, made habitable – besides, which is best of all, made to produce better pictures than he could make . . .

And the contented householder congratulated Maria and himself on their domestic achievement before describing further antics of the cats, and an errand he had run on behalf of the AGBI to take £4 to an artist's widow. He was still looking after 'old Fontaine' from time to time and sending on to him donations from other people 'so that he is almost out of the difficulties, having paid all his rent, and got many things out of pawn'. When the Constables' milkman lost one of his cows, Constable lent him £10, to be repaid when he could afford it.

His own financial condition wasn't prosperous but (he told Fisher in September) wasn't worse than usual. It was the year of a London banking crisis. Confidence had collapsed after a surge of reckless promotion of new companies, including one which was going to drain the Red Sea and find treasure left by the Old Testament Jews when fleeing Egypt.[7] Given the shaky times, 'not worse than usual' wasn't bad. Abram – though suffering losses of his own – was sending him £400 from the family business, and Constable meant to invest half of this in government funds in Maria's name. Back at his easel in Charlotte Street he felt that 'after 20 years hard uphill work' he had at last 'got the publick into my hands – and want not a patron'. Sir George Beaumont called in mid-September to look at his new paintings and tried to put the clock back; Constable told Maria that Sir George still wanted him 'to imitate pictures'. But Constable had commissions enough, including one to alter his small version of *Salisbury Cathedral* for the late Bishop's daughter Mrs Elizabeth Mirehouse, a painting of Hampstead Heath for a Mr Ripley and a version of *The Lock* for James Carpenter. He needed Johnny Dunthorne on hand to help for several months. Johnny came willingly and this time was boarded out with a local handyman called Ambrose, originally from Suffolk; Constable apparently wanted to spare the shy country boy the dangers of proximity to his maid Elizabeth. Johnny was invaluable, cleaning pictures, running messages, putting portfolios in order and working on a model boat for Charley. While Constable painted one copy of Mr Morrison's *Lock*, Johnny was at his side painting another copy. Johnny also helped with the outline of *Waterloo Bridge*, which was underway again, on and off, later in the year and which Constable hoped to have ready for the next show at Somerset House. Stothard, unlike Sir George a critic Constable listened to, came to see it and suggested an alteration of some sort that Constable called 'very capital'.

By the end of 1825 the commissioned works in progress amounted to £400 and Constable told Fisher 'four months will do them – God will help those who help themselves'. Self-help was again necessary because his French connections had gone awry. In mid-November Arrowsmith had turned up in Charlotte Street to find out about several pictures he had ordered from Constable; he had a friend in tow, an 'amateur'. Both artist and dealer were on edge. Arrowsmith was having money problems. Constable had just heard from Tinney that he would not lend *Stratford Mill* for an exhibition in Edinburgh and this irked the painter. Now, Arrowsmith wanted quick delivery of the paintings he had commissioned. His friend, the dreaded amateur, stood by witnessing the scene, along with Johnny Dunthorne and his father who was in town visiting his son. According to Constable, in a letter to Fisher, the French dealer was 'so excessively impertinent and used such language as never was used to me at my easil before'. Constable flew off the handle, startling Arrowsmith. The Frenchman backed down and apologised. Constable said he couldn't accept an apology. Arrowsmith departed with his friend, telling Johnny Dunthorne that he would gladly have given a hundred pounds to have avoided this scene.

Constable then wrote to Arrowsmith formally withdrawing from their arrangements and sent a draft of £40 for the amount he owed the dealer. Arrowsmith replied acknowledging that he alone was the sufferer. Constable said he would forget the affair; he left it to Arrowsmith to order or not order any more pictures. However, Arrowsmith was on the slide – bankruptcy was in the offing – and there would be no more orders. Charles Schroth also went under in mid-1826, forced to unload paintings at knock-down prices. Fisher thought Constable had let his impetuousness and paranoia get the better of him. He wrote: 'We are all given to torment ourselves with imaginary evils – but no man had ever this disease in such alarming paroxysms as yourself. You imagine difficulties where none exist, displeasure where none is felt, contempt where none is shown and neglect where none is meant.' Fisher could see that Constable might have some cause in the Arrowsmith dispute, but 'poor Tinney' was merely trying to achieve the return of something that he had paid for. He 'had rather see his picture on his own walls than hear of it in Edinburgh . . . He says you are a devilish odd fellow. For you get your bread by painting. – He orders two pictures[,] leaves the subjects to yourself; offers ready money & you declare off for no intelligible reason.'

Constable replied that Fisher's letter had done him good, but he was evidently still sure of his own case:

> It is easy for a bye stander like you to watch one struggling in the water and then say your difficulties are only imaginary. I have a great part to perform & you a much greater, but with only this difference. You are removed from the ills of life – you are almost placed beyond circumstances. My master the publick is hard, cruel, & unrelenting, making no allowance for a backsliding . . . Your own profession closes in and protects you, mine rejoices in the opportunity of ridding itself of a member who is sure to be in somebodys way or other.
>
> I have related no imaginary ills to you – to one so deeply involved in active life as I am they are realities . . . I live by shadows, to me shadows are realities . . . I am so engaged that Johny [*sic*] and I cant give up. I am in for a winters campaign.

Constable said that Johnny 'doated' on him. The young man was 'calm – gentle – clever – & industrious, full of prudence – & free from vice. He is greived at his master having so much of the devil about him.' Constable was, however, cheered by a visit from the actor Jack Bannister, who wanted to commission a Constable landscape. Encountering the artist at his door as he let out two chimney sweeps, Bannister – never lost for a wisecrack – exclaimed, 'What – brother brush!'[8]

He was off to Brighton over the Christmas season to be with Maria and the children. On New Year's Day he walked down to the beach and sat painting an oil sketch of the Channel, noting on the back of the picture: 'From 12 till 2 p.m. Fresh breeze from S.S.W.' He also painted Perne's Mill, at Gillingham, Dorset, which a local woman had been requesting since the summer of 1824. While he was at his easel

Maria read aloud from Nicolas Poussin's letters, recently redis-
covered and published in Paris. Maria was amused to find that
painters then and now had much in common: 'The letters are
apologies to friends for not doing their pictures sooner – anxieties of
all kinds, insults – from ignorance.'

It was very cold when he got back to London on 12 January. The
Thames was frozen over; his pictures, returned from Lille, were stuck
on a ship moored in the river. His sister Mary sent some fowls from
Flatford and Constable told Maria he would send them on to her in
Brighton – they would keep in this weather. Another gold medal had
been awarded to him in Lille and the painter of *The White Horse* was
lauded in the prefect's discourse. Constable tried to make things
right with Fisher, the absentee owner, by telling him, '*All* things
considered, the gold medal should be yours.' Fisher was probably
more pleased to hear that his picture was in perfect shape, 'without a
speck of injury'. But then Constable, unlike some of his famous
contemporaries, was technically an extremely sound painter whose
works stood up to time.[9] (Dunthorne Senior's early practice with him
must have helped.) Although he had told Fisher six weeks before that
*Waterloo Bridge* would be 'done for the next exhibition', and shortly
thereafter this said it was sticking to him 'like a blister' and disturbing
his sleep, he had to drop the painting from his campaign. He needed
to get on with pictures that might produce more immediate profit.

Sir Thomas Lawrence, the President of the Academy, came in
January to look at his works and, standing before the *Waterloo Bridge*,
pleased Constable by saying he had never admired his pictures so
much. This compliment evaporated quickly; when the Academy
elections took place on 10 February, Constable again got very few
votes. A consolation was that his younger friend Charles Leslie took
one of the two seats for painters and became a full Academician. But
Constable was used to disappointment in regard to Somerset House,
and as always ploughed on. Once more he heeded his own atavistic
affections, and Farington's ideas of how he should find popularity,
with a large upright of his old local scenery. *Waterloo Bridge* was put

aside (he claimed he did this partly because of 'the ruined state of my finances'). At the beginning of March his Brighton friend Henry Phillips, the botanist, provided some natural history for the new picture: 'I think it is July in your green lane. At this season all the tall grasses are in flower, bogrush, bullrush, teasel. The white bindweed now hangs in flowers over the branches of the hedge; the wild carrot and hemlock flower in banks of hedges, cow parsley, water plantain, &c.; . . . bramble is now in flower, poppy, mallow, thistle, hop, &c..' What was to be *The Cornfield* slowly came into existence, absorbing him completely. He told Fisher on 8 April, 'I could think of and speak to no one. I was like a friend of mine in the battle of Waterloo – he said he dared not turn his head to the right or left – but always kept it straight forward – thinking of himself alone.' The painting was roughly the size of *The Lock*, though 'a subject of a very different nature – inland – cornfields – a close lane, kind of thing – but it is not neglected in any part. The trees are more than usually studied and the extremities well defined – as well as their species – they are shaken by a pleasant and healthfull breeze.' And he quoted, more or less, from Thomson's *The Seasons*: 'while now a fresher gale, *sweeping with shadowy gust the feilds of corn* &c., &c.'[10]

The lane was Fen Lane. He had walked or run down it as a boy – the quickest way from East Bergholt to the river. He had sketches for it at hand, and pictures of it in his head. Whether he himself had ever lain prone on the dry summer ground and drunk from the cool spring, who knows? The boy doing so in the painting, while his dog paused, was perhaps a sentimental touch but he couldn't resist it; for a while he called the picture 'The Drinking Boy'.[11] The boy has taken off his hat to drink. He has a blue kerchief tied around his neck and wears a red waistcoat. He looks like a slightly younger version of the youth on *The Leaping Horse*. When he sent the painting to Somerset House it was entitled, in his usual way, *Landscape* and became *Landscape: Noon* for the British Institution (but people took to calling it *The Cornfield*, and that it became after 1838). Constable confessed to Fisher his hopes of selling it: 'It has certainly got a little more eye-salve than I usually condescend to give to them.' (His son Charles Golding Constable later remarked that the little church in the distance never existed and was put there by 'painter's license'.)[12] Constable worked at the Academy on at least one of the varnishing days. The sculptor Chantrey was as always prowling around and, noticing the dark shadows under the tails of the sheep, said in his usual jokey way, 'Why Constable, all your sheep have got the rot – give me the palette – I must cure them.' Chantrey's efforts made matters worse; he threw the palette rag at Constable and departed.[13] Constable himself remained in a good humour; he thought the exhibition that year was 'delightful'. He told Fisher, 'Turner never gave me so much pleasure – and so much pain – before.' Turner was showing four works, including the impressive *Forum Romanum* painted for Sir John Soane. His pain-provoking problem, according to the critics, was too much yellow. About this Constable noted generously, 'But every man who distinguishes himself in a great way, is on a precipice.'

*The Cornfield* was admired. Although it didn't find a purchaser then and there, it opened the gate through which a great number of people were to pass into Constable's country. *The Times* liked his *Gillingham Mill* as well, but thought *The Cornfield* 'singularly beautiful, and not inferior to some of Hobbema's most admired works'. Robert Hunt in *The Examiner* said, 'Mr Constable is not so potent a genius [as Turner]; but in the rural walk in which he has moved, he is one of the most natural Painters of his time . . . He has been faithful to his first love, Nature, from the commencement of his career. He is a chaste Painter, and goes hand in hand with her alone . . .' In 1850 Thackeray talked of *The Cornfield* as a piece which seemed to be 'under the influence of a late shower; the shrubs, trees and distance are saturated with it . . . One cannot but admire the manner in which the specific character of every object is made out: the undulations of the ripe corn, the chequered light on the road; the freshness of the banks, the trees and their leafage, the brilliant clouds artfully contrasted against the trees, and here and there broken by azure.'[14] As noted, corn was the term at the time for any cereal crop, but this looks like wheat, a thick golden carpet on the slope of the field, framed by trees and hedges and the river meadow beyond. The open gate reveals the lush crop growing nearly to the height of the gateposts.

The radiant field was a symbol of peace and fertility, an image of what fed people. But it was also a painting of money in the bank. Since Charles II's reign, for well over a century, the import of corn had been restricted, with bounties to encourage exports, and this had made for good times for farmers, landowners and grain dealers such as Abram. The long war with France caused further restrictions. The price of wheat rose 300 per cent in twenty years, and the poor, who depended largely on bread, suffered greatly. When peace came in 1815 corn prices began to fall, so more laws were introduced to keep out imports, prop up prices and restore the incomes of the 'landed interest'. This happened despite the complaints of consumers, particularly poor country folk, and the vehement opposition of townspeople, high and low.[15]

Constable was in East Bergholt unexpectedly in April. His sister Mary had written to say that Abram was very ill – would he come down? Mr Travis had called and found the patient in a profuse perspiration and eating nothing, though with a clear mind. Abram's staff had rallied round and Mary added the news which had much cheered Abram: 'Flour rose 5d. per sack to day which he likes to hear rather than the reverse.' In the village Constable spent three days with his brother and sister at Flatford Mill, and this gave him time to walk the river banks and along Fen Lane. On his return to town he wrote to Fisher that he had lately been in Suffolk and 'had some delightfull walks in the same fields'. Abram seemed better when Constable left East Bergholt, but he then had a week's relapse with chills and fever. Later, in the autumn, he wrote to thank John for having cheered him up in his illness: 'for sure I am you must have anxiety & care enough of your own, but your own vigour of intellect & energy of body has hitherto, aided by the Divine blessing, carried you through.' Hitherto, and for a while yet.

# 13. *Life Slips (1826–28)*

On 11 June 1826 John Constable turned fifty. If he had drawn up a balance sheet of his life to that date, he might have considered such 'same fields' paintings as *The Leaping Horse* and *The Cornfield* – and the deep commitment to landscape they represented – as making up for a great deal of disappointment. He was still not a full member of the Academy, though his five children, brought forth by Maria at a cost yet to be fully measured, continued to prove a splendid compensation for the slings and arrows of the art world. In mid-May, while Maria (pregnant again) was in Putney with Minna, staying with her sister Louisa, he wrote his wife a journal-like letter in which the other young Constables figured often along with other news – of Dr Gooch's poor health, a supper dance at the Chalons, and Charley's toothache, 'which hurts his nights'. On 24 May Mrs Roberts was still asleep when Constable wrote: 'Got up quite early to write to you before 8 – Saw the children at 7 – Emily's eyes were open & she was smiling – Isabel sitting up in her crib & saying, come here papa – & Charley was kneeling up in his bed which was full of things – cheifly boats . . .' A week earlier Constable's temper had been tested when one of the boys put a broom handle through a painting, but he was rarely cross with his children.[1]

Although he intended them all to stay in Charlotte Street during the summer, saving money by not paying 'for the privilege of sleeping in a hen-coop for the sake of country air', Maria's health made him change his mind. Brighton was again considered – Maria's father, now seventy-four, was convalescing there after an attack of apoplexy – but Constable decided to try Hampstead once more. He found a small house on Downshire Hill, half of a double house known as Langham Place, and 'an easy walk from Charlotte Street'.[2] He told Fisher about this and chided him for not keeping in touch: 'You once said "life is short," let us make the most of friendship while we can.' Constable also wanted to know what Fisher thought of an invitation he had received from Henry Phillips to contribute a paper on art to a literary journal Phillips was starting. Fisher was busy with ecclesiastical duties which he compared with Constable's exertions leading up to the annual RA exhibition, and he was anxious about the 'disturbance in the currency' that was rattling the country. But he replied at the end of September:

> I am doubtful about your Brighton Gazette. You are in possession of some very valuable and original matter on the subject of painting . . . I should be very sad to see this seed sown on an unvisited field . . . Throw your thoughts together, as they arise in a book (that they be not lost); when I come to see you, we will look them over, put them into shape, and do something with them . . . Set about it immediately. Life slips. It will perhaps bring your children in £100 in a day of short commons, if it does nothing else. Besides, I have been all along desirous of writing your life & rise in the art.

Constable went on painting through the late stages of Maria's next pregnancy, though a trip to Brighton had to be made to pick up young John from school. From there Constable wrote as if with hope to Maria in Hampstead, 'This is certainly a wonderfull place for setting people up – making the well, better – & the ill, well, so so . . . Old Neptune gets all the Ladies with child – for we can hardly lay it to the men which we see pulled & led about the beach here.' Maria presumably charged her husband rather than the sea god with her own condition and seems to have been fatalistic about it. Perhaps both she and her husband felt that the life-urge redressed the doom impending; they needed to create new life where for her it was beginning to slip away. But at his easel Constable could more or less shut out the world and its anxieties, particularly Maria's sickness, whooping cough

*The Hay Wain* (detail)

*Golding Constable's Kitchen Garden*

*The Road to the Spaniards*

*East Bergholt Fair*

*Maria Constable &*
*two of her children*
(detail)

*View of Dedham from Gun Hill*

*Hadleigh Castle*

*Fen Lane*

*Study of Cumulus Clouds*

*The Leaping Horse* (detail)

*Salisbury Cathedral* (from the south-west)

*Brighton Beach and Colliers*

*The Skylark*

*View of London from Hampstead*

*A Country Lane* ('Stoke by Nayland')

among the children, and his declining father-in-law continuing to complain about being hard up and having made many bad loans. ('It is his fate to be devoured by strangers', Constable told Fisher on 9 September.) The brush in his hand, the palette and canvas before him, created their own concerns, their need for solutions in terms of colour and form and light, brush stroke by brush stroke. In front of the easel he was in a bubble which lasted happily or unhappily as long as his concentration and physical energy. Painting was always hard physical work; he ended the day with weak arms and dirty fingers.

The Constables' sixth child, and third son, was born just after breakfast on 14 November 1826, 'a month before time'. The infant was christened Alfred Abram Constable; his godparents – among them two cousins – were Colonel Richard Gubbins and Mr and Mrs Lionel South. Maria had difficulty nursing the baby owing to her 'extream weakness', as he told his sister Ann just before Christmas, though Alfred was 'as pretty a little fellow as ever was seen'. Constable seems finally to have realised that children cost money; more children meant more expenditure. He wrote to Fisher about his increased progeny: 'It is an awfull concern – and the reflection of what may be the consequences both to them and myself makes no small inroad into that abstractedness, which had hitherto been devoted to painting only. But I am willing to consider them as blessings – only that I am now satisfied and think my quiver full enough.' If only he would follow those words with resolution!

The arrival of the new child determined Constable to find a permanent Hampstead home for his brood. His idea was 'to prevent if possible the sad rambling life which my married life has been, flying from London to seek health in the country'. He kept the lower part of his Charlotte Street house including the painting room and sub-let the top part to Mr Sykes, an 'agreeable' dancing teacher, and his wife. He told Fisher: 'I am three miles from door to door . . . & I can get always away from idle callers – and above all see nature – & unite a town & country life.' In the summer of 1827 he found what he had been looking for, a terraced house in Well Walk, Hampstead; it was on four floors with the kitchen in the cellar, cost one pound a week in rent, and was close to the Heath in one direction and to the centre of the village in the other. A supposedly health-giving chalybeate well was just across the road. Hampstead waters had brought the place to prominence as a spa in the previous century. The metallic-tasting water had iron-bearing properties; it was dispensed in a pump room and sold bottled at two inns, the Lower Flask and Upper Flask, and the retail price in the City of London was threepence per flask. (The water was declared undrinkable in 1903.)[3] Begging a loan from Fisher to help pay for moving-in expenses and workmen's bills, Constable described the house as 'to my wife's heart's content – it is situate on the eminence at the back of the spot in which you saw us – and our little drawing room commands a view unequalled in Europe – from Westminster Abbey to Gravesend. The <u>dome</u> of <u>St. Paul's</u> in the air, realizes Michael Angelo's idea on seeing that of the Pantheon – "I will build such a thing in the sky." ' Fisher was also hard-stretched at the time but exerted himself to find £30 to send Constable.

A large chunk of Constable's past had fallen away in early February 1827. Sir George Beaumont – 'the leader of Taste' – had died. Constable wrote to Wordsworth nine years later to say of Sir George, 'I feel that I am indebted to him for what I am as an artist.' He always remembered his first meeting with Sir George in Dedham in the mid-1790s and was grateful for the consequent instruction by way of Claude and Wilson, Girtin and Cozens, and Sir Joshua's *Discourses* that gave him a foundation on which to build his own natural painture. Moreover, even if he hadn't observed Sir George's 'Rules', he would never forget them – that in every landscape there should be at least one brown tree; and that every picture should have a first, second and third light. Sir George had once looked at a Constable painting and said, in his headmasterly fashion, 'I see your first and second lights, but I can't make out which is the third.'[4]

Alfred's whooping cough – a dreadful echo of his mother's – dominated the domestic scene in April. The doctors called frequently but couldn't cure it. Constable's sister Martha wrote from Dedham with a belated home remedy and the assurance that time would fix Alfred's cough. Constable kept on working, particularly on a Brighton beach scene showing the new Chain Pier, opened in 1823. This 'dandy jetty' as he had called it gave him some problems; the pier was too short so he decided to lengthen it; a sail on a boat had to be painted out to accommodate the new pier end; a boat being hauled up on the beach was deleted altogether. He finished the picture in time for the Academy exhibition. Fisher came to Hampstead the day before Constable sent it in and thought the painting 'most beautifully executed', so much so that 'Turner, Callcott, and Collins will not like it'. In *The Chain Pier, Brighton* one was aware of an onshore breeze, small combers crunching the shingle, a bright sun streaming down through a procession of woolly clouds, the smell of salt in the sea-damp air. But whatever the thoughts of his fellow artists and competitors, Constable failed to unload it. He wrote to Fisher: 'My Brighton was admired – "*on the walls*," – and I had a few nibbles out of doors. I had one letter (from a man of rank) inquiring what would be its "*selling*" price. Is not this too bad – but that comes of the bartering at the Gallery . . .' The press was mixed. *The Times* thought it one of Constable's best: 'He is unquestionably the first landscape painter of the day, and yet we are told his pictures do not sell. He accounts for this by stating that he prefers studying nature as she presents herself to his eyes rather than as she is represented in old pictures . . .' But *The New Monthly Magazine* declared that Constable's 'usual freshness of colouring, and crispness and spirit of touch' were out of place in a non-rural subject, and the *Morning Post* thought it looked as though streaks of ink had been dashed across it. His other two RA exhibits were *Gillingham Mill*, with much brilliantly observed vegetation on the nearside of a foaming millstream, and a *Hampstead Heath*.[5] This was the year Johnny Dunthorne exhibited for the first time at Somerset House with an early-Constable-like subject, *A Glade in a Wood*. Constable must have felt some vicarious pride.

It was also the summer in which George Canning, the Prime Minister, got Britain together with Russia and France in the Treaty of London to prevent the extermination of the Greeks by the Turks and Egyptians. And it was the summer in which William Blake – poet, painter, prophet – died. Constable was concerned about Blake's widow and wrote to John Linnell that the AGBI would act at once if the situation were urgent. In early September the Constables' Well Walk neighbour the comic actor Jack Bannister came to dinner. Constable had described Bannister to John Fisher as 'a very fine creature . . . very sensible, natural, and a gentleman'. The actor enjoyed Constable's paintings (he bought one of Branch Hill Pond) and Lady Dysart's venison. A great lover of puns, he had been a student at the Royal Academy and a pupil of de Loutherbourg when that artist – whom he nicknamed Lantern-bag or Leatherbag – was a scene painter at Drury Lane. Later, Bannister modelled for the figure of Sterne's Uncle Toby in Charles Leslie's *Uncle Toby and the Widow Wadman*. Constable seems to have shared the feeling expressed by William Hazlitt, when Bannister quit the stage in 1815, of a sense of the personal intimacy one feels with actors: 'We greet them on the stage; we like to meet them in the streets; they almost always recall to us pleasant associations.' But Leslie noted that although 'few persons more thoroughly relished good acting than did Constable', he seldom visited a theatre. On one occasion when he did, the machinery lowering the actor playing the ghost of Hamlet's father got stuck, and then was suddenly released, to much applause. Constable told the story to a neighbour named Pope, who said that he too would never forget it; he was the ghost.[6]

In October he decided it had been too long since his last real holiday in East Bergholt – nine years – and he wanted to fix the place in the heads and hearts of his children. Johnny Dunthorne was also in Suffolk, painting a portrait. But this time brother Abram took some convincing. He wrote to Constable at the end of September to say that he thought Flatford at this season a dangerous place for the young ones: 'It would be impossible to enjoy your company, as your mind would be absorb'd & engross'd with the children and their safety.' Abram clearly knew John was a worrier, but on this occasion he didn't change Constable's mind. Constable took only the two oldest, John Charles and Minna, and this perhaps caused a smaller impact on the solely adult household of Abram and Mary at Flatford Mill. In any event, the children at once made a good impression. Mrs Godfrey,

A barge on the Stour

wife of the squire, was much taken with them. The elderly widow Mrs
Hart, to whom Constable had given small sums for some years, was
the grateful recipient of his charity on this occasion by way of John
Charles. The locals were keen to see the fourth generation of the
family in East Bergholt: 'All heads are out of the doors & windows,'
Constable wrote proudly to Maria, telling her the children were
acclaimed as 'the best behaved ever'. Captain Bowen, a neighbour,
gave Minna a rose and young John a bunch of grapes. Brother and
sister were most entranced by the river. John Charles caught six fish
one day and ten the next, some of which they had for dinner. Minna
caught two.

    Minna must have thought the Stour valley was going to be a wild
place. When the Ipswich coach crossed Stratford St Mary bridge her
father had said, 'Now we are in Suffolk,' and she replied, 'Oh no, this
is only fields.' She found Suffolk at first 'very like Hampstead',
though she felt the blackberries here were better. The children were
kept busy calling on friends and relatives. Young John had ridden on

horseback to his uncle Golding's newly purchased small farmhouse, opposite the windmill, 'a sad tumble down place & very old', that Golding called the Pie's Nest.

Constable when relating to Maria the doings of the children didn't neglect any local gossip he thought might interest her, such as the bilious attack suffered by Mr Travis and the wedding in Dedham of 'Miss Bell & a Mr Spink a horse surgeon – God knows who they are – but the bells rang all day'. He would have news for Lady Dysart, too, about 'Mr Fitzgerald who has certainly behaved ill to Golding', by trying to get his hands on Old Hall Wood. When he was with his brother Golding, or writing to him, Constable sometimes fell into local patois or the sort of language brothers can use to one another: Bergholt was 'Bargell' and a bedbug-free bed was 'free from the buggery'.[7]

Constable appeared to relish telling Maria of the presents Minna and he had for her; his was 'a little pretty box for you for needles'. Perhaps he felt he had to tell her now about the gift; he didn't dare wait. But as though to show him there was nothing to fear, Maria went to church on Sunday 11 October ('I know you will *scold*') and paid for it by spending all next day in bed. She was again seven months pregnant. He couldn't stop getting her with child. She wrote to him that there had been a burglary in Downshire Hill (silver spoons, taken by a man dressed as a former sailor, selling pencils – he was nabbed for the theft). There had also been a delivery of coal Constable had forgotten to warn her of and – oh yes – old Mr Stothard had called, unexpectedly.

On his return, there was something to pay for the pleasures of the holiday. Constable was, or felt, broke. He was very down, as he often was when he got back home. He had sent *The Cornfield* to the Louvre to show at the salon, but there was no great acclaim this time, and no Arrowsmiths or Schroths came forward to buy it. Writing to Golding he said he envied him his sequestered life. Well Walk, though providing a comfortable house, was not living up to its name. When he, John and Minna got back from East Bergholt, Maria had been sure she would be 'quite well & happy'. The birth of Lionel Bicknell Constable, their seventh child, at 4.45 p.m. on 2 January 1828 at first produced no complications. Constable exulted to Fisher on 'the birth of a lovely boy' and wrote to Leslie that Maria 'goes on nursing famously, and went to church this morning'. On 23 February Henry Greswolde Lewis of Malvern Hall sent a game pie – a typical Dysart gift – and his hopes both that 'Mrs Constable will find it to her palette [*sic*]' and, unrelatedly, that Constable 'will be the British Claude in after time'.[8] But any reinvigorating effect of the birth was of short duration. Another letter to Leslie in early February remarked on Maria's most delicate condition; by spring Leslie was fully aware of Constable's alarm. Constable wrote to Samuel Lane: 'My poor wife is still very ill at Putney, and when I can get her home I know not. We talk of Brighton, but we only talk of it. She can't make such a journey. I am glad to remain quiet at my work, as I want to rid my mind of some troublesome jobs.'[9]

To add to his gloom *The Chain Pier, Brighton* – though hung prominently at the British Institution along with Bonington and Delacroix – got some harsh notices. The critic for the *London Magazine* said that under it might be written,

> '*Nature done in white lead, opal, or prussian blue.*' The end is perfectly answered; why the means should be obtruded as an eye-sore, we do not understand. It is like keeping up the scaffolding, after the house is built. It is evident that Mr Constable's landscapes are *like* nature; it is still more evident that they *are* paint. There is no attempt made to conceal art. It is a love of the material vehicle, or a pride in slovenliness and crudity, as the indispensable characteristics of national art; as some orators retain their provincial dialect, not to seem affected.[10]

Constable wasn't above lobbying this year at the Academy. John Flaxman had died, making a vacancy among the RAs. Constable went through the necessary motions and called on a number of the members, urging nothing (he said) but showing only his 'long face'. He wrote to both Charles Leslie and Thomas Phillips, hoping for support. As for Turner, Constable told Leslie, 'My call on him was quite amusing. He held his hands down by his sides – looked me full in the face (his head on one side) – smiled and shook his head & asked me what I wanted, *angry* that I called on a Monday afternoon. He asked me if I had not a "neighbour at Hampstead who could help me" – Collins. I told him we were no longer intimate & I know *nothing about him* – he then held fast the door . . .' After this Turner 'went growling to Chantrey.'\* Stothard and Leslie were firm Constable supporters but Phillips seemed to hold Constable's French fame against him. With most members Constable was still 'only' a landscape painter. William Etty, his main rival, was elected by a clear majority.[11]

While worrying about Maria, Constable went on with his paintings for the exhibition in May: two landscapes, one of Dedham Vale, the other of Hampstead Heath. His twin poles, you might say. The former showed the bridge at Stratford St Mary in the middle distance with some gypsies camped inconspicuously in the foreground; it conveyed a quiet tribute to Sir George Beaumont, whose *Hagar* had helped inspire his original *Dedham Vale* of 1802. In one respect, the Constables' lives were suddenly made easier. On 9 March Maria's father died, aged seventy-six. Charles Bicknell had resigned his post at the Admiralty in early January when his health finally collapsed and thereafter he appeared doomed, though in no great pain. Despite a long history of complaints about his straitened circumstances, the lawyer of Spring Gardens left a tidy fortune to his three surviving children: Sarah Fletcher, a daughter from his first marriage, and Maria and Louisa, the remaining children of the five from his second. Mrs Fletcher, previously widowed, had inherited a large amount from her first husband, Mr Skey, so the bulk of the estate was divided between Maria and Louisa, some £20,000 each.

Joy was not confined. Nor was this so only among the immediate beneficiaries. Abram wrote from Flatford on hearing the news, surprised by 'the extent of Mr B's property'. He was thankful that John was 'thus put into possession of the means of bringing up your family as you could wish'. (By the law of the day, a married woman's

---

\*Constable didn't like Turner's white-eyed glare or 'the shake of his head' and obviously didn't expect Turner's backing.

property was her husband's.) The benefaction was particularly welcome because the Constable businesses were going through a bad patch and Abram hadn't been able to send out the usual payments to his brothers and sisters. They were all thrilled at the Bicknell bequest. So was John Dunthorne Senior. 'How happy I have made old Mr D by telling them of your good fortune,' reported Abram. The word spread quickly around East Bergholt. Mr Revans was told and so was Mr Woodgate, two of the senior Mr Constable's executors. What would the Reverend Rhudde have said at this late tweak to the tale of the Constable–Bicknell connection?

Constable felt a great burden lifted from him. He said he intended to settle the money on Maria and the children. On 11 June he told Fisher that he could now 'stand before a 6-foot canvas with a mind at ease (thank God)'. Just as well, since Mr Sykes, the dancing master who had taken part of the Charlotte Street house, had failed to pay the rent. One other bothersome thing was that Johnny Dunthorne was spreading his own wings. Johnny's usefulness couldn't be minimised, but he was now thirty and had built up his own list of clients for portraits and restoration work. He had painting commissions in London and East Anglia – he had recently repainted the sign on the Duke of Marlborough Inn in Dedham, originally painted by his father in 1809. There were suggestions that Constable harboured some hurt feelings about this independence, and Abram once again tried to help. After seeing Johnny in East Bergholt when he was there for his sister Hannah's wedding, Abram tried to get across to Constable that Johnny's attachment was as strong as ever. However, Johnny also believed that Constable's 'natural temperament & ardent mind must & does harass anyone constantly with you'. Of course, nothing could obliterate Johnny's attachment and gratitude to Constable. Yet the younger man had his own jobs to do, debt was death to him, and – Abram implied – Constable ought to understand Johnny's feelings.

The exhibition at Somerset House that year generally disheartened Constable. He wrote to Fisher, 'Lawrence has many pictures, and never has his elegant affettuosa style been more happy. Jackson is the

most of a painter, but he does not rank with him [Lawrence] in talent
. . . Turner has some golden visions – glorious and beautifull, but they
are only visions – yet still they are art – & one could live with *such*
pictures in the house . . . Some portraits that would petrify you.' As
for Etty, recent victor in the RA stakes and contemporary cheesecake
artist par excellence, it was 'lady bums as usual'. Abram had hopes
that his picture of Dedham Vale would be ready in time, as it was, and
added, 'I somehow think they must elect you next time RA but you
don't much care about it I believe.' Abram reported that spring had
been early in the Stour valley; there was good feed in the meadows for
the cows – 'everything coming into life, & such greens, & the cheerful
rooks building & cawing, quite happy'. Chantrey liked Constable's
work and made an initial bid for the Hampstead landscape, but the
purchase didn't take place and the painting waited some years for a
buyer – John Sheepshanks.[12] Constable told Fisher the Dedham Vale
painting with its view from Gun Hill down to the estuary at Mistley
was perhaps his best; it had been 'noticed (*as a redeemer*) by John Bull
[the periodical]'. It went unsold during Constable's lifetime. The
paint sparkled as in a Rubens, but possibly a rare veteran viewer of
Constable's work might have detected that the light in his paintings
was beginning to grow sadder. The dark clouds were mounting.

# 14. *Darkness Visible (1828–29)*

Maria was sinking. In the spring while staying in Putney, she was for a while 'too weak to be moved'. Constable took her to Brighton in May and there, between visits to Charlotte Street, spent long periods sitting by her couch and bedside. Sometimes, coming up for air, he went to the beach and painted, but couldn't get her out of his mind. In late May he made several sketches of the collier *Malta* temporarily stranded high on the beach after a gale, with her cargo of coal being unloaded into a cart and a helping crowd shovelling shingle under her bilges to stop her heeling over; the *Malta* was refloated.[1] One oil sketch has inscribed on the back: '*Brighton. Sunday evening July 20 1828*'; for it he used his brushes hardly at all but instead squeezed out the paint in long blobs and brandished his palette knife savagely to evoke the rough waters of the Channel under low, threatening clouds, rain coming on, the light fading.[2] His state of mind doesn't need explication. The infant Alfred was also afflicted by illness, and this time Brighton seemed to do none of the invalids any good.

Maria's consumption was terminal. A number of their friends, including Charles Leslie, recognised this.[3] After increasingly brief periods of remission the disease had now reached the 'galloping' stage. Maria's last, disconnected letter to her husband was apparently written with a shaking pencil in late June when he was joined in Charlotte Street by Minna, now nine:

My Dearest John,
    I part with our sweet Minna with regret but she wishes it so much I would not keep her. I wish you likewise to send me Susan & I hope you

can come back yourself with Mrs A. I long to see you or would you like to wait till the next day & bring Isabel, perhaps Roberts & Emily. I look forward to the hope of [seeing you] coming at the end of this week, I trust I shall

    Yours ever, M.E.C.

On receiving this Constable immediately took a Brighton coach. He remained there with Maria for nearly six weeks of 'most untoward weather'. Then, giving up on the seaside's recuperative powers and hoping for 'sweet Hampstead' to make amends, he brought her and the children back to Well Walk. For a moment the change helped; their hopes were raised; how up-and-down everything was! On 22 August he wrote to Johnny Dunthorne, 'I believe Mrs Constable to be gaining ground. Her cough is pretty well gone and she has some appetite, and the nightly perspirations are, in a great measure, ceased.

Maria, towards the end

All this must be good.' Maria's doctors were suddenly sanguine and told Constable that Maria was on the mend. 'Pray God this may be the case,' Constable wrote to Dominic Colnaghi on 15 September, 'I am much worn by anxiety.'[4]

Unfortunately medical men at the time were powerless in the face of what would later be called tuberculosis. The doctors who came to treat Maria were not only without effective cures but subject to the same danger. Dr Robert Gooch, a small, dark-eyed man of thirty-four, an expert on women's diseases, came down with consumption himself; he had given up his medical practice two years before, retiring to Windsor to become the royal librarian. Born at Yarmouth, he used to put a Constable seascape on his sofa to look at while he breakfasted, saying he was at the beach enjoying the breeze. He died in 1830, having taught Constable a Latin couplet:

> *Eheu! quam tenui e filo pendet*
> *Quid quid in vita maxime arridet.*

> Alas! From how slender a thread hangs
> All that is sweetest in life.

Herbert Evans, the Hampstead physician, took Gooch's place in caring for Maria and the young Constables and became a friend of both the artist and Fisher.[5]

Maria's illness filled the house. Shepherded by Mrs Savage, the housekeeper, and Mrs Roberts, the governess, the children did their best not to be noisy. Constable sat with Maria, while the leaves from the trees in Well Walk fell on the dry, autumnal ground. From East Bergholt Abram wrote of the fine weather which he hoped was conducive to good health and certainly elevating and cheering for the mind. On 3 October he wrote again mentioning that wheat was expensive, 'a serious price for the poor', and expressing to his brother his hopes, within which lay his apprehensions: 'These things are in the hand of God.' Constable's sister Martha was already turning from hope to grief, and to trust in God's wisdom and patience. On

4 October a cry of distress from the painter (and a plea for company) came to Fisher in Salisbury; he replied, 'Your sad letter has just reached me . . . at a time that I fear I cannot move . . . I fear your friendship makes you over value the use I can be of to you; but what I can give[,] you shall have . . . Support yourself with your usual manliness . . .' Constable's newer friend Charles Leslie called at Well Walk in November and found Maria on a sofa in the sitting room, with its view over London. Leslie wrote, 'Although Constable appeared in his usual spirits in her presence, yet before I left the house, he took me into another room, wrung my hand, and burst into tears, without speaking.' Constable was too upset to function as an artist. To a client, Henry Hebbert, who wasn't happy with some aspect of a painting of Hampstead Heath, Constable wrote, 'I am intensely distressed & can hardly attend to any thing.'[6]

Leslie thought Maria endured her suffering with 'that entire resignation to the will of Providence that she had shown under every circumstance of her life'. In the late stages of consumption the coughing was intensely painful – and also dangerous to people nearby. Speech became a whisper. There were stomach pains, vomiting and bleeding, spikes of fever in the evenings and immense lassitude. The twelve-year-old girl with big dark eyes who had first caught the fancy of John Constable in a Suffolk village now lay 'sadly thin and weak', on a Hampstead couch, given up to her struggle to catch breath.[7]

Maria died on 23 November. The woman he had called his 'dearest life' was buried in the graveyard of St John's church, a short walk from Hampstead High Street. There Constable had a tomb erected against the wall of the cemetery. Dr Gooch's favourite Latin tag was inscribed on the stonework of the tomb: Life hangs from a thread. Constable might also have used the motto on the sundial over the doorway to East Bergholt church, *Ut umbra, sic vita* – Life is like a shadow.[8]

Friends and family rallied round. From East Bergholt sister Ann apologised for 'some passing clouds' which might have overshadowed the affection she felt for Constable; she offered her kindest love in his great trial. Abram came to London in person, bringing words of sympathy and of trust in God that their sister Mary had asked him to deliver. Martha Whalley paid tribute to Maria's patience and meekness, which she was sure would be rewarded. And John Fisher wrote from Osmington 'with the hope and intention of giving you comfort, but really I know not how. Words will not ward off irreparable loss; but if there be any consolation to the heart of man to know that another feels with him, you have that consolation, I do sympathize with you, my old and dear friend, most truly, and I pray God to give you fortitude.'

Constable, feeling hollow at heart, gathered his seven children around him. Leslie, stalwart friend, later observed that Constable continued to wear mourning for the rest of his life – but black was Constable's style. Maria, who had faced the possibility of Constable wearing black to their wedding, might have been touched but would probably have made fun of him.[9] (Leslie, with no funereal purpose, also wore black clothing as his day-to-day wear.)[10]

At this point Constable felt most able to pour out his heart not to Leslie, Fisher or Abram, but to his brother Golding, to whom he wrote, 'Hourly do I feel the loss of my departed Angel – God only know[s] how my children will be brought up – nothing can supply the loss of such a devoted – sensible – industrious – religious mother – who was all affection – but I cannot trust myself on the subject – I shall never feel again as I have felt – the face of the World is totally changed to me – though with god['s] help I shal endeavour to do my next duties –'[11]

Dr Evans had made friends with Fisher and on a trip to the West Country had called in Osmington to talk about their mutual friend. Evans reported to Fisher that Constable was in a state of 'complete self-possession'. The archdeacon and the physician agreed that applying himself to his painting would be best for Constable: 'Some of the finest works of art, and most vigorous exertions of intellect, have been the result of periods of distress.' When Fisher and Constable wrote to one another in early January about a visit the archdeacon hoped to make to Hampstead, Fisher thought Constable 'smitten, but not cast down'. Constable told Leslie that if he could get

Pen and ink
sketch of a
mermaid

afloat on a six-foot canvas, he might be carried away from himself; but
the job which was first offered him was a commission from Henry
Greswolde Lewis of Malvern Hall to draw a mermaid for an inn sign
in Warwickshire. Perhaps Lewis thought the task would cheer him
up. It afforded 'no small solace to my previous labours in landscape
for the last twenty years', Constable remarked sardonically to Leslie.
The buxom mermaid looked rather fetching in a sketch Constable
drew, but the actual inn sign, for the Old Mermaid & Greswolde
Arms, that a sign painter was meant to produce to Constable's
drawing, was never accomplished.

   When Fisher at last got to London in early February, it was to find
his friend at a strange moment. The Academician W.R. Bigg – 'Old

Bigg', painter turned restorer for reasons of a livelihood and a friendly admirer of Constable's works – had died, and Constable's name had once again gone forward for the vacant seat. Constable told Leslie, 'I have little heart to face an ordeal (or rather should I not say, "*run a gauntlet*") in which "kicks" are kind treatment to those "*insults to the mind*", which "*we* candidates *wretches* of necessity" are exposed to annually from some "high-minded" members who stickle for the "elevated & noble" walks of art – i.e. preferring the *shaggy posteriors of a Satyr* to the *moral feeling of landscape*.' Despite having little heart for it, Constable ran the gauntlet. In the preliminary voting he did well, but in the conclusive final round a strong rival appeared in the form of Francis Danby, poetic landscapist. Nevertheless, Constable scraped through to victory – by one vote. Alfred Chalon, a long-time supporter, called to let him know, and after him came George Jones and Turner with their congratulations. Turner stayed until 1 a.m., making up a little for long neglect. They parted, Constable said, 'mutually pleased with one another'. Whether Turner was really happy is less certain: he had been hoping to see his friend Charles Eastlake – later President of the Academy – elected.[12]

Just how much Constable gained from RA sympathy after Maria's death, we don't know. When he called on Sir Thomas Lawrence to pay his respects, the President let him know that he thought Constable had been lucky, being only a landscape painter, to be so honoured, when many meritorious history painters – a higher class of artist! – were on the waiting list. Constable of course thought differently. His election at last was an act of justice rather than favour, but – borrowing Dr Johnson's words to Lord Chesterfield – he let Leslie know that there was disappointment attached to the honour: 'It has been delayed until I am solitary, and cannot impart it.'[13] However, Fisher, who was staying in town at the Charterhouse, felt unalloyed pleasure at his friend's success. 'It is a double triumph,' he told Constable. 'It is in the first place the triumph of real Art over spurious art; and in the second place, of patient moral integrity over bare chicanery & misrepresented worth.' Another long-term supporter, his brother Abram, wrote: 'Now you are what you ought to have been years ago, RA . . . But your

Pictures will not need any other aid than their own intrinsic genuineness & worth.' The Dunthornes, father and son, were well pleased at his election. A few cavilled at Constable's victory, one commentator suggesting nastily that Mr Bicknell's money rather than Constable's painting ability had swayed the Academicians. The same writer in the following year attacked Constable's 'fantastic and coarse style of painting', by which he produced 'powerful effects, and sometimes a remarkable degree of natural truth; but he has certainly not improved in art as he has in fortune, to which latter he entirely owes the obsequiousness of the Academy, and the long struggled-for RA'.[14] It could be argued, to the contrary, that the lingering sense of Constable as a maverick artist supported by parental funds was one factor which kept him out for so long.

Whether any of the admonitions or encouragement made any difference to him other than to his sense of self-worth we can't be sure; he had to go on painting. Abram recognised this need: 'You will now proceed with your Picture of the Nore – & I think it will be beautiful.' This picture was to be big, just about a six-footer. It was a subject he had had in his memory for some time. He had made a small pencil sketch of it in 1814 during his trip to the Essex shore of the Thames estuary with the Reverend Driffield, then vicar of Feering. While Mr Driffield visited his other living at Southchurch, Constable explored the area, walking on the beach at Southend and the higher ground inland. The spot, Constable had told Maria at the time, contained 'the ruin of a castle which from its situation is a really fine place – it commands a view of the Kent hills, the Nore and North Foreland & looking many miles to sea'. The view also reminded him of his passage down river on the *Coutts* in 1803, when they had sailed past the Nore anchorage and rounded the North Foreland into a south-westerly gale. Hadleigh Castle at this time was two stumps of derelict thirteenth-century masonry, the biggest remnant resembling part of a huge cannon, split open and standing upright. This is the closest structure to the viewer in Constable's full-size sketch. Also in the left foreground is a shepherd with his dog. Cattle graze on the shaggy slopes that descend to the foreshore. Across the picture, from the centre to the right-hand side, stretches a broad belt of distant, glittering, choppy water. Above, a scumbled mass of small clouds fill a windy sky.[15]

The finished picture for the exhibition had some of the stir smoothed out of it; but it could still be taken for two pictures, foreground and distance, land and sea, which the artist hadn't quite tied to one another. And he referred to the painting for a while by either of two titles: *Hadleigh Castle* was one, *The Nore* the other. (At the Academy it was *Hadleigh Castle. The mouth of the Thames – morning, after a stormy night.*) The visible disconnection perhaps increased the sense of melancholy the painting provoked. When Constable had it ready to send to Somerset House, he asked Leslie to call in and tell him whether he should in fact enter it: 'I am grevously [*sic*] nervous about it, as I am still smarting under my election. I have little enough either of self-knowledge or prudence (as you know) and I am pretty willing to submit to what you shall decide – with others whom I value.' Clearly no one told Constable not to send in what he called, to Leslie, 'my crazy old walls of the Castle', or, to Fisher, 'the great Castle, such as it is'.

*Hadleigh Castle* was accompanied by one other painting, a small landscape showing a cottage. Constable described the exhibition, or 'pandemonium', to Fisher: 'Wilkie has 8 pictures – Lawrence 8, Jackson & Pickersgill 8 each. Callcott, though not 8, has one 8-feet long . . . Turner has some. They have an immense crash [of rejected pictures] in the hall – it is evident the Devil must vomit pictures all over London.' In the catalogue *Hadleigh Castle* was bolstered by some lines from Thomson's 'Summer' describing a sunrise over 'melancholy bounds':

> Rude ruins glitter; and the briny deep,
> Seen from some pointed promontory's top,
> Far to the dim horizon's utmost verges
> Restless, reflects a floating gleam.

On one of the varnishing days the mischief-making sculptor Chantrey – who had altered Constable's sheep in *The Cornfield* – approached *Hadleigh Castle*, saying the foreground looked too cold.

With Leslie for witness, Chantrey took the palette from Constable's reluctant hand and spread a glaze of asphaltum – derived from tar – over the offending section. Constable, alarmed, said to Leslie, 'There goes all my dew.' When Chantrey had moved on to make one of his improvements or practical jokes elsewhere, Constable wiped off the dark glaze and carefully restored the foreground glitter.[16]

Some critics were impressed by Constable's elegiac morning-after. The *Literary Gazette* thought it very powerful. *The Times* admired it as 'highly natural'. And the *Morning Chronicle* called it a noble picture in Constable's 'peculiar but forcible style'. (The writer of this, still showing some restraint, was Edward Dubois, who was to make almost a profession of increasingly acerbic commentary on Constable.) However, Leslie believed the picture 'received rather rougher usage than usual from the newspaper critics'. By some, Constable's 'disagreeable', 'disfigured' and 'mannered' surfaces were given prime attention: the *Gentleman's Magazine* said his scenes appeared to be scattered over 'with a huge quantity of chopped hay', and the *Sun* qualified its praise of the *Castle*'s 'nature and spirit' with 'though freckled and pock-marked'. As did *The Times*, noting the artist's habit of 'scattering white spots over the surface of his picture'.[17] Turner, too, was accused of splattering his canvases with soapsuds and whitewash, so there were ironies when he was credited that year with making similar accusations against the new RA member. (Constable returned the compliment by passing on to Fisher the gossip that one of Turner's pictures had been compared with a 'spitting box' at a hospital.) No one offered to buy the *Castle*. Perhaps no one wanted to feel the anguish that lay within the pockmarks produced by Constable's palette knife. The 'floating gleam' – indeed 'every gleam of sunshine' – was now blighted for him, as he was to write to Leslie in 1834. One also remembers his uncle David Pike Watts's remark to Constable in 1811 that 'cheerfulness is wanted in your landscapes; they are tinctured with a sombre darkness.' Surely this time with reason.[18]

Constable had some social engagements in spring that cheered him up a bit. On the penultimate day of the British Institution exhibition he dined with Wilkie, who was a delight as always, but the occasion wasn't all agreeable because among the company was Collins, in a masterful mood, and even more unfortunately Reinagle.[19] It was perhaps Constable's relief at getting through dinner and heading home that was displayed in a sketch attached to a letter to Leslie. Constable showed himself leaning out of the back of one of the new horse-drawn omnibuses rattling down the Strand, waving his exhibition catalogue at the animal painter Edwin Landseer and the collector William Wells, who were in the cab behind, waving their catalogues. (The first regular bus service began that year, from Paddington Green to the Bank of England.)[20] He also dined with Leslie and spent an afternoon with John Jackson, talking about art and artists; Constable said, 'The art is now filled with *Phantasmagoria*.' He had had a cold that lasted two months, and Fisher thought he was deranged to concentrate so much of his painting effort into that season: 'You choose February & March for composition, when the strongest men get irritable & uncomfortable, during the prevalence of the N.E. winds, the great destruction of the frame . . . in England.' Fisher added that London at that time was like 'a deep cellar in the infernal regions reserved for the most desperate . . . See Milton's *Cold Hell*.' Consequently he saw a good deal of Herbert Evans in Hampstead, the physician to whose medical skills he remained grateful. Evans accompanied him on a last look at the Academy exhibition and said he would join Constable and Fisher when they got together soon in Salisbury.

Such a trip had been talked about frequently since 1821. This time, despite Fisher's expectation that Constable would call it off, Constable booked places in 'the little Salisbury coach' for Tuesday 7 July for himself, John Charles and Minna, promising to be at Fisher's for teatime. He kept his promise. It was now seventeen years since Bishop Fisher first brought the two men together, and the younger Fisher had become Constable's best patron and best friend. Constable opened his heart to him about the Academy: 'as usual in bodies corporate – the lowest bred and greatest fools are the leaders'. And the acute and forthright Fisher, who was well looked after by the body corporate of the Church of England, had a like asperity, condemning Oxbridge missionaries for making 'Christianity a stern haughty thing. Think of St. Paul with a full blown wig, deep shovel hat, apron, round belly, double chin, stern eye, rough voice, and imperious manner, drinking port wine, and laying down the law of the best way of escaping the operation of the Curates Residence Act' – a piece of recent legislation designed to cut down on the multiple livings for senior clergy that produced many impoverished curates. Often lonely among his fellow painters in the crowded art world, Constable was lucky to have Fisher for confidant and supporter. In November 1824 Fisher told his friend, 'Your fame is your pole star.' When Constable became an RA, Fisher said, 'The event is important to me, since my judgement was embarked in the same boat with your success.' And on 30 April 1829 he wrote, 'Whenever I find a man despising the false estimates of the vulgar, and daring to aspire – in sentiment, language, and conduct – to what the highest wisdom, through every age, has taught us as most excellent, to him I unite myself by a sort of necessary attachment.'

Constable, John Charles and Minna stayed at Leydenhall, the large house in the cathedral close that Fisher had had since 1819. Archdeacon and prebendary, he had only to be in residence three months of the year. The garden contained a very tall alder tree, backed on to the River Avon, and had a distant view of Harnham Ridge. Constable painted an oil sketch from upstairs windows as he looked out to West Harnham. He painted the river itself, the water meadows and the pollarded willows on its banks, in a picture he was to submit, amid confusion, to the Academy the following year. He drew Fisher and his dogs in a riverside glade and went out on several trips in the nearby country, including one to Old Sarum, the hill which had once been the site of a 'city'; the first Parliament had been held there under King John in 1205, and despite now having only seven inhabitants, it continued to send two members to the House of Commons. Constable did several large sketches of the great mound; a wonderful watercolour followed. As Leslie noted, Constable had to be interested by 'a city turned into a landscape'. He made some sky studies, out of doors and from his bedroom, and sketched the cathedral again, once with a rainbow.[21]

At the end of July Constable went back to London, leaving twelve-year-old John and Minna, aged ten, with the Fishers. But Leydenhall suddenly became crowded. The Fisher's eldest son, Osmond, had come home from Eton. Two of Mary Fisher's brothers turned up, one with his wife and child. Fisher had to apologise that young John was first 'reduced to a leathern sofa' for a bed, and then sent home, though Minna, Fisher's godchild, got to remain. Fisher wrote to her father on 9 August: 'Minna grows into favour every day. Her spirits get more buoyant, & she skips about like a gazelle. Her manners are naturally very good, & a little stay where she will mix with company will ensure them.' Fisher's loving observations must have cheered Constable greatly about his motherless daughter. Mary Fisher saw that Minna's education wasn't neglected and sent her on improving jaunts, to the law courts, for example, to hear trials. Fisher wrote in early September: 'Minna is the nicest child in the house possible. Nobody would know of her existence if she were not seen. She improves in her French and otherwise – her *ear* is perfect.' Only that hint of Minna's near invisibility suggests that sometimes she was hugging her loss to herself. Minna added a postscript to a letter to Constable from Mary Fisher: 'I am so happy here that I should like to stay here as long as you like to keep me here,' and signed herself by one of her pet names, 'Ladybird'. When sickness ran through his house, Fisher thoughtfully kept the news from Constable, knowing he would worry about Minna. (The Fishers' youngest boy had scarlatina and a servant lad named Robert died of 'repletion' – which sounds like overeating.) Constable sent to Leydenhall a haunch of venison and a small painting which Fisher said he was going to hang over the piano, under the Claude, in the 'first drawing room'.

Constable managed another short trip to Salisbury in mid-November, when he came to take Minna home; he then gave Mary Fisher some painting lessons and made several drawings, one from the bottom of Leydenhall's garden. Fisher had told him that 'the Church under a cloud' was the best subject he could take, and Constable was apparently thinking of making another picture of the cathedral. They were to meet again elsewhere but, though of course neither of them knew it, this was to be their last meeting in Salisbury.

Their friendship had involved a number of money transactions, generally when Fisher bought Constable pictures and lent or advanced money if the painter's cash flow required temporary help. Now Fisher was hard-stretched. None of the land rent he was owed in Gillingham had been paid; he told Constable that his thoughts were 'compelled to run in the current of mere pounds & shillings'. By mid-December he asked a favour: could Constable take back two paintings, at least for the time being? Apparently, though he didn't name them, the pictures were *The White Horse*, the first six-footer, and *Salisbury Cathedral from the Bishop's Grounds*, which he had taken over from his uncle. Constable had to sell some government stock to obtain the agreed two hundred pounds but probably wasn't unhappy about regaining the paintings. He disliked losing control of any of his pictures, even for money. With Fisher and Tinney, as we have seen, he had often borrowed back his paintings and then been loath to return them to their 'owners'. On one occasion he gave the younger landscape painter F.R. Lee two reasons he didn't sell his works: 'When I paint a *bad* picture I don't like to part with it, and when I paint a *good* one, I like to keep it.'[22] As for John Fisher, he was grieved to part with his Constables. But six children made them 'valuable luxuries' he couldn't at that moment afford. In addition, Fisher hadn't been well; he complained of problems with his chest and larynx, and of heart palpitations.

In late October Abram had reported from East Bergholt the serious illness of James Inglis, married to a relative John Constable had painted as a girl, Jane Mason of Colchester; the Inglises had six young children. Abram was also distressed by the death of his 'faithful and sensible' dog, Pickle, aged ten. Fortunately Johnny Dunthorne had not long before done a portrait of Pickle that was now 'doubly valuable'. Pickle had accompanied Abram on a round of family visits the previous day, walking with him from Flatford into the village and to Golding's cottage. The dog was taken ill just before they got to sister Ann's and Abram was undoubtedly going to miss him – 'He was valuable & useful & very agreeable.' Constable wrote to Golding from Charlotte Street on 3 December thanking him for 'a most handsome present', perhaps for young John, whose birthday it was next day; he was happy to hear that all was quiet in the woods.[23] In family letters Constable had begun to sound a bit the way his mother had in her letters to him. However, to Golding he wrote with a fraternal frankness which would have horrified Ann Constable. Sending off to Golding some furniture for his rebuilt house near the windmill, Constable listed some of the items, including 'the shit pot . . . carefully packed . . . no bad thing . . . in a cold showery night on Bargell heath when taken short'.[24] Although Abram advised Constable to make allowances for Golding's 'singularity', preparing him for Golding's failure to thank Constable for his kindness – presumably most of all for getting him his job with Lady Dysart – there is no evidence Golding was anything but grateful.

It was a fierce winter. In Osmington Fisher said it had been Siberian. 'The snow drifted to ten & twelve feet between this place & Weymouth: and the road by the Sea-beach was completely blocked up.' Mary Fisher was a sad invalid during 'this most ungenial season', and the archdeacon was now unwell with what was thought to be gout, asthma and high blood pressure. Another victim of the season was Sir Thomas Lawrence. The President of the Royal Academy suddenly succumbed and died in early January 1830 – a man 'suited to the age, and the age to him', as Benjamin Haydon remarked. Lawrence was only sixty, and seemed to younger colleagues like Leslie to be painting better and better portraits. Constable, who had by no means been close to him, was distressed by Lawrence's death and went with Wilkie to the funeral in St Paul's. Haydon was there and recalled seeing them together: 'Cope, the city marshal, stood before them in a splendid cocked hat. Wilkie was fond of painting cocked hats; and while looking down with all the semblance of woe said to Constable, "Just look at that cocked hat. It's grand!" '[25] Turner was standing nearby and overheard the remark which he thought wrong on this solemn occasion. Constable noticed him looking away in disgust, and approved of Turner's reaction.[26] Although Lawrence hadn't classed landscape in the highest ranks of art, he had – according to the engraver David Lucas – thought Constable's paintings 'ferocious'. An unusual description for the time, and not a bad one.[27]

# 15. *Seven Children (1830–31)*

At the start of 1830 the Constable children ranged in age from Lionel, just two, to John Charles, twelve. Minna was ten and a half. She was ill in the spring, with a bad cold and a sore throat, and a doctor named Harris came to see her every morning for a week. She had been exchanging letters with Emma Fisher, who had recently had braces – a 'horrid gold machine' – fitted to her teeth, and the two girls discussed the *Keepsake* annual, copies of which they kept in locked drawers, so that no grown-ups could get hold of them. John Fisher thought the romantic stories in the periodical 'morbid' and didn't want Emma to read it; he was evidently unsuccessful in this. Perhaps to counteract the dreaded *Keepsake*, Constable gave Minna a prayer book in June. Minna was having music lessons with a Hampstead neighbour, Mr Frith, while attending Miss Sophia Noble's school. She had been going to Miss Noble's since 1827 and her younger sisters followed her. Constable was an indulgent and devoted father. His first-born John Charles was found as often in Constable's arms as in those of his nurse or even his mother. Leslie often heard Constable say, 'Children should be respected', and when the Leslies had another child in 1831, Constable confided to his friend, 'They were happy days with me when I had infants.'[1]

On 31 January 1830 Constable wrote to his friend expressing his disappointment that a planned visit from Leslie and his wife hadn't occurred, though he understood the reason: Leslie had toothache, which Constable knew all about. It was particularly sad because 'my little girls were all in "apple-pie order" to be seen. My dear Maria had been practising her steps and music all day that she might appear to advantage. All my boys were in their best, and had allowed a total clearance of the drawing room of their numerous ships, castles, books, bricks, drawings, &c . . .' Several years before, a doctor from Brighton, George Young, had encountered a permissive father on a visit to Charlotte Street. Constable took him to his painting room to show him a picture he was working on. When he got to his easel, so Young reported, Constable found that 'one of his little boys had dashed the handle of the hearth-broom through the canvas, and made so large a rent as to render its restoration impossible. He called the child up to him and asked him gently if he had done it. When the boy admitted that he had, he rebuked him in these unmeasured terms: "Oh! my dear pet! See what we have done! Dear, dear! What shall we do to mend it? I can't think – can *you*?" '[2]

Constable built for his boys a large playroom with a glass roof in the courtyard behind the house in Charlotte Street. Robert Leslie, one of Charles Leslie's sons, recalled among the toys there 'a most complete working model of a fire-engine'. One of the Constable boys cut holes in a large box meant to represent a house, filled it with wood shavings, and set fire to it. 'Another boy then rang a small bell, and the model engine appeared, but had scarcely begun to play upon the flaming box when Constable, to whose studio the dense smoke had found its way, came among us, and saying, "I can't have any more of this," looked for a can of water to put out the fire; while the author of the mischief coolly turned the hose of the little engine on the back of his father's head.' Instead of being furious with the boy, Constable treated it as a joke, and after the fire was extinguished went back to his easel. John Charles remained interested in fire engines for a number of years. When his younger brother Charles Golding was at school on the south coast, John Charles wrote to him and asked, 'Let me know what kind of fire engin [sic] there is at Folkestone.'[3]

Two indispensable people in the widower's house were Mrs Savage, the housekeeper, and Mrs Roberts – called variously Bob or Bobs – the children's nurse. Constable told his friends that Mrs Savage belied her name.[4] Mrs Roberts had come on the scene in 1821 after Charles Golding's birth and held things together thereafter; her caring talents were recognised by Abram in a letter to his nephew John Charles in 1839: 'She is a valuable friend & millions would not purchase such a one.' On one occasion she took John Charles down to Brighton to help him get over an illness, and her charge wrote home to Papa to say, 'Roberts as [sic] had a ducking in the see.' When Charles Golding was off at school in Folkestone Roberts wrote to him just before his birthday gently admonishing him to attend to his studies, 'for learning makes the man'. She told him to be careful of his clothes for 'salt water soon spoils them', and reminded him to write to his sister Emily for her birthday; she would be eight on the same day he was twelve. And lastly she urged him to write to his 'Poor Old Nurse. But out of Sight out of mind.' She went on sending parcels of clothes and food to the two older boys when they were away at school, and when Charles Golding – always interested in boats – finally went to sea, aged fourteen, one of his last letters from Portsmouth ended, 'Tell Bob she had made me very comfortable, what should I have done without her.' Constable felt truly 'helpless' when she had severe rheumatism in 1836.[5]

Constable took his motherless offspring on trips, a few at a time. They often visited the Leslies, and in 1829 he went with several of the youngsters to the Countess of Dysart, 'the last of the Tollemaches', at Ham House near Richmond; she was 'very kind to and pleased with my children'. They went on to Wimbledon to call on their aunt Louisa, now, since her marriage three months before, Mrs John Sanford. Constable thought Louisa hadn't married well; in fact she had 'sadly dished herself', and was feeling it. 'She cried & kissed the children a good deal.' Minna got to stay with 'her foolish aunt' on several occasions, 'a great sacrifice' on her father's part; he missed her exceedingly. Dear Minna was trying hard to fill her mother's role; at the age of eleven she was teaching her younger siblings the three Rs during the Christmas holidays. He wrote to Leslie, 'She is so orderly in all her plans, and so full of method – so lady-like by nature – and so firm and yet so gentle that you cannot beleive the influence of this heavenly little monitor on this whole house – but most of all on me, who look and watch on all her dear ways with mingled smiles and tears

. . . Should I live, and this dear image of her mother be spared to me, what a blessing and comfort to my old age.' In 1831 Constable took Minna, Isabel and Emily down to Dedham to stay with his sister Martha. Back at work in Charlotte Street he wrote at once to Minna. He told her about a great to-do caused by their black cat, which had got out of the attic window and prowled along to the roof of the Fitzroy chapel, where it spent all night in the rain (presumably howling), until rescued by a man sent aloft by their neighbour Mrs Johnson. And he let her know that John, Charley, Alfred and Lionel were quite well although Alfie had cut his finger several times while trying to make a model boat. Minna thoughtfully collected around Dedham a great many insects for her brother Charles. After telling her father about this, she closed one letter 'Good buy says Maria'.[6]

Allowing for the odd spelling idiosyncrasy (in which they followed their father), the Constable girls were well taught at Elizabeth House, Miss Sophia Noble's school in Hampstead. Handwriting, piano-playing, dancing and comportment were elements of instruction.[7] The boys' education was more of a worry. Constable's own early experience at Lavenham, where he had been beaten by the usher, led him to want to keep his sons close at hand. Fisher had told him how at Eton, where his son Osmond was a pupil, the 'pedagogues flog little boys' bottoms'. Constable thought that if his sons were sent away to school they would be 'plunged into <u>accumulative evil</u>'. Without Maria's guidance he was a softie. Charles seems to have been a normally rambunctious youth, who could take care of himself, but Constable was perhaps rightly worried about the oldest, 'my darling boy John', who was often ill.[8] He told Leslie, 'In this sweet youth I see all that gentleness – affection – fine intellect & indeed all those endearing qualities, which rendered his departed mother so dear to me – but I must not trust my heart on this subject – my greivous wound only slumbers.'

Early in 1831 Constable's cousin Jane South, née Gubbins, who lived just off the Strand in London and was the mother of six, suggested hiring an instructor for the two oldest boys. She had someone to recommend: young Charles Boner, a Twickenham youth of

German parentage, who was 'very *gentle* & very *clever*'. He could come
to Charlotte Street every day from nine to eleven to teach the boys,
'for a guinea a week the two'. Constable said yes. Boner was going to
be sixteen in April – barely two years older than John Charles. His
father was a German mathematician who was interested in – among
other things – the magnetic variation of compasses. Poetic, sensitive,
religious, serious: all epithets that fitted young Boner; and he was also,
what may have especially appealed to Constable, undemanding.
Boner agreed to the guinea a week though soon he was being paid £20
a quarter, which was roughly five shillings a week more. In late
October Constable, depressed and ill, suddenly felt he couldn't afford
Boner and gave him notice. But the 'termination' never happened.
The clouds cleared. Constable realised that Boner was already
invaluable. Though he acted older than his years and indeed sometimes seemed to lack humour – he took many of Constable's sardonic
sallies with unsmiling gravity – both John and Charles liked him and
referred to him as 'Old Bo'. And he soon became – following in
Johnny Dunthorne's footsteps – Constable's general assistant:
message-carrier, proof-reader, picture-packer, as well as part-time
tutor to the boys; he was always helpful, always amiable.[9]

Johnny Dunthorne – in some respects another of Constable's
children – was spreading his own wings. In 1828 Constable wrote
paternally to Johnny, who had been offered a restoration job at the
church in Nayland, 'I hope you will do it, but only in conjunction with
your father. It requires not a moment's hesitation. Take care of cold.
Work with the doors and windows of the church open; if it should
make it colder, it will drive out damp and the smell of graves.' Johnny
continued to work on Constable's pictures – Constable wrote to Leslie
in February 1830 that 'a sketch of the lane and cottage would be all the
better for a little of John Dunthorne's varnish'. This was possibly a
version of *The Glebe Farm* Constable had given Leslie.[10] Not long
before Martha Whalley had written from Dedham to say how
delighted they all were at Johnny's 'prosperity & promise, & doubt not
that he will continue to flourish – & please'. In 1831 Johnny brought
Constable a letter from his sister Ann and a batch of Bergholt stories.

John Dunthorne the younger. Self-portrait

She said, 'He is a very deserving young person and makes friends wherever he goes.' Johnny was increasingly in demand as a restorer. Fisher met Mrs Anne Michel, the wife of a general; she praised Dunthorne's cleaning of a Reynolds portrait and was surprised that Fisher knew Johnny already. More and more collectors were patronising him. Constable told Fisher in May 1830, 'John is much esteemed, for his integrity & skill – & what avails him more than either, he is not feared by them – his mildness disarms them of dread.'

By 1832 Johnny had his own studio/workshop in Grafton Street,
off Fitzroy Square, not far from Charlotte Street. He was never a very
original painter, but from 1829 to 1832 he exhibited at the Royal
Academy and British Institution. Some of Constable's works which
he had copied formed the models for his own unassertive pictures –
for example, an across-the-river view of Salisbury Cathedral and
Archdeacon Fisher's house in 1827, a work more detailed and less
naturalistic than his master's. Of course he painted Stour valley
scenes: various fieldscapes, river and lock views, rainbows . . .
Constable continued to promote Johnny's social life, when he could.
In August he took Johnny and his uncle Thomas Dunthorne who was
in town to an evening party at the British Institution so that Johnny –
who wasn't well then – could 'see the ladies and pictures by lamp light
. . . altogether a pretty sight'.[11]

On 6 November 1831 Constable sat down with the big family Bible
and entered on a flyleaf the names of all his children and the dates and
times of their births. John Charles was just coming up to fourteen and
Minna was twelve. In 1832 she had scarlet fever while at Miss Noble's
school and Constable was terrified. Mrs Roberts was tearfully
distraught, not being there to look after her. Bulletins from Dr Evans
or Mr Haines to Charlotte Street gave news of Minna's temperature
and pulse. The question was, would she live? But at last came a turn
for the better: John Charles, who had been much alarmed for his
sister, wrote from Well Walk to his father, 'Miss Noble says that
Miney has had a good night and is going on very well, we have sent
her a potel of strawberys.' Charles Golding, the second son, had good
health but high energy and a short attention span. For the studious
Boner he proved a somewhat disruptive pupil. Charles was sent to
school in Folkestone, and the seaside and harbour there gave him a
chance to expand his interest in boats. One of his first letters to Boner
from Mr and Mrs Pierce's establishment in Folkestone incorporated
a sketch of a merchant ship, an 'indiaman scudding along'.[12]

Constable, so long deprived of Academy rank, threw himself into the
workings of the institution. In 1830 he attended five council meetings

and general assemblies. He was on hand when Martin Archer Shee, Dublin-born portraitist and writer on art, was elected President in Lawrence's place. In the spring he joined the Arrangement Committee for that year's exhibition and this job as a 'hangman' meant putting up with criticism and requests for favours from colleagues, as well as – so he told Fisher – 'some scurrilities in the newspapers, the mouths of which who can escape who has others to please'. It was a task requiring diplomatic skills which he lacked. Some pictures were inevitably more visible and better lit than others. Constable was bothered by the immense frames of one exhibitor, but the offending artist said his frames were no different from those Lawrence had used. Constable told him, 'it is easy to imitate Lawrence in his *frames*.' His own entries gave him difficulty. He wrote to Samuel Lane while working on one, 'I am sadly harassed, and not being able to call on you is most vexatious. I cannot go out, lest my picture and my fire should go out too.' His exhibition pictures were a *Dell Scene* at Helmingham; a view of *Hampstead Heath with London in the Distance*, perhaps made from the upstairs back windows of Well Walk, showing the dome of St Paul's on the horizon and two donkeys in a dip in the foreground; and an unidentified 'landscape'.

A fourth painting should have been hung but ran into trouble. (Constable as an Academician had the right to exhibit up to eight paintings.) It was a painting he had done while sitting by the river at the end of the Fishers' Leydenhall garden some years before: a limpid, untroubled painting of the Wiltshire Avon, water meadows and a few pollarded willows on the far bank and reflections of the trees on the calm water surface moving slowly by. But this picture did not go forward with his other three as the work of Constable. Perhaps the porters made the mistake. *Watermeadows at Salisbury* got thrown in with the thousand or so works entered by non-members, and Constable listened while his fellow committee members discussed his picture. 'A poor thing,' said one. 'Very green,' said another. 'It's devilish bad – cross it,' said a third, meaning chalk-mark it for rejection. Abraham Cooper, who was on the Arrangement Committee, later told W.P. Frith that at that point Constable stepped forward

Water meadows near Salisbury

from his seat and faced his fellow judges. He said that he had painted the offending picture. 'I had a notion that some of you didn't like my work, and this is pretty convincing proof. I'm very much obliged to you.' Then, Cooper said, he made a low, ironic bow.[13]

Martin Archer Shee was upset and asked how the painting had got mixed up with the outsiders' paintings. The committee members muttered their apologies, expressed their embarrassment, and there was quick agreement that *Watermeadows* be admitted. But Constable wouldn't have this. He said, 'It has been properly condemned as a daub. Send it out.' He took it home with him under his arm. Some have suggested that this incident may have been contrived, either by RAs playing a joke on Constable, or by Constable himself, winding up his fellow members. But it seems more likely to have been pure mischance, a mistake by the carpenter who chalked the Xs or the porters who sorted and stacked the paintings. (Graham Reynolds notes that Constable told Fisher about a similar mistake the porters had made when they saw a cross on a frame and took it for the mark of rejection; but the cross turned out to have been made by the frame-maker. 'So much for chance in these things[,] on which perhaps hung the peace & livelihood of some respectable artist.') Constable didn't hold this incident against the Academy; at the sale of Sir Thomas Lawrence's effects in June 1830, he bought for twelve guineas the palette which had originally belonged to Sir Joshua Reynolds and which Sir George Beaumont had left to Lawrence – Constable presented the palette to the Academy. The Academy fixed a silver plaque on it, giving all the details of its provenance and mentioning that the palette and a handsome mahogany case had been presented by Mr Constable.[14]

Charles Leslie was among the early admirers of Constable's 'daub'; he told Richard Redgrave he would have given any of his own works for *Watermeadows at Salisbury*,[15] which John Sheepshanks later gave to the South Kensington Museum, now the V&A. But Constable was certainly aware that, although he hadn't agreed with the judgement of his fellow hanging judges in this case, his way of painting didn't satisfy everyone. He admitted to Fisher in May 1830, 'I have filled my head with certain notions of <u>freshness</u> – <u>sparkle</u> – brightness – till it has influenced my practice in no small degree, & is in fact taking the place of truth[;] so invidious is manner, in all things – it is a species of self worship – which should always be combated – & we have nature (another word for moral feeling) always in our reach to do it with – if we will have the resolution to look at her.'

# 16. *English Landscape (1830–32)*

The letter to Fisher of May 1830 went on to announce a Constable event. He told his old friend that he had a little book about to start coming out called *Various Subjects of Landscape, characteristic of English Scenery*; there would be four prints in each part, and it promised well. It was to be his summing-up. What it didn't promise – although he didn't know this yet – was an easy time for his health, finances and happiness.

*English Landscape* was a new experience for Constable, whose works had not been successfully reproduced at this point. It was a series of mezzotints, a form of engraving, invented in the seventeenth century, that became popular in the eighteenth when it was used to reproduce portraits painted by Gainsborough and Reynolds. The metal plate was chiselled into a blurred mesh of dots and this, when covered with ink, would produce a solid black printed image. The engraver then scraped off areas of the burr or burnished the plate smooth in the parts where he wanted half-tones and lights to create the picture he had in mind. The engraver Constable picked for his project was a twenty-seven-year-old craftsman named David Lucas.[1] Lucas's background was even more rural than Constable's – his father was a working farmer and grazier in Northamptonshire – but Lucas had been apprenticed to a leading engraver, Samuel William Reynolds. Reynolds had begun, but not finished, an engraving of Constable's *Lock*, of 1824, and he had also been asked by John Arrowsmith to make prints of some of Constable's Brighton drawings – another abandoned project. Lucas was living on the

Harrow Road, Paddington.[2] Constable had written to him in August 1829 when sending – so it seems – sketches for proposed plates. As the letter to Fisher of May 1830 demonstrates, the project was properly under way by the following spring.

In 1822 Fisher had recommended that Constable build up his reputation by lithographs. Constable's drawings always impressed people, Fisher said; therefore, 'Get one done on stone as an experiment.' Fisher wasn't keen on mezzotint, whose stubbly process he thought unsuited to Constable's 'evanescent effects' – 'Your charm is colour, and the cool tint of English daylight.' But his enthusiasm for the idea of Constable reproductions got to the artist. Fame of course was a spur, and other artists had found engraving a way of making a record of their works. Claude was the great inspiration, with his *Liber Veritatis*. Turner's *Liber Studiorum* was a more up-to-date exemplar – and Constable must have recognised the value of the book of engravings as an advertising tool, useful in disseminating Turner's work to a wider field. Constable could do with such an audience. Popularity, he kept claiming, was never going to be his, but this didn't stop him hankering after acceptance by his peers and greater recognition as a landscape painter. Did he know Hazlitt's essay 'Immortality in Youth'? – 'It is the simplicity and, as it were, abstractedness of our feelings in youth that (so to speak) identifies us with Nature and (our experience being weak and our passions strong) makes us fancy ourselves immortal like it.'[3] In the introduction Constable wrote for his book of mezzotints, he set those artists who had eyes only for 'what others have accomplished' against those who went to the primitive source, Nature, and added to Art qualities of Nature unknown to it before. They 'thus formed a style which was original'. The first type of artist merely repeated the work of others, and was easily comprehended and welcomed. But 'the rise of an Artist in a sphere of his own must almost certainly be delayed; it is to time generally that the justness of his claims to a lasting reputation will be left'. He intended to display the variety of nature and show how the landscape of England looked at various seasons, at various times of day.[4]

The effort of bringing forth *English Landscape* strained both artist and engraver. Constable wrote to Lucas in March 1831:

> I have thought much on my book, and all my reflections on the subject go to oppress me – its duration, its expence, its hopelessness of remuneration, all are unfavourable . . . The expence is too enormous for a work that has nothing but your beautiful feeling and execution to recommend it – the painter himself is totally unpopular and ever will be, on this side of the grave certainly . . . Remember dear Lucas that I mean not to think one reflection on you – every thing with the plan is my own – and I want to releive my mind of that which now harrasses it like a disease.

Nearly a year later Constable told Lucas:

> I am so sadly grieved at the proof you now send me of the Castle [Hadleigh, that is] that I am most anxious to see you. Your art may have resources of which I know nothing – but so deplorably deficient in all feeling is the present state of the plate that I can suggest nothing at all – to me it is utterly, utterly HOPELESS.'[5]

Lucas found it hard to measure up to Constable's standards. He thought Constable sometimes charged him with failures he didn't deserve. He told the painter, 'You seem to think I stick at nothing where my own interest is concerned, but I have made not a few sacrifices rather than act in a way that I anticipated would be disagreable [sic] to you.' But compared with the maker of the *Liber Studiorum*, who did much of his own initial etching of the plates and then had frequent rows with his engravers, Constable was patient and friendly. Both he and Lucas were often unwell during this period. Both were made anxious by sick children. Constable was aware that he kept changing his mind about which subjects to have engraved and how the prints should be composed, and he demanded reworkings from Lucas that were often counter-productive – the final states were much worse than the earliest.[6]

Yet despite all this Lucas found Constable a stalwart companion in their 'joint labours'. Between giving directions and then changing directions for printing the sets, Constable frequently expressed concern for Lucas and his family. When Lucas's little boy was very sick, Constable asked Dr Davis (who also attended Constable and his son John Charles) to visit the Lucases. On 4 January 1831 he sent Holland, the man who often carried messages for him, to find out from Lucas how things were with the boy: 'I feel for your distress, and I trust you have seen Dr Davis – for if human means can avail they are his. Don't think of me and my concern for a moment . . . I mention this only to releive your mind from all other anxiety, as I well know your great integrity, and that you are always too ready to devote yourself to others, or at least to me.' Ultimately Constable gave Lucas his support when he tried for election as an Associate of the Academy and told him they had 'a bond of friendship' brought about by 'the lovely amalgamation' of their works. Lucas was to remember instances when Constable reminded him of their common rural backgrounds. On one occasion in July 1830 Constable made a sketch for him showing the way English river valleys ran to the sea and in particular 'that which divides the counties of Essex and Suffolk'.[7]

Letters between painter and engraver tracked the uneven progress of the work. On 26 February 1830, for example, Constable chivvied Lucas – often in homely figures of speech – about the plates he was working on. 'I want to know how forward the "Evening" is and the retouched "Stoke",' he wrote. And: 'I have taken much pains with the last proof of the "Summerland", but I fear I shall be obliged to reject it. It has never recovered from its first trip up, and the sky with the new ground is and ever will be as rotten as cow dung.' And: 'I like your first plates, for they are by far (very far) the best, but I allow much for your distractions since, with these devils the printers – and your finances, and other matters, not in unison with that patient toil, which ought always to govern the habits of us both – but more perhaps yours . . .' And: 'Bring me another "Castle" or two or three, for it is mighty fine – though it looks as if all the chimney sweepers in Christendom had been at work on it, & thrown their soot bags up in the air. Yet everybody likes it – but I should recollect that no one but the elect see my things – I have no doubt the world despises them . . . Come early tomorrow evening, and bring what you can – & an account of the state of the next – I am nervous, & anxious about them . . . '

Sometimes Lucas got it wrong and aroused the painter's anger. After Lucas altered a 'Glebe Farm' plate without being asked to, and sent Constable a proof, Constable wrote in anguish to him, 'I frankly tell you I could burst into tears – never was there such a *wreck*. Do not touch the plate again on any account . . . I could cry for my poor wretched wreck of the Glebe Farm.' In one undated blast, at what was clearly a nervous moment (probably in 1833), Constable complained to Lucas, 'This dreadfull book must be my ruin . . . <u>You do nothing right</u> – not one thing that you say you will . . . It was the devil himself who first led me <u>step</u> by <u>step</u> to do it – thus to waste the sacred property of my children' – in other words Mr Bicknell's legacy. An apology to Lucas soon followed.[8]

Constable at first intended *English Landscape* to be eight plates in two parts each of four. Lucas was paid £15 and later £17 per plate. But Constable kept changing his mind about the subjects to be engraved and which plate should be in what part. Lucas was kept to the mark with admonitions about, say, the windmills. Constable was keen not to be added to the roster of 'uninformed artists' who created sails 'that no amount of wind would be able to turn round'. Constable went to visit Lucas now and then, tried out his printing press, and made drawings to show him how a windmill functioned.[9] However, the project went on growing like Topsy. In the initial series of 1830 to 1832 five parts or 'numbers' were printed, four of which had four prints and one six prints (several hundred impressions were apparently taken from each plate). A sixth part was contemplated but instead of this a further, differently arranged set of parts replaced the first, with an expanded title, an introduction and notes. Despite Constable's letter to Fisher of 24 May 1830 promising the first number the following week, publication was delayed until early July. Copies could be bought from 34 Charlotte Street and from the Colnaghis in Pall Mall East, though like Turner Constable resented the commissions taken by print dealers (the 'sharks', as he called them).[10]

A copy of the first number received a hospitable review from the *Athenaeum*. The subjects were more varied than expected from Mr Constable, 'who appears to have fed his genius, like a tethered horse, within a small circle in the homestead'. *The Spectator* faulted the 'extreme blackness and coarseness' of the engravings, while admitting that they displayed great feeling. Constable also presented copies to Peter de Wint, the landscape painter, who was grateful; to John Britton, antiquarian and topographical draughtsman, who like *The Spectator* thought the prints too black; and to James and William Carpenter, the father-and-son booksellers in Bond Street. Constable generally dealt with the son, in the hope that he would promote the work through the shop, rather than the father, with whom he had had his problems – not uncommon with those who bought or thought they had bought one of Constable's pictures and then found Constable hanging on to it, and allegedly improving it. James Carpenter went through this with *A Boat Passing a Lock*, exhibited at the Academy in 1829, and, not managing to acquire it, eventually agreed to accept a new Constable painting of the same size, for which he put up a deposit of one hundred guineas. Constable told Carpenter that *Helmingham Dell* – which he occasionally referred to as 'A Wood' – would be his but changed his mind just before he sent it to the Academy in 1830; he decided to keep it, forfeiting Carpenter's friendship and having to pay back the hundred guineas. It wasn't as if he hadn't painted the same scene several times, with a rather rickety bridge spanning a stream running towards the viewer through a dark, tree-shaded declivity, though this time there were deer, a cow, and a few small human figures that increased the sense of melancholy. Constable had no other purchaser lined up; he simply wanted to keep the painting.[11]

The 'Wood' figured in mezzotint-form in *English Landscape*; it was a spot to which he had been attached, as were most of the subjects in his 'book'. Others were East Bergholt common and its windmill for a plate named *Spring*; a view of West End Fields, Hampstead, entitled *Noon*; the shore at Brighton in surf and wind, *A Sea Beach*; and also

Brighton: a sea beach

Weymouth Bay, Hadleigh Castle, several Stour valley scenes and – a little more removed but meaningful to him – Old Sarum and the entrance to Yarmouth harbour. The frontispiece, which he and Lucas got around to in 1831 for the fifth part, showed the front of his parents' house and its grounds, with a man sketching, his dog nearby. The Latin epigraph below the title of *East Bergholt, Suffolk* was that translated in 1820 by John Fisher and his brother-in-law Christopher Cookson:

> This spot saw the day spring of my life,
>     Hours of Joy, and years of Happiness.
> This place first tinged my boyish fancy with a love of the art,
>     This place was the origin of my Fame.[12]

What some like *The Spectator* saw as Constable's extreme blackness or his fondness for the soot bucket was explained in his introduction. It was intended. He was seeking chiaroscuro as a main effect, and mezzotint was the technique best suited for this. The Italian term was briefly alluded to in the first series; in the second, in 1833, it was heralded in the subtitle, where the work being offered was said to be 'Principally Intended to Mark the Phenomena of the Chiar'Oscuro of Nature'. In a later lecture he defined chiaroscuro as 'that power which creates space; we find it everywhere and at all times in nature; opposition, union, light, shade, reflection, and refraction, all contribute to it'.[13] But it wasn't just an artistic means of creating space and bringing a picture to life; it was a natural thing, the 'medium by which the grand and varied aspects of landscape are displayed, both in the fields and on canvass' [*sic*]. Light and shadow were what counted, and the way these elements were balanced in a painting was all-important. Constable wanted his prints to direct the viewer's attention to this. Because mezzotint's rich blackness mimicked his own dark clouds (and possibly expressed his own black depressions), it was a suitable medium for him, particularly in the hands of David Lucas. In many of the most successful plates, Lucas got across the effects of Constable's broad and heavily paint-loaded brushwork. By vivid contrast and suggestive gradation, he caught Constable's solemnity and melancholy and the moments of glorious illumination. The antithetical elements, the light and the dark, were brought home by Lucas to the man who painted the original pictures. In 1834 Constable told Lucas, after being moved by the prints Lucas had made of *The Lock* and *The Cornfield*, 'Now . . . is every bit of sunshine clouded over in me. I can never now look at these two flattering testimonies of the result of my singularly marked life . . . without the most painful emotions.'[14] Mezzotint was right for the way he felt post-Maria: black-and-white emotions; darkness visible.

The descriptions that Constable wrote for some of the plates attempted to convey important matters, but the effort sometimes came across as stilted rather than spontaneous. For example, the plodding commentary for *Stoke-by-Nayland*: 'The solemn stillness of Nature in a Summer's Noon, when attended by thunder-clouds, is the sentiment attempted in this print; at the same time, an endeavour has been made to give an additional interest . . . by the introduction of the Rainbow.' Nature exhibited 'no feature more lovely nor any that awaken a more soothing reflection than the Rainbow'. He went on to analyse the phenomenon at length. He made a number of sketches and diagrams of rainbows; they seemed to be symbols of the hope he now sought. Other mementoes included a flight of rooks in a sunset at East Bergholt, the birds introduced possibly because he recalled an occasion at Osmington when a rook's cawing accompanied a walk with Fisher – and the rooks gave Lucas trouble, looking as they did like blemishes on the plate. Constable's printed prospectus for his book declared his desire 'to increase the interest for, and promote the study of, the rural scenery of England, with all its endearing associations, and even in its most simple localities; England with her climate of more than vernal freshness . . .'[15] And so on. He took an epigraph from Cicero: 'how much painters see in shade and protrusions that we do not see'. And he went frequently to his favourite poets – Shakespeare, Milton, Thomson, Akenside and Wordsworth – for helpful associations.[16]

If some of the attached writing was inflated, the twenty-two mezzotint prints engraved by Lucas served Constable's purpose. They showed rural England at its most winning time, a landscape shaped by use and craft, with hedges, copses, crops, locks, watermills and windmills, beach groins and harbour jetties, farmhouses and Norman churches. At one point he meant to dedicate *English Landscape* to John Fisher. Leslie later found in one of Constable's sketchbooks a draft of such a dedication:

> I know not if the landscapes I now offer to your notice will add to the esteem in which you have always been so kind as to hold me as a painter; I shall dedicate them to you, relying on that affection which you have invariably extended to me under every circumstance.

But, perhaps because Constable backed into the project in an irregular fashion, with the frontispiece appearing in 1831, a year after the first prints were made, and the letterpress commentaries two years after that, a dedication never appeared. Although Lucas produced more than four thousand prints, not many were sold. The Colnaghis got rid of a few and some individual buyers appeared, such as Lord Dover, who sent ten guineas for copies of the fifth number. Constable gave away a good many. At one point he added a ruin to the painting of the Glebe Farm he had sent to Lucas for transcription into mezzotint, saying '<u>not</u> to have a symbol in the book of myself, and of the "Work" which I have projected, would be missing the opportunity'. In 1832 numerous letters to Lucas from the painter expressed Constable's sense of ruination over *English Landscape*. The printer they were using for the letterpress, W.J. Sparrow, had been causing trouble. Sparrow was in love, waxing poetic, and his marriage plans got in the way of the humdrum work of printing. In June 1832 he sent Constable a large slice of wedding cake when the artist was impatient for proofs.[17] Gloom was piled on blackness heaped on gloom. Leslie put it well when he wrote that *English Landscape* ultimately proved to be, 'as Coleridge said of a work of his own, "a secret confided to the public, and very faithfully kept" '.[18]

# 17. *Clouds Overhead (1831–32)*

Through much of the period in which *English Landscape* was being brought to birth, Constable wasn't well; his ill health was both physical and mental. He wanted his book of prints to appear but the effort involved great depressions and weakened his resistance. He was fifty-four going on fifty-five in 1831, not an old man. Yet when Daniel Maclise, one of the Academy Life School students, sketched him at work that year as a Visitor at the Academy's Life School, Constable had an undoubtedly 'senior' look, the crown of his head bald and long sideburns only in part compensating for it. Disappointment with the paltry sales of *English Landscape* was multiplied by sickness: what he thought was his not unusual long-lasting winter cold turned into something worse. On 2 February 1831 he sent Lucas a message: 'I am so weak that I can hardly write.' And on 12 March, also to Lucas: 'I cough all night, which leaves me sadly weak all day.'[1] Did he wonder if he had Maria's disease? Dr Davis called, and Mr Drew the apothecary brought medicines and pills.

All this cut into his painting time, making for 'sad work' on a canvas for the RA exhibition; he was engaged on a new large *Salisbury Cathedral from the Meadows*. One visitor, Sir William Beechey, called on 23 March and gave him good cheer and bad: 'Why *damn* it Constable, what a *damned* fine picture you are making, but you look *damned* ill – and you have got a *damned* bad cold.'[2] Leslie thought Constable's 'redoubled application' on his exhibition pictures 'fatigued his mind', though the *Salisbury Cathedral* was only accompanied by a stop-gap *Yarmouth Pier*. He had apparently painted this

Daniel
Maclise's
drawing of
Constable,
*c.*1831

some years before but hadn't shown it at Somerset House; it would, as
noted, figure as one of Lucas's mezzotints for *English Landscape* in
1832. The sad work at the easel was enough, along with the easterly
winds and irregular meals, to disorder his health. Although Constable
generally liked his main meal at midday, the time varied if he was busy
painting. Leslie found him in mid-session sustaining himself on an
orange, and observed that Constable would finally 'sit down to dinner
ill with exhaustion, when it was too dark to paint'.[3]

Constable also threw a lot into his Visitorship at the Life School.
The job not only involved putting the model in a suitable pose but
advising the students. Constable, like Turner, was an innovative
teacher and a popular one. Both believed that models were better

posed not in isolation but in a real context.[4] Constable chose as the basis for his settings a scene from a celebrated old master or piece of classical art, such as a Last Judgement by Michelangelo, with two male figures, or a female nude as an Amazon. One of his first was based on a Raphael Eve and was appreciated by both the students and Academicians – particularly Etty, a persistent Life student and admirer of the unclothed female form. Constable told Leslie that he had set the girl in paradise, 'leaving out Adam'. He thought the students expected from him a landscape background, and so decided to have a bower made up of laurel branches with oranges attached. However, there were penalties attached. He said, 'My men were twice stopped coming from Hampstead with the green boughs.' The police thought, 'as was the case, they had robbed some gentleman's grounds'. The gentleman was Constable, but he had to go to the magistrates to get the men released and pay a fine of ten shillings, perhaps for wasting police time.[5] Constable invited Leslie to call at Charlotte Street and walk down to Somerset House with him and see the results of this wrong-doing for himself: 'It is no small undertaking to make a Paradise of the Life Academy.' Constable did an oil sketch of the Eve, seen from the rear, that his daughter Isabel later prudishly pruned to leave only the lovely head, with the girl's hair up in a loose bun.[6] Richard Redgrave thought that Constable was ambitious to prove to his Academy colleagues that, although a landscape painter, he could be an exemplary visitor in the Life School. The students evidently enjoyed his jibes and sallies.[7] Henry Sass, who also attended as a mature participant in the Life classes, on one occasion took along to Constable's studio W.P. Frith, a student from his nearby art school. Frith noticed that Constable had various natural items lying around – a bit of tree, some weeds, a bunch of dock leaves. They were apparently touchstones. Constable told him not to do anything without nature to hand. Walking away afterwards and discussing the neglect Constable's work suffered, Sass told Frith, 'The day will come when Constable will be understood.'[8]

By the time his Visitorship duties were over at the end of January 1831, Constable was plagued by his long-lasting cold. His six-footer of Salisbury Cathedral was slowed down. Several oil sketches had preceded the finished work and several drawings made on his last visits to the Fishers in 1829 came in handy. What John Fisher called the 'Church under a cloud' had long been a favourite subject. One oil sketch – roughly fourteen by twenty inches, now in Tate Britain – was in fact in his lightest manner, almost watercolour-like. In the finished work, a quadrant of a rainbow arches across the storm clouds and touches down on Leydenhall. Certainly Fisher's uncle the Bishop would have been perturbed by the mass of angry sky. It was the year before the passing of the great Reform Bill, and whether Constable was alluding to Church/State problems is uncertain. The good fortune suggested by the rainbow had perhaps a more personal implication. Constable knew Thomson's poem 'Summer', in which a thunderstorm passes over and a young woman named Amelia is struck by lightning and dies in her lover's arms. In the RA catalogue he quoted Thomson's lines about the storm's aftermath: tumultuous clouds, interminable sky, a purer azure 'and a clearer calm':

> . . . while, as if in sign
> Of danger past, a glittering robe of joy,
> Set off abundant by the yellow ray,
> Invests the fields, and nature smiles reviv'd.

The rainbow gives the impression that Constable was coming out from the storm he'd been in since Maria's death.[9]

Constable was on the Arrangement Committee again and in May found his hanging skills and honesty attacked in the *Observer*. Edward Dubois suggested that he had deliberately put the pictures of some of his landscape rivals in bad positions. Dubois allowed that Constable had few equals in depicting the scene before him 'with all its freshness and truth', before complaining that all his worst peculiarities were 'monstered' in his *Salisbury Cathedral*: 'coarseness and vulgarity are the marked characteristics of Mr C.'. 'The Great Salisbury', as Constable called it in a letter to Leslie, was hung close to Turner's *Caligula's Palace and Bridge*, and Turner was among those annoyed by

Constable's hanging arrangements. David Roberts, a young admirer of Turner, heard his hero sounding off at a party one evening about Constable's perfidy in moving Turner's picture to the benefit of his own. Despite Turner's sense of grievance, the *Morning Chronicle* thought the *Cathedral* showed his influence and Constable came out worse from the comparison. 'It is impossible to class among landscapes of the first order Mr Constable's coarse, vulgar imitation of Mr. Turner's freaks and follies.' Constable, thought the *Chronicle*'s critic (once again – as one might have guessed – Edward Dubois), had been painting with his toes. Both painters had been subject to jokes about their soapsuds and snowflakes and this continued, with *The Times* finding that the *Salisbury* – 'a very vigorous and masterly landscape' – had been spoiled by 'somebody' who had put in 'such clouds as no human being ever saw, and by spotting the foreground all over with whitewash. It is quite impossible that this offence can have been committed with the consent of the artist.' Yet the *Morning Post* and the *Literary Gazette* found the proximity of Turner and Constable a reason for compliments. The latter's critic was made to think of fire and water. 'If Mr Turner and Mr Constable were professors of geology, instead of painting, the first would certainly be a Plutonist, the second a Neptunist. Exaggerated, however, as both these works are – the one all heat, the other all humidity – who will deny that they both exhibit, each in its own way, some of the highest qualities of art?'[10]

Constable's palette knife had been strenuously employed on the *Salisbury Cathedral*, though after the Academy exhibition he went on reworking it with brushes only. In parts the painting was thick with impasto. Constable believed that in the future it would be considered his greatest picture, conveying what Leslie called 'the fullest impression of the compass of his art'.[11] A viewer in the early twenty-first century can cavil with that judgement. Forceful, yes; stormy, indeed; but the painting's intensity is dearly bought – other epithets that come to mind are mannered and rhetorical. An English El Greco? The late Bishop of Salisbury would have been more alarmed than ever by Constable's storm clouds. As a piece of painting it had wonderful parts but as a complete work it failed. No one bought the painting during his lifetime and this gave him the unchallenged opportunity to go on fretting about it.

Constable's health improved with summer. At the end of June 1831 he took the three girls to Dedham to stay with Martha Whalley and her family. Isabel cleverly brought along a kitten from Hampstead, hiding it in her bonnet. Constable himself lodged with Abram and Mary at Flatford for five days and then for another week in August; coming back from the first visit he wrote to Leslie, 'Nothing can exceed the beauty of the country – it makes pictures seem sad trumpery, even those that possess most of nature.' He had a chance to make some sketches, including one of a brown-and-white springer spaniel peering at a vole from a river bank. In early August the *Ipswich Journal* published an obituary by Constable of a farmworker from nearby Much Wenham, Thomas Chiverton. Chiverton left a widow and nine children. Although he was only a 'humble . . . day labourer', Constable

A dog hunting a water vole

wrote, Chiverton had 'a most extraordinary voice, one of the fullest, richest, and sweetest counter tenors ever perhaps heard'. He sang with the choirs of village churches and was acclaimed in that part of Suffolk. 'He was gentle and affectionate to his family', who were now bereft and lacking support. However, the locality rallied round and an appeal for funds to help Chiverton's family was successful.[12]

Back in town, the gift of half a buck from Lady Dysart provided the main dish for a dinner Constable gave in August, as if he were celebrating being out from under the cloud; his distinguished colleagues Martin Archer Shee and Henry Howard were there, along with Charles Eastlake and Charles Leslie, and Jack Bannister the actor. Writing to Leslie to tell him when Lady Dysart's 'haunch will be in perfection', Constable said he had bought a small drawing from John Varley. Varley had forthrightly told him 'how to do landscape', and kindly pointed out Constable's defects to him. When it came to naming a price for the drawing, Varley said, 'It would usually be a guinea and a half, but only a guinea for an artist.' Constable insisted on giving the larger sum, as Varley had made it clear to him that he was no artist.

George IV had died, and England was changing, sooner and faster than Constable might have liked. As one of the forty full Academicians, he was invited to the coronation of the new King. Constable was proud to be at the ceremony in Westminster Abbey, eleven hours long, to see with his own eyes 'the Crown of England put on the head of that good man, William IV – and that too in the chair of a saint'. He sketched for Leslie (who didn't attend) the Lord Chancellor, Lord Brougham, who had defended George IV's put-aside wife Caroline and further incurred Constable's animosity by favouring the reform-minded Whigs. Constable sketched him from the back, with his coronet perched like a tea cosy on top of an enormous wig, looking ridiculously like a Jack-in-the-green. Constable sat in the south transept commanding a view of the nobility: 'The moment the King's crown was on, they all crowned themselves. At the same instant the shouts of "God save the King," the trumpets, the band, the drums of the soldiers in the nave, and last – though not least – the artillery . . . made it all eminently imposing. The white ermine of the peers looked lovely in the sun . . . the tone of the walls was sublime – they were heightened, no doubt, by the trappings, like an old picture with a newly gilt frame.'

This upbeat moment was unfortunately short. In October he was ill and very depressed again. Things seemed particularly black because he thought the country was going to the dogs. The Duke of Wellington's government had been replaced by Whigs, bent on electoral reform. The new King was no longer that 'good man' but a reformer, Constable feared, and a great fool. Constable was worried that the Bicknell inheritance, needed for his children's future, would be snatched from him by radicals. He wrote to Leslie towards the end of October, 'What makes me dread this tremendous attack on the constitution of this country is, that the wisest and best of the Lords are seriously and firmly objecting to it – and it goes to give the government into the hands of the rabble and dregs of the people, and the devil's agents on earth, the agitators.' His illness kept him in Hampstead, and possibly the distance from his painting room in Charlotte Street magnified every problem; every difficulty was seen as an evil, every uncertainty as a calamity sure to happen. Constable's Tory tendencies were stirred to a boil by the movement for parliamentary reform. He was able to draw and paint Old Sarum (one of his subjects in *English Landscape*), enjoying it as a historic site and dramatic feature for a painting, while recognising that it was 'no continuing city' and without acknowledging that it was one of the most flagrant of rotten boroughs.

Constable's conservatism was rooted in Suffolk soil and family ties. It was part of his inheritance. He resisted change that might overturn the established order. It was a structure of things that included the family mills, the cornfields off Fen Lane, and Dedham church in the distance. Now the once unchanging plod of farming life was being shaken – there were new ways of tilling the soil, new machines for harvesting crops, new causes of unease and agitation. In protest at mechanisation, ricks were being burned in Suffolk as elsewhere. At one point both the rector – Dr Rhudde's successor – and the squire fled East Bergholt, fearing insurrection. Yet with Constable a hint of better health and a better outlook ran together. In early November he felt more fit and wrote to Leslie saying the Reform Bill now gave him 'not the least concern – I care nothing about it – & have no curiosity to know if it be <u>dead or alive</u>'. Among other things, the reformers got rid of the restrictions on killing, buying or selling game, and this pleased the rural poor. Trade unions were now legal. Although Peel's new police force kept Radical mobs from tearing London apart during the agitation for the bill, the pro-Reform crowds were incensed by the opposition of the spiritual peers to the bill in the House of Lords, and managed to stone the bishops' coaches and set fire to some of their palaces.[13] 'Disheartening times' indeed, as Fisher had complained the year before, but in 1831 the two friends found fewer occasions to grumble together. Constable's conservatism was in any event non-partisan – he called for a plague on all political bodies. In 1836 he remarked to his unrelated namesake George Constable, a brewer in Arundel, Sussex: 'I hate the Whigs, but the Tories have done the greatest mischeif, for it was they who passed the Catholic bill [emancipating Catholics from certain civil disabilities] – but I hate politics and never see a newspaper . . .'[14]

Constable meant to gather his family at Charlotte Street for Christmas but in the end Well Walk was favoured. Minna dressed the drawing-room mantelpiece with festive greenery and then, before going to Putney for a week to visit her aunt Louisa, set up a little table with decorations in the dining room to make things look pretty for her father while she was away. He missed her exceedingly. And the new year saw a severe relapse in his health. He was disabled by rheumatism, perhaps by rheumatic fever. His right hand, with which he painted, still functioned, but his left arm was useless and he couldn't work. Fourteen leeches were applied to his left shoulder to ease the pain, but this moved to his knee and he was unable to stand. He had to tell the Academy that he couldn't be a Visitor at the Life School this season. Etty stood in for him and enjoyed arranging the female models for a tableau of *Venus Sacrificing to the Graces*. Shee, the

RA President, wrote to say he was dismayed by Constable's illness.

Constable dictated to John Charles his correspondence to Lucas and Leslie.[15] The latter was staying at Petworth House and had tried to buck up Constable with an account of Lord Egremont's great collection. Constable responded, after several weeks of pain, to say he could now hold a pen again; he recalled some of Turner's early works, which included 'one of singular intricacy and beauty; it was a canal with numerous boats making thousands of beautifull shapes, and I think the most complete work of genius I ever saw'. And he went on, 'Your mention of a "solemn twilight" by Gainsborough has awakened all my sympathy. Do pray make me a sketch of it, if it is ever so slight a splash. As to meeting you in these grand scenes, dear Leslie, remember the great were not made for me, nor I for the great, yet, perhaps, things are better as they are. My limited and abstracted art is to be found under every hedge, and in every lane, and therefore nobody thinks it worth picking up, but I have my admirers, each of whom I consider a host.'

Constable was brought from Hampstead to recuperate in Charlotte Street. Johnny Dunthorne kept Martha Whalley informed about her brother's condition, and Abram came to town to talk about family matters; this cheered the invalid considerably. Abram, a lifelong bachelor, was a diligent uncle to the Constable children, as well as the indispensable administrator of the Constable grain-and-coal business. After his visit, Constable's doctor was impressed by the way Constable had perked up. Charles Leslie also heard frequently from Constable as he regained his strength. Constable wrote to him from his bed on 17 January: 'How heavenly it is to wake up as I do now after a good night – and see all these dear infants about my bed all *up early* to know how papa passed the night.' Constable claimed he was looking on the bright side of his illness and – like Robert Burton and John Milton – finding delights in melancholy. Constable's ups and downs were closely monitored by Leslie, who recognised Constable's ability to give in totally to his own feelings. 'He said of himself, "If I were bound with chains I should break them, and with a single hair round me I should feel uncomfortable." ' At one point the Leslie family got the impression that Constable in his bereaved state wanted a feminine companion, and Leslie's sister Ann, also an artist, was thought to be in line for the role.[16] But though she copied Constable's early *Church Porch*, which he lent her, visited Charlotte Street on several occasions with her brother and his wife, and often figured in Constable's invitations to dine with him and his children, nothing came of the putative attachment. The Leslies, however, went on providing close support, and vice versa. Constable felt able to tell Charles Leslie just after his wife Harriet gave birth to their third son, George: 'Don't let her *nurse* too long – nothing undermines a constitution so insidiously.'[17]

In early February Constable got to a meeting at Somerset House again and felt proud of the Academy. He worked himself back into his painting routine and told Lucas he was 'dashing away at the great London' – his Waterloo Bridge, his 'Harlequin's Jacket', his 'Lord Mayor's show'. He had been wrestling with the idea on and off since 1817 (though his first reference to a large canvas on the subject was in a letter to Fisher of 1 September 1820). In early March his knees were still so badly affected he couldn't manage the journey to Leslie's house. At the beginning of April he told Leslie that he was 'in a dreadfull state' about his picture, but his five-year-old son Alfred liked to 'help' by playing alongside his easel, sometimes creating mischief the doting father found delightful. His venerable and generally admiring friend Thomas Stothard called on 24 April to look at the Waterloo and said, like Dickens's Mr Jingle, 'Very unfinished, sir – much to do – figures not made out, sir.' The painting was finally called *Whitehall Stairs, June 18th 1817*, after the place on the river bank where the Prince Regent descended the stone steps and embarked for the bridge-opening ceremony. It was hung by the arrangers in the School of Painting, one of the smaller exhibition rooms. There, its creator thought, it could only be seen properly by visitors as they came through the doors; moreover the light was 'of the worst kind for my unfortunate "manner" '. He told Leslie he regretted sending in such a 'scrambling affair'. Constable had hoped to make the picture 'more finished' on the spot, but this was thwarted when the varnishing days, on which members could go on working on the field of battle, were reduced in number that year.

Constable was aware that the reduction in 'varnishing' time was directed mainly at Turner, the great competitor, who often turned what looked like a barely begun canvas into a recognisable painting on these occasions. This time a Turner painting, *Helvoetsluys*, hung next to the Constable river scene. Leslie recalled that Turner's was

a sea-piece . . . a grey picture, beautiful and true, with no positive colour in any part of it. Constable's 'Waterloo' seemed as if painted with liquid gold and silver, and Turner came several times into the room while he was heightening with vermilion and lake the decorations and flags of the city barges. Turner stood behind him, looking from the 'Waterloo' to his own picture, and at last brought his palette from the great room where he was touching another picture, and putting a round daub of red lead, somewhat bigger than a shilling, on his grey sea, went away without saying a word.

The intensity of the red lead, made more vivid by the coolness of the picture, caused even the vermilion and lake of Constable to look weak. I came into the room just as Turner left it. 'He has been here,' said Constable, 'and fired a gun.'

Turner did not enter the School of Painting again for a day and a half. 'And then,' said Leslie, 'in the last moments that were allowed for painting, he glazed the scarlet seal he had put on his picture, and shaped it into a buoy.'[18]

Constable's riverscape was the only picture he painted of the heart of London. He had used sketches for it that went back to the opening ceremony in 1817 and to visits to Lord Pembroke's terrace near the stairs he had made in July 1826, when he was seeking a better viewpoint for the painting. *Whitehall Stairs* showed John Rennie's new bridge as a pearly-grey structure of many spans, running in a straight line across the left side of the painting. The dome of St Paul's was a mere pimple in the distance downstream. Constable's final workings on the picture aimed to reproduce the sparkle on the river's surface. To achieve this his instrument of choice was a palette knife: thick blobs of white paint were plastered on to the canvas. Perhaps his crippling rheumatism made him favour the knife rather than the brush, as well as his desire for certain effects. Whatever, his methods aroused the wrath of some critics – several of whom also failed to get the significance of the title and date, an event fifteen years in the past. The *Morning Chronicle*'s Edward Dubois (who mistook the occasion for the more recent opening of the new London Bridge) thought the artist/plasterer 'might have been better employed in the erection of the bridge itself than in painting the subject'. However, the *Morning Post* got the picture: the right bridge, the right day, the right monarch. The paper noted the controversy over Constable's manner but sided with those who admired the painting and upheld it as 'a work of consummate skill'. *Whitehall Stairs* needed to be seen at a proper distance, the *Post*'s writer thought, not always easy in the crowded rooms of the Academy.[19] But even Turner's and Stanfield's productions shrank by comparison to it. Later critics have been puzzled by the weird balustrade in the foreground and the children beyond it suspended seemingly in the air. Charles Leslie, faithful friend, found his enthusiasm fully tested: he thought that in pursuit of 'the indispensable quality' of chiaroscuro, 'and of that brightness in nature which baffles all the ordinary processes of painting, and which it is hardly possible to unite with smoothness of surface', Constable had been led into 'a peculiar mode of execution', and had here 'indulged in the vagaries of the palette knife . . . to an excess'. Constable admitted to Leslie his restlessness about the picture – 'it has not my redeeming voice, "the rural"'. This lack of confidence may have led him to send in eight pictures in all, the most he had submitted since 1815; four were watercolours of rural subjects.[20]

Minna's bout of scarlet fever preoccupied him during June, and he was already alarmed about the condition of another person close to him – Johnny Dunthorne. On 22 June Constable wrote to Leslie, 'Poor John Dunthorne is getting daily, nay hourly worse – he cannot long remain to me.' Note the 'to me' – it would be a personal loss when it came. On 6 July, when Johnny's legs were so swollen he could hardly walk, Constable added: 'I shall lose a sincere friend, whose attachment to me has been like a sons from his infancy. He is without a fault & so much the fitter for heaven. I woke in the night about him.' Constable frequently went to Grafton Street to check on Johnny, but each melancholy visit took him a day to get over. Johnny knew he'd had it; he was saddened that he was being removed from the world just as he was succeeding in it. Leslie believed that Johnny had heart disease, though Constable thought a 'dropsical complaint' was involved.

The immediate calamity struck elsewhere. In the winter of 1829/30 John Fisher had been unwell with 'gout, asthma, and fulness of blood in the head'. The correspondence of the two friends seems to have faltered, though in 1831, before the RA exhibition, Fisher suggested some Latin tags for the catalogue, one of which Constable adopted for his *English Landscape* prospectus. In August 1832 Fisher went to northern France with his wife hoping for a change for the better. They had been in Boulogne a week when Fisher was seized by violent spasms. These began one day at 4 a.m. and went on for several hours. Then he slept almost continuously until eleven that night, when he suddenly stopped breathing. Fisher was forty-five. 'Suppressed Gout' was blamed first of all, though later Constable was told the cause of death was cholera. He wrote to Leslie of the 'sudden and awfull event':

> The closest intimacy had subsisted for many years between us – we loved each other and confided in each other entirely – and his loss means a sad gap in my life & worldly prospects – he would have helped my children, for he was a good adviser though impetuous, and a truly religious man – God bless him till we meet again . . .

Fisher – the privileged but perceptive cleric – had been Constable's first major patron and best friend. Their friendship hadn't suffered but rather had been reaffirmed when need for cash forced Fisher to sell paintings back to Constable. Although Fisher never got his

dedication in *English Landscape*, the letterpress describing its frontispiece recalled Fisher's uncle the Bishop, sometime vicar of Langham,
along with Sir George Beaumont, seasonal visitor in Dedham, as
influences in Constable's life. Through much of their acquaintance
the younger Fisher seems to have been a more spontaneous letter
writer than Constable, but it was to Fisher that the artist presented
some of his memorable thoughts: the sound of water escaping from
mill dams, and painting being but another word for feeling – thoughts
in which sensory detail and recollection were as bound up as in
Proust's remembrance of the madeleine. Fisher had resolutely backed
the hesitating painter when his prospective marriage to Maria seemed
in peril; he had applauded Constable for aiming high – 'your fame is
your Pole Star'; and he had for a long time helped hold Constable's
head above water. Bishop Fisher, 'the kindly monitor', had passed on,
and now so had the nephew who had frequently given Constable the
chance to show that he was not only a great artist but a good man.
Memories crowded in: Fisher conducting the marriage service in St
Martin-in-the-Fields; walking on the beach in Weymouth bay;
recommending Gilbert White's *Selborne*; making sermons, listening
to gossip, talking to wives and children . . . 'I cannot tell how
singularly his death has affected me,' Constable closed his letter to
Leslie.

Constable took refuge with his children in Hampstead where (he
told Mary Fisher a little later) he felt Maria's presence; he seemed
'still to live in the society of my departed Angel'. He spent a week
copying a winter landscape by Jacob van Ruysdael; the stay-at-home
Dutch painters were often in his thoughts at this time, as were the
works of the much-travelled Flemish artist-diplomat Rubens. The
Ruysdael had been lent by Sir Robert Peel, scion of a Lancashire
industrial family and Tory minister who had brought in Catholic
emancipation. Peel said Constable could borrow the Ruysdael as long
as he didn't copy it exactly; Constable added a dog. He also got
consolation from a copy of a small Pieter de Hooch that Leslie sent, a
painting of a room in Delft lit up by a sunbeam. He told Leslie that
the best proof of its excellence was that nothing in it could be changed,

'either in place, or light, or dark, or color – either warm or cold'. Trying to get through this bleak time, he wrote to Lucas saying he had added a ruin to the little Glebe Farm as a symbol of himself (and of his *English Landscape*).[21]

One person Constable encountered occasionally in Charlotte Street was his neighbour and one-time friend R.R. Reinagle. Reinagle was later to claim that Constable had been his pupil. He said he had taught Constable 'the whole Art of Painting' and that 'when his father, who was a rich miller at Bergholt in Suffolk, dismissed him from his house for loving the Art as a profession, I received him into my house for 6 months, & furnished him everything he wanted – even money'.[22] Reinagle was a skilful copyist of old masters and competent portrait painter. He had been a full Academician since 1823, six years before his so-called pupil. But he had qualities that Frith might have featured in a Road to Ruin. He often held sales of his own paintings and of purported old masters. On 20 and 21 June 1832, according to a sign nailed to his house at 54 Charlotte Street, three hundred extravagantly attributed pictures were to be auctioned there. Reinagle arranged an evening opening 'for the nobility', and laid on a band of drums, trumpets, and hand organs for musical entertainment. Constable felt a good deal of *schadenfreude* when the sale wasn't a success. He wrote to Leslie: 'The result of Reinagles puffing has been that nearly the whole of the pictures are left on his hands, enough not selling to pay his expenses . . . The whole mess has been (as I hope such things ever will be) a totall failure.' But he sounded genuinely sad in June 1835 when he wrote to young Boner that 'poor' Reinagle's bankruptcy had been announced. Reinagle continued to live by his wits. In 1848 he exhibited at the Academy as his own painting a marine picture by J.W. Arnold that he had bought at a dealer's and altered slightly. The deception was discovered, and Reinagle had to resign his RA membership.[23]

Meanwhile, Johnny Dunthorne was failing completely and by early October he was confined to bed. Constable looked in from time to time; he brought his copy of the Peel Ruysdael for Johnny to see.

Johnny died on Friday 2 November at 4 p.m., aged thirty-four. 'He fought a good fight,' Constable told Lucas, 'and I think must have left the world with as few regrets as any man of his age I ever met with.' He wrote to Leslie, 'His loss makes a gap that cannot be filled up with me in this world. So with poor Fisher. I am unfortunate in my friendships.' Constable went down to Suffolk to attend Johnny's 'last scene'; he stayed at Flatford with Abram and Mary. The Reverend Rowley delivered the funeral sermon taking his text from Isaiah IV, 21: 'In that day shall the branch of the Lord be beautiful and glorious, and the fruit of the earth shall be excellent and comely for them that are escaped of Israel.' Perhaps the stately language and high words flying over their heads gave some traditional comfort, but Johnny's distraught father told Constable not long after that he didn't care 'how soon he was laid in the same grave with poor John'. (It was 1844 when this reunion occurred; the Dunthorne tomb is on the street side of the East Bergholt graveyard.) Dunthorne Senior continued to prize a large telescope Johnny had made and thereafter made a point of showing it to callers at his house in the village. For Johnny there were no more stars.[24]

In the coach going back to London on 13 November Constable travelled with two other gentlemen. Passing across the vale of Dedham, he remarked how beautiful it was and one of his fellow passengers said, 'Yes, sir, this is Constable's country.' Constable then felt bound to introduce himself lest something more was said that spoiled the moment.[25]

# 18. *A Summer's Morning (1833–34)*

Early in 1833 Constable was working – not too happily – on two paintings. One was a house-portrait, not his favourite line of work, the subject being Englefield House which belonged to a wealthy Berkshire landowner, Richard Benyon de Beauvoir. 'My house tires me very much,' he wrote to Leslie. 'The window frames & chimneys & chimney pots are endless – but I shall fill the canvas beyond repentence.' The other was a painting of the monument commemorating Joshua Reynolds that Sir George Beaumont had set up in the grounds of Coleorton. But though the idea for this picture was, like that for the Waterloo, of long standing, dating from his first visit to Beaumont's estate in 1823, it seemed to bring on gloom and irritability. And this mood was accompanied by a cold. He put *The Cenotaph* aside and wrote again to Leslie:

> I am determined not to harrass [*sic*] <u>my mind</u> and HEALTH by scrambling over my canvas . . . Why should I – I have little to lose and <u>nothing</u> to gain. I ought to respect myself – for my friends' sake, who love me – and my children. It is time at '56' to begin at least to <u>know</u> 'one's self' – and I do know what <u>I am not</u>, and your regard for me has at least awakened me to beleive in the possibility that I may yet make some impression with my 'light' – my 'dews' – my 'breezes' – my 'bloom' and my 'freshness' – no one of which qualities has yet been perfected on the canvas of any painter in this world.

Painting it seems was also but another way of wrecking one's well-being.

Constable's children were once again among his main anxieties. Despite inscribing their names in the family Bible in November 1831,[1] as if to give them permanence, he knew by how thin a thread life hung for them all. He had taken the eldest boys to a lecture on volcanoes in mid-July 1832 that fascinated them but made Constable conclude, 'We inhabit a fearful planet'. His first-born John Charles still worried them with his frailty, although by March 1832 he seemed improved by the Hampstead air. Yet the boy often walked in his sleep and during one episode in midsummer hurt an arm – he had apparently been trying to move a chest of drawers. In July 1832 his second son Charley was sick, frightening Constable, though Dr Evans told him not to be alarmed 'for now'. Constable, trying to be father and mother both (with much help from Roberts), found it difficult to follow this instruction. Each child's birthday brought to mind their mother, his dear departed Maria: if she could see them now! But

Constable's son,
John Charles

thank God for Boner. When Pitt wasn't available Boner carried messages to Leslie and Lucas. At 35 Charlotte Street, where Constable attempted to pull his family together in early 1833, Boner opened the door to visitors and decided whom to let in. He also packed up sets of *English Landscape*, did proof-reading, and began to tutor Alfred and Lionel as well as the older boys.[2] Constable's own efforts at educating his sons included taking them to see John Beauchamp's foundry in Holborn: 'forges – smelting potts – metals – turning lathes – straps & bellows – coals, ashes, dust – dirt – & cinders – and every thing else that is agreable to boys'. Made happy by the place where Mr Beauchamp manufactured Britannia Metal, the Constable boys wanted their father to fit out such a workshop for them in the cellar under his painting room.

A proper full-time education was elusive. For a while in early 1833 Constable thought of putting young John Charles in the hands of Daniel Whalley, his sister Martha's son, a recent Cambridge graduate who was waiting for a curacy, to tutor him in maths and classics.[3] There was a plan to ship Charley off to Mr Wilkin's school near East Bergholt. But nothing came of these notions. Constable may have been school-hunting when he stopped at Hastings in 1833 and did a watercolour of East Hill near that town, a sketch designed to show the various strata that would interest the fossil-hunter John Charles. The school he eventually found was not far away in Folkestone, run by Reverend Thomas Pierce (or Pearce), recommended by Constable's cousin Jane South – her son Burton was a pupil there. Constable was in his usual two minds about this; his views on boarding schools were deeply embedded. But brother Abram encouraged the Folkestone scheme and Constable finally agreed. Boner took Charley down, calling at Dover to look at the castle on the way, and bearing a letter to Reverend Pierce expressing more than normal parental concerns. Charley's 'peculiar disposition and habits' were addressed, together with his 'natural ardor and activity of mind and habit'. (That is, he was an energetic, untidy, sometimes hard-to-control eleven- going on twelve-year-old boy who found it hard to concentrate.) 'He has never been treated with severity,' Constable told the headmaster, no doubt remembering the Lavenham 'lash'; and he enclosed a letter from Mr Drew about his son's health. Charley's prospects at the Pierce academy didn't seem to be dented by this flurry of fatherly concern or a subsequent admonition from Constable to 'pray be good and do not spoil your cloathes in sea water'. Charley was in fact attracted to salt water from the start. His sketch of an East Indiaman running up the Channel showed that he was soon getting down to the beach at Folkestone. The experiment with Charles worked to such an extent that Constable decided that John, now fifteen, could go to the Reverend Pierce's, too.[4]

Young John had taken up science – he was particularly interested in anatomy and geology, in minerals and fossils. He wrote to his brother Charles in May telling him he had been dissecting a frog and in early June asked him to look in 'stratum super stratum if there is any chalk, you will find the best fossils there'. When he joined Charley (who was more interested in insects than chalk) at school in Folkestone in the autumn, he requested Boner to make sure new issues of the *British Cyclopedia* and a periodical on botany were kept for him at Charlotte Street. 'No wonder the ancients worshipped the sea! I wish you would go and look in the clay they dig up out of the wel [the Weald] for fossils.'[5] Darwin, at that point a believer in the Bible's view of Creation, set sail on his nearly five-year voyage on the *Beagle* at the end of 1831, but taking with him Volume I of Charles Lyell's *Principles of Geology*, which proposed that the earth had been produced by geological forces over aeons of time – and not in an Old Testament timescale. Many thoughtful people, like Philip Gosse, were examining nature intently while trying to make their findings fit traditional religion. Constable himself had become interested in geology. When he went with the two eldest boys to East Bergholt at the beginning of August, he told Leslie that 'we ranged the woods and feilds, and searched the clay pits of Suffolk for the bones, and skulls, & teeth of fossil animals, for John – & Charles made drawings and I did nothing at all.' Doing nothing! – a novel admission for Constable. Was the spring winding down or was he truly happy, as he claimed, not to be painting but simply watching the boys enjoying themselves?

That Charles was drawing gave him immense pleasure. Leslie had heard in April from the proud father the good news about 'dear Charley – my son who is transported. He has sold his first picture – a drawing (God knows what it is) is bought by the *Curate* of Folkestone for one shilling – ready money, I dare say.' When Constable's new acquaintance George Constable came on the scene, two of his qualities that Constable approved of were that he was interested in the *English Landscape* prints and was 'a sensible man in all matters of science'. The Arundel brewer specially endeared himself by sending young John a box of fossils, which the boy prized. Constable thanked his near namesake and added: 'To me these pieces of "time-mangled matter" are interesting for the tale they tell; but above all, I esteem them as marks of regard to my darling boy . . .'[6]

Young John's new-boy period at the Pierces made Constable nervous. He told Leslie, 'To part with my dear John is breaking my heart – but I am told it is for his good.' He wrote to the boy enclosing 'a hasty sketch' of a great stone his uncle Abram had sent down for him from Flatford, but was soon more than usually alarmed when young John, in the new circumstances of the school, went sleepwalking again, fell, and injured his leg and hip. For a time this injury seemed to get worse. On 10 October Constable travelled to Folkestone to be with his sons, bring fruit and cakes Boner had sent, and stayed a fortnight. Young John wrote to Boner (now tutoring Alfie and Lionel) reminding him to guard his precious magazines and adding, 'You must not think my leg is quite well. Yesterday Mr Knight cut it to let the matter out. I can not put my foot to the ground, it has been allmost 3 weeks, and I have had on it a 114 leaches, and for a week I had nothing to eat . . .' The leeches were Mr Knight's method of reducing inflammation. Boner then sent down some money, for Constable was 'almost high & dry', and had had to borrow from John – he, his father noted, 'is always prudent & carefull – so like his Mother and so little like me'. Constable was also forced to take an interest in the behaviour of Burton South, young John's cousin and fellow pupil. Burty had a scapegrace reputation and was blamed for encouraging Charles Constable to spend all his pocket money on 'eatables and such like foolings'. Burty seems to have been the instigator of an extra-curricular walking expedition with Charles to Dover. This, the older brother told the younger, might have given him a fever from walking fast in the heat of the sun 'and might have kild you'. Burty was arraigned but the Pierce sentence allowed him to join Charles on the trip to London at the start of the summer holidays. Boner met them off the coach before they had a chance to abscond elsewhere.[7]

After his unusual Suffolk holiday – 'gone fossiling' – Constable got some drawings and watercolours done while in Folkestone looking after John Charles. And he had been busy earlier in the year, preparing *Englefield House* for the Academy. He had worked on it through the winter with his usual peaks and troughs of morale. Despite his success with *Wivenhoe Park*, a happy resolution of the possibilities and pitfalls of the type, the genre was not for him. He had written loftily to Fisher, 'A gentleman's park is my aversion. It is not beauty because it is not nature.' (Nowadays we are more tolerant, finding many a great estate a thing of beauty, a zone of cultivated

Folkestone, 1833

landscape – possibly reminiscent of Constable's Suffolk – amid hedgeless expanses run by agribusiness.) But Constable's aversion hadn't caused him to refuse de Beauvoir's commission. The job seems to have come to him by way of Samuel Lane, Sir Thomas Lawrence's former assistant, who had done a portrait of the mansion's owner. Constable and Lane had visited the house near Reading in August 1832 and Constable sketched it. In mid-December, busy with the painting, he wrote to Leslie that he had made all the cows in the foreground bigger. 'This has had all the effect you anticipated and sent the house back and also much enhanced & helped to realize my foreground, which indeed this blank canvas wants to aid it. But I must try at one of the elements – namely air – & if that include light, I ought not to despair.' His brother Abram visiting London reacted with enthusiasm to the painting: 'I think your House Picture will be beautiful, a faithful representative of "9 o'clock in the morning, in [summer]" '.[8]

However, in late February he had to put up with the collector William Wells, who enjoyed telling Constable how much better he liked the work of other artists. On this occasion Wells looked over a number of Constable's paintings. As Leslie learned:

> I sincerely beleive nothing amongst them made any impression upon him [n]or did they come into his rules, or whims, of the art. I told him, that I had perhaps other notions of the art than picture admirers in general – I looked on *pictures* as things to be *avoided*. Connoisseurs [such as Wells] looked on them as things to be *imitated* . . . and serve only to fill the world with abortions . . . Good God – what a sad thing it is that this lovely art – is so wrested to its own destruction – only used to blind our eyes and senses from seeing the sun shine, the feilds bloom, the trees blossom . . . – and old black rubbed-out dirty bits of canvas, to take the place of God's own works.

Constable said he wanted to see Leslie again. Like Jaques in *As You Like It*, he loved to cope with Leslie when he, Constable, was in one of his 'sullen moods'.

Towards the completion of the painting for de Beauvoir he cheered up. Even though the chimney pots were endless, he wrote to his son Charles that Englefield House – named after a 'great battlefeild of the Danes' – looked bright and cheerful, and that 'all like it who see it'.[9] One such admirer was the Countess of Morley, who visited Charlotte Street in early April and on seeing *Englefield House* declared, in words he might have picked himself, 'How fresh – how dewy – how exhilarating!'[10] A discordant voice was that of Mr Wells, making a second visit; he stayed two hours and this time was really annoying, not least because he had taken up the rival landscape painter F.R. Lee. Constable wrote to Leslie, 'Mr Wells saw nothing in my house to approve – but much to disparage. I had "lost my way" – Turner was "quite gone" – lost and possessed by a yellow which he could not see himself, therefore could not avoid. Mr Wells looked not at any of my pictures – only by glances of contempt – but on seeing some of my studies, he kept saying, this would be of use to Lee – & this – & this might be of service to Lee – & so on.' Wells sent Lee to Charlotte Street to ask about the prices of Constable's studies – Wells would pay for them. Constable told Lee they would have to wait for the final sale, presumably on Constable's death or bankruptcy. 'This most kind and benevolent Mr Wells would gladly put the last shovel of earth on my coffin with his own hands.'

The Arrangement Committee at the Academy had shovels or knives of their own. Reinagle was one of the three arrangers that year and Constable tried to get him to hang the *House* in a good spot, in a good light. In early April Constable told Boner that Reinagle 'has made me quite easy about my picture and that all is going right in the great house [i.e. Somerset House] at this most selfish time of all, when cutting a man's throat is considered really an act of kindness'.[11] Indeed it was, and Reinagle and his associates, Briggs and Westall, put *Englefield House* in a place where, Constable thought, it was 'quite destroyed'. Sir Martin Archer Shee rubbed in the salt by telling Constable it was 'only a picture of a house, and ought to have been put in the Architectural Room'. Constable replied, echoing Abram, that it was 'a picture of a summer morning, including a house'.[12]

The reception by the press wasn't too horrid. The *Morning Chronicle*'s writer was snippy as usual, saying that *Englefield House* – entered with six other smaller oil and watercolour landscapes by Constable – was merely topographical map-work. *John Bull* – in a review forwarded by Abram – exclaimed, 'Constable is either laughing at the public or wishes to be laughed at himself.' But the *Morning Post* was enthusiastic:

> We have seen nothing to compare with this from the hand of Mr Constable for a long time. There is so much freshness and truth and such a mass of bright but sober colour, that it is quite a gem in its way. Mr Constable has evidently forgotten to put on his last layer of whitewash . . . We hope he has lost the brush. The whole picture consists of an ancient castellated mansion on a lawn, with a thick shubbery behind.[13]

Unfortunately, the person most concerned after the artist, the owner of the mansion, wasn't among the painting's admirers. Richard Benyon de Beauvoir thought the cattle in the foreground made it seem as if 'he had his farm yard before his Drawing Room windows'. Could Constable please replace the cattle with deer? Mr de Beauvoir wanted the house – *his* house – which was of Elizabethan origin, to be the object of attention. And he complained to Samuel Lane of the 'specky or spotty appearance' of Constable's painting. In an early sketch Constable *had* put deer, not cows, and he had no objection to replacing the cattle in that way. But even with deer in place de Beauvoir still didn't like the picture, and it was another year before he paid the hundred guineas due to the artist. He also rejected Constable's offer to try again and to 'enter minutely into its elegant detail'. De Beauvoir eventually gave the offending painting to a nephew. At this point it is possible to side in part with the viewers who found *Englefield House* wanting. It has a detailed deadness or ghostly blankness; the air and light Constable hoped for were better suggested in one of his preparatory watercolour sketches made the previous August. As Constable had noted, the windows and chimneys were

innumerable and he couldn't get round the fact. It was not a
Wivenhoe Park or Malvern Hall where acquaintanceship made for
attachment. Thereafter his aversion to gentlemen's parks was fully
maintained. Some of his smaller but more personally connected
entries at Somerset House – a heath, a windmill, a landscape at sunset
and one called *A Cottage in a Cornfield* – better presented his
strengths.[14]

He found time for small and often happier jobs. He coloured in 'all the
little pictures in Dr Watt's Hymn Book for dear Emily'.[15] He oversaw
the making of a new title page and introduction for *English Landscape*.
He gave a talk at the Hampstead Assembly Room and did illustrations
for an edition of Gray's *Elegy Written in a Country Churchyard*. He
also spent a night at Lady Dysart's, sent twenty-eight bottles of port
to Abram and Mary for Christmas, and shipped via cousin Sidey's
vessel a quantity of blankets for the needy of East Bergholt. At a
meeting of the AGBI he took up the miserable situation of one Russell
Sharp, 'hard up'.[16]

In June 1833 he had had a blow to his pride worse than de
Beauvoir's rejection. An oil by him of *Helmingham Dell* was knocked
down at Christie's for two pounds ten shillings. The picture had
belonged to James Pulham, had been bought back after his death by
the artist, and then recently sold to a collector named Robert Ludgate.
Ludgate died in turn while the picture was on show at the British
Institution and his widow swiftly and naively put it and other pictures
up for auction with no reserve price. But the *Dell* arrived late for the
Christie's sale and failed to get listed in the printed catalogue – this
put off many dealers and potential buyers. Some thought it couldn't
be a real Constable. On its sale to Charles Scovell for a mere fifty
shillings, Edward Dubois, the *Morning Chronicle*'s hatchet man, said
this indicated the proper value of Constable's works. An aggrieved
Constable asked various friends and the solicitor Anthony Spedding
whether he should sue the *Chronicle*. Spedding advised taking no
action. Mr Christie said it was all unintentional – he had thought he
was knocking it down and thus saving it for the vendor's widow – and

Mrs Ludgate claimed she had been talked into the hasty sale by a friend, Major Chapman, who had apparently profited by securing the Ludgate collection for little money; she now called Chapman 'base'. Constable in Hampstead wrote to Boner about the 'villany' of Dubois: 'What can such a man be but an assassin, to destroy character, livelihood, & every thing else, & let himself out for hire to write against everything good, for pay.' After 1834, Dubois' venom was dropped from the *Chronicle*, though he was absent from the *Observer*, too, in 1836 and 1837.[17]

The number of Constable's old friends lost to death had increased again. In early March 1833 his early mentor J.T. 'Museum' Smith, whom Constable had first met in 1796, had died – inflammation of the lungs was given as the cause.[18] Towards the end Smith was in 'great debt and poverty' and borrowed thirty pounds from Constable.[19] Constable made one attempt to get repaid but soon relented. Smith told Constable he would never regret his goodness to one he had known so long,[20] and Constable wrote to Leslie on Smith's death, 'How glad I am at the result of my conduct to him (for I did not know it, but he was then dying) now that he has reached that bourne whence no traveller returns.' Constable sent five guineas to Smith's widow, who had been left without a shilling, but he asked Leslie not to mention it. Leslie noted that although Constable didn't have a large circle of friends, he had a few who were very good friends indeed. Those who got to know him liked him very much. And his best friends took a lot out of him. After a time-consuming ten-day visit from Fisher in 1824, Constable wrote to Maria, 'I am almost glad Fisher is out of town.'

Now he was threatened with the departure of his closest remaining friend. Leslie, born in London but an American by parentage and upbringing, was offered a part-time job teaching art at the United States Military Academy at West Point, on the Hudson River in New York State. A house, a steady income, a healthy situation, good prospects for his children, a studio – all the advantages were paraded, and Leslie's American relatives pressed him to accept. Constable was dismayed. He wrote to Leslie on 11 June 1833 (his own birthday and possibly a day for weighing up his own career), 'The loss of you is a cloud casting a shade over my life, now in its autumn . . .' In mid-August, when Leslie and his family were getting ready to sail, Constable wrote from Well Walk: 'The thoughts that I am to be deprived of [the] society, at least of the happy hours of your and Mrs. Leslie's several interviews, of our communications on art, and on many things else – weigh very heavily on my heart – so much so as to depress my mind, and prevent the enjoyment of even the little that remains of your countenance to me.' But the letter continued with a sudden enthusiastic exclamation: '<u>What beautiful silvery clouds are rolling about today</u>!!!'

The Leslies sailed in September, taking two presents from Constable, a watercolour of a windmill near Colchester and – specifically for Harriet Jane Leslie, Constable's god-daughter – a copy of Isaac Watts's *Divine Songs* illustrated with woodcuts by Stothard that Constable had hand-coloured. Constable sent to the *Athenaeum* an unsigned and somewhat obituarial note about Leslie's departure, mentioning Leslie's liking for English art, 'including the works of Chantrey, of Wilkie, of Turner, the native freshness of the landscapes of Constable, and the grace and freshness of the portrait composition of Chalon . . .'[21] (Too much freshness, perhaps, but the puff for Chalon redressed the puff for himself.) When Constable in Hampstead next wrote to Leslie (in West Point), in January 1834, he said, 'I have been sadly ill since you left England, and my mind so depressed that I have been scarcely able to do any one thing – in that state I did not like to write to you . . . I wish enough I had been with you, never more to set foot on old England again . . . I find it hard to touch a pencil now that you are not here to see [it].' From one who had so far never let England out of his sight, the suggestion that he wanted never to set foot in it again was serious stuff, but probably expressed only his mood of the moment. In fact, according to Lucas, Constable predicted that Leslie would soon come back. This proved correct. Leslie found his new quarters at West Point a tight fit. He was expected to help with his students' examinations and this cut into his time for painting. Everything cost more than he had been led to believe it would. His wife wasn't well. And so in mid-April he and his family sailed again for England on the *Philadelphia*, the ship commanded by Captain Elisha Morgan, the Yankee skipper who became a friend of Dickens and Turner and other artists.[22] A new house for the Leslies was found off the Edgware Road, on the edge of town, and there Constable was happily reunited with them, and visited often. Leslie's son Robert recalled an occasion when Constable and his father had sat in the front room, sipping tea, and admiring a sunset beyond a fine row of oaks and elms, after which they spent the rest of the evening talking over pictures in Leslie's painting room.[23] Leslie regretted the time it had taken for him to get to know Constable, to understand 'his worth as a man, or his true value as an artist'.[24]

While Leslie was in the States, Constable's social circle was constricted. As he got older and life seemed to accelerate, friends dropped away. One such colleague, John Jackson, had died in 1831 – a fellow RA student, a protegé of Sir George Beaumont, a fine portrait painter, and a man Constable regarded as having 'no enemy'. (Jackson was coming home in a coach from a dinner party and gave up his inside seat to a lady; he caught a chill and never recovered.)[25] There was still Stothard, but the book illustrator (and butterfly collector) was now seventy-eight (in 1833) and in failing health. He had voted – without being lobbied – for Constable's election to the Academy. On one sultry day, according to David Lucas, when Stothard and Constable were sitting 'in the shadow of a tree of rich foliage, Stothard looking up through the branches to the clear blue sky remarked . . . "You see, Constable, it's all glazing, glazing".'[26] Stothard had given useful advice for improving *Waterloo Bridge* and had called to see Constable when he was ill. His deafness was less of a handicap when he was with a companion, but he was on his own in the autumn of 1832, out walking, when he apparently didn't hear a carriage approaching and was knocked down. There was no visible injury, but Stothard never fully recovered. Constable repaid past kindness and sometimes called to see Stothard. In April 1833 he wrote to George Constable that he had just spent an hour or two with Stothard: 'Poor man! The only

Elysium he has in this world is found in his own enchanting works. His daughter does all in her power to make him happy and comfortable.'[27] Stothard died on 27 April 1834.

One other old acquaintance had fallen away. Benjamin Haydon, ten years Constable's junior, had got to know him at the Academy Life School. Even pricklier than Constable, Haydon had dreams of glory as a historical painter. For a while he was taken up by Sir George Beaumont, whose patronage could be mercurial. But Haydon's flamboyant dedication to 'high art' and his bumptiousness caused trouble. In 1808 Constable had told Farington that Haydon 'is possessed with a notion that the eyes of the world are upon himself'.[28] His patrons vanished. The Royal Academy declined to elect him and was savagely condemned. He remained friends with Wilkie, however, and in 1828 expressed admiration for Constable's use of colour in his *Dedham Vale*, on show at the chief den of iniquity, Somerset House.[29] In April 1832 Wilkie told Haydon he had just run into Constable who had recalled dining with them in Slaughter's Coffee House on St Martin's Lane twenty-six years before. Haydon recorded this in his journal, which now seems to have a better claim to immortality than his stagy, bombastic paintings.

Wilkie – wide-eyed, startled-looking – went on being a good friend of Constable's. After Maria's death, Wilkie's house in Lower Phillimore Street was one where Constable first came out of his seclusion. Artists were often neighbours, as in Charlotte Street, and frequently landlords or tenants of one another. Leslie had rooms in Charlotte Street for a while, and when he moved to Lisson Grove it was to the house of the sculptor J.C.F. Rossi, in which Haydon had rented a studio before his bankruptcy. Artists also modelled for each other: Haydon donned a monk's robes for a Wilkie painting and Constable at least twice posed as a doctor for Wilkie, in 1809 for his *Sick Lady visited by her Physician*, and in 1834 for the physician in *Columbus*.[30] With Constable, friendship took precedence over what he thought of his friends' art. Wilkie's literary sort of painting would not have seemed a natural thing for the landscape painter to like, but he stood by Wilkie even as his early fame diminished and the effect of studying old masters abroad altered his style.[31] In April 1833 Wilkie was at work on a full-length portrait of William IV in military uniform, and Constable wrote to Leslie that Wilkie 'is too fond of rancid old art, but his soul saves it all – so grand & fine'.

Jack Bannister still came to dinner from time to time; the actor was delighted with the print recently made of Leslie's painting of the *Tristram Shandy* characters, *Uncle Toby and the Widow Wadman* – Bannister had modelled for Uncle Toby.[32] And John Linnell, Hampstead neighbour, who was, like Constable, a landscapist and portrait painter, was frequently encountered in the village or going to and from London by coach. Relations had been edgy between them. Linnell was, as noted, a Baptist, and Constable tended to take against Dissenters. Linnell had blamed Constable for spreading stories about Linnell's antagonism to the Salisbury drawing master David Read in the early 1820s; Linnell had thought this gossip had scuppered his chances of being elected to the Royal Academy. (Despite his talent, he never was, though he went on exhibiting there.)[33] His religious beliefs and ostentatiously shabby dress were also held against him, but as far as Linnell was concerned, the blame for his rejection belonged to Constable. Some, like Linnell's biographer A.T. Story, thought Constable was jealous of his 'young competitor' and – soured by the long time he himself had waited to be recognised, 'with lesser men preferred before him' – didn't tolerate his rivals. William Collins had been drawn into the argument and for a long time ceased to be a friend of Constable's. After Constable's election to the Academy in 1829, Collins declared that the value of his own diploma had gone down by 50 per cent. The following year Constable told William Carpenter, Collins's brother-in-law, 'I despise no man but Collins.' In fact, he admired Collins's skill but thought his work sentimental. With Linnell matters slowly mended. Linnell had befriended old William Blake and seems to have introduced Blake to Constable. Anyone wanting to make friends with him had to persevere.[34]

By 1831 Linnell and Constable were on good terms again. Linnell sent Constable an engraved portrait of Robert Gooch, Maria's gynaecologist, who had died the year before, and Constable was grateful. A few years later Constable bought several of the early parts of Linnell's work, *Michael Angelo's Frescoes in the Sistine Chapel* (1833–7) and suggested to Linnell an exchange of a copy of *English Landscape* for the remaining parts.[35] As for Collins, he too eventually softened. Leslie wrote to him after Constable's death asking for any thoughts he had about the departed, and Collins replied, tactfully if ponderously, 'The charm of our lamented friend's conversation upon art, was not only its originality, but its real worth, and the evidence it afforded of his heart-love of his pursuit, independent of any worldly advantages to be obtained by it.'

More handicapped and less talented than Stothard, Samuel Lane was a frequent visitor to Charlotte Street. He lived not far away in Greek Street and often came with problems that he hoped Constable would solve. He may have hoped that his efforts to promote the *Englefield House* commission would be a form of repayment. But what Lane wanted most, to be made at least an Associate of the Academy, proved beyond Constable's powers. Farington, Lane's early sup-porter, might eventually have managed it, but he had now been dead for twelve years. If communicating with Lane using sign language took patience, so did dealing with Lane's many grievances and his recourse to the wine bottle to relieve them. Constable sometimes went over to Greek Street late in the evening to answer one of the *cris de coeur* and found Lane stupefied. Nevertheless he went on trying to help. He let Lane know when he was going to be out of town and when he had returned from, say, East Bergholt.[36] Lane seems to have called at Charlotte Street in October 1833 hoping that Constable would support him in the November elections for the Academy, but Boner told him truthfully that Constable was in Folkestone visiting John and Charles. When Constable heard from Boner about Lane's visit, he replied to Boner: 'I have written to poor Lane to sooth him if possible about the Academy. I wish for his sake it was at the bottom of the sea I am beholding so magnificently displayed and that these noble breakers would wash it from his mind.'[37] Constable must have felt on occasion that the Academy, like many a club, was better belonged to and ignored than kept out of and annoyed by. But Lane didn't have that privilege.

One friend came late on the scene: the brewer and amateur painter George Constable. He was sixteen years younger than the artist who shared his surname and he had come across the *English Landscape* mezzotints while up in London in December 1832, staying coincidentally at 58 Charlotte Street. George Constable pleased John Constable by buying the most expensive prints of the engravings at a time when the latter felt gravely out of pocket from the venture. Soon, despite an arm injured after he was thrown from his gig, George was urging John to visit him in Sussex. He wanted to acquire one of his versions of *Salisbury Cathedral from the Bishop's Grounds*. And a week before Christmas 1833 he asked Constable, 'Could you without much trouble enclose me a bit of your sparkling colour to copy?' – a request that Constable's heirs should have known about when a number of unknown 'Constables' later came on the market.[38]

By 1834 Constable had become vice-president of the Artists' Fund, the AGBI, and he went on being concerned with hard-up artists, their wives, widows and children. As noted, early the year before he had taken up the desperate case of Russell Sharp, whose wife had been 'an actress of <u>notoriety</u>'. Constable continued to be interested in the condition of Mrs Theresa Hopkins, widow of the miniature painter John Hopkins, and carried small sums from the Fund to the house in Hampstead where she lay ill. He made a generous and apparently personal subscription to the orphaned children of a Mrs Hall in Grafton Street. Loans from him helped many he didn't give directly to, though he complained to Leslie that some recipients – not only Museum Smith – took advantage of him; he was more annoyed by their deception than the loss of the money. He often got other benefactors involved in his good causes: 'old Fontaine', the needy Swiss organist, was assisted by donations via Constable from Lady Dysart and John Fisher. Fisher was told by Constable on one occasion that his 'account' with Constable had been debited five shillings to help save Fontaine from near starvation. Nor was East Bergholt neglected. Early in 1834 his sister Mary wrote from Flatford about Constable's plan to send from London 'winter comforts' by way of cousin Sidey's coasting vessel. She said she would be pleased to be Constable's agent in seeing that old and needy villagers received the blankets he was sending.[39]

## 19. *Fever and Fire (1834)*

In late December 1833 Constable was again taken sick in Hampstead. Unable to leave Well Walk, he wrote in January to Leslie in America to say how ill and depressed he had been since Leslie departed from England. But worse was to come. He spent most of February and March in bed. His doctor, Herbert Evans, wrote to their mutual friend William Purton, one of several amateur painters Constable became friends with, to say it was a severe attack of rheumatic fever: 'In the early part of this period the suffering was very great; all the joints became the seat of the diseases two or three times over, and the pain and fever were of the most aggravated kind. These sufferings he bore with great patience for one of so sensitive a frame.' Constable generally cheered up when Evans made one of his twice-a-day visits. But Evans said, 'I think he was never so well after this severe illness; its effects were felt by him, and showed themselves in his looks ever afterwards.'[1]

There was a family history of this illness, too. Constable had had what he described to Leslie as an acute attack of rheumatism in December 1831 and his son John seems also to have had rheumatic fever during the 1833 Christmas holidays. Fortunately the devoted young Boner looked after Constable, ran errands, took dictation, and sat up all night in attendance.[2] Rheumatic fever can affect not only the joints but the skin and central nervous system. It produces symptoms like arthritis: swollen joints, making the wrists, elbows, ankles and knees hot and painful. Nodules and protuberances may form, and rashes appear. Sometimes the muscles jerk involuntarily. Most seriously, the heart can be inflamed and damaged. In Constable's case, painting was impossible, and for him this must have been as painful as the illness. His sister Mary had her own ideas for alleviating his symptoms: warm seabathing, avoiding cheese and very hot coffee, drinking camomile tea, walking in the sunshine and fretting at nothing.[3]

When it came time for the Academy exhibition, he had only three watercolours and a pencil drawing to submit. *The Spectator* noted: 'The exhibition is not rich in Landscape this year; which makes us miss Constable the more: he spoils better landscapes than many can paint.'[4] One of the watercolours was Old Sarum from the south – very grey green and a sky frothing with rain clouds, with what looks like a downpour beginning on the right and, the motif he had used in *Hadleigh Castle*, a shepherd with his crook and a dog chivvying a flock of sheep along the sloping hillside; the giant mound, a seemingly inevitable shape, dominates the centre of the picture.[5]

He was unable to go down to Suffolk for a promised spring visit or call in Colchester on the Masons, his cousin Anne and her husband, as

Old Sarum

he had intended. In June his spirits weren't lifted when a Landscape with Figures of his was bought in at Christie's at fifty guineas; at least Mr Christie ensured it wasn't knocked down for fifty shillings.[6] He was better enough to travel to Sussex in early July, joining young John at George Constable's. His host won young John's heart with the gift of 'an electrifying machine', whose arrival in Charlotte Street Constable dreaded. He was thinking about another big painting, 'either a canal or a rural affair', he told George Constable,[7] and the fresh landscape of West Sussex was saluted in a letter to Leslie:

> The chalk cliffs afford John many fragments of oyster shells and other matters that fell from the table of Adam in all probability . . . The castle is the cheif ornament of this place – but all here sinks to insignificance in comparison with the woods, and hills. The woods hang from excessive steeps, and precipices, and the trees are beyond everything beautifull: I never saw such beauty in *natural landscape* before. I wish it may influence what I may do in future, for I have too much preferred the picturesque to the beautiful – which will I hope account for the *broken ruggedness of my style*.

If the southern 'hangers' were new to him, the succulent meadows along the Arun River were similar to those beside the Stour. Constable collected samples of the rich-coloured sand and soil of Fittleworth common to take back to Charlotte Street. He told George Constable he'd like bits of the slimy posts he'd seen near an old mill – would the brewer cut them off and send them to him?[8]

He also visited Petworth House. Lord Egremont, the great collector, asked him to stay for a few days, and Constable said he would when Leslie was there. Looking at the art there, Constable came across a Gainsborough awaiting hanging. He wrote to Leslie, 'I placed it as it suited me – & I now, even now think of it with tears in my eyes. No feeling of landscape ever equalled it. With particulars he had nothing to do, his object was to deliver a fine sentiment – & he has fully accomplished it.' Leslie often spent part of the autumn with his family at the 'house of art', as Constable called it. After some dithering about the Earl's invitation, Constable finally – encouraged by Leslie – took it up. As painter and patron John Constable and Lord Egremont might have been thought meant for each other. But Constable had earlier got into one of his awkward moods and decided that Lord Egremont wasn't fond of landscape painting. In 1824 the Earl had seen some of Constable's work being painted for Arrowsmith, and, Constable told Fisher, 'He recollected all my pictures of any note, but he recollected them only for their defects . . . The truth is landscape affords him no interest whatever.' (A comment that might have made Turner smile.) However, by 1834 the noble Lord's generosity to artists – Turner and Leslie included – seems to have swayed Constable, and on 30 August he told a rather infirm Lady Dysart with some pride that he was going down to Petworth for a few days. Leslie, there already, continued to recommend the attractions of the house: 'Today forty people dine here, most of them magistrates, and the house is as full as it can hold. Among them is the Duke of Richmond. I have just been looking at the table as it is set out in the Carved Room, covered with magnificent gold and silver plate.'

Chantrey and Thomas Phillips, the portrait painter who was one of Lord Egremont's favourites, were among the guests Constable found at Petworth. The Phillipses and Leslie took him to Cowdray Park to see the ruins of the castle, and Constable sketched.[9] He stayed not 'a few days' but a fortnight. The hospitable Earl arranged for a carriage to be at Constable's disposal for trips in the locality. Constable went with Leslie to sketch an old farmstead known as Wicked Hammond's House. A woman living in the former home of the alleged villain told them that some bones had recently been found in the well that a local doctor said were 'the arm bones of a Christian'. Leslie sketched the interior, Constable (as one might have expected) the outside, with its tall chimneys. Leslie observed his friend's daily habits: 'He rose early and had often made some beautiful sketch in the park before breakfast. On going into his room one morning . . . I found him setting some of these sketches with isinglass. His dressing table was covered with flowers, feathers of birds, and pieces of bark with lichens and mosses adhering to them, which he had brought home for the sake of their beautiful tints.'[10]

Lord Egremont had also invited Turner, but the Earl told Constable that Turner was unable to come. 'He was off to the *North* on a bookseller's job, that was a profound secret.'[11] Lord Egremont may have thought it would be instructive and amusing to throw the two landscape painters together, the celebrated and the less so, chalk and cheese. Or as Mary, one of Charles Leslie's children, once noted in a handwritten so-called 'lecture', 'The too [*sic*] most oposite modern painters, namely <u>Constable and Turner</u>, painted two metals much alike, Constable painted silver, Turner painted gold. That is the remark I heard pappa say when compareing a Constable with a Turner.'[12]

Turner's one-year seniority in birth (and twenty-seven-year seniority as an Academician) gave him plenty of scope he might have assumed anyway to act superior to Constable. Young Robert Leslie, then about eight, encountered Turner later that September at Petworth, presumably just back from his northern journey, down by the lake in the park – one of Turner's favourite haunts. He had just caught a large pike. Robert had with him a toy sailing ship, a flat piece of board his father had cut out and which Constable had rigged for him with sticks for masts. When he heard the name Constable, Turner muttered crossly, 'Oh, he don't know anything about ships. This is how to do it.' Tearing some pages from his sketchbook he made some paper sails for the craft that struck Robert as really shipshape. Constable was never the owner of his own sailing boat, the way Turner was, but from his life on the Stour, his knowledge of his father's barges and coasting vessels, his voyage on the *Coutts*, and his observations from the beach at Brighton and Weymouth, he certainly knew about the sea and sailing vessels – pulled up on the shingle, rolling at anchor, or running before a Channel breeze. He drew or painted them as well as any man – except possibly the great competitor. (Turner, it may be noted, as if not to be outdone produced a Brighton *Chain Pier* a year after Constable's.) Robert Leslie wrote later, 'Though I think Constable never loved the sea, he was always at home with his pencil among shipping and boats. And I remember a simple but valuable lesson of his to me upon the first principle in drawing the hull of a man-of-war. "Always think of it," he said, "and draw it first as a floating cask or barrel – and upon this foundation build up your ship, masts, and rigging." As he said this, he rapidly evolved a stern view of a line of battleship upon the sketch of a half-immersed cask.'[13]

During his Petworth stay Constable filled a large sketchbook with drawings, some highly finished. Two were pale watercolours, one of the great house from across the lake, the other of the rolling parkland and downs with Chanctonbury Ring in the eastern distance – fawn, light green, blues, barely coloured. How Constable got on with the motley company in what some referred to as 'Liberty Hall' – the Earl's wife, mistresses, children, distinguished guests, and sundry artists and their families – is not known. The length of his stay suggests that he got over his pre-visit nerves and feelings of reluctance and awkwardness but was then glad to get home to his chicks. He never went to Petworth again. And Lord Egremont, already in old age, never bought a Constable painting.[14]

Constable and Turner were both on hand in London on the evening of 16 October 1834 when the Houses of Parliament caught fire. They were among a number of Royal Academicians drawn to the spectacle. Wooden tallies once used as exchequer receipts were being burned in the furnaces of the House of Lords and the heat in the chimneys ignited structural timbers. A greater part of the medieval palace of Westminster was devoured by flames. Turner made sketches first from a boat on the river that he shared with Stanfield and some RA students, then from the Surrey bank opposite. Constable brought his two oldest sons in a hackney coach and got the driver to park it on Westminster Bridge so they could watch the inferno. Fire, heat and flame were very much in Turner's line; the river, and river water used by the firemen for their pumps, more in Constable's – and young John Charles as a youthful fire-engine enthusiast would have been excited. Soldiers were brought in to reinforce the police attempting to control the gawping crowds. The correspondent of the *Gentleman's Magazine* noted that when the roof of the House of Lords fell in, the spectators 'involuntarily (and from no bad feeling) clapped their hands'.[15]

Constable may have felt that divine intervention had struck the newly Reformed Parliament. Early the next year he wrote delightedly to his son Charles after attending the election in Suffolk for the House of Commons: 'People are truly sick of the Whigs. The Tories are the best people, the Whigs next best – but as the Whigs always join the Radicals, we are not safe in their hands.'[16] Two weeks after the fire, he described it to Charles Leslie. As he did so, Leslie said later, 'he drew with a pen, on half a sheet of letter paper, Westminster Hall as it showed itself during the conflagration; blotting the light and shade with ink, which he rubbed with his finger where he wished it to be lightest. He then, on another half sheet, added the towers of the Abbey and that of St Margaret's Church – and the papers, being joined, form a very grand sketch of the whole scene.' Inky fingers were an unavoidable by-product of art.[17]

Towards Christmas the black dog gripped him again. He begged off a visit he planned with Leslie to see their colleague Gilbert Stuart Newton, whose mind was gravely unhinged. Newton – born in Nova Scotia and raised in Boston – had told Leslie as a matter of fact that the seventeenth-century Lord Strafford was still with them – he had escaped death on the scaffold and was, to boot, the same person as Lorenzo de Medici. (The number of artists who cracked up perhaps only *seemed* greater than average.) Constable's depression wasn't helped by trouble he was having with Alaric Watts, editor of the *Literary Souvenir*. Constable had been invited to write an essay for this annual, and Watts had so chopped up his material that the painter refused to let it appear. He was also having an altercation with David Lucas. He told Leslie that he was only kept going by work: 'My canvas soothes me into a forgetfulness of the scene of turmoil and folly – and worse – of the scene around me.' He seemed cross about and almost jealous of the engravings Lucas had done of *The Lock* and *The Cornfield*; they made him feel, perversely, that his creations, and he along with them, were being sold to 'low publishers'; and consequently he no longer felt the gratification of his own work. 'The two beautiful prints by Lucas are in the windows [of the print sellers], but every gleam of sunshine is blighted to me in the art at least. Can it therefore be wondered at that I paint continual storms? "Tempest o'er tempest rolled" – still the "darkness" is majestic . . .'

Nevertheless, he sent notes to Lucas by way of Boner, apologising for his 'impetuosity', and Lucas kept his temper – or at least kept silent – when, despite having apologised, Constable once again went off the deep end. (Lucas took a modest revenge every now and then by requesting the loan of a pound or so.) Constable's state of mind indeed seemed blighted by his participation in what he called the 'dreadful book' with its 'worthless & bad proofs' which Lucas sent him. He had been here before, as he had made clear in a paranoiac memorandum to Lucas giving all the reasons he should never have gone down the profitless path of print publishing:

1. Great interruption of my time – & peace of mind.
2. An anxiety that ought not to be with me.
3. Selling off the prints in lots or detail – a trouble.
4. Nobody will ever pay me what they owe me.
5. I never was able to get money of[f] a printseller yet.
6. I must supply the trade with property.
7. I confer all the benefit – they not equally to me.
8. I commit myself with faithless and low people.
9. A disrepute in joining with them in trade.
10. Advertizing very disagreable – & disreputable.
11. A great anxiety and disturbance of mind.
12. Better to pay money out than in a bad job.
13. Consider the first loss as mostly the least.
14. Not to volunteer into all the above or
15. any of it – above all consider the weight on the mind.

This screed continued, without further numbering, for some twenty more lines to do with the hopelessness of making money from print-making and print-selling. His feelings about *English Landscape* had been summed up in a note to Lucas in late June 1833: 'The whole work is a dismal blank to me, and a total failure & loss.'[18]

However – and there was generally a however with Constable – he had bounced back enough to make improvements to his 'book'. Early in 1834, before the rheumatic fever really hit him, he wrote to Leslie at West Point that he was making 'a flyleaf for each of my prints', a page of historical and topographical information about each subject 'with Poetical Allusions applicable to the scenery'. His reasoning was that 'many can read print & cannot read mezzotint'. In fact he completed six such pieces: they dealt with the plates for *East Bergholt*, his birthplace and family home; *Spring* – the view of East Bergholt common; *Stoke by Nayland*, a picture of a thundery noon, with church and rainbow; another *Noon*, this one showing West End Fields at Hampstead; *A Sea Beach, Brighton*, with fishing boats and waves rolling in; and finally *Old Sarum*, the subject he said embodied the words, 'Paint me a desolation.'

By the end of 1834 Constable had sold fewer than a hundred copies of his book of prints. (One buyer was General Rebow, of Wivenhoe Hall, who paid Constable seven guineas for a copy on India paper.) But when he blamed Lucas for the ensuing tribulations he soon regretted it. He explained to Lucas that he was 'watchful & jealous' of his own style but admired the engraver's 'mode of rendering that style'. He had no doubt of Lucas's regard for him and his love for Constable's 'things in landscape'. And Constable went on, 'There can be no greater proofs than the manner in which you have rendered them . . . at your own risk, and that of your family and reputation . . . We have a bond of friendship . . . that all do not possess – a unison of feeling in art.' When Lucas was at work engraving *Stratford Mill*, Constable explained to him 'the natural history of the painting' – the way the changes in river level caused the roots of plants or trees to thrive or die (hence a dead tree on the right bank); the way the prevailing wind led the trees in the water meadows to lean in one direction.[19]

He encountered Lucas one day at an exhibition of Rembrandt drawings and thought of talking to him about how he should remain open to engraving portraits; but he realised that Lucas just then was in another world. Constable wrote to him next day, 'You availed yourself of Rembrandt's light and shadow, and were lost.' When

Lucas wanted to stand for election to the Academy in 1835, Constable supported him, but told Lucas to 'remember that most of the Royal Academicians know as much of landscapes as they do of the Kingdom of Heaven'. And when Lucas lost to the engraver Samuel Cousins, who was well known for his work after Lawrence portraits, Constable consoled Lucas as well as he could on the four votes he had received. He knew how it felt.[20]

## 20. *The Appearance of the Day (1833–36)*

The 'dreadful book' was one means by which Constable hoped to make a claim for landscape painting, and his role in it. A second method now appeared. In mid-June 1833 he delivered his first lecture on the subject. He wrote to Leslie a few days before: 'Remember I play the part of Punch on Monday at eight, at the Assembly Room, Hampstead.' The audience were members of the Literary and Scientific Society of Hampstead; the lecture was entitled 'An Outline of the History of Landscape Painting'. No exact transcript of the talk (or its successors) exists, though Constable made notes for them and, after the first occasion, an abstract of what he remembered he had said. The lectures expressed the obligation he had once written to David Wilkie about – his need 'to <u>tell</u> the world there is such a thing as landscape existing with Art' because he had so far largely 'failed to <u>show</u> the world that it is possible to accomplish it'.[1] Perhaps he remembered what John Fisher had said to him seven years before when Henry Phillips, the Brighton botanist, asked him to write a paper for his proposed literary magazine. Fisher had suggested that Constable put down in a book his thoughts on painting, on his life and his opinions, and set about it without delay.[2]

Fisher of course was no longer alive but Leslie was on hand in George Romney's old house[3] to hear Constable getting to grips with the matter, the substructure of art that distantly underpinned his own painting. Constable had brought along reproductions of works he was going to mention; he had asked Lucas to help him find a large copy of *The Mill*, then thought to be by Rembrandt, that Samuel Reynolds,

Lucas's teacher, had engraved. Constable evidently failed to live up to his self-characterisation as Mr Punch. One lady house guest of the Purtons was there and – according to the speaker – 'fell in love with my lecture'. He began modestly, suggesting that the committee of the society be exonerated for choosing so inefficient a speaker. He wanted to trace the history of landscape – to separate 'this department of art' from 'the mass of historical art in which it originated', and show how 'it became a distinct and separate class of painting, standing alone'. Early landscapes were painted on the walls of Herculaneum, 'part of their arabesques', with 'trees, like candelabra, formally spread on a plain blue sky'. Pliny claimed that something like chiaroscuro was understood at this time, but Constable saw no evidence of this in the landscapes of the period. In any event, in the early Middle Ages 'all was lost . . . in the general wreck of Europe'. The Bayeux Tapestry was 'little better than a Mexican performance'. When illuminated manuscripts represented Christ's agony in the garden of Gethsemane, they showed the place 'only by a flower or flower pot, the rest of the field of the picture being dark'. But this, however rude and imperfect, was the origin of landscape painting. And in its infancy the art was 'nursed in the hands of men who were masters of pathos' – Cimabue and Giotto, followed by Ghirlandaio, Barnardo, Uccello, and eventually Raphael. 'Thus was landscape cradled in the lap of history . . . and it thus gained a strength and a dignity which has never since wholly forsaken it.'[4]

The early German and Netherlandish painters came next in Constable's pantheon, among them Dürer and Lucas van Leyden, but it was in Venice that he found 'the *heart* of colour'. Thence landscape spread its future excellence throughout Europe. The Bellini brothers schooled Giorgione and Titian in 'a servile manner' but a true way nevertheless, to judge by the result: at their best, Giorgione and Titian 'never lost their respect for nature' or wandered 'into the vacant fields of idealism'. Constable took Titian's 1520 painting showing the martyrdom of Peter the Dominican as an admirable union of history and landscape; he hadn't seen more than a print of it but judged from 'the level and placid movement of the clouds . . . seen under the pendent foliage of the trees which overhang the road' that the attack on the monk occurred towards evening. Time of day always mattered with Constable. He dealt next with Annibale Carracci and Domenichino, with Nicolas Poussin, Claude Lorrain, and a 'more minute imitation of particular nature'. Claude's 'chief power consisted in uniting splendour with repose, warmth with freshness, and dark with light'. There followed the romantics Salvator Rosa and Sébastien Bourdon, the first wild and terrific, the second more visionary. Constable later quoted Sir George Beaumont on Bourdon: 'He was *the prince of dreamers, yet not without nature.*'[5]

This remark was in an expanded recapitulation of his Hampstead talk that formed four lectures he gave – at the suggestion of John Charles's chemistry professor, Professor Michael Faraday – at the Royal Institution in Albemarle Street in May and June 1836. He sent Leslie an invitation with the message: 'I enclose a card of the Royal Institution that you may be convinced of my folly . . . but I have not *yet* commenced making spruce beer in the streets like RAs of our neighbourhood.' In these lectures – which he made without fee – Constable moved on to Rubens, Rembrandt, and Ruysdael. Rubens's rainbows and 'dewy light and freshness' greatly appealed to him, as did Rembrandt's chiaroscuro, 'that power which creates space'. He showed his audience copies of some Ruysdaels: one was of the mouth of a Dutch river, 'without a single feature of grandeur in the scenery; but the stormy sky, the grouping of vessels, and the breaking of the sea, make the picture one of the most impressive ever painted . . . *We see nothing truly till we understand it*. An ordinary spectator at the mouth of the river, which Ruysdael has here painted, would scarcely be conscious of the existence of many of the objects that conduce to the effect of the picture.' His own awareness he further demonstrated with another Ruysdael – what Leslie called 'a small evening winterpiece' – that represented the beginning of a thaw. The once-apprentice miller observed:

The ground is covered with snow, and the trees are still white; but there are two windmills near the centre; the one has the sails furled, and

is turned in the position from which the wind blew when the mill left
off work; the other has the canvas on the poles, and is turned another
way, which indicates a change in the wind; the clouds are opening in
that direction, which appears by the glow in the sky to be the south . . .
and this change will produce a thaw before the morning. The
concurrence of these circumstances shows that Ruysdael *understood*
what he was painting.

In 1812 a print of the 'shoar at Skeveling by Ruisdael' that pleased
Constable greatly was hanging in the room in his parents' house at
East Bergholt from which he was writing to Maria. To Leslie,
Constable had once praised a Ruysdael which seems to have been a
direct progenitor of his own works: 'It haunts my mind, and clings to
my heart, and stands between you and me while I am talking to you;
it is a watermill; a man and a boy are cutting rushes in the running
stream (the tail water); the whole so true, clear, and fresh, and as brisk
as champagne, a shower has not long passed . . . '[6]
One or two Dutch painters didn't make the grade with him. After
his second Royal Institution lecture, Constable wrote to his friend
William Purton about the reception of the first: 'Faraday said it
pleased him – Sir Martin [Shee] and [Thomas] Howard liked it . . . I
trust you will follow me through my sermons . . . I hope to murder
Both and Berchem on Thursday next at quarter to four o'clock.'[7] He
disliked Nicolaes Berchem's 'bastard style of landscape' which was
'wretched art . . . produced under the very worst stimulus'. This
remark caused one collector in the packed audience to ask Constable
afterwards if he should sell his Berchems. Constable said, 'No, sir,
that would only continue the mischief. *Burn them*.'[8]
Yet generally the Dutch moved and haunted him. The works of Jan
Steen and Pieter de Hooch for instance seemed 'put together almost
without thought; yet it would be impossible to alter or leave out the
smallest object, or to change any part of their light, shade or colour,
without injury to their pictures – a proof that their art is consummate'.
There had been the copy of a de Hooch that Leslie had sent him after
Fisher's death, showing a room with a shaft of sunlight falling on the

floor, and Constable's praise: 'How completely has he overcome the art, and trampled it underfoot, yet how full of art it is.' At the Royal Institution he summed up the Low Country artists: 'The Dutch painters were a *stay-at-home people* – hence their originality . . . We derive the pleasure of surprise . . . in finding how much interest the art, when in perfection, can give to the most ordinary subjects.' Cold critics might wish the Dutch artists told more elevated stories, but those they chose to tell were 'told with an unaffected truth of expression that may afford useful lessons in the treatment of the most sublime subjects'.[9]

Constable found the start of the eighteenth century much less enticing. The 'French taste' was emasculated. Vernet was offensive and the landscapes in Boucher were the pastoral equivalent of the opera house. Boucher told Sir Joshua Reynolds that 'he never painted from the life, for . . . nature put him out'. Then David and his contemporaries produced art which sprang from the terrible Revolution: 'stern and heartless petrifactions of men and women, with trees, rocks, tables, and chairs, all equally bound to the earth by a relentless outline, and destitute of chiaroscuro, the soul and medium of art'. In England, the eighteenth century had been full of similar degradation until Hogarth, Wilson, and Reynolds came along. Wilson struck Constable as a particularly reviving spirit: he opened 'the way to the genuine principles of landscape in England; he appeared at a time when this art, not only here, but on the Continent, was altogether in the hands of the mannerists . . . He looked at nature entirely for himself . . . [but he] might have starved had he not been appointed librarian to the Royal Academy.' The Stour valley now figured in Constable's account. Gainsborough had been born in Sudbury, ten miles inland from East Bergholt, and both his art and his character were appealing. In his landscapes Constable discovered 'the stillness of noon, the depths of twilight, and the dews and pearls of the morning'. They were the canvases of a 'most benevolent and kind-hearted man'. (Constable at some point bought in a Suffolk junk shop a plaster horse which Gainsborough had modelled, a 'tired old horse', but a treasure.) He concluded his roll of honour with Cozens and

Girtin, stressing that he had tried 'to draw a line between genuine art and mannerism, but even the greatest painters have never been wholly untainted by manner. – Painting is a science, and should be pursued as an inquiry into the laws of nature. Why, then, may not landscape painting be considered as a branch of natural philosophy, of which pictures are but the experiments?'[10]

Earlier it had been 'Painting is but another word for feeling'. This 'Painting is a science' may have been less a recantation than a nod to the times, to his own increased interest in geology, to John Charles's interests, and to some of the scientists in his large audience. Over the four lectures, the number of his Royal Institution listeners averaged 233.[11] (NB: the Hampstead group which heard his sermons was from the Hampstead Literary and *Scientific* Society.) Wordsworth was among the celebrities invited to Albemarle Street, and Samuel Rogers, the banker-poet, gave Constable advice on presenting his talks.[12] Leslie made memoranda at some of the lectures and later acquired Constable's notes for others. But Constable told his friend before the second Hampstead lecture in July 1836, 'I have written little and I certainly shall depend on being conversational.'[13] Of the occasion itself Leslie remembered that 'the sky was magnificent . . . As I walked across the West End fields to Hampstead, towards evening, I stopped repeatedly to admire its splendid combinations and their effects over the landscape, and Constable did not omit in his lecture to speak of the appearances of the day.'[14]

To Boner, then in Germany, he wrote of this lecture, 'It went off immensely well. I was never flurried – only occasionally referring to notes – spoke what I had to say off hand – was an hour and a half – and was "novel, instructive and entertaining," as the committee . . . told me.' He added, 'Mr G[eorge] Young [the surgeon] was there and said I had much in me to make a lecturer – & he gave me a few lessons & will continue his hints. He said I had the main thing – I could command my audience.'[15] Leslie thought his friend an interesting speaker – constantly referring to the pictures he had brought along and indeed better impromptu than when reading from a text. 'Many of his happiest turns of expression were not to be found in his own notes, they arose at the moment, and were not to be recalled by a reporter unskilled in shorthand.' Leslie was charmed by Constable's voice, though it was pitched 'somewhat too low', and by the play of 'his very expressive countenance' and his off-the-cuff felicities.[16]

In October 1835 he went to Worcester to deliver his 'sermons', this time three in number. He wrote to Lucas, 'who would ever have thought of my turning Methodist preacher . . . but I shall do good, to the Art for which I live'. To his host in Worcester he expressed some reservations: 'I feel myself in the situation of the lobster as very pleasant at first, but as the water got hotter and hotter, was sadly perplexed.' But he later told Boner that he performed with éclat. He struck a personal note in his survey of landscape painting by mentioning his Suffolk origins and first job as a miller. He was annoyed by the *Worcester Guardian*'s report, which 'mangled and mixed up' his remarks, although 'it was all well meant'.[17] While in Worcester he went out to Bewdley to stay overnight at Spring Grove, the home of Maria's half-sister Sarah, formerly Mrs Skey, who had married a clergyman. It was twenty-three years since he was there, wooing Maria.

His third and last Hampstead lecture took place on 25 July 1836. He meandered around many loosely related topics, among them the effects of patronage, the bad habits of mannerists, how to draw from nature, the growth of trees and the contemplation of scenery. His illustrations for what he had to say about trees included a drawing of a tall and elegant ash which had stood near the road into Hampstead and according to Constable 'died of a broken heart', with a sign directed against vagrants attached to it by two long spikes 'driven far into her side'. (For him the tree was feminine.) He quoted from two poets, Thomson and Milton, and declared:

> There has never been an age, however rude or uncultivated, in which the love of landscape has not in some way been manifested. And how could it be otherwise? For man is the sole intellectual inhabitant of one vast natural landscape. His nature is congenial with the elements of the planet itself, and he cannot but sympathize with its features, its various

aspects, and its phenomena in all situations. We are no doubt placed in a paradise here if we choose to make it such . . .

And towards the end: 'We exist but in a Landscape and we are the creatures of a Landscape.'[18]

Compared to Turner – whose last disjointed lecture at the Academy as Professor of Perspective had been given in 1828 – Constable seems a model of lucidity. He obviously put a lot into his talks. He borrowed pictures to use at them and got back from his cousin Jane Inglis a copy he had made from Claude. He borrowed books, such as Bryan's *Dictionary* from William Carpenter in order to find out more about John Cozens. Samuel Rogers lent others to him. His painter's library was increased for research purposes, though his authorities were not always impeccable, and as a stay-at-home artist unfamiliar with Continental collections he had to depend on prints of many old master paintings. Constable the lecturer was much more conventional than Constable the painter, his lecturing style somewhat stilted and ponderous. Although much in his discourses now sounds like received wisdom, a lot of it may have shocked his contemporaries, followers of the Taste and the portraitists and history painters who were the majority of RAs and the critics who applauded them. The wisdom only became received because of Constable and those who eventually saw things his way. He was overcritical of Boucher, whose landscape-as-fantasy didn't appeal to this inhabitant of the natural landscape. But he ploughed his own memorable furrow. For example, 'What were the habits of Claude and the Poussins? Though surrounded with palaces filled with pictures, they made the fields their chief places of study.' And on Mannerists: 'To this species of painting belong the works that have filled the intervals between the appearances of the great artists. They are productions of men who have lost sight of nature . . .', men who were sometimes talented, sometimes feeble: Wouwermans, Berchem, Both, Vernet, Loutherbourg; Jacob More, Philipp Hackert . . . Ultimately, Constable declared:

Manner is always seductive. It is more or less an imitation of what has been done already – therefore always plausible. It promises the short road, the near cut to present fame and emolument, by availing ourselves of the labours of others. It leads to almost immediate reputation, because it is the wonder of the ignorant world. It is always accompanied by certain blandishments, showy and plausible, and which catch the eye . . . As manner comes by degrees . . . all painters who would be really great should be perpetually on their guard against it. Nothing but a close and continual observance of nature can protect them from the danger of becoming mannerists.

His sermon was perhaps intended not just for his audience but for himself.[19]

# 21. *A Portion of England (1835–37)*

The year began fine and remarkably illness free. Constable went up to Suffolk to see his brothers and sisters and to vote.[1] He wrote enthusiastically to Boner that 'the Blues', the Tories, had been triumphant in that locality. Moreover, 'The birds are singing, the rooks busy, the meadows green, & the water & skies blue.' (A few months later he expressed via Boner his anti-Radical thanks to the Almighty for removing 'the restless spirit, old Cobbett'.) Boner wrote back to East Bergholt on 19 January to give him the London news, to hope his Suffolk stay did him good, and to say, 'We are all well.'[2] While he was out of town John Dunthorne Senior called and talked to Alfie. On getting back to Charlotte Street Constable wrote to Dunthorne asking if he could borrow several drawings that his son Johnny had made: one of some plants and two of 'the ashes in the town meadow'. Constable explained, 'I am about an ash or two now.' He said he was sending his old friend care of Flatford two large mezzotints which Lucas had just engraved of *The Lock* and *The Cornfield*. Constable had told Lucas he had heard good things about the pair of prints; it was thought they would sell.[3] But an early reaction from *The Spectator* gave with one hand and took with the other. The engravings were done 'with great vigour and freedom, and in successful imitation of the painter's peculiar manner'. Moreover, mezzotint wasn't well suited to landscape and brought out Constable's faults more strongly. It made 'his cold, dark colours appear blacker, and his scattered lights whiter; thus exaggerating the raw tone of his later works'.[4]

*The Spectator*'s review is worth dwelling on because it gives a good idea of what Constable was up against now that his eccentricities were well known enough to be mocked. The writer agreed that Constable's pictures had 'the germ of a strong feeling for nature', but this was hidden beneath an 'unpleasing mannerism'. (Evidently his own 'close and continual observance of nature' hadn't protected him from this.) The reviewer continued:

> His early works are admirable for the sober truth and identity of their imitation of nature; and notwithstanding he scatters a shower of snow over every landscape he paints, he cannot entirely conceal the traces of merits that he seems determined to obliterate. We know he means these little spots of white to represent the glancing particles of light that are reflected on every glossy leaf in a bright sunshiny day, or after a clearing-shower; but all the world save only himself mistake it for a representation of snow, or meal scattered over the canvas.

The writer described the two scenes as faithfully and feelingly conveying the English countryside, but of the two he preferred *The Lock* for its more forceful effect. In the lane of *The Cornfield*, 'the numerous little white lights produce a spottiness instead of a sparkling brilliancy, cutting up the general effect, and destroying the tone of the picture'. Moreover,

> The shepherd-boy lying down to drink at the spring, instead of making us feel how welcome is the cold draught on a sultry day, causes us to shiver as if he were dipping his face in an iced pool . . . The glowing warmth of Turner's paintings subsides into sober brilliancy in engravings; the crude and cold colouring of Constable translates into harsh blackness and whiteness.[5]

His only entry for the RA exhibition that year was *The Valley Farm*, a version of an old subject, much painted by him, Willy Lott's house and the stream that ran past Flatford Mill. It was a large canvas, if not quite a six-footer. He worked on it through the winter and spring of 1835 and in the end didn't use Johnny Dunthorne's drawings but his own of a Hampstead ash, with added boughs. The prominent collector Robert Vernon (wealthy as a result of selling horses to the British Army) was happily spending some of his fortune on British paintings; in the last couple of years he had bought two Turners, *The Bridge of Sighs* and *The Golden Bough*. Vernon came to Charlotte Street in March and saw *The Valley Farm* on the easel. He asked Constable whether he had painted the picture for any particular person and Constable replied, 'Yes, sir, it was painted for a very *particular person* for whom I have all my life painted.' Vernon bought the painting then and there. Leslie may have had a hand in setting the price, for Constable was unsure what to ask. Turner's standard price for a three-foot by four-foot canvas in the late 1830s was two hundred guineas. Vernon paid Constable three hundred pounds for *The Valley Farm*, more than the artist had ever got for a painting before.[6]

But Constable went on working on it. He wrote to George Constable a few weeks later to say happily, 'I have got my picture into a very beautifull state. I have kept my brightness without my spottiness, and I have preserved God Almighty's daylight, which is enjoyed by all mankind, excepting only the lovers of old dirty canvas, perished pictures at a thousand guineas each, cart grease, tar and snuff of candles . . .'[7] It seems to have been at one of this year's varnishing days that Constable encountered Clarkson Stanfield at work on a canvas and told him, 'I like your picture very much.' 'Pooh,' said Stanfield, 'that won't do, Mr Constable. I know what you say behind my back – you say of my pictures, *they are all putty!*' 'Well,' admitted Constable, 'well I did say so – but Mr Stanfield, I *like* putty.'[8]

The sale of *The Valley Farm* insulated Constable from some of the criticism the picture engendered. Although the *Athenaeum* declared that Constable, 'an original in everything, . . . must be compared with nature, and not with art', the *Morning Post* found that 'neither in sunshine nor in shower did we ever see anything so speckled and spotty'. The *Literary Gazette* thought, a touch more kindly, that his habit of sprinkling flake-white over the wet surface of his pictures and thereby concealing their beauty was here only partially successful: 'The truth and vigour of his work manifest themselves,

notwithstanding all his insidious and suicidal effects to hide them.'
Abram with brotherly kindness wrote to say that he had seen *The
Valley Farm* 'well-mention'd' in *The News*, but failed, tactfully, to
pass on the news that the paper not only said the painting was 'full
of talent' but that 'the daubs of white give it a cold, wiry, chalky look
– which a friend remarked set his teeth *on edge*'. *The Spectator*
believed Constable preferred 'his mannerism to his fame'. The
Reverend John Eagles, the amateur artist and knockabout critic
whose attack on Turner the following year inspired a seventeen-
year-old John Ruskin to passionate defence of his hero, wrote in
*Blackwood's*: 'There is nothing here to designate a *valley* nor a farm.'
Eagles saw 'something like a cow standing in some ditch-water . . .
Such conceited imbecility is distressing.' As for the difficult Edward
Dubois, in what seems to have been a final attack in the *Observer* on
Constable as an artist who was wealthy enough to be eccentric,
Dubois said that *The Valley Farm* excelled in chiaroscuro, and had
more than usual of Constable's reputed power. Yet this was by
contrast with his characteristic ability to maim his landscapes – as in
the sky here, the 'tossing about of the stuffings of pack-saddles
among remnants of blue taffeta'.[9]

Dubois seems also to have been the first to draw attention to the
presence in the painting of an intruder – a cat sitting on a milk pail. A
few weeks later the *Literary Gazette* thought the offending animal was
the accidental result of atoms falling from Constable's whiting bag.
Academicians were heard asking one another, 'Have you seen the cat?'
The guilty party was named as Edwin Landseer, who on a varnishing
day had mischievously converted several of Constable's white blobs
into 'a very pretty and intellectual cat'. Although the cat on the pail
soon vanished, as the artist went on reworking his picture, another cat
has since been spotted by a sharp-eyed observer, a tiny shape on the
window sill of the farmhouse. Constable's revenge?[10]

*The Valley Farm* was another example of what had become a true
Constable failing: his inability to leave well enough alone. It had
always been a tendency; it was now a bad habit. He asked Leslie to
drop by after he got the picture back from the Academy; he admired

Leslie for his reworking of his own paintings, and he wanted him to
see *The Valley Farm* 'now, for it has proved to me what *my* art is
capable of when time can be given sufficient to carry it home'.
Constable spelled out to John Chalon his improvements to Mr
Vernon's picture: 'Oiling out, making out, polishing, scraping, &c.
seem to have agreed with it exceedingly. The "sleet" and "snow" have
disappeared, leaving in their places, silver, ivory, and a little gold.' In
mid-December *The Valley Farm* was back with Mr Vernon at his
great house in Pall Mall but Constable told William Carpenter that he
hadn't finished with it; it was coming back to him for 'more last
words'. Once in a while Constable recognised that his mania to rework
things was counter-productive. Henry Syer Trimmer reported that
Constable kept Lucas at work altering time and again a large plate –
for a Salisbury Cathedral engraving, apparently – but finally
exclaimed, 'Lucas, I only wish you could bring it to the state it was
nine months ago.' Too many 'last words' made for the downside of his
perfectionism.[11]

   Comparing this view of Willy Lott's house with other versions of
the subject did *The Valley Farm* no favours. Pictures he had done of
the spot at various times both early and late had much more life, for
example *The Mill Stream* of 1811–14, *Scene on a River* of 1830–7
(V&A) and *Farmhouse near the water's edge* of c.1834 (also V&A).
Despite Constable's belief that he had preserved 'God Almighty's
daylight', the painting lost its sparkle; the bitumen he used to glaze it
perhaps helped its attraction when he painted it but soon cracked and
faded.[12] It now seems a dead-end picture, a tired re-enactment of his
Stour valley days in which – rather than daylight – gloom, gloom,
gloom is the prevailing feature. Gothic was of course à la mode. Some
recent viewers have detected elements of anguished nostalgia in it.
'The tortured surface . . . suggests an almost desperate attempt to
recreate the past,' writes Leslie Parris, while for David Hill it is a
scene from a nightmare, the man ferrying the bonneted young woman
a sort of Charon, using his quant pole to push his boat across a murky
Styx rather than rippling Stour.[13]

                                    *

It was a year of family upheaval once again – this time centred on Charley going off to sea. The boy had brine in his blood. His early drawings had been of boats and at the Pierces' school in Folkestone he had kept one eye on his books, the other on the Channel. Boner accompanied Charley on a river trip to Gravesend in July 1834. 'A glorious piece of happiness for me,' Charley wrote to his father. 'We spent a very pleasant day there, it was very rough, we went in a little boat after we came down in the steamer and nea[r]ly we ship[p]ed several good seas.' (The Reverend Pierce hadn't had much success with Charley's spelling.) Charley wrote to his brother John enthusiastically, 'You can have no idea of the opposition of the Gravesend steamers on Gravesend Pier, such a pulling and fighting between the sailors, it was tremendous.'[14] Pursuing his vocation, Charley – fourteen that year – returned to Gravesend to stay for several days with the Brenchley family and in the autumn of 1834 went up to Suffolk on Sidey Constable's coasting barge *Telegraph*; he wrote to his father on 10 November of the excitements of the voyage to Mistley: 'We ran through the Swin [channel] on Sunday morning & I heaved the lead for 7 miles[.] Side had a bath in the Thames rather more than he liked but I pride myself of his catching hold of an oar which I held out to him. He went bang under & was very much frightened.'[15] On his return, Constable's sister Mary wrote to her brother from Flatford:

> Your clever son Charles Golding took leave of his Suffolk friends, & set off with Captain Sidey to join the ship . . . yesterday – the young waterman was in high spirits & he seemed without care or any earthly trouble & I trust we shall soon hear from you of his safe arrival under your roof.
>
> We found him a very interesting youth, *even* if he had not been your son . . . We *all* did *all* we could to make him happy & his company was quite *beyond* his age . . . The wind being fair the voyage will most likely be a . . . quick one.

The *Telegraph* voyage confirmed Charley's nautical ambitions. He was studying mathematics with a new tutor, W.E. Bickmore, to help with his navigation. Constable considered the navy for him but was told that in this now twentieth year of peace the Admiralty list for would-be midshipmen was long.[16] The East India Company was the next option. Family connections were brought into play. In East Bergholt Abram got some personal details of Captain William Hopkins, who commanded the *Buckinghamshire*: 'I call'd at Mrs Clark's this morning & told her what you said of Captain Hopkins, & they speak very highly both of him & the service, he is the brother of Miss Hopkins who was with them several years as Governess . . . and he has work'd his way up to his present situation from small beginnings, & why should not Charles, with his good conduct & abilities . . .?' As Abram no doubt knew, Charley's abilities were apparent, his good conduct somewhat more potential.

The household was put into a frenzy as Charley's departure loomed. Constable wrote to Leslie on the longest day of 1835: 'I wish Charley well at sea – for his own sake. He is an extraordinary boy, and if his genius does not destroy him it will be the making of him – but my *fear* is more than my *hope*!!' Constable proudly painted a portrait of Charley in his new merchant marine uniform – Mr Vernon's purchase of *The Valley Farm* helped pay for the necessary seagoing clothing, and his rigging-out kept Mrs Roberts and the maids more than usually busy.[17] In early August Leslie heard again from Constable:

> My poor Charley's time is now very short in the land of comfort. The ship sails this week. The house has been long in a stir with his 'outfit' – there seems no end to the wants . . . What would Diogenes or an old sow (much the same thing) say to all this display of trousers, jackets, & by dozens – blue & white shirts by scores – and a supply of ratlin for the hammock, as he expects to be often *cut down*.

Constable was trying to be light-hearted but he felt stricken at the prospect of saying goodbye to the lad, who was 'full of sentiment & poetry & determination & integrity'. Nine-year-old Robert Leslie was allowed to accompany Constable, Alfred, and Mrs Roberts to look around the *Buckinghamshire* in the East India Dock, with Charley, according to his father, promising to 'show how the planks are laid, and the "timbers" and all'.[18] (Robert Leslie, as noted, became a skilled amateur sailor and boatbuilder as well as a professional sea-painter; this visit – together with Turner's rigging of his toy-ship at Petworth – may have helped determine his life.) Charley hung close to his father and asked him to stay until the next day, but Constable couldn't bear to prolong the farewell; he shook hands and said goodbye.[19] But he was happy with his view of the *Buckinghamshire*: 'A noble ship, the size of a 74.'[20]

By the end of August Charley's real sea life had begun. He wrote several letters home while the *Buckinghamshire*, bound for Bombay, called at Gravesend and Spithead. The ship had been held up in the Thames by thick fog. On 30 August: 'We anchored a few miles below Woolwich late in the evening because we went against the tide. We had two large foreign steamboats tow us down on each side. When the anchor went [down] it brought to my mind exactly how you had described it to me on board the Coutes.' Charley observed that when the anchor was raised next morning, the sailors heaved at the capstan while a fiddle was played to encourage their efforts. He'd found the only disagreeable thing so far was to be awakened out of a sound sleep 'to keep two cold hours watch'. Luckily he'd got a well-ventilated berth near a hatch. From the anchorage at St Helens, off the Isle of Wight, they had collected cargo and passengers, and glimpsed the *Victory* moored in Portsmouth harbour. Then they set off down Channel in a hard blow, with Charley aloft on the mizzen topsail yard, reefing the sail, letting go one line, hauling on another, while the ship pitched, rolled, and lurched in the heavy seas. Charley told his father in a last note sent with the pilot as he was dropped off Start Point: 'We have a great many gentlemen passengers on board . . . Some of them had a hearty laugh at seeing my cap blow far away to leeward from the mizen and just after went my right shoe.'[21]

Constable proudly told Leslie that his son was 'a true sailor – he makes up his mind to combat all difficulties in calms or storms with an evenness of mind – which little belongs to me, a landsman. They have had a rough business of it so far.' And to George Constable in Arundel, where Charley's brother John had been staying, Constable wrote frankly about his anxious time:

> I have done all for the best, and I regret all that I have done, when I consider that it was to bereave me of this delightfully clever boy, who would have shone in my own profession, and who is now doomed to be driven about on the ruthless sea. It is a sad and melancholy life, but he seems made for a sailor. Should he please the officers and stick to the ship, it will be more to his advantage than being in the navy, – a hateful tyranny, with starvation into the bargain.[22]

Constable's early experience in Lavenham apparently still left its mark. Those in authority could well be tyrants. But perhaps he also remembered his own struggle to follow the path he had picked out, and his father's acquiesence in and support for what he chose to do.

Charley had preoccupied him this year but not to the exclusion of all else, though the other children got less dramatic attention. The girls were still at Miss Noble's in Hampstead. Emily, now ten, wrote in June 1835:

> My dear Papa,
>   I hope you will be pleased with this my first letter and I will try that my next shall be better. The holidays will very soon begin, and I trust you will find me improved in my studies. Give my love to my Brothers, and to Roberts,
>     And believe me, your affectionate child,
>       Emily Constable[23]

Minna seized any chance to be maternal and tidied up her father's possessions to a point where he couldn't find anything. Constable took Minna and young John down to George Constable's for a few days in July and was happy walking among the riverside willows and hanging woods of the Arun valley. Alfie was also at a Hampstead school, run by Mr Brooks. Constable told Leslie, 'He plays first fiddle there in everything but his books – but poor boy, his whole life till now has been one of afflictions, which as well as his drollery . . . has endeared him to me – perhaps unduly so.' Lionel went for a while to a dame's school kept by a Mrs Rawley but then joined Alfie at the Brooks establishment. As for young John, now studying in London, he went off happy and well on a trip to France, though he didn't care for the food there: too much vinegar in everything. He visited the Louvre but wasn't marked by the experience. The only picture he remembered, when being debriefed, was (Constable reported to Leslie) 'the Watteau, "where ever so many cupids & people were flying about the sky & climbing up the mast of a boat." As to Ruisdael, Claude, Poussin & Titian, he knows little and cares less.' Constable himself was still set against the Continent; he wrote to Boner in late June declining an invitation to Germany to see the mountains. 'Such a range of scenery . . . would expand my ideas of landscape' but also cause him, he feared, 'to lose his character as a painter'.[24] That character was to some members of the public still uncertain. Constable was asked to testify at this time in a dispute about the genuineness of a purported Claude. In its report on the matter, *The Times* called him an 'amateur painter'.[25] In March 1836 he wrote again to Boner to say things were going smoothly: 'My own "oneness" of pursuit leads to little change, more than the subject on my easil, but thank God all the children are well.'[26]

His son John was studying 'Chymistry, Anatomy & Materia Medica', with lectures and anatomy lessons in the daytime and extra tuition in Latin from Charley's tutor Mr Bickmore in the evenings. John had thoughts of becoming a clergyman or doctor or even both after Cambridge. Now that Boner had departed, he was also serving as his father's personal assistant. John told Constable about the visitors who called when he was away lecturing and kept him up to date with household finances: 'The money will hold out very well.' Constable in turn did his best to keep his son informed, telling him, for example, 'Mr Vernon paid me for the picture.' In December 1835 young John was entered as a future student of Corpus Christi College, Cambridge. A few days later Abram called at Charlotte Street with six gallons of linseed oil for David Lucas, 'as pure as the seed can produce it', Abram said. (The family firm continued to be useful.) Constable and John went to Flatford for a week at Christmas and Mary thought the occasion was 'a very happy one'. (The girls went to stay with their aunt Louisa Sanford in Wimbledon.) Constable had been consulted by Abram on works at Dedham Mill – the shaft of which needed repair – and Abram was next involved in what Mary called 'vast works' on the lock gates there: 'His heart well nigh *fails* him under all his cares.'[27]

While at Flatford, Constable discussed with his brother and sister a proposal Mary had put forward – 'between hope and fright' – to buy some local land. Abram, as always cautious about spending capital, had reservations at first but didn't discourage her when she got interested in part of the Coleman estate, which included Old House Farm and land called Fishers. Mary asked: What if she took the former and Constable took the latter? 'A small portion *of England in East Bergholt* . . . would prove a *harmless* link of worldly pleasure,' she suggested. It was on the east side of the village, south of the road from the centre, some way beyond the lane that went down to Flatford, and next to the Dodnice River and some beautiful woods. The timber was excellent though brother Golding didn't altogether approve of the soil. The price being asked was £4,000. She thought it a benefit, should they become 'Easterns', that the new rail road wouldn't cross the land. (This was the Ipswich section of the Eastern Counties Railway, designed to run eventually from London to Yarmouth, and then built as far north as Colchester.) In May 1836 Abram wrote to Constable to say the purchase had been agreed – a deposit of £200 paid and completion to be at Michaelmas. Mary intended to farm all the land and pay rent to Constable for his part of it; she anticipated much pleasure from it. By 20 May 1836 she had engaged an elderly couple, Mr and Mrs Crosbie, to help with the farm and dairy.

Constable thus became the owner of Bergholt land. The family's former house was still owned by Mr and Mrs Walter Clerk who had bought it in 1818. Abram in May 1836 said that he had spent 'a most agreeable evening . . . at the *Old House*', and that Mr Clerk – with long-term health problems – was 'much better, but tender'. The new Constable land was shown on the local tithe map for 30 December 1837, with Mary as the occupier, and a tithes and rent charge of £32 6s 0d paid to the incumbent rector, Reverend Joshua Rowley. Various buildings and pieces of land owned by Constable and Mary were specified on the map. They included Little Taylor's, Whins, Flax Field, Barn Field, Gar, Bean Field, Cross Path Field, Bridge Field, Lays, Long Meadow, Long Fen, Stoneland's, Coleman's, Fisher's Fen, Forty Acres, Broom Knoll, Quaking Fen, Fisher's Field, Wright's Fen, Great Taylors, Park Field, Spooners, an allotment, some yards, some buildings and a garden. Bergholt names. But for the moment Constable didn't have the chance to visit his new property.[28]

# 22. Two Monuments (1836)

Constable had only one complaint against Leslie: his good friend, even though back in the same city, lived too far away. His house in Pineapple Place was on the east side of Edgware Road, just beyond the old Kilburn Gate.[1] It was on the edge of open country, with hayfields that extended to Harrow-on-the-Hill. Constable insisted the place was fatal to Leslie's friendships, but nevertheless got himself there quite often. Leslie also came frequently to Hampstead or Charlotte Street. He dined with Constable on Christmas Eve 1834, when Samuel Rogers, David Wilkie and Jack Bannister were among the company. Leslie and Constable were different as artists but in some ways similar as men. What brought them together may have been that they were both somewhat out of the London swim and at a distance from their roots. Both favoured black clothing; both were warm individuals under a surface severity. Yet Leslie might not have taken to Constable if he hadn't admired his paintings. He cultivated Constable's friendship because he liked his art.[2] And because Constable in turn liked Leslie so much – and felt for Leslie's wife and children an immense affection, almost as if they were reflections of his own lost Maria and his own chicks – he admired Leslie's paintings more than might have been expected. Leslie was essentially an illustrator, whose narrative pictures dealt with literary or historical subjects, such as his *Uncle Toby and Widow Wadman* or his *Autolycus selling his wares*. Constable lent him sky studies and, in March 1836, for the *Autolycus* sent him a rough sketch of a mountain ash he thought might be helpful. Leslie took the hint and introduced such a tree with its red berries to a sliver of landscape behind his shepherd and young woman.

In time Leslie would be accused of creating in his memoir too deferential a portrait of Constable, as if he were a superior being; but Leslie often wrote acutely about his friend. Although Constable didn't have a very large circle of friends – or a great number of admirers of his pictures – they 'compensated for their fewness by their sincerity and their warmth'. Leslie thought that Constable's genius, in both his character and his art, didn't suit his time. His stand-offishness was a problem, but despite it 'no man more earnestly desired to stand well with the world; no artist was more solicitous of popularity'. On the one hand he desired approbation, on the other he couldn't conceal the candid opinions that made people find him disagreeable. 'What he said had too much point not to be repeated, and too much truth not to give offence; so some of his competitors hated him and most were afraid of him . . . He was opposed to all cant in art, to all that is merely specious and fashionable . . . He followed . . . his own feelings in the choice of subject and the mode of treat-ment. With great appearance of docility, he was an uncontrollable man.' When people accuse Leslie of seeing Constable through rose-coloured spectacles, they should recall that remarkable epithet, 'uncontrollable'.

Among Constable's acquaintances at this time was Samuel Rogers, well known for his breakfast parties for the great, good, and talented at his house in St James's Place, who was also to be encountered at Lord Egremont's in Petworth along with Chantrey, Beechey, Turner, and Leslie. Constable had a memorable London morning with the banker-poet in March 1836. Rogers told Constable he was on 'the right road' as a landscape painter and that nobody could explain its history so well. Constable thought Rogers had the best private collection of paintings in London and particularly admired his Rubens. Rogers was pleased when Constable noticed the falling star in it. Constable watched his host feed some sparrows from the breakfast table; the sparrows seemed to know him well. Yet Rogers seemed also to tap into Constable's dissatisfaction and melancholy. He told Constable that genius had to put up with the burden of being hated. Constable surprisingly demurred at this, though he agreed it could be true 'in nature'. He wrote to Leslie afterwards, 'I told him if he could catch one of those sparrows, and tie a bit of paper about its neck, and let it off again, the rest would peck it to death for being so *distinguished*.'[3]

The Royal Academy was in its final days at Somerset House. Leslie was on the Arrangement Committee in 1836 and Constable was pestered by 'sparrows' of a different sort, artists so-nicknamed who were hoping to get their works shown and who believed that a good friend of Leslie's might sway the selection process. Some hopefuls sent not only supplications but their actual canvases to Charlotte Street, adding to the pressure on Constable. Among the 'Hammatures' (as he called them) seeking approval was the devoted Reverend Judkin; another was the French artist Auguste Hervieu, who had helped *The White Horse* get to Lille in 1825. Constable, aware from his own experience that he was being a nuisance, put in a word not only for Hervieu but for J.M. Nixon, a historical painter who had provided display placards for his lectures, for William C. Ross, a miniature artist, and for Samuel Lane, his old, handicapped, portrait-painting friend. That a painter was, like Nixon, 'a kind and good father', or like W.H. Fisk, from Thorpe-le-Soken in Essex, not far from the Stour, 'a kind, good, amiable man' (whose wife moreover had once made 'some beautifull salve for Maria's chilblains'), all made a difference to Constable, whose high standards vis-à-vis Berchem and Both didn't come into play when it was a matter of the Academy and people he knew. However, his caustic tongue wasn't completely subdued. One Brighton property owner, W.W. Altree, who was concerned to ensure that an architectural drawing of some villas he proposed to build was prominently hung, was – Constable told Leslie – 'a great fool, and very ignorant, & forward in consequence'.

Constable entered two pictures for the exhibition, the last at Somerset House: *The Cenotaph* and *Stonehenge*, two sorts of monument. The first was a painting of a memorial to Sir Joshua Reynolds in the park of Coleorton Hall, but was also by the way a

Memorial to Sir Joshua Reynolds at Coleorton, 1823

memorial to Sir George Beaumont, who had placed it there, and to the
Academy itself. Constable had made a drawing of it back in November
1823, and wrote to Fisher about his visit: 'In the dark recesses of these
gardens . . . I saw an urn – & bust of Sir Joshua Reynolds – & under it
some beautifull verses, by Wordsworth.' The Beaumonts had laid the

first stone for it on 30 October 1812, with Joseph Farington on hand. Constable had quoted Reynolds's *Discourses* ten years before, to the effect that there was no *easy* way of becoming a good painter. In 1813 he had written to Maria about his liking for Reynolds's paintings: 'Here is no vulgarity or rawness and yet no want of life or vigor – it is certainly the finest feeling [for] art that ever existed.' *The Cenotaph*, like *The Valley Farm*, is an elegiac, even funereal, painting, with a tiny robin and an alert deer the only life in it; the trees are bare, the sky mostly masked by their branches. Constable wrote to George Constable that it was 'a tolerably good picture for the Academy, [though] not The Mill, which I had hoped to do . . . I preferred to see Sir Joshua Reynolds name and Sir George Beaumont's once more in the catalogue, for the last time at the old house . . . The Exhibition is much liked. Wilkie's pictures are very fine, and Turner has outdone himself; he seems to paint with tinted steam, so evanescent and so airy.' The deer was probably meant to evoke Sir George's fondness for *As You Like It*, the play set in the Forest of Arden, where melancholy Jaques observed a wounded stag.[4]

While he was at work on *The Cenotaph* two young brothers, Alfred and Robert Tidey, visited Constable. Robert, the younger of the artistically inclined pair, wrote later:

> I was interested and amused by his mode of work and the way in which he produced such wonderful effects in his pictures by dabbing on splashes of colour with his palette knife in lieu of brush and stepping well back into the room now and again to view the result, remarking to my brother in an absent sort of way, 'How will that do, Tidey, eh? How will that do?' He seemed to me, as I believe he was, a man of extreme gentleness and simplicity of character.

*The Cenotaph* got a fairly good press. Abram told his brother he heard well of it. Constable wrote to George Constable, 'I hear it is liked, but I see no newspaper, not allowing one to come into my house.' In fact, the *Observer* (with Edward Dubois departed) was coming on side: 'The peculiar manner in which Mr Constable's pictures are painted makes them appear singular at first, but by choosing a proper distance for observing them, by degrees the effect seems to grow upon us until we are astonished that we did not like them better before.' *The Times* seemed to like the somewhat sententious lines by Wordsworth that Constable quoted in the catalogue more than the 'singularly finished' picture itself.[6] But the *Morning Herald* and the *Morning Post* both approved of the painting, the latter deciding that 'like all the pictures of Mr Constable, the present is marked by peculiarities, but they are the peculiarities of an original style, without the tricks of mannerism'. It was a word that kept coming up, even when it was being denied. Indeed, the *Athenaeum* thought the picture 'less mannered' than Constable's works usually were; and *Bell's Weekly Messenger* declared the painting had much beauty, albeit with 'a singularity of style in the execution that rather approaches to mannerism'.[7]

As for his second offering, it was a watercolour which Constable had told Leslie about the previous September: 'I have made a beautifull drawing of Stonehenge. I venture to use such an expression to you.' *Stonehenge* was large for a watercolour, about fifteen by twenty-two inches. The standing, tilting, and fallen stones, and a few small figures, were spotlit against a tempestuous purple-black cloud with the inner and outer bands of a rainbow arching down in the background. (He told Lucas about this time that he had been 'very busy with rainbows, and very happy doing them'.) A hare scuttled across the sheep-trimmed grass. In the Academy catalogue Constable described part at least of what he had in mind: 'The mysterious monument of Stonehenge, standing remote on a bare and boundless heath, as much unconnected with the events of past ages as it is with the uses of the present, carries you back beyond all historical records . . . ' The watercolour made use of preliminary studies, two drawings and two watercolours, several of which he squared up for transfer, together with a pencil drawing he had done in 1820 while staying with the Fishers in which the great stones cast black shadows in the same way as the gnomon of a sundial. In the Academy water-colour he made the stones slightly smaller in terms of the whole picture, though the sky and weather increased the sense of surrounding drama. The contemplative shepherd and speeding hare offered a contrast to the stones: time present, time past. The hare seems to have been a late arrival; it was painted on a small piece of paper cut to a more or less hare-shape and pasted on. (Turner's *Mortlake Terrace* of 1827 had a pasted-on dog; his *Rain, Steam and Speed* of 1844 contained a hare that seemed, like Constable's, to suggest natural vitality.) Constable's sky was unique; it showed no obvious influence of his 1820s sky studies. The *Literary Gazette* declared 'the effect with which Mr Constable has judiciously invested his subject, is as marvelous and mysterious as the subject itself'. It is interesting to see him reinvolved with watercolours at this stage, perhaps finding them easier to manage than oils following his rheumatic fever.[8]

A farewell dinner for the Academy took place on 20 July in the Great Room at Somerset House after the close of the exhibition. Constable was on hand in 'the dear old house' along with the President. Sir Martin Archer Shee was about to defend the RA before a parliamentary committee inquiring into its procedures and Constable was among those who applauded Shee's staunchness.[9] (Haydon – no friend of the Academy – would give evidence in August before the committee and while he approved of the instruction in the Antique School, he totally disapproved of the rotating system of Visitors in the Life School, citing as an extraordinary example of the teaching methods 'a very celebrated landscape painter' who caused laughter by bringing in some lemon and orange trees and setting them round a naked Eve. Constable's 1831 arrangement had, as noted, been popular with the students.)[10] In any event, at the farewell dinner Constable dined with many of his fellows, including Wilkie, Callcott, Stanfield, Leslie, and Etty. Chantrey gave the toast: 'The Old Walls of the Academy.' Turner, believed to be opposed to the move to Trafalgar Square, was among the absentees. He had set off on one of his frequent summer tours abroad, this time through France to the Alps with Hugh Munro for company.[11] The Academy Life School stayed on at Somerset House until March 1837 when it moved into the Academy's new quarters in the same building as the National

Gallery. Constable was one of the members chosen to be Visitors of the Life School in its last Somerset House session.

Constable was sixty on 11 June 1836. How old did he feel? He was looking forward to Charley's return from his first voyage. Minna and Isabel were in Wimbledon and Constable visited them there, before they rejoined Emily, Alfred and Lionel with Mrs Roberts in Hampstead. Young John had gained a certificate for his chemistry studies and went off to spend five summer weeks at Flatford, 'fishing and rowing all day and reading when it is wet', his father told Emily in a letter from Charlotte Street written with a cat called Kellery perched on his shoulder. He went on, 'A little black and white kitten was let down into the area in a woolen bag yesterday morning early' – evidently by someone who knew the Constable family liked cats. 'It is very thin . . . Kellery is very jealous.'[12] Constable still hadn't got up to Suffolk to see his new property. He delivered his last lecture in Hampstead on 25 July and arranged to have nine pictures sent to an exhibition in Worcester. The local paper there was struck by 'the wonderful effect' made by *Salisbury Cathedral from the Meadows – Summer Afternoon* and *A Farmyard by a Navigable River in Suffolk – Summer Morning*, painted by 'the same great master'.[13]

Charley had a short spell of shore leave when the *Buckinghamshire* docked. His first voyage had left its mark on the boy, so his father told George Constable in Arundel. 'All his visionary and poetic ideas of the sea & a seaman's life are fled – the reality now only remains, and a dreadful thing the reality is, a huge & hideous floating mass.' Charley's self-discipline and sense of order had been improved, however – 'an advantage [to] a youth of ardent mind & one who has never been controlled'. The *Buckinghamshire* was now going to China. Constable paid a firm of shipping agents the sizeable sum of £75 for Charley's accommodation and mess bills as a midshipman.[14] He asked Lucas to send a copy of the new engraving of *Dedham Vale* (or the painting itself) so Charley could see it before he sailed, but if Lucas couldn't manage this, 'never mind – only he may never see it again'. Constable feared losing Charley rather than Charley losing him (his misgivings also surfaced in several ink sketches of ships in storms done at this time). Yet an awareness of the possibility of his own demise could be found in a profoundly gloomy letter written to a collector friend, a Mr Stewart – apparently a Hampstead neighbour – for whom he had painted a small picture of the Heath. Charley's ship was still in the Thames estuary in late November, held up by bad weather rather than fog this time. Constable told Stewart that he himself was 'so much invalided that I have not been <u>allowed</u> to leave the house . . . I am not in the best of spirits. The parting with my dear sailor boy – for so long a time that God knows if we ever meet again in this world – the various anxieties and the fear of the world, & its attacks on my dear children after I am gone & they have no protection, all these things make me sad.' And he added, 'I want to stick to my easil – but cannot.'[15]

When the *Buckinghamshire* got away, it was to run immediately into more fierce weather. Charley reported to his father shocking scenes in their storm-refuge anchorage off the Nore. Constable wrote to Leslie: 'One large ship floated past them bottom upwards, & after the gale he saw 7 large hulls in tow with steamboats & some on the Goodwins [sandbanks] and some on the beach under the Foreland. The captain [Captain Hopkins again] gave him praise for his conduct in the weather mizen topsail ear-ring, and getting down the rigging in the gale, Charley's <u>post of honor</u>.' Constable felt fear, and pride, for Charley, and a vicarious excitement. He accompanied his words with a nervously messy little sketch of Charley's station aloft, attending to the mizzen topsail. The sketch would have left Leslie little the wiser despite his passages with Captain Morgan – whose *Philadelphia*, Constable reported, was a miraculous survivor of the same storm.

Jack Bannister, good old friend, had died on 7 November; this didn't improve Constable's morale. There would be no more of Bannister's songs and puns. Constable dined with Leslie and Wilkie on 1 December and recalled meeting Wilkie when they were students at the Academy. He remembered Wilkie saying that he was following his Scottish master's advice, borrowed from Reynolds, to be industrious if you were short of genius. Wilkie was as modest as always and as usual seemed to put Constable into a nostalgic frame of mind.[16] Wilkie around this time told Constable that he ought to paint 'a large picture for over the line' for the next Academy exhibition.[17] Constable a week later heard from the collector and clothing manufacturer John Sheepshanks that he wanted Constable's *Glebe Farm*, 'one of the pictures on which I rest my little pretensions to futurity'. Would it be all right to ask 150 pounds for it, Constable enquired from Leslie. Sheepshanks's gesture was generous, since Constable had just declined to paint a companion picture for a William Collins the collector owned, a painting which Constable said had 'nothing to do with the *art*'. At Sheepshanks's mansion in Blackheath he viewed the many pictures: Wilkie's two looked beautiful; the more than a score of Mulreadys were 'less disagreeable than usual'; Turner's five were 'grand' but evidently not long for this world – some of his best work, said Constable, was 'swept up off the carpet every morning by the maid and put onto the dust hole'.[18]

Constable was again in the midst of a tormented attempt to alter – or get Lucas to alter – a large mezzotint of Salisbury Cathedral. Dark clouds loomed behind the spire; the whole thing was 'too heavy'. A number of corrections were still required in November. On 9 December he said the most recent proof was effective but 'the flash of lightning over the north transept' should be emphasised. On the last day of 1836, although he was once more sadly disturbed by the stormy sky, he couldn't think why he had suggested a change. Lucas needed money and asked for a loan of two pounds. With an hour and a quarter to go before midnight, and 1837 imminent, Constable wrote enclosing two sovereigns and his good wishes to Mrs Lucas, who was about to have a baby. 'God preserve your excellent wife, and give her a happy hour – I have not forgot my own anxieties at such a time though they are never to return to me.' He ended with the words, 'You have caused the Old Year to slip through my hands with pleasurable feelings . . . Farewell.' But six weeks later the print, now called *The Rainbow – Salisbury Cathedral*, was still a bother. He wrote to Lucas, 'I hope that obliging – and most strange & odd ruffian your printer, will be allowed to have just his own way in printing this plate – that is, now we see we must not be "too full." It is as [he] says only fit for "a parcel of painters." It will not be liked, any more than the English landscape, if it is too smutty.'[19]

Constable went for a New Year's celebration at the Leslies' on 2 January. For the Constable children it was like an 'excursion into the country'. He insisted the Leslies allow him to return the hospitality two days later and that they come to share some venison the Countess of Dysart had sent. The other guests would be the family solicitor Anthony Spedding and Miss Spedding, who was fond of Minna.[20] Constable closed his invitation with the words he said John Fisher had used to him in a request that he make a visit: 'Prithee come – life is short – friendship sweet.'

# 23. *Engaged with the Assassin (1837)*

With the New Year past, it was back to the easel. The canvas Constable worked on was to be called *Arundel Mill and Castle*. Mills never ceased to interest him and perhaps as he painted he heard the wheel going round, the rush of river water, the stones grinding within. While staying with the George Constables in July 1835 he had sat on the banks of Swanbourne Lake near Arundel and sketched this ancient powerhouse,[1] which was far older than the stage-set castle. In 1836 he had borrowed back the sketch – a gift to George Constable – saying young John wanted him to make a painting of it, but *The Cenotaph* had come first.[2] In mid-February 1837 he wrote to the Arundel brewer telling him he was indebted to him for the new work, 'a beautiful subject . . . It is, and shall be, my best picture.' He had six weeks before the Academy exhibition and felt easy about completing it in time. In the *Mill and Castle* he used a scene which he had told Leslie several years before was a wonderful natural landscape – 'the trees are beyond everything beautifull'. One can see in the painting hints of his early addiction to Gainsborough, but even more, and less happily, reverberations from his other old hero, Rubens, to whom many of the painterly effects seem indebted. Not only Arundel Castle but the *Chateau de Steen* looms over *Arundel Mill*. There are of course Constable motifs – the boys fishing in a little creek at the lake's edge remind us of other boys fishing in the Stour. Yet in recovering such things he gave the impression of trying too hard to improve on his old works, to improve the unimproveable, and the result was unnatural. The Swiss art historian J. Meier-Graefe later wrote that Constable, in his last larger pictures, 'felt expression slipping away from him, and tried to indemnify himself by exaggeration of method'. Consequently he lost the freshness that existed in his sketches.[3] The word 'mannered' once again came to mind. Even Constable began to have doubts about his 'best picture'. On 25 February he told Leslie that he had been 'sadly hindered . . . my picture is not worth any thing at the moment'.

Titian, not Rubens, was in Constable's thoughts as he set up a scene for the Academy's Life students to draw. He took over from Turner as Visitor at the end of February, and he wrote to Leslie that he would be 'engaged with the "Assassin" all the following week' – that is, with the figure of the murderer in Titian's *St Peter Martyr*. A man named Fitzgerald was to be his model for the assassinated Dominican and another named Emmott the fleeing murderer, 'an obliging well behaved man . . . who is anxious for a turn at the Academy'. He had to hand a print of the same subject based on a painting by Jacobello del Fiore, done five years before the Titian. He had made a point in his landscape lectures of the Titian's significance in the process by which landscape painting unlinked itself from history painting and became an independent branch of art.

Constable's tour of duty lasted until 25 March. He looked after the Life students from five p.m. until nine p.m. every evening in front of a model lit by oil lamps. The scene he set to follow the Assassination required a young woman. Etty, naturally interested in helping out, sent a note which amused the recipient:

Dear Constable,
    A young figure is brought to me, who is very desirous of becoming a model. She is very much like the Amazon and all in front remarkable fine.

The apprentice model was seventeen. For her, Constable put aside a more experienced female named Welham who had been promised the job but had in some way misbehaved; moreover (he told Leslie) she was 'a sad story teller, and gossip, & old and worn out in figure'.[4] Clearly not remarkably fine.

Looking after the Life class was a strenuous job after a day's painting. It was a long winter, with deep snow in Charlotte Street, the fogs thick with coal smoke. There was much influenza about and Constable advised Samuel Lane to keep his children at home because of the bitter weather – 'nothing breeds whooping cough so much'. His own family escaped illness although he worried about young John, 'the most tender of us all', still working hard for his Cambridge entrance. His girls were all well and happy at 'that excellent woman's, Miss Noble', where Mrs Roberts went to see them from time to time. He attended the first RA general meeting to be held at 'the new house'. Many thought William Wilkins's building too low-key and by no means big enough for the National Gallery (in the west half) and the Royal Academy (in the east), crammed in together.[5] But Constable called it 'very noble'. His last Life class session took place in Somerset House on 25 March, a Saturday. He treated it to his usual humorous interjections. Richard Redgrave, who was there along with Etty, painting from the model, said that Constable 'indulged in the vein of satire he was so fond of'.[6] At the end of the evening – not just his last evening as Visitor but the last such get-together in the old house – he gave a brief talk to the students about what caused the arts to prosper or fail. One factor that led to success was the right sort of instruction; one that led to disappointment was trust in false principles. The Academy had advantages as the cradle of British Art; students shouldn't rush to European schools instead. The best school of art existed where the best artists lived, not where the largest number of old masters were displayed. Some people thought the French were best at drawing. Yet remember what Stothard had said: 'The French are very good <u>mathematical</u> draughtsmen, but life and motion are the essence of drawing, and their figures remind us too much of statues.' Constable asked the students to show in their work that they had imbibed the Academy principles which would honour the new establishment and their country, then he thanked them for their diligent attention during his Visitorship. At this the students stood and cheered him heartily.[7]

After this he had a busy few days. Among his visitors in Charlotte

Street was a recent Academy student, Alfred Tidey, who had watched him working on *The Cenotaph*. Tidey became a painter of miniature portraits, his subjects including Minna and Charley. On 28 March Tidey found Constable happily absorbed in his *Arundel Mill and Castle*. He gave it a touch here and there with his palette knife and then stepped back to judge the effect, saying, 'It is neither too warm nor too cold, too light nor too dark, and this constitutes everything in a picture.' Constable asked Tidey to stay to dinner and answered questions about the Academy's new quarters by sketching a rough floor plan.[8] On the following day Constable wrote to Lucas about the Salisbury Cathedral mezzotint; he was particularly pleased with the rainbow, which they had been fussing over. He said that he was planning to go to a general assembly of the Academy the next evening, Thursday, and would dine on Saturday with John Fisher's father at the Charterhouse, the school and almshouse in a former City monastery.[9]

On the Thursday Constable met Leslie at the Academy and after the assembly walked part of the way home with him. It was a fine night but very cold. In Oxford Street they heard a child crying and Constable crossed the street to see what was wrong. It was a little beggar girl who had hurt her knee. Leslie watched as Constable gave her a shilling and some sympathetic words. These, Leslie said, 'by stopping her tears, showed that the hurt was not very serious'. As they walked on, Constable – perhaps thinking about the giving of money – complained about some losses he had had recently, small enough but a nuisance because the people involved took advantage of his good feelings. Constable had gone well out of his way for Leslie but they parted cheerfully at the west end of Oxford Street to take their separate routes home.[10]

On the last day of March he worked on *Arundel Mill and Castle*; it would soon have to go to the Academy exhibition. Several people who called in Charlotte Street had the impression Constable wasn't well, but put the malaise down to his being cooped up in his painting quarters, worried about his picture. In the evening he went out on an errand for his favourite charity, the Artists' General Benevolent

Institution. He got home about nine and ate a good supper. At bedtime, however, he said he felt chilly. He asked for his bed to be warmed; the maid thought this was unusual for him. From ten until eleven he read in bed as he always did. On this occasion he was reading Robert Southey's *Life and Letters of Cowper* – William Cowper, poet of religion and nature, as far as Constable was concerned a fellow spirit, author of 'John Gilpin's Ride' and 'The Task' (which Constable particularly liked). In a letter to his friend the Reverend John Newton (3 May 1780) Cowper wrote:

> I draw mountains, valleys, woods, and streams, and ducks, and dabchicks. I admire them myself, and Mrs. Unwin admires them; and her praise, and my praise put together, are fame enough for me . . . I amuse myself with a greenhouse which Lord Bute's gardener could take upon his back, and walk away with; and when I have paid it the accustomed visit, and watered it, and given it air, I say to myself – 'This is not mine, it is a plaything lent me for the present; I must leave it soon.'

After Constable had fallen asleep the maid removed his candle.[11]

Because he had rented out much of the upstairs of the Charlotte Street house to help cover the costs of Well Walk, he and his son John were using two adjoining bedrooms in the attic.[12] Young John had been at the theatre and when he got home and went to bed, he heard his father call out. Constable was in great pain and felt giddy. His son suggested a doctor be called but Constable said no. He agreed to take some rhubarb and magnesia; this made him feel sick. He then drank some warm water, which made him vomit. The pain got worse. Constable asked John to get hold of their neighbour, Mr Michele, a medical man. He moved from his bed for a while to an upright chair, then back to bed where he lay on his side. By the time Michele arrived, Constable seemed to have fallen asleep, so his son thought, although in fact he had lost consciousness. Michele said brandy was needed as a stimulant. The maid ran downstairs to get some, but she was too late. Young John heard Constable gasp several times and then, nothing – he had stopped breathing. His hands became cold. Half an hour after the onset of the pain he was dead.[13]

Constable's trusted messenger Pitt came to Leslie's house early the next morning. It was 1 April. Leslie saw Pitt from a bedroom window as he was dressing and went downstairs, expecting to be handed a note from Constable, perhaps an invitation.[14] But the message was to say that Constable had died during the night. Leslie and his wife hurried to Charlotte Street. They found the painter lying in his little attic room, looking as if he were asleep, with his watch still ticking on the bedside table and a volume of the Southey *Life of Cowper* alongside it. Among the many engravings hung on the walls was a print near the foot of the bed that Samuel Rogers had lent him of a moonlight scene by Rubens.[15]

*

Constable's death mask

Leslie remained for the rest of the day. Several death masks were made while he was there. A post-mortem was conducted by Professor Partridge of King's College in the presence of Michele and George Young, the surgeon who had given Constable advice about how to present his Hampstead lectures. The results of the post-mortem were inconclusive. The doctors found no indication of any disease that might have killed him. His pain was thought to be from indigestion.[16] Michele later told Leslie he thought that if the brandy had been given promptly it might have kept Constable alive. Nowadays we know that indigestion-like pains – 'heartburn' – can be signs of what is in fact a heart attack. We also know that rheumatic fever, which Constable had suffered a severe bout of, can do serious cardiac damage, can indeed be life-threatening: Dr Evans of Hampstead thought Constable never fully recovered from his rheumatic fever. Some sort of heart failure was generally suspected by commentators in the press. The *Morning Chronicle*'s short obituary on 3 April said the cause of death was 'an enlargement of the heart'. The *Morning Post* declared that Constable died of 'an affection of the heart'. On 9 April *Bell's Weekly Messenger* said the cause appeared to be 'spasm of the heart'. One other condition that might be taken into account was Constable's proneness to anxiety, which John Fisher had pointed out 'hurts the stomach more than arsenic'. He might have died of a perforated ulcer, though an ulcer should have given painful signs of its presence earlier on. He might simply have burned out his allotted store of vital spirit.[17]

For Leslie, the shock slowly accumulated. The suddenness of Constable's death felt like a blow which at first stunned him and then gave him pain. He gradually learned how much he had lost in Constable, and it was more than he supposed at the time of his friend's death.

The funeral took place in Hampstead parish church and at the tomb where Maria was buried in the graveyard. His brothers, Golding and Abram, led the mourners. Many of Constable's friends and Hampstead neighbours were on hand. Of family members, his son John was the most noticeable absentee; he was still overwhelmed by his father's death and too ill to attend. Perhaps as a child, close to his mother, he had lived with death too long. That most persistent of Constable's 'loungers', the clergyman and amateur artist the Reverend Thomas Judkin, recited the Order for the Burial of the Dead: 'I am the resurrection and the life . . . The Lord gave, and the Lord hath taken away . . . Man that is born of woman hath but a short time to live . . . He cometh up, and is cut down, like a flower . . . earth to earth, ashes to ashes, dust to dust . . . Amen.' Judkin wept over the Book of Common Prayer and his were not the only tears that fell. Constable's coffin was laid in the tomb alongside Maria's. Some of the mourners noted again the Latin lines he had borrowed from Dr Gooch and had had inscribed for her on the stone side of the tomb:

Alas! From how slender a thread hangs
All that is sweetest in life.[18]

## 24. *The Other Side of the Grave (1837– )*

The first Academy exhibition in the new buildings on what was becoming Trafalgar Square was also the first in thirty-four years not to have John Constable on hand. His son John was now head of the family, but Charles Leslie had his work cut out as friend, adviser and protector to the Constable children. For a start, Leslie ensured that Constable was represented at the Academy exhibition. An RA rule allowed an artist's hitherto unexhibited work to be hung at the first exhibition after his death, and so *Arundel Mill and Castle* was entered by Leslie on Constable's behalf. So were two smaller pictures, but the selectors seem to have thought these weren't sufficiently finished. At the exhibition, *Arundel Mill* was received in the light of its creator's passing, for the most part kindly. *John Bull* declared that the painting showed how great a loss the public had suffered. In recent years, its writer said, Constable had spoiled some of his beautiful works by whitewashing them. Yet now he stood high as a draughtsman, colourist and artist 'of feeling, science, and power'. The paper presciently concluded: 'His early works are truth and nature themselves; and, unless we much mistake, *all* his works, now that he is gone, will be held in very great estimation.' (Constable would have noted ruefully that he was indeed on the way to being a popular artist, even if *going*, i.e. dying, had to be part of the process.) The Reverend John Eagles, reviewer for *Blackwood's*, moderated his usual offensiveness by saying the painting was unfinished and it was therefore unfair to exhibit it. But Eagles was sorry at the loss of Constable and said 'some of his earlier pictures were both sweetly and vigorously painted'. *Arundel Mill and Castle* was among the works put up for sale by the artist's administrators on 16 May 1838 and was bought in on behalf of John Charles Constable.[1]

Leslie cautioned the young man to lock up all the sketches that had been left lying loose on the floor of his father's painting room. Leslie also set about organising a committee to buy one of Constable's larger pictures as a permanent memorial and donate it to the National Gallery. Clarkson Stanfield was among several warm supporters of the plan. Reverend Judkin, William Carpenter and William Purton joined in. The 'large Salisbury' – *Salisbury Cathedral from the Meadows* – was considered; Leslie asked John Charles to leave the key to the Charlotte Street studio with Mrs Roberts so that would-be donors to the gift fund could look at it and other Constable paintings there. Eventually the large Salisbury was judged to be too boldly executed and not suitable for 'the general taste'. *The Cornfield*, Purton's recommendation, was chosen instead. The estate valued it at three hundred guineas. Sir William Beechey was appointed chairman of the money-raising committee and over a hundred people subscribed. David Wilkie sent five guineas; William Wordsworth and Michael Faraday gave too. On 9 December 1837 the Trustees of the National Gallery gratefully accepted the painting to which the artist had once given 'a little more eye-salve than usual'. One old friend of the artist who visited Charlotte Street, the miniature painter Andrew Robertson, felt melancholy at the great number of works Constable had left; this showed how little his merits had been recognised. But he thought the presence of *The Cornfield* in the National Gallery would prevent Constable's works being buried until, eventually dug up, they were 'brought to live in another age'.[2]

At his death Constable was worth about £25,000. He had £528 in his bank account with Cocks Biddulph at Charing Cross. The Bank of England held in his name £12,000 in annuities that Charles Bicknell's legacy had purchased for the benefit of Maria and the children. Abram owed him £4,000 on which 4 per cent interest was due. Others, including Dr Herbert Evans and Lancelot Archer-Burton, owed him more than £1,000. The contents of his houses – both leased – were worth over £500 and his 'Books Pictures Prints Drawings and other Articles relating to the Fine Arts', £1,900. Yet the administrators of his estate felt more should be raised to cover the future needs of his children, and so some works would be auctioned.[3]

The sale occurred during thirteen days in May 1838. Beforehand Leslie and Mr Foster of the auctioneers came to Charlotte Street to list items for the catalogue. Leslie varnished some of the paintings, starting with *The Chain Pier, Brighton*. John Charles had transferred from Corpus Christi to Jesus College, Cambridge, to be with Osmond Fisher, and during his Christmas and Easter vacations he began to 'set the pictures to rights', listing all the oil sketches, drawings and prints he found at Well Walk and Charlotte Street, while trying to pursue his algebra studies, a task that laid him low. Meanwhile, Foster's advertisements for the sale were appearing in the press and visitors began to call at Charlotte Street to look at the pictures, among them William Carpenter, the Hampstead amateurs Henry Hebbert and W.G. Jennings, General Rebow and several friends of Leslie's.[4]

At the time the sale didn't seem a great success. Prices obtained were generally low. The art trade was obviously uncertain about bidding for works – thrown suddenly on the market – of a landscape artist whose reputation wasn't clear cut. However, on the first day of the sale, 10 May 1838, many of the 5,000 prints and drawings were sold. They included prints of works by Titian and Claude, and original drawings by Richard Wilson, Gainsborough and George Frost. The prints and drawings fetched a total of £648 12s 6d. Most of the buyers were in the trade, but John Sell Cotman was one bidder who entered the fray with the dealers. Twenty-nine of the cloud and sky studies sold for £3 11s. As for the Constable/Lucas venture *English Landscape*, the copyright, plates and more than 7,000 unsold prints were offered but bought in for £100. Perhaps just as well, for the prints proved useful in a few years' time to Charles Leslie. Lucas himself was ill-served by Constable's death. The loss of his patron took place as photography advanced. With a declining practice, the talented printmaker eventually took to drink and spent some time in the Fulham workhouse before his death in 1881.[5]

The paintings put up for sale on 15 and 16 May included copies
Constable had made of some of his favourite old masters and his own
original works. Nearly 150 of these paintings were sold and twenty-
five bought in; the proceeds £1,764. Some of his full-size oil sketches
were now seen in public for the first time, among them two sketches
for *The Hay Wain* and *The Leaping Horse*, bought in for £14 10s to be
given by Purton and Carpenter to the Constable children. The large
oil sketches weren't valued highly: the *Hadleigh Castle* exhibited in
1829 sold for £105 and the full-size sketch for it for £3 13s 6d. Many
of Constable's works raised doubts; no one knew enough about him or
about all these pictures suddenly released on the art world. What was
typical? What was a sound investment? *The White Horse* went to the
children's legal guardian, Lancelot Archer-Burton, for the highest
price of the sale, £157 10s. (Archer-Burton, who had changed his
name from Lancelot South on inheriting property, was married to
Constable's cousin Jane Gubbins; their son Burton, Folkestone
schoolmate of Constable's two oldest sons, followed John Charles up
to Cambridge.) John Charles attended the sale and bought three
paintings, one a *View of London from Hampstead Heath*. The number
of dealers on hand indicated that some in the trade suspected a rise in
Constable futures. Samuel Archbutt bought fourteen paintings. J.H.
Smith, acting for John Sheepshanks, tussled with a collector named
Anderton for *Water Meadows at Salisbury*, the 'nasty green thing' the
RA selectors had wanted to reject in 1830; Smith obtained it for
Sheepshanks for £35. 14s. Despite the many pictures returned to the
family, and despite the less than dramatic prices, the Foster sale got
many Constables out into the world and gave the name resonance.[6]

The houses in Well Walk and Charlotte Street were emptied of much
material that had sustained them. The children weren't badly off: to
the Bicknell legacy and their father's funds was added a bequest from
Constable's older brother Golding, warden of Lady Dysart's woods,
who died in March 1838 aged sixty-four. The children moved to 16
Cunningham Place, St John's Wood, where they were closer to
Archer-Burton (in Grove End Road) and Charles Leslie (in Pine

Apple Place). There Mrs Roberts went on putting her heart and soul into their care. Charley referred to 'Old Lady Ribbons' in a letter in 1846, and in 1853 he asked Minna to give 'Old Bob' two sovereigns from him as 'a little remembrance'. She was mentioned in family correspondence as late as 1862. Uncle Abram came to Cunningham Place to see his nephews and nieces in February 1839 and found it, though smaller than Charlotte Street, 'comfortable' and 'convenient'. (Hints of discord appeared between the heirs and Uncle Abram.) Charley had learned about his father's death on arriving in Bombay after a gale-ridden voyage. He wrote to his brother John, 'How hard it seems that the Almighty should have snatched so kind and good a Father from us.' Charley wanted to know that some of the drawings and sketchbooks were safe, and mentioned them anxiously again in his next letter: 'I mean the Book of Sketches in the Coutes Indiaman and the two Brighton sketch books.' The drawings dealt with the sea, which was now Charley's world. At the end of August 1838 he came back to England and quit the *Buckinghamshire*. However, he went on learning navigation, studied steam engineering, and talked of becoming the mate of a brig and serving in the Mediterranean. But as with many a Conradian hero, the East had seduced him. He was commissioned a midshipman in the Indian Navy in April 1839. In India he met a naval lieutenant who recalled riding in a Hampstead coach with John Constable some years before. The artist had in his lap a toy cutter, a gift for his son, who he said was passionate about ships. The lieutenant begged him not to let Charles go to sea. He would be away from his family for long periods; promotion was so slow. And Charley ran into both problems. He made lieutenant in 1845 and commander eighteen years after that. He conducted surveys of Eastern waters – the chart he drew of the Persian Gulf was still used in 1936.[7] He married in 1861, the only Constable child to do so, his wife a Maida Vale girl, who died in childbirth. Charley's second wife was the daughter of next-door neighbours in Cunningham Place. Five of his children, Constable's only grandchildren, survived childhood. Charley retired in 1863 with the honorary rank of captain and came back to England for good.[8]

*

John and Maria Constable's family was generally neither robust nor lucky. Minna had survived her bout of scarlet fever, but two of her siblings didn't. Emily – who shared the same birthday as Charley – caught the disease in May 1839, aged fourteen. Dr Evans came frequently, as he had done for Minna, and Mrs Roberts looked after her day and night (she too caught scarlet fever but was tough enough to live). Emily – Emma – Ema – died on 8 May. Scarlet fever used to kill more children in Britain than any other disease; it brought on a very high temperature, strawberry-red tongue and face, painful throat infection and rashes. Emily's brother John once again stuck his head in the sand. He wrote from Cambridge, 'There is nothing that I dislike so much as to be present on such occasions, besides while I am away it seems more dream like.'[9] John was now interested in the chemistry of photography, but was also caught up by religion – he hoped to obtain a curacy after taking his degree. He was engaged to Mary Atkinson, daughter of the Surrey couple who had looked after him when he broke down after his father's death. His rooms at Cambridge were full of Constable's paintings and sketches. He told Mary about a dream one of his university friends had had about him. A service was being held in the college chapel and the congregation were looking at a lancet window in which young John was seated, wearing episcopal robes, with a mitre on his head. But there was neither curacy nor bishopric to come. His forebodings kept him from funerals, but for other people John didn't duck reality; his medical studies involved working in Cambridge hospital wards, and while getting such hands-on experience he too contracted scarlet fever. John Charles died on 21 March 1841. He was buried in Jesus College chapel, the last person to be buried there. Osmond Fisher arranged for a tablet in John's memory over the grave.[10]

Loss piled on loss, therefore. Charley as the oldest surviving son was now head of the family. But Minna, two years older, was on the spot and effectively in charge of affairs, with legal help from J.D. Haverfield, a friend of her father's. Borrowings of drawings and prints made her anxious; she missed having someone close by to comfort her.

'I begin to feel the loss of a mother now more than ever,' she said. And the children seemed to have inherited from their father some of his prickliness. Charles in the late 1860s denounced as fakes a number of Constable pictures that were in fact genuine. He also bore a long grudge against Minna and Isabel for the way they shared out Constable's works among the surviving children in five supposedly equal parts at the end of 1847. He said they had divided among themselves all the shipping pictures he believed belonged to him. Later, when he was twenty-six, Minna twenty-eight, and Isabel twenty-five, he recorded his problems with his sisters and noted 'all love has been quenched in their lonely hearts'. They thought he had taken advantage of them. The sniping and griping was passed down. Charley's second son Hugh Golding Constable relayed the memories of his side of the family of how small-minded his aunts had been: 'They had been belles & asked everywhere & spoilt and besides that they lived in London.' At least it was clear as they squabbled over the pictures that they knew they had inherited a treasure.[11]

The habit of art was attached to them all. John Charles and Charles Golding both drew ships. Isabel attended the School of Design at Somerset House where 'classes for Females' were held and she went on to paint skilful plant and flower studies. Alfred and Lionel had a reputation of being hard to handle when together – 'unsettled wild boys', Minna called them in a letter to Charley in India – but both studied painting and showed strongly their father's influence as landscape artists. Alfred, on leaving school aged sixteen, went to stay with Uncle Abram and Aunt Mary in Flatford where he fished and boated and sketched the meadows below Fen Bridge. He had thought of going to sea like Charley but after a period of drawing from the Antique at the British Museum enrolled at what had been the Sass Academy, now moved to Bloomsbury Street and run by F.S. Cary, a former Sass pupil. Lionel, after dallying with farming, also went to Cary's Academy and drew the plaster casts. When Alfred exhibited at the Royal Academy in 1847, Charley wrote to Minna to say, 'It is a great comfort though to see Alfa actually exhibiting, this looks as if he was all right, but I remain very anxious about Toby.' Toby – that is

Lionel – was in fact the most talented; he had four paintings at the RA in 1850; his works sometimes showed original flair but were also on occasion taken for his father's. He and Alfred sent samples to each other and also to Charley who wrote, 'I should like wild bits or coast bits, racey of course . . . let them have "breadth".' By 'racey' Charley seems to have meant something not tame, something with punch. Raciness was a term Constable had used in writing to John Fisher.[12]

But the promising careers of both young Constables were abbreviated. Robert Leslie later described how Alfred and Lionel were rowing across the Thames above the weir at Goring Mill when their home-made boat upset. 'It was in November, 1853, on a dark, frosty evening, and, though able to swim, he [Alfred] sank before reaching the river bank, overcome probably by cold and shock. His brother Lionel narrowly escaped being carried over the weir, and, on looking round after reaching shore, was horrified to find that Alfred . . . had disappeared.' The family believed that Lionel suffered a stroke following his brother's drowning. He gave up painting and occupied his time with carpentry, photography, sailing, and making fireworks. By 1885, towards the end of his life, he was living in St John's Wood again with Minna and Isabel.[13]

After John Constable's death, it wasn't long before his life was given literary shape. John Fisher in 1826 had already seen his friend as a *subject* and said that he had always wanted to write about Constable's life as an artist,[14] but he never managed to do so. His own life slipped away before Constable's. Charles Boner, who went off to become a tutor to a princely family in Germany, and who composed well-regarded poetry and travel books, also missed his chance, though he had preserved a store – almost a shrine – of Constable memories. '*I* ought to have done it,' he said years later (in 1865). 'No one could write such a life of Constable as I might have done. To know all the beauty and sweetness of that man's mind one must have been with him *always*, as I was.'[15]

The person who got in first, forestalled Boner, and seemed for many years to have written the only necessary Life was Charles Leslie.

He started pulling together material not long after Constable died. He obtained recollections from the children. In 1840 he went to Flatford, accompanied by William Purton, visited the mill and saw the old family house up in the village; what Leslie described as a handsome mansion was then unoccupied and was soon to be pulled down. Leslie talked to Abram, who had once claimed his brother John would be famous, after death if not before. He visited Constable's sisters and had for guides to the locality young John and his cousin the Reverend Daniel Whalley.[16] Leslie did a first-rate job of assembling anecdotes and letters and converting them into the *Memoirs of the Life of John Constable, Esq., R.A.* The first edition of around two hundred copies, brought out in 1843 with James Carpenter as the nominal publisher, was illustrated from the overstock of *English Landscape* prints, supplied by Minna in return for thirty free copies of the *Life*. (In 1843 Minna still had 186 sets of *English Landscape*, several thousand prints in all.)[17] Although her brother Charles was annoyed that Leslie had related some of his adolescent adventures on the *Buckinghamshire*, he approved of the general thrust: 'The good, quiet, character of poor Papa is kept up throughout.' One hundred and five copies of the book went to subscribers. Leslie might have noted once more that Constable's friends 'compensated for their fewness by their sincerity and their warmth' – and their willingness to shell out for the book. A second 'popular' edition was called for, smaller in format, and illustrated only by two portraits of Constable and one mezzotint, that of *Spring: East Bergholt Common*. Longmans published it in 1845. Although it was slow to sell, other editions eventually followed.[18]

Leslie was praised for the skill with which he let Constable tell the story in his own words, although in fact he often modified or polished Constable's language. He omitted names where he feared people might be embarrassed. He wanted to show Constable as a genius, but not one who was too earthy or rough-hewn. Maria's protests against her husband's overlong stays with the Beaumonts weren't mentioned. This rose-tinting was later to be held against the biographer. Leslie's 'kindlier nature' had clothed his portrait of Constable, Richard Redgrave thought in his *Century of Painters* of 1866. Elsewhere

Redgrave suggested that Leslie's *Constable* was agreeable but insufficient: 'He appears all amiability and goodness, and one cannot recognise the bland, yet intense, sarcasm of his nature: soft and amiable in speech, he yet uttered sarcasms which cut you to the bone.'[19] Even Leslie seems to have recognised that the portrait needed darker shading. In his *Autobiographical Reflections* of 1860, he drew attention to Constable's love of approbation and insistence on getting his own way. Unlike Turner, who wasn't so articulate and never talked of his own art if he could help it, Constable couldn't be prevented from talking of his feelings and views on art. Leslie noted, 'This made him extremely interesting to those who could feel with him, but either tiresome or repulsive to those who could not.'[20]

By mid-century Constable was the subject of increasing interest, and in the pros and cons of what was said about him we discern a radical rather than conservative artist. The art critic P.G. Hamerton confessed to failing to recognise what Constable was up to early on, but waking up to it in the mid-1860s. Constable, he wrote, 'did not see lines but spaces, and in the spaces he did not see simple gradations, but an immense variety of differently coloured sparkles and spots. This variety really exists in nature, and Constable first directed attention to it.' Hamerton pointed out that the French had not only taken up Constable earlier but continued to admire him. Paul Huet, Théodore Rousseau, Eugène Delacroix and many others claimed him as a messiah. For Delacroix, in 1858, Constable was 'the father' of modern French landscape painting, a 'real reformer', and, with Turner, one of the glories of English art; had the French but known it, the sparkles and spots of impressionism were shortly to appear. Théophile Thoré, the French writer who first cast a spotlight on the identity and works of Johannes Vermeer, wished *The Cornfield* were in Paris rather than London; in the Louvre, he thought, Constable's painting would have been more greatly appreciated.[21]

One vocal and discordant voice was also heard. John Ruskin did not like Constable. It seemed to be almost personal, though they never met. It was as if Ruskin found in Constable's work a direct affront to his hero Turner. For Ruskin wild mountain scenery was the thing;

Constable was morbidly enamoured of a well-tended landscape and other subjects of a 'low order'. Constable's 'early education and associations were . . . against him'. He couldn't draw. 'His works are also eminently wanting both in rest and refinement.'[22] He was unteachable – by which Ruskin seemed to mean unaffected by the great authorities of the past; for instance, he wouldn't let himself be instructed by the Scriptures. Moreover, his devotion to chiaroscuro and its shadows contributed to his damnation. His works were 'mere studies of effect without any expression of specific knowledge'. And his effects, Ruskin complained (following Fuseli), were 'greatcoat weather and nothing more'. Turner looked at a landscape and godlike saw 'at a glance the whole sum of visible truth open to human intelligence'. Constable saw in the same scene merely what might be observed by an intelligent fawn and a skylark. Ruskin allowed that Constable might be original, honest, and free from affectation, but he was ultimately 'nothing more than an industrious and innocent amateur blundering his way to a superficial expression of one or two popular aspects of common nature'. Ruskin was interested in skies, and in the neglect of them by contemporary painters; but he completely ignored Constable's contribution to the subject.[23]

Leslie defended his old friend while he was Professor of Painting at the RA from 1847 to 1852. In his *Handbook for Young Painters* of 1855, based on his Academy lectures, Leslie declared that Constable filled a place among British painters that Turner, however great, couldn't fill. Constable was 'the most genuine painter of English cultivated scenery, leaving untouched its mountains and lakes'. Far from being unteachable, Constable from start to finish learned from previous masters; he made copies of Raphael cartoons, of etchings after and paintings by Ruysdael, and of paintings by Wilson, Rubens, Teniers and Claude. As for Ruskin's charge that Constable was unable to draw, Leslie suggested that Ruskin had never seen a genuine painting by Constable – his impressions were perhaps founded on some of the forgeries that were now circulating or – a real dig – he had seen Constable pictures 'without looking at them, which often happens when we are not interested'. Unlike Ruskin's hero, 'Constable never fell into the common mistake by which even Turner appears to have been influenced, namely, that what are called warm colours are essential to convey the idea of warmth in a landscape. The truth is, that red, orange, and yellow, are only seen in the sky at the coolest hours of the day, and brown and yellow tints, in the foliage of England, prevail only in the spring and autumn. But he [Constable] fearlessly painted midsummer noon-day heat, with blues, greens, and grays forming the predominant masses. And he succeeded.'[24]

Despite Ruskin, Constable's stock was rising. John Charles and Minna had suspected that some visitors – aware of the increased value of his pictures – were 'borrowing' his works with no intention of returning them; James Brook Pulham, the son of a Constable patron, was a possible culprit. Moreover, fakes now began to appear. Charles Leslie wrote in 1843 to warn Francis Darby (who had bought two Hampstead paintings Constable had exhibited at the RA): 'Constable's pictures have so risen in value, that they are now eagerly sought for, and the consequence is there are many forgeries on the market, particularly of his small works, and it is dangerous for any one to buy a picture, professing to be his, unless they are sufficiently acquainted with his style.' Leslie thought that George Constable, brewer and amateur painter, was the author of some clumsy and 'wretched imitations' – and had no explanation of why the recent good friend would do this. A number of what Leslie's son Robert called 'extreme palette knife' forgeries came to light in the 1840s, the paint still soft on them. Meanwhile, collectors of the real thing began to add to the inflationary impulse. Colonel James Lenox, the American who had in 1845 bought, via Leslie, Turner's *Staffa, Fingal's Cave*, three years later bought (with Leslie's advice again) a small version of *The Valley Farm*. Lenox's transatlantic lead was followed by John G. Johnson, J.P. Morgan, H.E. Huntington, Henry Clay Frick, and Andrew and Paul Mellon. *Salisbury Cathedral from the Meadows* went for £600 in 1850. *The White Horse* fetched £630 in 1855. *The Hay Wain* was auctioned by Christie's in 1866 and sold for £1,365 – a Benjamin West sort of price.[26]

It wasn't just millionaires; a wider public was discovering

Constable through works exhibited in museums, particularly the National Gallery and the South Kensington Museum, later the Victoria and Albert, the 'V&A'. The Ashmolean in Oxford acquired a Constable in 1855, and the Royal Academy began to show his work outside the exhibition season. At the same time writers – among them Tom Taylor, P.G. Hamerton and the Redgrave brothers – expressed in print the new awareness. Ruskin may have provoked some, and others were encouraged by Constable's reputation in France. There, his gold-medal status still reverberated. The Barbizon painters couldn't have managed without him. As for the Impressionists, to take one example Monet's Hyde Park scenes were in his debt.[27]

Isabel was the last of Constable's children to die – unmarried and childless – in 1888, at the age of sixty-six, the same not very great age Minna had been when she died. Isabel had inherited the bulk of Minna's and Lionel's estates and was left with a large number of their father's oils, watercolours, and drawings. She, Minna, and Lionel apparently agreed that the nation should be their heirs in this respect, and she gave the National Gallery six Constables and one of his palettes in 1887 and 88. (Henry Vaughan had also given it *The Hay Wain* in 1886.) The South Kensington Museum received what Isabel called 'Landscape Sketches' – ninety-two oils, 295 drawings and watercolours, and three sketchbooks. The British Museum got forty-seven drawings and watercolours and the Royal Academy fifteen oil studies. In her will Isabel bequeathed a further five paintings to the National Gallery: *Scene on a Navigable River (Flatford Mill)*, *The Cenotaph*, *The Glebe Farm*, *Hampstead Heath with a Rainbow*, and *Harwich Lighthouse*. She left to the South Kensington Museum the oils *Trees at Hampstead*, *Cottage in a Cornfield* (which Constable had exhibited at the RA in 1833) and *A Watermill at Gillingham, Dorset*, together with the splendid watercolours of *Old Sarum* and *Stonehenge*. Visitors to London now had nearly 130 Constable oil paintings and some 350 drawings to look at, a far more generous collection of his work than had ever been seen. Two particular favourites for copyists were *The Cornfield* and *Hampstead Heath with Harrow in the Distance*

– in 1891 the latter was the most copied 'modern' painting of the year. And Constable prices were still soaring. *The White Horse* went in 1894 for £6,510 to Agnews, who sold it to the banker J.P. Morgan. In 1895 Agnews bought *Stratford Mill* for £8,925 and Sir Samuel Montagu, another banker, acquired it from them.[28]

Constable was bankable; indeed, in the public press he was finally – in the words of the London *Standard* – 'a great man'. Scholarly writers, led by Charles Holmes, began to consider his works. The critic Julius Meier-Graefe, in his 1908 book *Modern Art*, struck what was to become a common chord when he named what he – like Delacroix – saw as the twin peaks of British Art: 'Turner draped the inartisitic in the most enchanting robes, and Constable presented the artistic in the simplest guise.' Meier-Graefe was reminded by Constable of some contemporary artists, including 'the best of these, Manet'. The French connection was still being made in 1937 when some sketches of Brighton beach by Constable led Kenneth Clark to think of Matisse.[29]

Although by the early twentieth century Constable was everywhere – on fire screens and tea cosies, jigsaws and biscuit tins, mass-produced prints and posters – his fame required closer definition. There was on the one hand the Constable of Constable Country, of *The Hay Wain* and *The White Horse*, the artist whose Flatford had become a national shrine; but there was also the Constable of the clouds, the views from Hampstead and the deeper recesses of Fen Lane, a much more private, low-key painter. And by then taste was coming round to judging Constable's sketches and studies as superior to the paintings he finished for exhibition. Meier-Graefe, Holmes, Clive Bell, and Roger Fry all agreed on this. Fry wished Constable had spent less time elaborating the great machines which he intended to make an effect at the Academy. Fry found the 'real Constable' in the full-size studies for the exhibition pictures. Meier-Graefe was content with Constable as an artist who had never fully established himself: 'a quiet spirit' who 'never knew the glory of the conqueror'. This Constable 'lacked the kindling quality of astounding per-sonalities. His art . . . had that simplicity of perfection, which repels the public and the public's painters . . . His gift attains the abstract purity of the scientific fact, and its benefits are so universal that the giver is scarcely remembered.'[30]

The simplicity was also sincerity. The contemporary British painter Lucian Freud, German-born and Dedham art-school trained, selected Constable's works for a large Paris exhibition in 2002–3; he said that 'in Constable there is no false feeling. For me, Constable is so much more moving than Turner because you feel for him, it's truth-telling about the land rather than using the land for com-positions which suited his inventiveness.' The 'natural painter' wasn't into bravura. But truth-telling can be painful. Freud noted that it was impossible to think of van Gogh without recalling Constable's dark-shadowed late paintings.[31] And Constable's celebrity creates its own feeling of déjà vu. Barges, farm wagons, slimy posts, lock gates, cornfields . . . all lead to critical close-down. Social historians con-demn him for looking at landscape through a landowner's eyes. Anita Brookner complains that none of the workers in his landscapes saunters easily through them: 'all his characters have the appearance of serfs'.[32]

His territory also carries its burden. 'Constable Country' has become a real-estate term, albeit one in which the National Trust as well as developers and estate agents have a stake; the Trust owns a good deal of the land around Flatford. The ancient core of East Bergholt is now surrounded by executive housing for commuters to Ipswich and Colchester. But the centre of the village remains the curiously disjointed coming together of roads it was in Constable's childhood, with church and pub prominent, and the main street curving in a way that makes visitors question their heading. St Mary's church sits at a right-angle bend of the road, with the Dunthorne tomb standing near the graveyard wall and the sundial, still fixed over the church door, that John Dunthorne Senior kept painted. The old Constable family house has gone, but Constable's little gambrel-roofed studio, Moss Cottage, stands nicely preserved next to a car-repair garage and across from the Red Lion. East Bergholt took its somewhat inchoate form from its large tract of common land and the

lanes that radiated off around it to the 'ends' – the scattered
dependent hamlets at Flatford, East End and Burnt Oak. The lane
down to Flatford now decants tourist traffic into a fairly secluded
National Trust car park. From here those looking for the scenes that
made John Constable a painter can walk to the mill and the miller's
house, now a nature study centre, to Willy Lott's house, and to the
lock and a footbridge over the Stour with a riverside footpath through
the meadows. From the slopes above the river the tower of Dedham
church can still be seen, though when the leaves are off the trees you
can also glimpse on the four-lane A12 the tops of the trucks whose
sound just carries. However, autumn and winter are not Constable's
seasons.[33] Spring and summer are, with the trees in leaf, the wheat
ripening, any storms passing away, the white clouds scudding, and
England as it never will be again.

# *Notes*

In order to suppress what might become a tsunami of notes, I have not cited every reference to letters appearing in four volumes of the *Correspondence*: Volume I, *The Family at East Bergholt 1807–1837*; Volume II, *Early Friends and Maria Bicknell*; Volume III, *The Correspondence with C.R. Leslie, R.A.*; and Volume VI, *The Fishers*. From the context it will generally be clear in which of these volumes a reader in search of further sources ought to look. His parents, brothers and sisters are present in Volume I. John Dunthorne Senior and Maria Bicknell figure greatly in Volume II. (The editorial material by Ronald Beckett introducing and surrounding the letters also contains many useful biographical details and these are also not 'afternoted'.) However, if I have suspected that for some unusual reason there is a need to specify a reference to one of these volumes, I have cited the volume as CI, CII, CIII or CVI, and the page number. Further information about specific pictures can be got from the Reynolds volumes, *Early* and *Later*, or the catalogues to the Tate exhibitions of 1976 and 1991. My last chapter is particularly indebted to *The Discovery of Constable* by Ian Fleming-Williams and Leslie Parris.

**Preface**
1   CIV p325; Leslie p210.
2   C:FDC p103 n1.
3   Mosley p399.

## 1. Day-Spring

1  Victoria History of the County of Essex; letter to the author from Angela Green.
2  Leslie p22.
3  Reynolds in Salander–O'Reilly 1988 p5; Leslie p23.
4  Owen & Brown p69.
5  *Discourses* p94.
6  Leslie pp24–5; Reynolds *Early* p1.
7  Albus p148; Shirley 1949 p43.
8  Farrer, *The Dunthorne Mss.*
9  C:FDC p54; CVI p78.
10  Freda Constable p14.
11  Freda Constable p21; Leslie p25.
12  Whitley 1930 p169; Owen & Brown p219.
13  C:FDC pp196, 199–200; Reynolds *Early*, p7.
14  C:FDC p31; Freda Constable p22.
15  Reynolds *Early* p21; Farington IV p1164.

## 2. A Hero in Distress

1  C:FDC pp201–2.
2  Gilbert pp126–7.
3  Reynolds *Early* p27; Gadney p20; Farington IV p1380.
4  G. Leslie pp6–9.
5  K. Clark 1976 p49.
6  Farington IV p1365.
7  Owen & Brown p151.
8  C:FDC p55.
9  Leslie pp32–3.
10  C:FDC p55; G. Leslie p7.
11  Farington IV p1544.
12  Farington IV p1516.
13  Farington IV pp1515, 1568, 1576.
14  Reynolds *Early* p37.
15  CVI pp6–7.
16  Farington V p1764.
17  Farington V p1764.

## 3. Nature's Proper Interest

1  Farington VI pp2082–3.
2  Farington VI pp2202, 2238.
3  Farington VI p2340.
4  Owen & Brown p152.
5  Leslie p37.
6  Reynolds *Early* p60.
7  Farington VII p2712.
8  CV pp2–3.
9  Leslie p37.
10  CV p6.
11  Keats pp131, 162.
12  Johnson p97.
13  Farington VIII pp3162–5.
14  Keats p83.
15  Tate 1991 pp21, 398.
16  Tate 1991 p21 fig 4.
17  Whitley 1928 p122.
18  Farington VIII pp3001, 3080–1.
19  C:FDC pp134–7.
20  Leslie p38.
21  CIV pp12–14, 19–23.
22  6 February 1808 document in R. Constable collection.
23  Reynolds *Early* p58.
24  A. Lyles *Burlington* March 1999 p181; Payne pp32 & 63.
25  Farington X p3620.
26  Ivy pp64–5.
27  CIV pp236–7; C:FDC pp202, 222.
28  C:FDC p314.
29  Farington IX p3280.
30  CIV pp31, 236–7.
31  Reynolds *Early* p121.

## 4. A Cure for Love

1  *Discourses* pp93–4.
2  Elam p47.
3  Farington XI pp3916, 3921.

4   Farington XI p3944.
5   Gombrich p316.
6   Parris & Shields *Constable: the Art of Nature* 1971 p7.
7   CIV p16.
8   CIV p27.
9   CIV pp28–9.
10  CIV p31.
11  C:FDC p314.
12  Farington XI pp4025–6.
13  Tate 1991 p23.
14  Farington XII p4250.

## 5. Avoiding Notice
1   Tate 1991 pp131-2.
2   Farington XII p4291.
3   Tate 1991 p132.
4   C:FDC p33.
5   Farington XIII p4495.
6   Tate 1991 p25.
7   Tate 1991 pp153–5.
8   CIV p218.
9   Whitley 1928 pp244–5; Ivy p70.
10  Farington XIII p4364.
11  Freda Constable p65.
12  Rosenthal 1983 p83.

## 6. Ready to Marry – Perhaps
1   Tate 1991 p25.
2   Colley p158.
3   CIV p45; Tate 1991 p315.
4   Whitley 1928 p258.
5   CIV p46.
6   Farington XIV pp4864–6.
7   Leslie p85.
8   Gombrich pp48, 299, 387–8; J. Clarkson, et al pp13–20.
9   City of Westminster archives; CVI p7 n1.
10  Farington XIV p4844.

11  Farington XIV pp4921–2.
12  Whitley 1928 p256.
13  Tate 1991 p26.
14  Tate 1991 p430.

## 7. Housekeeping
1   Farington XIV p5035.
2   Freda Constable p72.
3   Leslie p91.
4   Leslie pp90–1.
5   Whitley 1928 p269.
6   Flora Thompson *Lark Rise* p257.
7   Tate 1991 pp26, 179, 184–5; Leslie p32.
8   Farington XV pp5174–5.
9   Ivy pp74–8.
10  Farington XV pp5284-5.
11  C:FDC p322.
12  Tate 1991 p27.
13  Farington XV p5345.
14  K. Clark 1976 p150.
15  Reynolds *Later* p28; Whitley 1928 pp300–1; Leslie pp92, 94–5.
16  *John Constable and the Fishers* pp37, 43; Tate 1991 p27.
17  Cook p2.
18  Tate 1976 p108; Farington XV p5400.
19  F. Redgrave p56.
20  Collins I pp56, 168–170.
21  Leslie p8.
22  Leslie p9.
23  K. Clark 1960 p117.
24  Ivy p23.
25  See *Sense and Sensibility* pp83–5: 'Everybody pretends to feel . . .'
26  Whitley 1930 p35.

## 8. All but the Clouds
1   Gadney p34.
2   Farington XVI p5487.
3   Ivy p84.

4   Farington XVI pp5532-3.
5   *Discourses* p6.
6   Cobbett 31 August 1826 pp61, 84.
7   CIV p310.
8   Farington XVI pp5582–3.
9   C:FDC p52.
10  Farington XVI p5645.
11  Ivy pp88–91.
12  Whitley 1930 p9; Ivy p93.
13  C:FDC p87.

## 9. Skying
1   Gilpin p34.
2   C. Leslie 1860 I p183.
3   K. Clark 1976 p59.
4   Leslie p112.
5   Badt p49; *Constable's Clouds*, pp42, 136, 154; Hamblyn, p228; *Constable's Skies*, p47.
6   Badt pp47–8; *Constable's Clouds*, p167.
7   *Constable's Clouds* pp76, 81, 87, 140, 154; Hamblyn p223.

## 10. At the Summit of Earthly Ambitions
1   CIV pp246–7.
2   CIV p218; *London Encyclopedia*; *Survey of London* XXI; Frith 1957 pp31–3.
3   Whitley 1930 p29; Ivy pp92–5.
4   St John 2005 p7.
5   Whitley 1930 p40.
6   CIV pp288–90.
7   Ivy pp99–100.
8   CVI p116.
9   Owen & Brown p107.
10  Owen & Brown p2.
11  Leslie p132.
12  Owen & Brown pp218, 220.
13  Leslie pp135–6.
14  Leslie p185; Trimmer in Thornbury; see also CV pp66–72 which

quotes a memorandum about Constable that Trimmer gave Thornbury, mentioning Maria's death by consumption.

15  Cockayne & Stow pp112-13; Dickens *Nicholas Nickleby* ch 6; D. & R. Porter pp198–9, R. & J. Dubos ppviii, 38–39, 69–101; Dormandy pp2, 14–16, 39, 58.

16  Dormandy ppxiv, 14–16.

## 11. Trying the Sea

1  Tate 1991 pp206-11, 369.
2  Tate 1991 pp284–92.
3  Whitley 1930 pp61–2; Ivy p107.
4  Gadney p66.
5  C:FDC p75.
6  *Discovery* pp195–200; Reynolds NY 1983 p104.
7  Leslie p145.
8  CIV pp182-3.
9  Ivy p111.
10  Tate 1991 p267; Warrell in *Brighton Revealed*; Cobbett I p206.
11  Leslie p144.
12  See CII, beginning 19 May 1824.
13  Tate 1991 p274.
14  Tate 1991 pp270–1, 274; Warrell in *Brighton Revealed* pp19–29.
15  CIV pp183–4, 197–8; C:FDC p330.
16  Whitley 1930 p76; Ivy pp103–11.

## 12. The Leaping Horse

1  Tate 1976 p142; Tate 1991 pp296, 464–5.
2  Rosenthal 1983 p166.
3  CV p148.
4  Whitley 1930 pp86, 97; Ivy pp111–16.
5  CIV p98.
6  Warrell in *Brighton Revealed* pp30–1.
7  Sheppard p57.
8  C:FDC pp77–8.
9  Sarah Cove, Constable Trust lecture 28 April 2005.
10  Leslie p170.
11  CIV p404.

12    Whitley 1930 p102.
13    Tate 1991 pp301–2; C:FDC p59.
14    Whitley 1930 pp101–2; Ivy p119.
15    Payne p6; Rosenthal pp110–12; Trevelyan pp220–1, 465.

### 13. Life Slips
1    CV p128.
2    Cook p8.
3    Cook p10; Colville pp59, 62.
4    Owen & Brown pp2, 87; C. Leslie 1855 p50.
5    Tate 1976 pp148–9; Tate 1991 p31; Ivy pp122–4.
6    Angelo pp203–4; Hazlitt p690; Leslie p175.
7    C:FDC p80.
8    CIV pp71–3.
9    Leslie p182.
10   Ivy pp125–6.
11   Tate 1991 p32.
12   Reynolds *Later* pp189–90.

### 14. Darkness Visible
1    Fleming-Williams pp212–19.
2    Reynolds *Later* p193.
3    Leslie p185.
4    CV p71; Leslie pp184–5.
5    Smith p44.
6    CIV p101; Leslie p185.
7    Leslie p185; Dormandy p221; CI p250; CVI p238.
8    Rhyne notes that CCI p450 and CIV p76 have, wrongly, 28 November for the date of Maria's death.
9    Leslie 1843 cited Beckett CII p450n.
10   Leslie ed. Shirley 1930 p234.
11   C:FDC p81.
12   Tate 1991 p32; Leslie p189.
13   Leslie pp188, 190.
14   Ivy pp132, 138.
15   *Hadleigh Castle* is 48¼ × 65⅞; Tate 1991 pp312–13; Reynolds *Later* p199.

16  Leslie p194.
17  Ivy pp133–4.
18  K. Clark 1960 pp112, 114–17.
19  CIV pp227, 317; C:FDC pp168, 228.
20  Fox p202.
21  Tate 1991 p41.
22  F. Redgrave p284.
23  Letter in Osborn Collection, Beineke Library, Yale.
24  C:FDC p80.
25  Haydon p611.
26  Thornbury I p177; Bailey p262.
27  CIV p330.

## 15. Seven Children

1  CV pp123–5; Leslie p299.
2  Leslie p200; CV p128; J. Young, cited CV, p134.
3  R. Leslie, footnote in his edition of C. Leslie's *Constable*, first page of ch V; CV pp145, 153.
4  CV p117.
5  CV pp30, 117, 125–6, 149, 153, 168–70, 191; C:FDC pp87–8.
6  CV pp28, 53, 127, 131, 133, 135.
7  CV p122.
8  CV pp122, 125, 128, 134.
9  CV p129, 134, 142–3, 165.
10  Rhyne p148.
11  CV p140.
12  Tate 1991 p34; CV pp132, 137–8, 149.
13  Reynolds *Later* p209.
14  Tate 1976 pp159–60; Frith 1887 I pp237–8; Whitley 1930 p189; Reynolds *Later* p209.
15  F. Redgrave p285.

## 16. English Landscape

1  CIV p314.
2  CIV p317.
3  Hazlitt p312.
4  Tate 1976 p160; *Mr Constable's English Landscape*, 1830 (Henry

Bicknell's and later Paul Mellon's copy, Yale Center for British Art library); Parris, *John Constable and David Lucas*.

5 CIV p344; Wilton p10.

6 Wilton p10; CIV p322.

7 CIV pp327, 339; Wilton pp10–11.

8 CIV p325; Tate 1976 p163; Tate 1991 p35.

9 CIV pp318, 321.

10 CIV p328; Wilton p11; Tate 1976 p160.

11 Tate 1991 pp33–4, 291–2, 316; CIV pp329, 333.

12 Tate 1991 p329; CVI p54.

13 *Discourses* p12.

14 CIV p414.

15 Leslie p196.

16 Tate 1976 pp161–3, 165; Tate 1991 p336; Cicero *Academica II* p20, quoted Gombrich.

17 CIV pp378, 381–2.

18 Leslie pp197–8; CIV pp364 et seq, 378, 381–2.

## 17. Clouds Overhead

1 CIV pp341, 345.

2 CIV p346.

3 Leslie p206.

4 A.P. Oppé in *Early Victorian England* vol. II 1934 p146.

5 G. Leslie p44.

6 Reynolds *Later* p231.

7 F. Redgrave pp56–7.

8 Frith 1957 pp195–6.

9 Thomson *Summer*, lines 1223 et seq.

10 Ivy pp149–52.

11 Leslie p254.

12 *Discourses* p81; *Ipswich Journal* 6 Aug 1831.

13 Trevelyan pp507, 482–3.

14 CV p35.

15 CIV p364.

16 P. Leslie plx.

17 C. Leslie 1860 I p116.

18 CIII p69; C. Leslie 1860 I pp202–3.

19 Ivy pp158–63.
20 Tate 1991 pp369–72.
21 CIII p81; CIV p80.
22 Autograph letter to W.H. Ince 11 February 1846 inserted in Grainger's copy of Leslie *Constable*, Yale Center of British Art.
23 CIV p216, 220, 222; C:FDC pp22–6.
24 Leslie pp228–30, 237; C:FDC p61 n1.
25 Leslie p230.

## 18. A Summer's Morning

1 Tate 1991 p34.
2 CV p142.
3 CV p141.
4 CV pp141–3, 145; re *East Hill, Hastings* 1833: Fleming-Williams 1990 pp264–5 and Tate 1991 nos 330, 331.
5 CV pp159–60, 166.
6 Leslie p243; Darwin ed. Engel pxv.
7 CV pp159–61, 166–7.
8 Tate 1976 pp171, 174–5.
9 CV p150.
10 CIV p112.
11 CIV p111; CV p155.
12 Leslie pp238–9.
13 Ivy pp168, 172–3; CIV p111.
14 Tate 1991 p167; CIV pp114, 117; Rhyne p174.
15 CV p150.
16 CIV pp146, 397, C:FDC pp10, 92.
17 CV pp163–5; Reynolds *Later* pp174–5; Ivy pp178, 210.
18 CV p106.
19 CIV p383.
20 CV p105.
21 Holcomb *Burlington* 1982 pp628–9.
22 Bailey pp85–6.
23 CIV p110.
24 C. Leslie 1860 I p64.
25 CIV p223.
26 CIV pp242–3.

27   CV p12.
28   CIV pp230-1.
29   CIV p235.
30   Tate 1976 p177.
31   CIV p229.
32   Leslie p246.
33   G. Leslie pp4, 111.
34   Story p137; CIV pp287–8, 293.
35   C:FDC p33; CIV p295; Story pp139–40.
36   CIV pp247–9.
37   CV pp167–8.
38   CV pp9–10, 13–16.
39   CV pp108–11; Leslie pp95, 248.

## 19. Fever and Fire

1   C:FDC p332; Leslie p247; CV p173.
2   CV pp172–3.
3   Leslie pp246, 248.
4   Ivy p190.
5   Leslie p248.
6   Tate 1991 p36.
7   CV pp16–17.
8   Leslie pp249, 253–4.
9   CV p19.
10   Leslie p253.
11   CIV p419.
12   Mary Leslie 'lecture' inserted in Grainger's copy of Leslie's *Memoirs*, 1843, Yale Center for British Art.
13   Bailey p314; R. Leslie 1894 p57; R. Leslie footnote in C. Leslie, *Life & Letters of John Constable* 1896, p20; Ruskin *Praeterita and Dilecta I* pp534–6.
14   Leslie p253; Tate 1991 p480.
15   Whitley 1930 p293.
16   CV p178.
17   Leslie p254.
18   CIV pp395, 400–1, 403, 405–6.
19   CIV pp402, 414, 416–17, 421–3.

20 CIV pp420–1, 423–4.

## 20. The Appearance of the Day

1 *Discourses* p28.
2 Leslie p308.
3 *Discourses* p29.
4 Leslie pp308–11.
5 Leslie pp312–13, 317.
6 C:FDC p8; Leslie pp178, 333–4, 337–8.
7 *Discourses* p34.
8 *Discourses* p56.
9 Leslie pp228–9, 336, 338.
10 Leslie pp331–2, 339–43; Gainsborough's model horse in Gainsborough's House museum, Sudbury.
11 Shields & Parris *John Constable* Tate 1985 p15.
12 C:FDC p8.
13 *Discourses* p30.
14 Leslie p344.
15 CV pp184–5.
16 Leslie p350.
17 Ivy p209.
18 *Discourses* pp35, 71–2; C:FDC p22.
19 Leslie p258; *Discourses* pp29–30, 34, 36, 53, 58.

## 21. A Portion of England

1 C:FDC p96.
2 CV pp179, 185.
3 CIV p419.
4 Ivy pp197–8.
5 Ivy pp198, 200.
6 Tate 1991 pp376–8.
7 CV p20.
8 Ivy p210.
9 Ivy pp199–202.
10 Ivy pp203–4.
11 CIV pp149–50, 278, 427.
12 CV pp20, 25–6; Tate 1991 p378.

13   Parris Tate 1976 p182; Hill p21.
14   CV pp173, 175.
15   C:FDC p95.
16   CV pp181, 187.
17   CIV p128 n4.
18   CV p187.
19   CIV pp130–1.
20   CV pp189.
21   CV pp189–92.
22   Leslie p262.
23   CV p183.
24   CV p185.
25   Shields & Parris *John Constable* Tate 1985, p15.
26   CV p196.
27   CV pp191, 193–5; CIV pp426–7.
28   CI pp300–1; Suffolk Record Office, map P461/27.

## 22. Two Monuments

1    CIV p151.
2    C. Leslie 1860 I pp113–16.
3    Leslie p269.
4    CV p92; Tate 1976 pp49, 136, 185; Leslie pp270–1.
5    Reynolds *Later* p286.
6    Leslie pp270–1.
7    Ivy pp214–16; Tate 1991 p37.
8    Tate 1991 p490; Ivy p217.
9    CIV p285.
10   Ivy p221.
11   CIV p285; Whitley 1930 p319; Bailey p330.
12   CV p199.
13   Ivy p218; Rhyne p202.
14   CV pp200–1.
15   CIV pp123–4, 429.
16   CIV pp229–30, 431.
17   G. Leslie p77.
18   CIII pp141, 143–4.
19   CIV pp427, 431, 433, 436; Parris, *John Constable and David Lucas* p9.

20 CIV p106.

### 23. Engaged with the Assassin
1 CV p36–7.
2 Tate 1991 p384.
3 Salander–O'Reilly 1988.
4 Leslie p277.
5 CV p37.
6 *Discourses* p77.
7 Leslie pp277–8; *Morning Post* 4 April 1837.
8 CIV p303.
9 Reynolds *Later* pp298–9; CIV p438; Leslie p279.
10 Leslie p281.
11 Leslie p282.
12 *Discovery* p1.
13 Leslie p282; see Thomas Churchyard account in Morfey; Tate 1991 p38.
14 C. Leslie 1860 I p158.
15 Leslie p282.
16 *Discovery* p3.
17 Leslie p282; C. Leslie 1860 I p158; Tate 1976 p190; CV p128; Ivy p224.
18 Leslie pp292–3.

### 24. The Other Side of the Grave
1 Reynolds *Early* p39; Tate 1991 pp384–5; Ivy pp233–4.
2 *Discovery* pp9–10; CIV p308.
3 *ODNB*, Ivy on Constable; C:FDC p96 n7; *Discovery* p11.
4 *Discovery* pp13–21.
5 *Discovery* p15; Shirley 1930 pp10–14.
6 *Discovery* pp15, 17–18, 20–1.
7 CV pp203, 205, 207–8.
8 *Discovery* pp12, 68–9.
9 CV p206.
10 *Discovery* p24.
11 CV pp207, 213–14; *Discovery* pp11–12, 57, 61–2, 64.
12 *Discovery* pp26–7, 42, 55–7, 59–60, 64–5.

13    C. Leslie *Constable* 1896 edn pp263–4n; *Discovery* pp66–7.

14    CVI p226.

15    CV p207; Boner I p13.

16    CV p206.

17    *Discovery* p30; Tate 1976 p161; Shirley 1930 p146.

18    Vaughan, *Oxford Art Journal*; C. Leslie 1860 I pp114–15; *Discovery* pp24, 30, 48.

19    R&S Redgrave II p346; F. Redgrave p56.

20    C. Leslie 1860 I pp115–16.

21    *Discovery* pp48, 52–3; Hamerton p315; Leslie, intro by B. Nicolson p10; Delacroix *Selected Letters* ed. J. Stewart, London 1971.

22    Ruskin *Modern Painters* I pp99–100.

23    Ruskin *Works* III pp191, 603; A.P. Oppé in *Early Victorian England* p143; Badt p5; C. Leslie 1855 pp273, 277; *Discovery* pp49–51.

24    C. Leslie 1855 p273; Ruskin 1897 *Modern Painters* I pp99–100, Tate 1976 p24.

25    C:FDC pp247–8.

26    *Discovery* pp42–4, 46; Parris, *John Constable and David Lucas* p1.

27    *Discovery* pp48, 52–3; Gage p191.

28    *Discovery* pp85–7, 138; Painter.

29    *Discovery* pp122–3; Salander–O'Reilly 1988 citing Meier-Graefe I pp68, 71, 129.

30    *Discovery* pp123–4; Salander–O'Reilly 1988 p90.

31    William Feaver interview with Lucian Freud, *Sunday Telegraph* 29 September 2002.

32    *TLS* 27 February 1976.

33    Constable to Fisher, October 1823, from East Bergholt: 'I want to get to my easil in Town – & not witness rotting melancholy dissolution of the trees . . . which two months ago were so beautifull.'

# Bibliography

I have had close to hand the *Correspondence* edited by R.B. Beckett; the Tate catalogues of the Constable exhibitions of 1976 and 1991 (cited in my notes as Tate 1976 and Tate 1991); the indispensable catalogues of Constable's work by Graham Reynolds; *The Discovery of Constable* by Ian Fleming-Williams and Leslie Parris (cited as *Discovery*); and Charles Leslie's *Memoirs of the Life of John Constable Esq., R.A.* (cited as Leslie, with page numbers). There are a number of editions of this, all out of print, but I have, unless otherwise noted, used that introduced by Benedict Nicolson and published by John Lehmann, London, in 1949. The Victoria County History, the *Survey of London* (1949) vol. 21, the *London Encyclopedia*, and the *Oxford Dictionary of National Biography* have also been frequently consulted.

## Books

Anita Albus, *The Art of Arts*, New York, 2000

Henry Angelo, *Reminiscences of Henry Angelo*, 2 vols., London, 1828

Kurt Badt, *John Constable's Clouds*, London, 1950

Anthony Bailey, *Standing in the Sun: a Life of J.M.W. Turner*: London, 1997; New York, 1998

Thomas J. Barratt, *The Annals of Hampstead*, 2 vols, London, 1912

John Barrell, *The Dark Side of the Landscape: The Rural Poor in English Painting*, Cambridge, 1980

R.B. Beckett, *John Constable and the Fishers*, London, 1952

R.B. Beckett, ed., *John Constable's Correspondence*:

    I.   The Family at East Bergholt 1807–37, London, 1962

II.  Early Friends and Maria Bicknell, Suffolk, 1964
III. Correspondence with C.R. Leslie RA, Suffolk, 1965
IV.  Patrons, Dealers and Fellow Artists, Suffolk, 1966
V.   Various Friends, with Charles Boner & the Artist's Children, Suffolk, 1967
VI.  The Fishers, Suffolk, 1968

R.B. Beckett, ed., *John Constable's Discourses*, Suffolk, 1970

Charles Boner, *Memoirs & Letters of Charles Boner*, London, 1871

James Clark, *Treatise on Pulmonary Consumption*, London, 1836

Kenneth Clark, *Looking at Pictures*, London, 1960

Kenneth Clark, *Landscape into Art*, London, 1976

William Cobbett, *Rural Rides*, 1830 reprinted, 2 vols, London, 1908

E.E. Cockayne & N.J. Stow, *Stutter's Casebook*, Suffolk, 2005

Linda Colley, *Britons*, New Haven, CT and London, 1992

W. Wilkie Collins, *The Life of William Collins Esq. R.A.*, 2 vols, London, 1848

R. Colville, *London: The Northern Reaches*, London, 1951

Freda Constable, *John Constable*, Suffolk, 1975

Olive Cook, *Constable's Hampstead*, London, 1976

G.H. Cunningham, *London*, London and New York, 1927

Charles Darwin, ed. Engel, *Voyage of the Beagle*, London, 1839, reprinted New York, 1962

Thomas Dormandy, *The White Death*, London, 1999

René & Jean Dubos, *The White Plague*, London, 1953

J.F. Elam, *St Mary's Church, East Bergholt*, Suffolk, 1986

Joseph Farington, *Diaries*, 17 vols, New Haven, CT and London, 1978–1998

Revd Edmund Farrer, ed., *The Dunthorne Mss.*, Vol. XX, Part 2, Suffolk Institute of Archaeology and Natural History, 1929

A. J. Finberg, *The Life of J.M.W. Turner*, Oxford, 1961

H. A. L. Fisher, *A History of Europe*, London, 1936

Ian Fleming-Williams & Leslie Parris, *The Discovery of Constable*, London, 1984

Ian Fleming-Williams, *Constable and his Drawings*, London, 1990

Celina Fox, ed., *London – World City, 1800–1840*, New Haven, CT and London, 1992

W.P. Frith, *My Autobiography*, 2 vols, London, 1887

W.P. Frith (N. Wallis, ed.), *A Victorian Canvas*, London, 1957

Roger Fry, *Reflections on British Painting*, London, 1934

Reg Gadney, *Constable and his World*, London and New York, 1976

John Gage, *J. M. W. Turner: 'A Wonderful Range of Mind'*, New Haven CT and London, 1987

Josiah Gilbert, ed., *Autobiography & Other Memorials of Mrs Gilbert (formerly Ann Taylor)*, London, 1874

William Gilpin, *Three Essays on Picturesque Beauty*, London, 1792

E.H. Gombrich, *Art and Illusion*, London and New York, 1960

Richard Hamblyn, *The Invention of Clouds*, London, 2001

Philip G. Hamerton, *Thoughts About Art*, London, 1873

J.L. & B. Hammond, *The Village Labourer*, 2 vols, London, 1948

Benjamin Haydon, *Autobiography & Journals*, London, 1853, reprinted 1950

William Hazlitt, *Selected Essays* (includes 'On Actors & Acting' from *The Examiner*, 1817), London, 1930

Elizabeth K. Helsinger, *Rural Scenes and National Representation*, Princeton, NJ, 1997

David Hill, *Constable's 'English Landscape Scenery'*, London, 1985

E.J. Hobsbawm & G. Rudé, *Captain Swing*, London, 1969

Charles Holmes, *Constable and his Influence on Landscape Painting*, London, 1902

Luke Howard, *The Climate of London*, London, 1820

Leigh Hunt, *Autobiography*, 1850, reprinted London, 1949

Sidney C. Hutchinson, *The History of the Royal Academy:* London, 1968; 2nd edn, 1986

Judy Crosby Ivy, *Constable and the Critics 1802–1837*, Suffolk, 1991

E.D.H. Johnson, ed., *The Poetry of Earth*, London, 1966

John Keats, *Letters*, Oxford, 1954

Charles Leslie, *Memoirs of the Life of John Constable Esq., R.A.*, London, 1843 and 1845

Charles Leslie, *A Handbook for Young Painters*, London, 1855

Charles Leslie, *Autobiographical Reflections*, 2 vols, London, 1860

George D. Leslie, *Inner Life of the Royal Academy*, London, 1914

Peter Leslie, ed., *Letters of John Constable R.A. to C.R. Leslie R.A., 1826–1837*, London, 1931

Robert C. Leslie, *A Waterbiography* (1894), reprinted Southampton, 1985

Robert C. Leslie, ed., C.R. Leslie, *Memoirs of the Life of John Constable*, London, 1896

W. Morfey, *Painting the Day: Thomas Churchyard of Woodbridge*, Woodbridge, 1986

Nicholas Mosley, *Julian Grenfell*, London 1976, reprinted 1999

Charles Nodier, *Promenade from Dieppe to the Mountains of Scotland*, Edinburgh, 1822

Felicity Owen & D.B. Brown, *A Collector of Genius: Sir George Beaumont*, New Haven, CT and London, 1988

Colin Painter, *At Home with Constable's Cornfield*, London, 1996

Leslie Parris, Conal Shields & Ian Fleming-Williams, eds, *John Constable: Further Documents and Correspondence*, London and Suffolk, 1975

R. Paulson, *Literary Landscape: Turner and Constable*, New Haven, CT and London, 1982

Christiana Payne, *Toil and Plenty*, New Haven, CT and London, 1993

Nikolaus Pevsner & Enid Radcliffe, *Suffolk*, Harmondsworth, 1974

Cyrus Redding, *Fifty Years' Recollections*, London, 1858

D. & R. Porter, *Disease, Medicine and Society in England 1850–60*, London (1987), 2nd edition Cambridge, 1995

Roy Porter, *Patients' Progress*, Cambridge, 1985

F.M. Redgrave, *Richard Redgrave – a Memoir*, London, 1891

Richard & Samuel Redgrave, *A Century of British Painters:* 2 vols, London, 1866; one-vol. edn, London, 1947

Graham Reynolds, *The Later Paintings & Drawings of John Constable*, 2 vols, New Haven, CT and London, 1984

Graham Reynolds, *The Early Paintings & Drawings of John Constable*, 2 vols, New Haven, CT and London, 1996

Charles Rhyne, *John Constable: towards a Complete Chronology*, privately printed, Oregon, 1990

Michael Rosenthal, *British Landscape Painting*, Oxford, 1982

Michael Rosenthal, *Constable – the Painter and his Landscape*, New Haven, CT and London, 1983

Michael Rosenthal, ed., *Prospects for the Nation: essays on British Landscape*, New Haven, CT and London, 1997

John Ruskin, *Praeterita and Dilecta* (1885–1889), reprinted Oxford, 1978 (Ruskin I)

John Ruskin, *Modern Painters* 6 vols (1843–1860) reprinted London, 1897 (Ruskin II)

John Ruskin, *Works*, ed. E. T. Cook & A. Weddenburn, 39 vols, London, 1903–1912 (Ruskin III)

Ian St John, *Flatford*, Suffolk, 2000

Ian St John, *East Bergholt*, Suffolk, 2002

Ian St John, *Dedham*, Suffolk, 2005

W. Sandby, *The History of the Royal Academy of Arts*, 2 vols, London, 1862

Norman Scarfe, *The Suffolk Landscape*, London, 1972

Francis Sheppard, *London 1808–1870: the Infernal Wen*, London, 1971

Andrew Shirley, *Published Mezzotints of David Lucas after John Constable*, London, 1930

Conal Shields & Leslie Parris, *John Constable*, London, 1969, reprinted 1985

Andrew Shirley, *John Constable R.A.*, London, 1944, reprinted 1948

Andrew Shirley, *The Rainbow*, London, 1949

Katharine Sim, *David Roberts R.A. 1796–1864*, London, 1984

F.B. Smith, *The Retreat of Tuberculosis*, London, 1988

Robert Southey, *Works of William Cowper*, 15 vols (Vol. 1 includes Southey's *Life of Cowper*), London, 1836

A.T. Story, *The Life of John Linnell*, 2 vols, London: 1892

John Taylor, *Records of my Life*, London, 1832

Flora Thompson, *Lark Rise to Candleford*, Oxford, 1939, reprinted 1973

Walter Thornbury, *Turner*: 2 vols, London, 1862; 1 vol., London, 1877

G.M. Trevelyan, *English Social History*, London, 1942, reprinted 1946

Barry Venning, *Constable*, London, 1990

Kit Wedd (with Lucy Peltz & Cathy Ross), *Creative Quarters: the Art World in London 1700–2000*, London, 2001

R.J. White, *Life in Regency England*, London & New York, 1963

William T. Whitley, *Art in England 1800–1820*, Cambridge, 1928

William T. Whitley, *Art in England 1821–1837*, Cambridge, 1930

Selby Whittingham, *Constable and Turner at Salisbury*, Salisbury, 1972

Andrew Wilton, *Constable's 'English Landscape Scenery'*, London, 1979

James Woodforde, ed. J. Beresford, *Diary of a Country Parson*, Oxford, 1935

Ian Yearsley, *Dedham, Flatford and East Bergholt*, Chichester, 1996

Arthur Young, *General View of Agriculture of the County of Suffolk*: London, 1797; revised edn, 1813

G.M. Young, ed., *Early Victorian England 1830–65* incl. article by A.P. Oppé, 2 vols, Oxford, 1834

## Exhibition Catalogues

*Constable: The Art of Nature* by Leslie & Conal Shields, Tate Gallery, London, 1971

*John Constable*, with essays by Ian Fleming-Williams, Leslie Parris & Conal Shields, Tate Gallery, London, 1976

*Constable's Country*, introduction by Michael Rosenthal, Gainsborough's House, Sudbury, 1976

*Constable's England*, with essay by Graham Reynolds, Metropolitan Museum, New York, 1983

*John Constable, R.A.*, with essays by Julius Meier-Graefe, Graham Reynolds, et al., Salander–O'Reilly Gallery, New York, 1988

*Constable*, with essays by Ian Fleming-Williams & Leslie Parris, Tate Gallery, London, 1991

*John Constable and David Lucas*, with essay by Leslie Parris, Salander–O'Reilly Gallery, New York, 1993

*Brighton Revealed through Artists' Eyes*, ed. David Beevers, with essay by Ian Warrell, Royal Pavilion Art Gallery, Brighton, 1995

*Constable and Wivenhoe Park*, J. Clarkson, N. Cox, M. Rosenthal, J. Nash et al., University of Essex, 2000

*Constable's Clouds*, ed. Edward Morris, with essays by John Gage, Anne Lyles, Martin Suggett, John E. Thornes & Timothy Wilcox, Liverpool and Edinburgh, 2000

*Constable: Le Choix de Lucian Freud*, with essays by William Feaver, John Gage, Anne Lyles, Oliver Meslay et al., Paris, 2002

*Constable's Skies*, ed. Frederic Bancroft, with essays by Sarah Cove, Anne Lyles, Peter Power, Graham Reynolds & Conal Shields, Salander–O'Reilly Gallery, New York, 2004


**Magazines and Periodicals**

*Apollo*, LXXXI, 1965: R.B. Beckett, 'Constable at Epsom'

*Burlington Magazine*, October 1982: Adele M. Holcomb, 'John Constable as a contributor to the *Athenaeum*'

*Burlington Magazine*, March 1999: Anne Lyles review of Reynolds, *Early*.

*Burlington Magazine*, September 1999: F.G. Notehelfer, 'Constable and the Woodbridge Wits'

*Journal of the Warburg Institute*, XX 1957: Michael Kitson, 'Constable 1810–16'

*Oxford Art Journal*, 19:2, 1996: William Vaughan, 'Constable's Englishness'

*Turner Studies*, 8:1, 1988: Louis Hawes, 'Wordsworth & the Age of English Romanticism'

# Index

346
JOHN CONSTABLE

and death of his dog 198; advises
Constable to make allowances for
Golding 199; praises Mrs Roberts
202; has Constable to stay 225,
236, 274; cheers Constable when
ill 229; as uncle 229, 241; and
Charley's schooling 239; receives
Christmas port from Constable
246; and Constable's reviews 277,
290; gets Charley posting on ship
280; brings linseed oil for Lucas
283–4; involved in 'vast works' on
lock gates 284; and Mary's land
purchase 284; at Constable's
funeral 303; money owed to
Constable 306; discord with
nephews and nieces 309; has
Alfred to stay 311; on his brother's
paintings 9, 243, 244, 313
Constable, Alfred Abram ('Alfie'; son):
birth and christening 175; illness
176, 185; childhood 203, 230, 280,
311; education 239, 241, 282–3; in
Hampstead 293, 296; exhibits at
Royal Academy 311; death 312
Constable, Ann (*née* Watts) (mother):
marriage 2–3; and Constable's
schooling 4; her 'connections' 7,
11–12, 19; and the Dunthornes 10,
11, 68–9, 75; and J.T. Smith 17;
her hopes for Constable's future 8,
17, 58, 73; keeps Constable abreast
of village news 20–21, 25, 43–4,
46–7, 74; portrait (*c.* 1803) 35, *35*;
worried about husband's health
43; approves of Constable's
courtship of Maria 49, 57–8;
recognises the importance of Dr
Rhudde 50–51, 58–9, 75; maternal
worries 51–2, 56; offended by
Maria's brother 63; stroke and
death 75, 80
Constable, Ann (sister): childhood 3,

5–6; and father's death 86; runs
dog kennels 87; invites the
Constables to stay 94, 95, 98; and
sale of family house 103, 104;
portrait *105*; as godmother to
Maria Louisa 108; in a prickly
mood 121; house burgled 135;
apologises to Constable for 'some
passing clouds' 188; praises
Johnny Dunthorne 204–5
Constable, Charles Golding ('Charley';
son): birth 120, 162–3; childhood
144, 164, 166, 173, 203, 238, 240;
portraits *238*, 300; and Mrs
Roberts 202, 309; tutored by
Boner 203–4, 206; at school in
Folkestone 206, 239–40, 241–2;
interest in drawing 240–41, 311;
goes to sea 279–82, 293–4, 309;
marriages 309; children 309;
friction with sisters 310–11;
denounces Constable pictures as
fakes 311; and his brothers' artistic
talents 311–12; approves of
Leslie's *Life* 313; on *The Cornfield*
170–71
Constable, Emily ('Emma'; daughter)
162–3, 173, 202, 203, 225, 246,
282, 284, 293, 310
Constable, George (friend) 228, 241,
253, 257, 297, 316; Constable to
249–50, 276, 282, 290, 293
Constable, Golding (father) 2; marriage
2–3; business 6, 11, 73; and
Constable's future 4, 8; and
Constable's artistic career 10, 15,
17, 19–20, 28, 29, 34, 42, 43; ill
health 52, 56; repairs Dedham
Mill 47; saves employee from
press gang 52; sends Constable
advice and cash 57; worried by
criticism of Constable's work 59;
approves of his portrait work 60;